SOARING
WITH THE
PHOENIX

SOARING WITH THE PHOENIX

RENEWING THE VISION, REVIVING THE SPIRIT, AND RE-CREATING THE SUCCESS OF YOUR COMPANY

JAMES A. BELASCO & JERRE STEAD

WARNER BOOKS

A Time Warner Company

Warner Books, Inc., 1271 Avenue of the Americas,
New York, NY 10020
Visit our Web site at http://warnerbooks.com

W A Time Warner Company

Printed in the United States of America
First Printing: March 1999
10   9   8   7   6   5   4   3   2   1

Library of Congress Cataloging-in-Publication Data

Belasco, James A.
   Soaring with the phoenix : renewing the vision, reviving
the spirit, and re-creating the success of your company / James A.
Belasco and Jerre Stead.
      p.   cm.
   Includes index.
   ISBN 0-446-52400-X
   1. Corporate turnarounds.   I. Stead, Jerre L.   II. Title.
HD58.8.B454   1999
658.4'063—dc21   98-34785
                                                            CIP

Book design by Giorgetta Bell McRee

ACKNOWLEDGMENTS

What a trip!! Sixty years ago no one—not my parents, my siblings, nor myself—could have imagined the roads I'd travel, the places I'd visit or the heights I'd scale. I am in awe of where I stand today and the road I've traveled. I have gone further, done more and reached higher than anyone—including me—ever expected.

I am blessed with my fellow travelers on this road of life, folks who choose to share a piece of their travel time with me. First and foremost is my wife, Candy. She is my best friend, my life partner, my thought colleague and my love. When I think of Candy's contribution, the words of the poet Robert Browning run through my head: "Grow old with me, the best is yet to be . . . the last of life, for which the first was made."

My children and grandchildren fill the landscape of my journey with the variegated patterns of sunshine and shadow that characterize life's journey. They are at once both a great joy and a big challenge. They teach me valuable lessons about leadership in the twenty-first century, how to lead a world I do not control. They are my progeny, my gift to tomorrow—and I am inordinately proud that they carry my dream into the future. My legacy is safe in their hearts.

Then there are all the business associates who hired me to teach them and, over time, became my mentors and close personal friends. There are names like Gil, Jack, Richard, Tom, Michael . . . but the roll call goes on and on, so I can't even begin to list them all. Their names fill my walls with cards at Christmastime, my e-mail log during the year and my heart forever. Close friend and co-author of *Flight of the Buffalo*, Ralph Stayer, occupies a very special place in my life. He is a very dear friend who helped me see further by allowing me the privilege of standing on his giantlike shoulders. All taught me something valuable about myself, life and business. They made the trip challenging and exciting.

Meredith Kunsa, my business partner and director of my business, is a special blessing. For more years than most marriages endure, she and I have been busy working and learning together. Her caring straightforwardness and deep sense of ethical behavior are beacons for me in an often confusing and blurred world. She keeps me straight, on time and in tune with my own personal vision of excellence. Without Meredith I might still be at the starting gate.

My students and business partners are extraordinary blessings on my journey. They are great teachers and role models for me. I am pleased (and a little embarrassed) when a former student stops me in the street in Helsinki or a restaurant in Sydney and thanks me for a life-changing experience. I need to be as acknowledging of their contribution to me as they are of my contribution to them. Similarly, I sit at the feet of my business partners around the world and drink deep from the cups of their wisdom that they so freely offer to me.

All of these fellow travelers offered me their hands to pull me, their eyes to guide me, their shoulders to carry me and their brains to educate me. The accolades from the past and the present belong to them. You can thank them for the wisdom and insight contained in these pages. Blame me for the oversights, overstatements and other inadequacies of the text.

The road to the future stretches broad and wide ahead of me. There is so much to learn, so much to do. As I turn and start up that road I want to continue to reach for the stars, build on each individual's unique contribution and help others to be all they are capable of becoming.

As good as it all is now, what is now is all past. I am eternally grateful to all those who brought me to this place. As I turn my face toward tomorrow, I know that the best is yet to be. I am excited and ready to soar into that future.

—James A. Belasco

Helping great people do great things is really fun. I've spent my career with six corporations—all in different markets, all with different products and services, all with very different cultures— and yet one thing was the same: really great people trying hard to be successful and to do their very best. I thank each and every associate for helping me to learn how to coach and how to lead. People truly are the only sustainable advantage any organization has. By giving people power, permission and protection, there are no limits to what they can accomplish. The real measure of success is whether, after you leave a position, the organization keeps getting better and better as a result of the environment you have created. I've tried hard to do that with every job I've ever had. Being surrounded by great people has made every day fun. Today I'm enjoying my career more than ever before, and it's because I'm so fortunate to lead great people doing great things.

Forty years ago, at the age of fourteen, I started dating a wonderful person named Mary Joy. Four years later we got married, went through the University of Iowa together, had both of our sons during our time in college and have been together ever since. I'm so very proud of Mary Joy as my partner and, in fact, the center of my life. She is deeply understanding and has done an awesome job of running our household and helping me in a million ways, as well as being an accomplished musician, medical technologist, pilot, athlete and a super MOM and grandmom. I would have accomplished little without her.

Our two sons, Joel and Jay, make us so proud in their family and business successes. I love sharing ideas with them and listening with joy to their ideas and accomplishments. Our daughters-in-law, Michele and Robyn, are great daughters and moms, growing up and living all over this marvelous world. My two brothers, my brother-in-law and their families have always been special people, of whom we are very proud. And finally our wonderful grandchildren: Sydney, Madeline and Sam. I hope that this book someday helps them to flourish and soar as they create their mark on society. Living today in this continually changing world is wonderful. May every person enjoy it, and please remember: Work is really play with a purpose!

—Jerre Stead

SPECIAL THANKS

Michael O'Sullivan deserves a very special recognition for his role in the creation of this book. Michael worked with us at AT&T/NCR/Global Information Solutions (GIS), adding pepper and spice to the usually boring corporate presentations and writings. People were forever asking Michael to "spice this up a bit." He always succeeded in turning dull corporatese into lively, understandable, motivational words. That's why we asked Michael to work with us in our Phoenix undertaking.

Michael exceeded our every expectation. The three of us would talk, usually by phone, with Michael recording our musing. Somehow he'd work his magic and turn the transcript into a working draft, from which we wrote, rewrote and rewrote, every time passing it through "Michael's Miraculous Wordsmithing Machine." Time and again we'd hear ourselves saying, "Michael, spice it up a bit, can you?" He'd do it every time.

Furthermore, it was a joy to work with Michael. He possesses an unerring sense of right and wrong that resonates and reinforces our own deeply held values and ethics.

Many of the charming and clever words in this manuscript belong to Michael. We hope they outshine the sometimes turgid corporate and academic words of the authors.

—James A. Belasco
Jerre Stead

CONTENTS

PART I

INTRODUCTION TO PHOENIX PRINCIPLES

CHAPTER 1

The Continually Renewing Phoenix: The Herald of Revivolution

HEAVY HUMAN TRAFFIC: SEARCHING TO BE SOMETHING AND SOMEBODY

Once More, with Feeling: Rewind, Playback, Pump Up the Volume

It is dark—well past our 7:00 P.M. dinnertime—by the time I slip into my car to make my way home after another twelve-hour day. "This is Thursday, isn't it?" I ask myself. "No, it's only Wednesday." The days all run together. "It's been seven months since I signed on as plant manager. I've been hard at it, seven days a week, twelve hours a day. And what do I have to show for it?

"Why is this plant so tough to move?" I ask myself. The boss told me it was in bad shape, and everyone else seemed to agree. But it's been like moving through molasses. Everything is harder, takes longer, and gets less than enthusiastic execution. People smile a lot and agree in meetings, and then go back and do it the same old way.

I review today's events. I walk through the plant on my way in. The housekeeping is still poor, a sure sign of low morale. The on-time shipment chart that I insisted on is three days behind. "A good example of foot dragging when the boss insists upon something," I tell myself. I pass lots of people hard at work making parts. These are good people looking for good leadership.

I'm ten minutes late for my 8:00 A.M. operations meeting. The knot tightens in my stomach when I tune into the conversation. It's about our production planning system. Haven't we settled this issue already? It seems to me we've been talking about this topic forever. Everyone agrees about what we have to do. We just can't get on with doing it.

The second half of the meeting consists of each production line head presenting their three-year plans. The first one is a disaster. I wait for others to speak up—having learned early in my career that I need to speak last to maximize the input from the group. Thirty agonizing minutes later we're still doing the corporate minuet. I ask a few sharp questions and others pick up the scent. "With some prompting these people are really good," I think. "How do I get them to prompt themselves?"

But the real issues don't ever get addressed. We're falling further and further behind in our manufacturing technology base. We tried a lean manufacturing approach and scrapped it before I came. Inventory is sky-high and the financial folks are screaming that we need to cut it in half. Whenever I mention the inventory concerns everyone just shrugs their shoulders and says, "It can't be done." Employee turnover is the highest in our industry. We're just not doing the right things to get and keep a high-quality workforce. I know these issues will get worse as the competition closes in on us. I just can't get anyone else to be concerned. The knot in my stomach tightens still more.

Beginning with a working brown bag lunch, my afternoon is bumper-to-bumper meetings. I spend one hour with the production staff of our chief component supplier and our own executive staff. Then I spend another hour with just the plant manager of that supplier. We go round and round the same issues. Talk seems to be the currency of choice in his organization and mine—not action. Neither of us can get our people to face up to the serious issues confronting us.

Several managers drop by to discuss personnel issues. These conversations go well, but again, we tend to *talk* more than *do*. We've been talking about replacing one of the production line heads—the one who made such a poor presentation this morning—for almost five months.

My shoulders hurt. The pain in my lower back won't quit. And the knot in my stomach is a constant companion. Home is a safe haven. Hovering in the foyer is the savory aroma of dinner. I hear the kids arguing down the hall as a DJ babbles vacuously. My wife is talking on the phone as I enter the kitchen. Still in her company attire, she uses her free hand to take a dish from the microwave—waving at me with a smile. Things seem intact. No paramedics. No police. All is well. I thumb through the mail, nothing serious there, then pitch right in to move dinner along: set the table, round up the kids, help my wife get the food on the table and watch the minutes spin by.

Several roller-coaster conversations and verbal exchanges later, I have dined, relaxed, pontificated, warned and even apologized. I shake my head and ask myself, "Have I really done enough today?" Still, tomorrow is another day.

"Nuts," I think to myself. "Got to review those policy changes before I hit the hay." I wave good-night to the family as I trundle off to the den for what has become my daily after-dinner work session.

In Search of Meaningful Change: The Ethereal Golden Fleece

The day recounted above never exactly happened. But versions of it take place every day. Some days are better, many are worse. They're unfortunately too typical for those of us trying to create more productive, more satisfying offices, factories and living rooms.

From the workplace to the community to the family, we (Jerre and Jim) see real human issues to resolve, communications to improve and commitments to keep. Everywhere we look there are people with hopes and dreams, fears and anxieties. Real, earnest, authentic people with attitudes and stubbornness and nuttiness and affection who want to be "something" and "somebody" for other people. These personal human issues play out on the stage set by traumatic, dramatic changes in industry and business. The search to be something to somebody becomes even more complicated by the global business earthquake zone in which we all live.

NOW IS THE HOUR: HEED THE NEED FOR REVIVOLUTION

We live in an uncertain world. Old countries and political entities are breaking apart and new ones are forming. Industries are changing dramatically right before our very eyes. Jobs we thought were sacrosanct disappear in the twinkling of an eye. We confront a world in which personal and organizational change is revolutionary, not evolutionary. That is why we refer to the phenomenon as *"revivolution": renewal through revolution (or rapid evolution that looks a lot like revolution).*

Shopping malls morph into amusement parks. Amusement parks look like Jurassic Parks. The Web makes it possible to create multimillion-dollar businesses almost overnight. Corporate giants are spawned in home basements and garages. Rapid renewal—or revivolution—is everywhere.

Monumental Change Drives the Need for Revivolution

Tomorrow arrives too quickly for most of us. Stuck in the mire of today's rules that no longer work, we flail around in our search for security. But the answer is right before our eyes. Invent a new tomorrow and change the rules! The January 1997 edition of *Fast Company* reports how Moses Znaimer, the owner of a start-up TV station in Toronto, Canada, called Citytv, created a whole new set of rules for television news broadcasting. He created local and interactive TV that was real-time with real people. Instead of talking-head news anchors who read TelePrompTers to audiences, Citytv offers television where the street is the studio and the real-time experience is the program. People love it. When the rules don't allow you to do what you think is best to do, change the rules. Moses Znaimer did!

And it's not just businesses that revivolute. Today, churches don't act like conventional churches in many places. They meet in huge community centers—or drive-in movie locations. They provide a variety of creative enterprises where members participate, create, learn and meet others. They use the Internet—and cruise the streets in vans to reach out in mobile high-tech and high-touch configurations to meet the needs of people who can't/won't come to them. If Muhammad won't come to the mountain, the mountain will come to Muhammad.

Jack Welch, chairman of General Electric Company, recently said: "If your change isn't big enough, revolutionary enough, the bureaucracy can beat you." He recognizes the need for monumental change that overrides our own mind-sets that cling to the security of today. Welch's monumental change, in turn, drives the need for revivolution.

Businesses regularly get blindsided by new competitors, new technology, new industries or a sudden shift in what customers value. Banks—and bank tellers—disappear, new automobile nameplates emerge like weeds in a garden, plants open and then close again in the twinkling of an eye. Individuals are similarly surprised by radical changes in jobs and markets. We can be sure of only one thing. The head-spinning rate of global, technical, social and personal change will continue to accelerate. Incremental adjustments will never be enough.

Phone-Genesis: Revivoluting at the Speed of Sound and the Death of Distance

A September 1995 special supplement of *The Economist* pointed out that this is the best of times for telecommunications firms. Everywhere around the world people are scrambling to get a telephone. Millions of new subscribers—both wireless and wired— join the rate-payer rolls every year. Prices often rise faster than costs, yielding large profits for many telco firms.

Yet this is also the worst of times for telco organizations. Tomorrow is coming too fast for most of them. As the world telecommunications companies deregulate, there is a competitor hiding under every rock. Everyone wants a piece of the $500 billion global market. In the U.S., competition for the local franchise includes not only the local telcos, like Southwest Bell, and national telco firms, like AT&T, but also international telco firms, like British Telcom. And that's just counting telephone companies. To that witches' brew of competition across the world add cable companies (Time Warner and TCI), electric utility companies (Utilicorp), railroads (Deutsche Railroad), water companies,

banks (Société Générale), software/hardware computer companies (Microsoft and Intel) and even chemical companies (Bayer).
From a monopoly market, telecommunications is becoming a
classic free-for-all market of which Adam Smith would be proud.

The increase in competitors fuels the switch from scarcity to
glut in communications capacity. Counting the rapidly expanding
wireless capacity, less than one fifth of the total global telecommunications capacity is currently utilized.

The telecommunications cost structures pose another strategic
challenge. Operations costs continue to fall. Already the cost of a
call from New York to New Delhi is about the same as a call to the
neighborhood pizza place. When telephone costs are no longer
distance-related, tariffs will inevitably change. The time-related,
distance-related rate structure will likely disappear. You'll pay as
much to call for that pizza delivery as you will to talk to Uncle Ivan
ten time zones away across the pond and half a continent beyond.

All of these swirling changes pose the potential for a major
price war in the telco business. The war is already underway.
Consider what's happened in the long-distance business in America. Rates are cheaper now in real terms than they were in 1984.
And mailboxes are filled with mail from AT&T, from MCI, from
Sprint urging you to switch to them for your local service. Tele-
marketers call twice a week, offering free weekend calls and other
incentives to switch local and long-distance service.

The old-line telcos who die by atrophy or as war casualties will
do so because they were unable to revivolute themselves to create new organizational forms. Incremental change in service offerings and products will only work for so long. Without both
organizational and individual monumental change from the inside, there will continue to be many résumés out on the street
that list telco experience.

Metal-Genesis: Revivolution in the Big Steel Business

The steel business has been through the revivolution mill. Originally, the huge, integrated steel companies set up near the
sources of their raw material. The plants turned out semifinished
products that went to customers for finishing. Big steel was es-

sentially in the commodity business. Managers ran tight, centrally managed hierarchical organizations.

Japan attacked first, using new and more efficient technology to produce the same commodity. Then Korea combined newer technology with cheaper labor. For a while, it looked as though the American steel industry was dead. But along came the new mini-mill industry, complete with a whole new way of doing business, characterized by a flat organization centered around the needs of the customers it served.

Mini-mill operators bought recycled scrap, used computer-aided design and computer-aided manufacturing, and produced finished products to customer specifications. Scrap steel was available almost everywhere, so they could move closer to their customers. They encouraged employee empowerment, which led to dramatic productivity improvements. Today, mini-mill operators, like Chaparral and Nucor, not only produce more steel than the integrated steel companies, they also rank high on the "Most Admired Corporation" list—a feat never accomplished by US Steel and Bethlehem.

Avoid the Quicksand of Incremental Improvement: Improving Today Almost Never Creates a Successful Tomorrow

Most organizations fail largely because they are focused on incremental improvements of the present, not a revivolution creation of the future. General Motors invested $121.8 billion in capital equipment and research and development during the 1980s, only to see its stock value fall $22.9 billion in the same period. We jokingly recall the picture of robots spray-painting other robots in Roger Smith's "Factory of the Future" as the classic example of misguided investments.

The General Motors experience exemplifies the need for revivolution and why investments in improving the present don't pay off. In the automobile business, as in many others, hectic speed and quantity of change create a deceptive illusion of dramatic improvement. Actually, most organizations are only making incremental changes at a whirlwind pace. The carousel whizzes by on spin cycle, and people think: "Wow. I'm really going places!" Not the case.

Revivolution spans the face of economic, political and organizational life. Everywhere we turn, every institution in our lives cries out for revivolution—now.

THESE ARE THE BEST OF TIMES—
FOR REVIVOLUTING FUTURES!

We live in a time of unparalleled abundance and prosperity. A 1996 study by David W. Moon for *Barron's* reveals that Americans today enjoy not only the highest standard of living, but also more disposable income than any preceding generation. Family income, adjusted for inflation, grew steadily throughout the 1980s. Real disposable income per capita rose steadily throughout the past two decades.

America is the job creation envy of the world. We've created more than 70 million new jobs since 1970, at least 10 million of them in this last half decade alone. And these are not "hamburger-flipping" jobs, either. More than 60 percent of the new jobs are high-paying managerial and professional positions.

All of this job creation goes on despite headline-grabbing stories about "downsizing." A recent black-bordered *Newsweek* cover story "Job Killers" is just plain wrong. Announced downsizings totaled 3 million workers since 1989. Compared to the 10 million new jobs, that means a net gain of 7 million new jobs, better than all the countries in Europe combined in the same time period. For instance, former AT&T CEO Bob Allen announced 40,000 reductions (which later shrank to 24,000). However, in the last decade, in the same industry, MCI added 36,000 new jobs and Sprint 25,000. IBM cut 135,000 people during the 1990s. In 1996, they hired 10,000 new people. The bottom line: America's unemployment rate—about 5 percent—is less than half that of the rest of the world. There are lots of high-paying jobs out there.

Americans are earning more, too. Real wages increased 9.3 percent since 1959, while wages as a percent of total income rose from 68.6 to 73.1 percent. So wage earners like you and me are getting a larger share of the economic pie these days. More important, real per capita personal income rose an average of 3.7 percent every year in the 1990s, enabling just about all of us to buy more of the things we like.

As a result of this economic prosperity, more and more poor people make it into the middle and upper class today than ever before. A University of Michigan study found that over a fifteen-year period (from 1974 to 1991) only one in twenty poor Americans stay poor, thirteen become middle-class, and six become rich. The U.S. Treasury found similar results. That's the best upward mobility rate ever.

But good-paying jobs rely upon education. The pay difference between those with and without college degrees continues to widen. In 1979, there was a 49 percent wage difference between college and noncollege wages. Today that difference is 89 percent. The message: if you want a brighter future, go to school. That's a good news message, though, because more educational opportunities exist in the United States than anywhere else in the world.

JOIN THE REVIVOLUTION: FOLLOW THE FOOTPRINTS OF OTHER REVIVOLUTING INDIVIDUALS

Many people are enlisting in the revivolutionary army. They are proactively, revolutionarily creating new futures for themselves. Are you ready to join up? Follow these footprints.

The Surplus Executive Finds a New Home

Imagine the challenge confronting Ned, a fifty-eight-year-old marketing executive laid off from a large company. Ned spent all of his thirty-six years of gainful employment with large organizations. He found that large organizations don't often hire people his age for executive positions.

He finally found a spot with a much smaller organization. He told us, "It's sort of like it used to be in my old organization, with one basic difference. I know now that every day I have to sell something, make something, ship something and collect something—or I don't eat. There is no big Deep Pockets Daddy to finance me for a while or some assistant to make my calls or prepare my handouts. I've got to rely upon doing it myself—every day." Ned revivoluted himself in order to create his future in the midst of continuous upheaval.

New Life Chasing White Balls on the Greens

Dan was forty-seven when we met him—a senior vice president for information technology for a major money center bank. Dan had it all: a top job in a cutting-edge profession with a growing company, and a new beautiful wife and three wonderful children. Two years later we encountered Dan at an information technology conference. He still had the beautiful wife and family, but was now with another company. "My former company decided to outsource IT, so I became excess baggage. A great outplacement package enabled me to land with this smaller company, at just about what I was making, with a real opportunity to make a difference. My family loves the new location. I'm set for life."

Maybe. But "life" turned out to be a lot shorter than Dan was thinking about. We ran into him at a restaurant recently and got caught up on his activities. "I left that company within a year. They wanted ninety hours a week from me. It was too much. Talked it over with my wife and kids and decided that life was too short to invest that much in somebody else's future. Why not invest it in my own, we figured. I quit the job and went to golf school to become a pro golfer. At age fifty-one I decided to do what I've always wanted to do—play and teach golf. Cut back on our expenses and lived on our savings for the year I went to school. Now I'm the assistant pro at the big course in town and loving every minute. Come on out and play a few holes. Who knows what you might decide to do."

Talk about revivoluting. Dan seized the moment and created his own future.

Do I Have to Go Back and Sit in a Classroom Again?

We met Jonathan at a seminar some years ago. He was almost forty years old and had worked his way up to a mid-level management position at a large industrial naval installation in town. But he was unhappy. "I've been marking time for the past ten years. I've just got to do something else. There's talk of privatizing the base, or moving our work to some other location. I could be on the street—and not know what to do."

We urged him to consider one of several education programs that might give him a non-navy perspective and set of skills as well as getting him into a network of people working in the private sector.

"What, you want me to go back to school?" he exclaimed. "It's been eighteen years since I've sat in a classroom. I don't think I can do it." Much conversation later, Jonathan agreed to talk to an MBA admissions counselor.

Jonathan dropped off the radar screen for several years, until we ran into him in a shopping mall. We shared a cup of coffee and his revivolution story. He signed up for and completed the Executive Masters of Business Administration program. He applied a number of ideas to improve his section at the base that he developed as part of his master's, got recognized by the captain and then the admiral for his improvements and wound up leading the reinvention task force team.

"It was the biggest kick in my entire life. I got several offers from folks in private industry. One finally was too good to pass up. I'm leaving next weekend to begin my new life in Oklahoma."

We smiled as we went looking for our family members in the mall. We midwifed another successful revivoluteer.

So, You Think One Person Can't Make a Difference, eh? Ask Carol About That

Carol worked as a technical writer for a large engineering/architecture firm. She was good at what she did. But it didn't bring her much joy. Her boss was very supportive. "Why don't you try your hand at design," she suggested. Carol did a little design work on a project and liked it (as did the architect on the project).

Carol signed up to go to evening school to learn design. Six long years later, balancing night school, a day job and a growing family, Carol finally graduated and became state-certified. Just recently we saw an article in the local paper that Carol's firm won the "orchid of the year" award for the best-designed building, and Carol was mentioned as the project designer. Who says one person can't make a difference? Carol did!

Calling the Doctor: Information Please

Greg was an impressive figure sitting in the rear of the seminar room at the executive MBA class we recently taught. With a full head of silver hair, an easy smile and a soft and reassuring voice, it was easy to see why he ran one of the most successful gynecology practices in town. Why was he in this expensive, intensive, self-paid two-year education program?

He told us. "I've been delivering babies in this town for almost twenty years, and get Christmas cards from more than a thousand people every year. But I make less today to deliver a baby than I did twenty years ago, while my expenses are up more than 2,000 percent. Beyond the money, the practice has changed. People are less courteous, more demanding, less willing to listen to advice. It's just not as much fun anymore. I'm going to open a chain of stores providing products, services and information oriented toward middle-aged women. My wife and I researched the field and decided that there is a huge unmet need out there. More importantly though, this will give us a chance to recapture our life together. We're not getting any younger, and if we don't do it now I'm afraid that we'll be too locked into the practice to give it up. At forty-seven these flowers can still bloom in a new garden."

We'd wager that the fragrance from their revivoluting blossoms fills the air. By the way, he's one of six physicians in that class, all looking to use the lever of additional business education to revivolute themselves into new careers.

Pink Cadillacs and Green Dollars

Then there's the woman who took her life savings of $5,000 and renewed her personal and professional world. After working for years in direct sales, she launched a new life as an entrepreneur, opening a small storefront. She later became an author. She branched out into helping other women become financially independent and personally more fulfilled. Today, that little family business has grown to a nearly $2 billion cosmetics company with an international presence. Her name: Mary Kay Ash. Her company: Mary Kay Cosmetics. She is one of *Forbes* magazine's "Greatest Success Stories of All Time." She now devotes her time to helping other women become the beautiful living legends they deserve to be.

Right, I can hear you saying. That's just a once-in-a-blue-moon experience.

But think again. Today there are 3.5 million female-owned, home-based businesses in the United States, employing 14 million people on a full- or part-time basis. And they're making very good money.

Leading Active Revivoluteer Lives

We—Jerre and Jim—have lived active revivoluteer lives ourselves. One of us started out in personnel in a large company. (Actually yearning to be a teacher, just like Dad, but didn't because of a severe stuttering problem.) Then revivoluted into a college professor (after taming the stuttering somewhat), researcher and writer. All the while maintaining a strong business connection, working as both a consultant and business owner. In retrospect, both of us have revolutionarily revived our careers at least half a dozen times in the course of forty-five years. For us, revivolution is a personal way of life.

THE PHOENIX METAPHOR FOR
REVIVOLUTIONARY SELF-RENEWAL

"Okay, okay," you say. "I got it. I've got to revivolute—change dramatically. But I've tried that before and failed. I've quit smoking nineteen times. I've been on seventeen crash diets that only *add* inches to my waist line. How do I revivolute?"

Look around you for the answer. Self-renewal is the way. See self-renewal in living color blossoming before your eyes. From the ever-renewing sunrise to the season-changing colors on the trees, we live a life that continuously rejuvenates itself—and ourselves. Renewal is a natural and permanent part of life. Plants renew themselves. People renew themselves. Organizations renew themselves. Revivolute yourself through self-renewal.

Now is the time for self-renewal. Robin Williams standing on desktops in *Dead Poets Society* shouting, "Carpe Diem"—seize the day. There is no time like the present. We live in good times— good economic times, and good times to move on to new lives. One executive we know told us recently, "I'm going to die in six months. Not a physical death. But my life in this job will end in six months. Once I complete the projects on which I'm working— and that will take about six months—I will stop doing what I'm doing. I will have made the last big payment on my retirement annuity. The last child will be out of school. At fifty-two, it's time to think about what I want to do with the rest of my life. I may take on another role in this organization, may keep the same role but change the way I think and do this job. I may move on to another organization or change professions altogether. Whatever I do, it won't be what I'm doing now." The same "What do I want to do with the rest of my life" question resounds over and over again in executive suites, plant floors, classrooms and living rooms. The answer to the question will be found in the pages of this book.

The Phoenix is the mythical symbol of the continually renewing life force. Throughout history and across many different cultures, humans have told stories about, fantasized about and worshiped the forever-renewing Phoenix. Each culture paints a similar picture of the self-renewing Phoenix: beautiful sunrise-sunset gold and crimson feathers, a bird which renews itself, a soaring spirit that periodically emerges in newly re-created forms. The great scarlet and purple creature continually soars past its yesterdays on its way to brighter tomorrows. For all of humankind's history, the Phoenix embodied a core attribute of time and life itself: the renewal of all living things. The Phoenix is a symbol of hope for the future—and of our enduring capacity to create infinitely better tomorrows for ourselves and others.

The Roman poet Ovid wrote: "There is one bird which renews itself out of itself. The Assyrians call it the Phoenix." But there is no need to go back 2,000 years to see examples of the self-renewing Phoenix. Look at the sun every day or the changing colors of the leaves and the seasons to see renewal played out in living color. From the spring festivals of Easter and Passover to the fall and winter festivals of Thanksgiving, Christmas and Hanukkah, we order our lives, our work, and our celebrations around the recurring cycle of renewal.

The economist Joseph Schumpeter talked about the phoenix-like characteristics of our economic system that cyclically leaves the "old order" behind in order to create a better "new order." We believe that this same life cycle exists for organizations and individuals. In fact, we've seen it, and lived it.

Look around you today and see, feel and hear self-renewal taking place. Turn every page in this book and you'll read about self-renewal. It is a constant theme. It represents the overpowering reality with which we deal, day in and day out, minute in and minute out. In a world rent by change, Phoenix self-renewal is the path to a more secure future. Renew, revitalize and re-create yourself. Be a soaring Phoenix.

PREVIEW OF COMING ATTRACTIONS

To soar, the self-renewing Phoenix utilizes the five principles discussed on the following pages.

First, Renew Yourself: Create a Future That Makes a Difference and Leaves a Legacy

"Change an organization"—now there's an oxymoron. Years of working to "change" organizations—either our own or others—convince us that "change" is an elusive rare species, often talked about, seldom observed and rarely captured. Look around. Read the business press. Talk to your colleagues. The instances of successful long-term organizational change are as rare as polar bears in Peru.

Why the poor record? And, given the poor record, why the repeated efforts? The answer: each and every one of us shares the deep desire to learn, to grow, to make a difference. We are filled with the wonder and awe of what can be—along with the terror of what might be. The questions swirl through heads—and hearts—and dog our every step. Like a resounding bell in a endless series of valleys, they echo through waking and sleeping hours. Will tomorrow be better than today? Will I be better off tomorrow? Will my children? My grandchildren? Can I make a difference in my life and in the lives of those around me? What do I want the rest of my life to be like? What do I want my work environment—my organization—to be like? Can I really make a difference?

In the answers to those questions lies the kernel of this book, and our promise of a better tomorrow. We're on a journey—an exciting adventure into tomorrow. We are optimists. We believe that earnest, hardworking folks can create their own future, make it better, leave a mark and help others. We know that one person with courage can make a revolution. It takes hard thinking and hard working. Sir Edmund Hillary didn't take a Sunday stroll and wind up at the top of Mount Everest. We are ready. Are you?

It Is Easier to Create Tomorrow than Change Today. Everywhere we look, there's a need to change: "The morning bathroom line is killing me: we need a bigger house. The car is rattling: time to trade in and up. Why can't the children get better grades in school and be better behaved? Got to change their attitude. The job looks dicey: better look into changing jobs before the reduction in force comes."

On and on it goes. Change rears its ugly head in every aspect of our lives.

We busy ourselves trying to "change things." Virtually every change effort begins with a simple assumption that colors everything: we can change what other people do. At home, we micromanage the kids, grounding them when they misbehave or get poor grades, and even do their homework with them to make certain it's correct and gets turned in on time. At work, we install customer service programs to change the way employees treat customers. We adopt simultaneous engineering to change the way engineers develop products. We establish lean manufacturing techniques to change the way production workers produce products. We reengineer systems to change the way people process the reams of data in our world. All these efforts rely upon the simple assumption that we can change the way people perform.

"Nonsense," shouts the more than a century of experience between us. Rather than attempting to change an ongoing situation, we've discovered that it is far easier to create a brand-new one. "Green field" organizations and situations almost invariably are more successful. Yet we go merrily on our way trying to "change things." "Insanity is doing the same things and expecting different outcomes," Einstein said. Judged by that standard, most of us are certifiably insane.

Self-renewal Is Job No. 1. Nothing is forever. Today's star is forgotten tomorrow. Today's market leaders become tomorrow's also-rans. Yakov Smirnoff is an example of successful self-renewal. The Russian comedian, of "Oh, What a Country!" fame, had a very successful career in the 1980s—a weekly sitcom, parts in several movies and a highly visible Best Western commercial. His satirical way of looking at things Americans take for granted, combined with his trademark laughter, made Smirnoff a famous, successful celebrity.

But, as in all businesses, times changed. The Wall fell, the Soviet Union imploded and being a Russian comedian no longer had a mystique. The canceled TV show and diminished bookings convinced Smirnoff that he needed a new act. He moved to Branson, Missouri, renewed himself and relaunched his career. He's now a very successful theater operator/performer. Self-renewal was Job No. 1 for Yakov—and it paid off.

Mother Earth's Self-renewal in Bright Red and Black. Visit the big island of Hawaii and watch the earth renew itself. On the southeastern side of the island, 3,000-degree lava spills out of *Kilauea* destroying tropical forests, covering the land with smoldering black lava and creating hundreds of acres of new land. Just thirty miles to the north up the coast, too-many-to-count waterfalls spill the two hundred or more inches of rainfall into the ocean carrying in their muddy waters the remnants of thousands-of-years-ago lava flows now softened into rich, fertile soil.

Self-renewal is Job No. 1 for the earth. Molten rock boils up from beneath the oceans and eventually forms land, hard crusts of moonscape-like barrenness. The wind, rain and sun weather the land, transforming the hard rock into fertile soil. Plants, animals, birds and insects populate the forest, taking it into another renewal stage. The wind and rain ceaselessly wash the now soft and fertile soil back into the ocean, causing yet another renewal phase. In time, the land will disappear again beneath the waves to be renewed in another place and time.

As it is with the earth, so it is with humans. In fact, our life's story is the story of continual renewal: from child to student to husband to parent to grandparent, from engineer to manager to executive to president to friend. And we're not done yet. We know the value of continual renewal. We know that we must continue to create our own future—seize the moment—be in charge. That's why we choose the Phoenix as the symbol for our book.

Create a Tomorrow That Makes a Difference and Leaves a Legacy of Which You Can Be Proud. But what kind of tomorrow is worth creating, worth spending the long hours toiling in the salt mines? What kind of "new order" do you want? It certainly isn't the "new order" of the dark ages where civilization almost disappeared. Neither for us is it the "new order" of fear for one's job that characterizes so much of the downsizing and right-sizing that passes for corporate revitalization these days.

What "new order" do we want? Hard question, easy answer. Like most of you, we yearn to leave a legacy, something that makes a difference in the world and makes our children proud to carry our name. We collect our children's prizes and prominently display them throughout our home and office. We are not unique. A neighbor's son is a very good soccer player. Soccer trophies decorate their fireplace. Pictures of their son in action on the soccer field, along with his numerous "My Child Was Citizen/Scholar of the Month" bumper stickers, line the guest bathroom walls. Part of their legacy is their award-winning soccer-playing son.

Our neighbors are no different than President Bill Clinton, who frets about his place in history, or Jack Welch, who wants to create a General Electric that continues to grow and prosper after he leaves. At the deepest point in our souls, each of us wants to leave something worthwhile behind. We "Soar with the Phoenix" when we keep creating new futures that will help us leave a legacy that truly makes a difference.

Second, Plug into Your Connections

Ah, What a Web of Business and Personal Connections We Weave. We are connected to many people: some we know, most we don't. Connections tie us together as members in the human family. Follow the connection lines for Sally, an engineer at Boeing Aircraft. Sally is connected to other Boeing employees: the eighteen members of her engine casing development team for the Boeing 747 airplane, the 2,400 members of Boeing's product development department who develop other components of the 747, the 6,200 product development employees working on other aircraft like the 737 and the 777, the other 12,400 members of Boeing's commercial aerospace division, and the balance of Boeing's 42,000 employees. She knows only 500 of her 42,000 Boeing connections, but she is intimately connected to them all. If one mechanic forgets to complete the solder on one rivet and that causes one Boeing 747 to fall out of the sky, Sally's job is at risk—as are all 42,000 employees' jobs.

Sally is also connected to the thousands of suppliers who provide more than 60 percent of the components that compose the 747. And she's connected to the airlines who buy 747s and the airlines' customers (you and me) who occupy those jumbo jet seats. Sally also has many connections in her home community of Seattle, including neighbors, teachers, grocery clerks and insurance brokers. Many people across the world own shares in Boeing, and thus Sally is connected to all of them.

Sally also has a wide range of personal connections. She's connected with her primary and extended families. Friends are im-

portant to Sally. Her personal telephone book bulges with the
names of hundreds of fellow MIT graduates. She's active in several professional associations and those names fill her book as
well. Sally serves on a planning subcommittee in her community.
Through that work she's met a number of the local officials and
businesspeople.

Sally's connections are many and complex, numbering in the
hundreds of thousands. She knows personally only a few of the
many people who influence her life and whose lives she touches
in one way or another. Sally is interconnected with others in the
way the air molecules inside a balloon are connected to each
other: push one side of the balloon in and it moves all the molecules around and changes the shape of the entire balloon. Sally
lives in a connected world. We all do.

John Donne, the famous English poet, articulated connectedness four hundred years ago when he wrote, "No man is an island." The Internet is today's manifestations of Donne's poem,
where everything is connected to everything and everyone is
connected to everyone. You can't see the Internet, you can't
touch it. Yet the Internet, like the personal and business network
connections in which we all participate, is one of life's most fundamental facts.

**All Business Connections Are Personal, and Personal Connec-
tions Are Another Form of Business.** People don't buy from a
business. They buy from a person. We buy a car from a salesperson, not a dealership. After all, there are lots of dealerships selling identical automobiles. Walk down the street and listen to the
pitchmen. Pick out one you can trust and that's whom you'll do
business with. That's true buying cars, homes and components
for 747s. Sally will tell you that. She works hard to build trust
with her customers and her teammates. She delivers what she
promises and works to only promise what she can deliver. Business is relationships, and all relationships are personal.

"Balance" is a popular word these days: balance between family and work, between work and exercise, between career and
personal development, according to Sue Schellenberger in the
Wall Street Journal. She cites the example of Randall Tobias,
chairman and CEO of the large pharmaceutical company Eli
Lilly, who says: "I don't want to be defined solely by the boxes I
happen to occupy on organization charts. I also want to be de-

fined as the father of my children." J. Michael Cook, CEO of Deloitte Touche Tohmatsu, a large accounting and consulting firm, said, "I wish that over the years I had more control over my time and more opportunities to be involved in family things. I wish I'd understood the importance of that Thursday afternoon soccer game. . . . At Deloitte we say to people, 'Though client demands drive our days, we have the flexibility of having multiple clients and the freedom to make our own schedule and to decide how and where to spend our time. Take advantage of that flexibility.'"

Those words strike a chord with us. We understand the importance of balance between personal and business life all too well. Some years ago we lost our top financial person because his wife died and he just fell apart. His personal life so impacted his business life that he lost both. Every day we encounter people struggling with personal issues that affect their business day. Tobias's words ring true for us. We, too, want to be more than a box on an organization chart. Don't we all? We've said words similar to Cook's to ourselves and the folks with whom we work. As the leaders of our organizations we know that we must be concerned with the personal as well as the business life of our teammates. As we'll say repeatedly throughout this book, "You can't hire a hand, or a brain. You hire the whole person and all of that person's business and personal connections."

Recognize and Honor Your Connections. Connectedness and interdependency are not new concepts. We borrow them from our colleagues in biology and in physics. We see them today, in living color, as the Internet, read about them as the "network organization" or the "virtual organization." It's a popular topic, because beyond the hype, this vital interconnectedness drives a great deal of our behavior.

Each of us—like Sally—has many connections that are like ever-widening ripples caused by a stone in a calm lake. Our point: we live lives connected to many others. These connections form the framework within which each of us plays our part. Identify your connections and the role you play in their lives and the complementary role they play in yours. Leverage these connections to create a future that leaves a legacy that makes a difference.

Third, Create Success for All Your Connections

Hands need bodies. People need communities, nations and this planet. We are all interconnected—and interdependent. A healthy hand depends on a healthy body. A healthy person depends upon a healthy community, a healthy nation and a healthy planet. Since we're all connected, my health depends upon your health. My success, therefore, depends upon your success. I am as committed to helping you succeed as I am to helping me to succeed. Isn't that logical? Of course.

That's why good "capitalists" are concerned about the health and success of employees and community members—as well as shareholders. James Gwarty, Robert Lawson and Walter Bark of the Cato Institute point out that free market activities exist within a democratic context. Research clearly supports the reality of this interdependence. On the most macro level, economic freedom produces national prosperity. Political freedom is a necessary prerequisite to economic freedom. Democracy fosters a market economy that, in turn, creates prosperity. Political democracy in a community, then, is the driving force that enables economic prosperity for any given organization within that community.

Freedom creates the opportunity for people to generate innovative ways to help customers succeed, while a totalitarian state limits both the range of options available to create customer success and the sole customer for whom success must be created: the state. Successful American business organizations today can thank the framers of the Constitution two hundred years ago. To ensure their future success, organizations today must work to strengthen political freedom and the long-term viability of the market economy.

Take the "create success for others" mandate to the more personal level. Teaching is the best way to learn. Medical training is based on the "see one, do one, teach one" philosophy, where the doctor-in-training sees a procedure done, does the procedure himself, and then, to reinforce the knowledge, teaches the procedure to the next group of doctors-to-be. We've learned a lot about life teaching scouting to our kids. Our wives learned a lot about faith teaching Sunday school. Helping others learn helps the teacher learn. What a win-win deal. And a great example of how our "create success for others" philosophy helps create success for you.

Fourth, Learn More in Order to Contribute More to Others' Success

"How Safe Is Your Job?" the headline agonizes from the cover of *Fortune* magazine. "Job Killers," the cover of *Time* wails in angst above the scapegoated "Rogues Gallery" of corporate presidents who announced substantial job reductions. From the six o'clock news, to the drive-time talk shows, to the business press, the media howl of economic instability reverberates.

Those misleading headlines do, however, present truth in one regard: gone is the idea that organizations create job security. Writers of every stripe, from the union press to the "Capitalist Tool" *Forbes,* convinced us for years that "The Company" or "The Union" or "The Government" would take care of us. Recall the words of Tennessee Ernie Ford's song "Sixteen Tons": "He mined sixteen tons of Number Nine coal . . . but he owed his soul to the company store." Is that the job security we want? Obviously not.

In truth, there never was security in any job—except the security of indentured servitude that Tennessee Ernie Ford sang about. Union or nonunion—it never mattered much. There were jobs in good times and no jobs in bad times. And the bad times came frequently.

"Okay, okay," you say. "I see what you mean. I've got to create my own job security. But how do I do that? It sounds like an impossible task." Make no mistake. It isn't easy. But it is doable. The solution is simple to articulate, and hard to do: keep learning more so you can create more value for others.

In the 1960s Sonny Werblin, owner of the AFL New York Jets, paid an astronomical $400,000 to Joe Namath, a gimpy-kneed quarterback from Alabama. He was vilified in the press for spending ten times what other leading quarterbacks were receiving at that time. Yet, using the draw of Joe Namath's name, Werblin increased season ticket sales by more than $2 million. What would you do if someone offered to give you $2 million tomorrow if you could scrape up $400,000 today? You'd mortgage the house and everything you owned to the max. A 500 percent return in one year is better than the tables at Vegas. Was Namath worth $400,000? Absolutely. He created value five times his cost for his "customers"—the owners who paid him and the fans in the seats.

The Namath principle applies in organizations as well. The best job security in any organization is to create so much value for others that they see you as essential to their own success. How do you do that? By learning more. Joe Namath not only had a strong arm, he also worked hard studying defenses. He worked hard learning—and it paid off for himself, Sonny Werblin and the millions of football fans he entertained every Sunday afternoon. Use his lesson—learn more—to create success for everyone in your network—including yourself. We will talk about how to do these easy-sounding but difficult-to-execute activities in later chapters.

Fifth, Take Ownership of Your Company and Your Life

We hear it all the time. "That's all well and good for you to say take ownership. After all, you're the CEO. But I'm a middle manager. I work for a Neanderthal. We just announced a 12 percent reduction in force and I'm not certain I'll make the cut. Look, I need this job. I've got a mortgage to pay and hungry mouths to feed. I'd better keep my nose clean and not make waves." Or, "Me? A leader? I'm just a machinist around here. I just do what they tell me to do. 'Leave the engineering to the engineers. Just do what you're told,' the foreman told me last week after chewing me out for making a small adjustment in my machine to make it easier to use and faster."

Yet who gets hurt when the business goes south and customers tell us to get lost? Look in the mirror for the answer. If each and every one of us does not assume responsibility for making tomorrow different, none of us has a place there.

The old movie *High Noon* says it best. In that movie a bunch of bad guys ride into town and cow the merchants. There are more merchants than bad guys. The merchants have more guns than the bad guys. But the merchants cannot get themselves together. Along comes the hero, Gary Cooper. The merchants talk him into saving them. Though he tries mightily to get them involved in the fight, at high noon there he is, on that dusty street, packing iron, facing the bad guys alone as the merchants hide behind their counters.

Of course, Coop the hero wins and the merchants come out of hiding and cheer him. In a moving ceremony, they offer him their sheriff's badge. He throws the badge in the dirt. He knows that without the merchants' taking responsibility for their own protection, it is only a matter of time until he winds up in a wooden box. The message of the movie is clear: everyone must assume responsibility for his or her own success. How to do that is found in the chapters that follow.

The message is very important. Each and every one of us can make a difference. You are responsible for your life and your career success just like each of us—Jerre and Jim—is responsible for his life. One person can—and will—make a revivolution. Are you ready?

THE ROAD MAP

The self-renewing Phoenix soars, renewing its vision, revitalizing its spirit and re-creating its success when it spreads its leadership wings and takes charge. The self-renewing Phoenix leads his or her network of interconnected people to create another symbol of the legacy of continuing success: the Pyramid, itself a symbol of enduring greatness and creativity. We've divided our book, like ancient Gaul, into three parts.

Part 1: Introduction to Phoenix Principles. In this section we spell out the basic principles for becoming a soaring Phoenix: renewal is the natural way to create a future, we are all interconnected and interdependent, and creating success for others is the best way to create success for yourself. The Phoenix soars utilizing these principles.

Part 2: Phoenix Leadership. We soar like the Phoenix when we take ownership of our organization and our lives and become a leader. A soaring Phoenix seizes the moment, takes charge and helps everyone with whom he is connected achieve their dreams and aspirations. Phoenix leaders make five critical contributions to the success of their interdependent, interconnected people: they surface issues, engage the people, prioritize resources, unleash ownership and energize learning.

Part 3: The Phoenix Pyramid. The Phoenix leader then creates the new foundation for future success. That solid new foundation is represented by a Pyramid, itself a symbol of strength and creativity. We'll lay out the systematic way a Phoenix leader builds that solid Pyramid base for the future success of vision, mission, values, goals, strategies, disciplined management infrastructures, business processes and communication systems.

Throughout, we'll challenge you to renew yourself, develop your leadership skills and build your strong Pyramid base for future success.

Authors' Biases:
Do What Actually Works, Do What's Really Right

Just so you know. We are primarily businesspeople. Our focus is: "Does it work?" We are practical folk, more impressed with the elegance of work ability than the elaborate articulation of philosophy.

We are also emotional people. We think with our hearts as well as our heads. We are more concerned with the question "Is it the right thing to do?" than "Are we doing it right?" We have often walked away from "good" business deals because there were "bad" strings attached.

And we are doers. We believe that people learn by doing, not talking. So, let's get on with the doing.

CHAPTER 2

We Are All in This Together: People Need People on the Global Net

Self-renewal is Job No. 1. That's the first Phoenix principle. Connectivity, or we are all connected, is the second principle. That's what this chapter is about.

One of the best examples of connectivity is the Net—the ubiquitous Internet. Millions use it and populate it; the number of users grows at double-digit rates *a month* and is projected to reach one billion by the end of the twentieth century. The Internet fundamentally changes business, communications, politics—life as we know it. Yet no one can see it, touch it or feel it. The Internet revolutionizes our lives, and we can't even draw a picture of it.

But the Internet is only one example of the networks that connect people. The network of graduates from our university is another example of connectivity: everyone who graduated from the university is connected to everyone else who graduated from it. Our church is another network that connects people all over the world. We live in a network world where these networks form the warp and woof of life.

We will talk in this chapter about how to use this network thinking to soar with the Phoenix. Three key threads are woven throughout this chapter: we are interconnected; we are interdependent; we are tied together by the common purpose of creating success for all those we serve.

WE ARE ALL CONNECTED:
EVERYONE IS LINKED TO EVERYTHING

"The knee bone's connected to the thigh bone. The thigh bone's connected to the hip bone, the hip bone's connected to the back bone . . . now hear the word of the Lord," the old spiritual went. That's also the word of the self-renewing Phoenix, looking over the landscape of the globe and seeing a mosaic of interconnected networks.

The Power of Interconnectedness: The NCR Experience

NCR (at the time part of AT&T/NCR) implemented a new organizational concept, customer focused teams (CFTs). These cross-functional teams from sales, finance, marketing and professional services organized around specific customers. CFTs were either assigned to major accounts or a limited number of medium-sized accounts. There were about 500 teams globally. The new model changed everything, not only within NCR, but also with all the interconnected customer and supplier systems.

In dealing with Wal-Mart, for instance, many things changed as a result of the new CFT organization structure. The NCR CFT leader held regular meetings with Wal-Mart's CIO, his staff and the heads of the major operating units. Together they set mutually agreed upon objectives for the installation and implementation of a series of computer-aided merchandise-ordering processes. The CFT leader was the only vender to participate in Wal-Mart strategic planning sessions. Members of the CFT spent many hours working side by side with Wal-Mart employees at store locations across the country solving installation problems, training store personnel and actually operating the system during busy times. "I thought they were on Wal-Mart's payroll. I even issued them an employee badge," a store manager said about her NCR CFT members. The CFT system change fundamentally altered the relationship between NCR and its interconnected customer, Wal-Mart.

The shift to CFTs changed the interconnected systems within

the organization as well. For example, the human resources senior vice president realigned his organization to support the CFTs. He decentralized much of the HR function out of headquarters, placing them geographically closer to the CFTs. He gained significant productivity improvement by focusing the objectives, measures and rewards for all HR associates around creating success for client CFTs.

Some of the interconnected changes caused by the switch to CFTs were not as positive. The CFT leaders in the field set pricing for their customers. They pressured the finance department to create a pricing book and a pricing model for their use in the field. The finance associates were in a difficult spot. Initially they could not meet their internal customers' request because their data wasn't good enough to produce the pricing book quickly, and they did not have the resources to fix the data shortfalls. NCR associates experienced difficult times making the new system work because a key interconnected system was missing.

The CFT model also redefined NCR's relationships with its interconnected suppliers. For example, NCR held monthly video teleconferences with Intel, a key supplier of chips. As a result of those meetings, Intel sped up their development of the high-performance chips NCR needed for their massively parallel-processing equipment they sold to Wal-Mart.

The bottom line: change one network, how the field organization is structured—from a functional structure to CFTs—and you impact every other interconnected network both internally and externally. The NCR story is a good-news story. They grew their revenues more than 20 percent during the next twelve months, the largest growth at NCR in many years. The effects of the new CFT model reverberated outward through hundreds and thousands of interconnected networks, renewing roles, relationships and tomorrows for all the people it touched.

The Butterfly Effect: Every Person Has Unforeseeable Power to Create Tomorrow

We touch an array of global networks every day. It is easy to feel overwhelmed and powerless. That feeling was expressed by one machinist we know who said, "Hey, I'm just one person. How much of an impact can I really have?"

Actually, you can have amazing impact that is unpredictably far-reaching. Systems research is based upon the core principle that small causes have large consequences. The "butterfly effect" in meteorology is one of the best examples. We've often heard it said (in fact, in truth we've often used the same metaphor) that the butterfly flapping its wings in Peking contributes to the tornado in Kansas. This suggests that every individual person (a butterfly) can influence major complex systems. One person can make a difference.

Individual Butterflies Taking Small Actions That Make Big Differences. A shipping supervisor at a Square D factory in South Carolina was one such butterfly. One weekend, the company received an emergency call from a nuclear power plant on the East Coast. They needed a critical part immediately. The supervisor took it upon herself to use her own personal credit card to fly the part to the Boston area in a heroic effort to delight the customer with a lightning-fast response. The part solved the problem, and the plant continued to operate. Square D kept the customer, which contributed to keeping a 2,000-person plant operating. Two million people kept their lights on. One person took a small action that made a big difference.

One Butterfly Designs a Truck. *Business Week* in its July 29, 1996, issue reports the work of James C. Bulin, another butterfly. He lived his working life buried in the bowels of the Ford Motor Company. His offbeat ideas were often ignored or laughed at. Imagine his surprise when he was singled out for his contribution to the success of Ford's best-selling F-150 truck. Rather than beginning from the traditional benchmarking of other successful cars, mid-level designer Bulin focused on customer desires. He identified six generational groups and their values and tastes. For instance, "Depression Kids," born between 1920 and 1934, plan for rainy days and look for status in automobiles. They like "new" and "powerful" and "colorful," so they trade up each year. The "Birth Dearthers," born between 1970 and 1977, on the other hand, grew up with a silver spoon, but don't have the income yet to support their tastes. They look for sport utility vehicles and practical cars like sedans.

Bulin convinced the designers to narrow the cab by two inches and lengthen it by five inches to give it the more lean and muscular look that would appeal to the "Baby Boomers." Virtually every detail of the F-150 got redesigned using Bulin's generational value groups data. Ford increased the wheel size to make the truck taller and give it greater presence (something desired by the "Lost Generationers" and the "Birth Dearthers"), while also smoothing out the tire tread to give it a softer ride (something desired by the "Baby Boomers"). Bulin's ideas may produce the next category killer automobile for Ford and over $1 billion in net earnings. Not bad results from one small idea.

Billiard Balls Create Great Music. Oftentimes unrelated activities have large unforeseen consequences. What's the relationship between billiards and music? None, you say. Perhaps that's true for ordinary mortals like us. But for the great composer Mozart, there was a close relationship between his two loves, billiards and music. Mozart found great relaxation—and inspiration—in billiards. Standing at the edge of the table waiting to shoot, he was captivated by the sequence, rhythm and pitch of the clicking balls. His scribbled notes at the pool table became transcendent musical experiences. Perhaps your scribbled notes will be as valuable one day. Never doubt that you will make a difference. Only time will tell how great.

Each of us *can indeed* have a significant impact on tomorrow, like that butterfly in Peking influencing the weather halfway around the world.

The Butterfly and El Niño. Because everything is connected to everything, small changes in one area produce major changes in many other areas. Take the current that runs off the coast of Chile in South America. Every so often it decides to move to the north. Oceanographers and meteorologists do not know what causes the movement. They do know, however, that when the current moves, it triggers droughts and firestorms in Australia, floods and forest fires in California. We all know that "butterfly" current as El Niño. A little ocean butterfly changes half the world's weather.

In short, the knee bone is connected to the thigh bone, and every other bone as well. That interconnectedness offers each of

us great potential to make a big difference. Remember that butterfly, and Mozart . . . and soar with the Phoenix.

INTERDEPENDENCIES: PEOPLE NEED PEOPLE
WHO NEED PEOPLE

Share Your Value or Perish: Connect Intelligence and Talent

None of us is as smart as all of us. The collective sum of all our
knowledge and talent is greater than that of any individual. No
single individual in an organization knows all that the organization knows. On his way out the door one day for an important job
interview, I remember Dad asking me, "Where are the Yankees
these days in the standings and how are they doing?" I knew
more than he about sports, and he wanted a "door opener" comment from me for his job interview. Together, we got that job—
and the increased standard of living that went with it. At that
moment he needed my information.

Interdependencies create and sustain life. We need each other.
We need help—not only to survive and grow—but to live fulfilling
lives and spread success. We cannot live in isolation.

Whenever Two or More Are Gathered in His Name . . . Whether
it's a profit or nonprofit organization, interdependent groups of
folks are the basic building blocks of organizations. Take Ginghamsburg United Methodist Church. Once a tiny congregation in
a minuscule Ohio village, the organization grew dramatically—
from ninety to more than 2,000—in little more than ten years.
The secret? Small "cell" groups that meet in homes and develop
interdependent, meaningful, productive relationships.

Once a small, steepled country kirk in a rural countryside,
Ginghamsburg is now a sprawling, bustling community-worship,
activities and counseling center. It includes a resale clothing
store, women's counseling center, a food pantry, a community-
crisis outreach program, a furniture warehouse, three children's

clubhouses and many other critical support services. The church holds four worship services each weekend—with attendance averaging over 3,000.

In his book, *Spiritual Entrepreneurs: Six Principles for Risking Renewal*, the church's pastor, Michael Slaughter, underscores the importance of small groups of interdependent parishioners as catalysts for successful growth and meaningful spiritual experiences. These small groups "have the power to break addictions, overcome co-dependent tendencies, and restore broken relationships." They are also the key to rapid growth.

Ingenious Interdependencies: Rise of a Roman Empire. In the Prato region of Italy between Florence and Pistoia is a "virtual organization" made up of interdependent businesses. President Massimo Menichetti launched a revivolution that exploded a large, hierarchical textile organization into small chunks. But how those chunks flourished! Each one became a business. *Strategy and Leadership* journal, in its July-August 1996 issue, reported how he did it.

"I wanted the finishing department to specialize in what they were good at; I broke up the spinning and weaving departments and let them excel in whatever they wanted to specialize in, unencumbered by the rest of the specialities," explained Menichetti. He reasoned: "If they innovate and are good at what they are doing, they can always sell their products to somebody in Prato." The large, informal Prato network is interconnected by "impannatores" who act as the network's liaison with customers. The impannatores connect the interdependent small businesses—as well as create new markets and develop the infrastructure. The interdependencies make the whole business region stronger.

How did he do it? Menichetti sold almost half of the company stock to employees—and allowed them to pay with profits over the following three years. The disaggregation worked—in spades. So much so, in fact, that the pattern repeated itself over and over throughout the region. Today, there are more than 15,000 interdependent firms with five or fewer employees. Their textiles produce millions in revenues—and have added 20,000 people to local supplier businesses in the area as well.

A Time for Choosing: A Thousand Networks, a Thousand Options

Interdependencies help us cut through the clutter of overlapping networks. Each of us faces many interconnecting networks. In a theoretical sense, everything is connected in some way to everything else. No one of us, even with the help of the biggest computers, can function in that nightmare of too many interconnected networks. We would not know whom to pay attention to or what to do.

To cut through the fog of interconnected system overload, identify your most important interdependencies. Ask, "Who (or what network) has the most important resources I need and is my most important customer?" In that way interdependencies help to focus energies on the few most important interconnected people and networks.

Interdependencies, like interconnectednesses, help us plan our renewed future. Each and every one of us faces an enormous array of choices. We must choose the customers to work with, the energies to expend, the activities to involve ourselves in. Creating the right future requires us to understand the complex web of choices confronting us.

CUSTOMER SUCCESS IS THE FOCUS AND THE GLUE

All networks share a common focus on creating success for customers. The focus is the same for the leaf creating life-giving nutrients for its mother tree and the engineer helping an end-user solve a problem. The more effectively each of us creates success for our customers, the more essential we are to their success, the more personal security we will enjoy.

Creating customer success pervades all networks. It is the golden thread that holds the interconnected and interdependent networks together. Successful networks think like their customers think, see what they see, hear what they hear. They inhabit the worlds of their customers and their customers'

customers, share their aspirations and know their progress toward their goals.

Customer focus requires the ability to constantly renew to meet constantly changing needs. After all, customers change; situations change; needs change. All networks are in continual flux, engaged in producing new outputs to meet the new needs of customers.

Like the Phoenix, individuals must continually renew themselves to produce the new outputs demanded by their customers.

Just Who Are All These People—And Which Ones Are Our Customers?

At first blush the question is almost too easy. They are family, friends, people we work with, the people we directly supply. But there's a much longer list of all those people we serve throughout our interconnected network.

Imagine: Brian builds massively parallel processor computers in California. A network services provider in New Jersey buys the computer. Brian's niece Donna who lives in California accesses the Internet through that network service provider to gather some information for her twelfth-grade advanced biology report. Donna earns an A on the report. Her teacher calls Donna's parents to praise Donna's performance. Encouraged by Donna's biology performance, her mother sends off the completed application to an Ivy League school with a top-rated premed program. A doctor is born.

The connections continue. Brian's server enables connections across the globe, as countless people use it to access the Internet. A company developing a cologne in Paris uses the Internet to gather data about creating a new fragrance that will be produced in the company's New Jersey plant. The fragrance is soon being sold in Sydney, Australia, and it sparks a romantic relationship in Singapore.

Everyone is a potential customer.

Now That We Have Identified Who They Are, What Are Our Customers' Needs?

Do we truly understand our customers, their business, their interests and their definition of success?

ABC Community Bank has thousands of customers. During its hundred-year-old history it provided valuable traditional consumer banking services. But customers' needs changed. Customers wanted remote access, through ATMs. ABC installed three offsite ATMs, but customers wanted as many as a dozen more. Customers also wanted personalized investment services, but the bank couldn't figure out how to provide them without running too great a risk. As a result, many customers took their business elsewhere.

Family members are important customers in our network web. We've sometimes misread a family member's needs. For instance, one of our son's English grades dropped. We pushed him hard to improve, spending hours each night reviewing his work. He resented the increased pressure and our relationship soured. Then we went to school and saw the problem. His teacher was new and ineffective. Every student in that class was struggling. There were many great teachers in his school. This teacher wasn't yet one of them. We arranged to transfer our son to another class. His grades improved, so we stopped hassling him about studying harder. Our relationship improved, and we now go to ball games together. Our son was our customer and we had failed to listen to his needs.

How Will We Measure Delivering Success for Our Customers?

It's not enough to throw products and services at them. It's not enough to make the deal and walk away. This is a relationship, and it's personal. We owe it to our customers to help them create a successful tomorrow.

The answer relies upon direct and continuous communication with all customers. Learn from open communications, not osmosis. Surveys help; so do direct conversations. We measured our son's success (and our own) strictly in terms of grades. His measures of success are far broader. They include spending time with his friends, getting to use the car, doing fun activities with selected family members (his siblings mostly, not his parents). We need to hear, and use, his measures, not just our own. Mind-set is crucial. To truly create success for your customers, see yourself as a student, and your customer as your teacher.

What You See Is What You Get: Establish Line of Sight to Your Customers

All that we've written thus far is answered through line of sight to all customers. Every employee/supplier needs a clear line of sight to all customers, to see which actions deliver the best results. What matters is not just the immediate effect, but the total series of actions across the network. Look as far as you can see.

For example, when you play pool, you have a goal of getting the billiard balls, one at a time, into the pockets. Difficult positioning may require complicated shots. For some of us, every shot is complicated. You may choose to bank the ball off other balls, or the table side rails, or off your opponent's chin. You survey the possibilities, make mental connections and use your skills to cause the chain of events that results in getting a specific ball in the pocket. You need to see the whole table, and the locations of every ball in order to choose a successful strategic path.

Sally leaves General Electric to go into business for herself. She leaves behind an entire network of customer and supplier systems. Her leaving impacts them. She needs to be replaced in their web of customer-supplier systems. Her decision to start a home-based business impacts an entirely different set of customers, mainly her family. She's around home more and the kids expect her to do more "Mom" activities like driving them to sports events. Sally's husband hopes that she'll prepare dinner more frequently now that she's home more. Her new clients may expect to hold meetings at her office, not realizing that it's now in the unfinished basement of her home. Sally's decision changed her world. She now confronts a whole new interconnected set of customer networks, and must anticipate reactions like those at the pool table.

Customer-Focused Transformation at Warp Speed

The senior vice president of marketing launched a major strategic reassessment of NCR's market position and value proposition. The results were not unexpected. Customers wanted business solutions that helped them improve relationships with *their* customers and increased their operational efficiencies.

The emerging customer information solutions market promised enormous opportunities for NCR's customers to accelerate profitable growth and reduce costs. NCR identified that market as their future growth engine. They recommitted to provide customer-focused solutions—their name for information technology solutions—that would help their customers better understand and serve *their* customers. We reengineered a worldwide, $7 billion organization of 46,000 associates and over 600 products and services to deliver those products and services. A daunting but necessary task.

NCR put in place a set of strategic focusing tools and a clear framework for creating the future. The model aligned measures and rewards to drive new objectives and new behaviors. It established rewards to reinforce behaviors that would implement the company vision, mission, values and goals and strategies—all of which were customer-centric. We will describe how to build this framework, called the Phoenix Pyramid, in Part 3.

The new model represented major changes in roles, relationships and processes. NCR changed from a vertical hierarchy to a team-centered model; from a command-and-control mode to facilitative leadership; from centralized decisions to empowered associates; from internal competition to external focus on customers; from marketing as a support function to marketing as a play caller; and most of all, from a product-oriented focus to a customer solutions focus. All NCR associates focused on serving external customers, not just supporting internal activities. All processes were aligned to support the new customer focus.

Senior management launched a global communication campaign to create associate engagement and buy-in. It's one thing to design process charts and write job descriptions on paper. It is quite something else to change roles, relationships, values and behaviors for 46,000 associates in hundreds of different offices, cultures and environments. The communication plan included global satellite network broadcasts to associates around the world, distributed print materials, department and business unit meetings, and an Associate Response Team to provide quick e-mail replies to associate questions.

A special cross-functional transition team of associates and consultants championed and guided the organization change process itself. In addition, teams of eighty to a hundred of the company's senior coaches traveled all over the world to conduct small-group strategic framework "road shows."

The point: by working from the outside in with their customers and carefully listening to them, NCR was able to create for them the kinds of support they needed. NCR agreed with customers on standards and measures of satisfaction and success, and then worked backward to determine what they needed to do internally to create it.

You already know the ending. In the first year of the new model, NCR grew its revenues by over 20 percent—the largest growth in revenue at NCR for many years. It all began with listening carefully to customers and then turning that data into a whole new systems model.

Realizing the revenue growth meant revivoluting a global organization at warp speed. Certainly NCR did not create a perfect organization. Nor did it solve all of their customers' problems. The NCR story demonstrates the two critical points in this section: focus on customers and hold the interconnected systems together. Revivolution is de rigueur for survival.

Summary: Alignment Across Your Personal Network

The biggest challenge today: aligning overlapping interconnected networks to meet ever changing customer needs. Everyone is focused on their little piece of the elephant, believing that it is the whole animal. People often act as though every other person or organization is an interference on the set of "My big movie." They don't see their critical interdependencies. Their narrow view is like a puzzle missing several large pieces. In fact, it isn't

really a puzzle at all—because the picture of the big picture is
missing!

Each of us owns the responsibility to hold that picture of the
big picture high enough that all other network members can see
it. Given the complexity of overlapping networks, life today is
like bowling blindfolded. How can you ever expect to score a
strike if you can see neither the alley nor the pins? Every one of
us is responsible for providing the eyes to the others so they can
know where and how to roll the ball and how many pins they
knocked down. We are our brother's keeper. We are his eyes.

And that is perhaps the most fundamental fact of life: we are all
members of interconnected, interdependent voluntary webs of
human participation called organizations. Each person chooses
in his or her heart and head to establish the connections—and
architect the relationships. We all share the responsibility to
make those relationships successful. It's not about egotism, nor is
it altruism. It's realism.

PHOENIX WORKSHOP

DESCRIBE YOUR NETWORK:

Professional and personal network connections	Interdependencies	Their definitions of success	How can I help them succeed?

CHAPTER 3

Imprinting the Success Equation: The Phoenix's Mentality

The self-renewing Phoenix recognizes, honors and leverages its interconnected networks. All of these networks are focused on delivering success to its various customers. The soaring Phoenix focuses every thought and action on creating success for all its customers. We refer to this "create success for all customers" preoccupation as the Phoenix's mentality, and it's best expressed in the "success equation" that we'll show you how to adopt and implement in this chapter.

Mentality: Life's Powerful Behavioral Code

Every company has its own unique mentality, its own embedded, automatic responses to life in the marketplace. An organization's mentality determines what it does, how it reacts in situations, how it thinks and acts in all of its daily activities. In short, an organization's mentality creates its identity throughout all its interconnected systems. Exponentially replicated and magnified throughout the organization, mentality is the organization's internal mental imprint, and its marketplace differentiator.

Think about the Pepsi-Cola Company. Competition is Pepsi's organizational mentality imprint. Every activity is influenced by its view of the world as a competitive arena in which, to quote Coach Vince Lombardi, "Winning is the only thing." Executives run up stairs. They keep *big* charts tracking weekly market share movements and trends. They see the world as a battlefield—and Coke as the enemy. Competition is Pepsi's mentality imprint. Every new employee at Pepsi soon learns that beating the competition, whether outside or inside the company, is the surest path to success.

Contrast that mentality imprint with Procter & Gamble's consumerism. Terrence Deal and Allan Kennedy in their book *Corporate Cultures* wrote that P&G "glories in listening and listening well to customers. Furthermore, they have developed more ways to listen to customers than anyone else." Consumerism is P&G's mentality imprint.

All organizations have a mentality imprint that conditions behavior. Some imprints create great success. Witness Pepsi and Procter & Gamble. Other mentalities lead to failure. That's likely what happened to the almost 50 percent of firms that dropped off the Fortune 500 list in the last decade.

Individuals, families, athletic teams and communities have their own mentality that shapes their collective attitudes, responses and aspirations. Every individual and organization has its singular operational signature.

The important question for you: does your mentality help you be a soaring Phoenix?

Altering the Mentality Code

Are we all victims of our current mentality, forever trapped into being what we are? Is there no hope of being different? Absolutely, there is hope, lots of it. Mentality can be changed along with its subsequent behaviors. In biology, genetic engineers change DNA by splicing together strands of DNA from different sources, to produce tomatoes that don't spoil, cotton that resists the dreaded boll weevil and drugs that cure previously incurable diseases. Like editing videotape to create a new movie, we splice together different DNA strands and produce new biological creations. So it can be with mentality. We can change our mentality, which will lead to a change in behavior.

Similarly, we can splice together new mentality strands into our organizational and personal lives and create a new self-renewing Phoenix that becomes a leader and creates the Pyramid base for future success. We can choose how we will communicate, behave and conduct relationships.

Imagine the power. You can create the answer to the following questions: What do I want my organization to be like? What do I want the rest of my life to be like?

Reshaping Our Worlds by Introducing a New Mentality

That's exactly what Jim Sims did when he became president and CEO of Cambridge Technology Partners (CTP) as reported by Eric Matson in the August-September 1996, issue of *Fast Company*. Sims knew Cambridge's business of designing mission critical application software. He knew that only 16 percent of all software projects came in on time and on budget. He knew that nearly a third were canceled before they were completed. He also knew that most executives trusted used car salesmen more than they trusted software designers. Into this maelstrom Jim Sims created a new mentality for Cambridge Technology Partners: the mentality of speed. Sims was a Phoenix leader helping create success for all his customers—and helping his firm and his fellow Cambridge employees become soaring Phoenixes.

He asked, "How can you have two-year development cycles for software when most industries change every two to three years?" So he created an organization that focused on speed and delivered projects in six to nine months, instead of the usual two years. "Speed is the only way to get economic payback from technology," he says.

Cambridge's new speed mentality changed its relationship with customers. Rather than a six-to-nine-month front-end design specification cycle, Cambridge developed a three-week intensive Rapid Solutions Workshop. In these workshops Cambridge employees helped the customer identify the features that yielded the biggest economic benefits. The customer could then see clearly the economic benefits of starting right now with Cambridge, and realizing millions of dollars of additional profit, as opposed to taking an additional six to nine months evaluating competing bids, hoping to save a few hundred thousand in development costs.

The speed mentality altered internal processes at Cambridge as well. Take hiring. They set up sixty-day hiring cycles. Senior Vice President Susan Locker monitors weekly such key speed indicators as job acceptance rates and employee referrals to make certain that they are on the sixty-day track. To stimulate employee referrals (more than a third of all current employees came as referrals) Cambridge created a new policy paying a $3,000 referral bonus.

Consider this strategy. The emphasis on speed in opening new offices to fuel their dramatic growth led Cambridge to develop a step-by-step procedure to open new offices in sixty days and get them to profitability in nine months. The emphasis on speed, generated by the new mentality, pervaded every aspect of Cambridge's internal life and its relationships with its many interconnected systems. The new mentality helped their Phoenix soar. Cambridge grew revenues twenty-two times and employment fourteen times in a five-year period; and their stock increased thirteen times in value over the same period.

Tony's New Movie: From Protein Chemist to Bio-Infomatics

Individuals can also develop new mentalities that help them become a soaring Phoenix. That's exactly what Tony Kerlavage did. As reported by Kate Kane in the August-September 1996 issue of *Fast Company,* Tony was a protein chemist, working as one of the army of researchers at the National Institutes of Health in the 1980s. He got fascinated with the cloning process, particularly the powerful cloning computerized sequencers. He set out to build his own new mentality, combining his protein chemical background with newly acquired molecular biological and database management skills.

Today, he directs the seventeen-person Bio-Infomatics Department at the Institute for Genomic Research, where he and his staff use more than forty computerized DNA sequencers generating medical breakthroughs—and beat off the weekly calls from headhunters looking to attract him to pharmaceutical and biotech companies. According to Craig Venter, president of the institute, Kerlavage's background is "in the hottest demand in the field." Not bad for an ordinary NIH researcher less than ten years ago who used his new mentality to renew himself into doing fascinating, leading-edge work and great personal success.

Get Out Your Scissors and Edit Your Future

Tony's story, and the millions of other individual and organizational stories, demonstrate that you can create a mentality that enables you to create success for all of your interconnected network customers. The Success Equation is the mentality of the soaring Phoenix. It imprints "create success for: employees, end-user customers, suppliers, communities, shareowners."

THE SUCCESS EQUATION

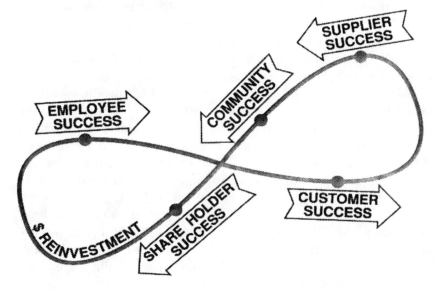

THE SUCCESS EQUATION: THE MENTALITY OF THE SELF-RENEWING PHOENIX

This mentality imprints the signals that create success for those networks with whom you are interdependent. You serve five major groupings of networks: employees, end-user customers, suppliers, communities and shareowners. We will show you how to identify and enhance the key activities in which you can engage that will implant and enhance the Phoenix mentality of "create success for all customers." We've found that the Success Equation applies to all organizations, as well as to all individuals.

THE COMPONENTS OF ASSOCIATE SUCCESS

The Success Equation begins with employees, today more commonly called "associates." A restaurant manager we know put it this way. "It's funny, but true. The better I treat my associates the better they treat the guests—and the healthier the bottom line is. I don't understand why it works that way, I just know that it does." We know why. Both academic research and personal experience validate the conclusion that associate success drives individual and organizational success.

We were panel members at one of those high-profile meetings recently. One of the other panel members, an absolutely brilliant CEO of a highly successful company, said, "Constantly creating new technology is the only sustainable competitive advantage." When it came our turn to speak, we turned to him and asked, "And who creates that new technology? Get and keep the best people, Bill, or else you can't sustain that technology advantage." He smiled knowingly. He's aware that people create his leading-edge technology, without which he'd be a sad footnote in tomorrow's newspaper. He works hard to attract—and retain—the best people. He knows the basic truth: great people build a great organization, not the other way around.

Effective organizations begin with effective associates. There are three key drivers of associate success; three ways you can help associates succeed so that they and the organization can win. They are: provide line of sight to customers, provide the tools and training associates need to succeed with customers, and help associates make a difference in their working environment. Do these three activities and you will implant and enhance the Phoenix's "create success for all customers" mentality.

Tune into Your Customers and Don't Change That Channel

You must know what your customers want, need and demand. You must know how they live and how they think. Get them up on your screen and watch closely. That's what line of sight to customers is all about: getting direct, firsthand information about what customers do, say and think so you can know more about your customers than they know about themselves. Line of sight requires direct feedback from customers so you know how well you're doing in meeting their needs. Line of sight involves having those who make the product talk directly with those who use it and hearing directly from them what's working and not working, not relying upon some third or fourth party like a customer service department or a direct marketing research firm. Johnsonville Foods, for instance, has plant-level associates do taste tests in supermarkets so they can talk directly to end-user customers. Complaints come directly to the plant-level associates who made the product, rather than going to the customer service department. All of these activities provide associates with direct line-of-sight information and communication with end-user customers. Without that vital knowledge, you are absolutely disconnected, dysfunctional and disposable.

Tom Warner, president of the Warner Company, understands the importance of line of sight to customers. Founded in the 1940s, the Warner Company is the largest plumbing contractor and the second-largest heating, ventilating and air-conditioning company in the Washington, D.C., area. During the last seven-year period sales grew from $19.8 million to $31 million. In that same period, margins went from zero to 15.5 percent. Warner's story was chronicled in the August 1994 issue of *Inc.* magazine.

What's the magic formula Tom Warner used? He organized his business so each and every one of his associates had line of sight and responsibility to a given set of customers. Warner set up each of his plumbing, heating and air-conditioning associates as semi-independent businesspeople responsible to their own set of customers. For example, Ron Inscoe is an area technical director for the Warner Company in Bethesda zip codes 20814 and 20817. These are his territories. Ron pays close attention to the folks in these two zip codes. He knows who they are, what they prefer and want, and he services their needs and gets direct feedback (in the form of sales orders or complaints) from his customers. They have his truck phone number, his pager number and his home number. He works for them. Ron is the Warner Company to his customers.

Pay Outrageously Close Attention to All Kinds of "Customers"

It is not enough to understand your current customers. How about present noncustomers? And future customers? All of those "customers"—present, nonpresent and future—are members of your marketplace network. So you need to understand all of them.

Department stores didn't, and they paid dearly for their oversight. Even in their heyday, department stores only captured less than half of total retail sales dollars. They were happy with that. After all, they had a very profitable and exciting business. But how about the other half of the retail sales that didn't wind up in department stores? They never bothered asking the question "Why isn't the other half of the business coming to us?"

Not looking at the noncustomer cost the department stores the insight into understanding shopping patterns and shopper preferences. With that information maybe they could have anticipated the trend toward convenience and entertainment that today sends so many dollars to catalogue sellers and the Disneys of the world. Today less than 20 percent of all retail dollars go through department stores. Not focusing on the noncustomer left the department store ignorant of the coming shifts in customer demands that decimated their ranks. Focus on the whole customer set, not just the current set.

While you're focusing on noncustomers, don't forget to look for tomorrow's potential set of customers. The average age of Cadillac buyers is more than sixty-five. Cadillac executives worry a lot about that demographic statistic. That's why several years ago they brought out the Cimmeron, a mini-Cadillac, aimed at the late forties and fifties crowd. They were concerned that they could miss the entire next generation. That model failed and still leaves the Dearborn folks studying the obituaries and worrying about their future.

Individual soaring Phoenixes also need to develop line of sight to their customers so they can understand their needs. Stasia was a student in our Masters of Business Administration program. She was looking for an organizational development/human resources position. She saw lots of potential customers including local firms and local/national consulting firms. She sent out résumés to them all. We helped her see some other not-so-obvious potential customers. We identified the opportunity for her to work at our university as a freelance trainer and consultant. There were many other colleges and universities in our town who might also use her freelance services, if she pitched them on it. Stasia's potential customer list was much broader than she originally thought. She discovered that she needed line of sight to all of these potential customers in order to get the best job offer.

Most individuals and organizations have many more noncustomers than customers. Develop line of sight to all customers— even those who currently don't even know they might be customers of yours—and get to know them intimately.

Give People the Training and the Tools— And Then Let 'Em Rip

Associates usually ask the same questions, "What do I have to do? How do I get the tools to do it effectively? How will I know how well I did?" The associates' answers to these questions—not the boss's answers—drive the associates' satisfaction and productivity.

We worked with a large telecommunications company. For many years they measured associate satisfaction at least once a year for several hundred thousand associates. That databank helped us help a mid-level accounting manager in one of their divisions dramatically improve the productivity in his area.

When we first met Bob his associate satisfaction scores were atrocious. In Bob's area overall associate satisfaction was 29 percent, the lowest in the finance group, which was the lowest in the division, which was the lowest in the company. Bob was a typical traditional "tell-'em-what-to-do" manager. Bob was in his mid-forties, and that style had worked in the past. But today, it was working in reverse. The more he practiced his tell-'em style, the lower his scores fell. Worse, a new senior management team changed the bonus plan, tying bonuses to associate satisfaction scores. It sure looked like it was time for Bob to polish up his résumé and find another home before it was too late.

Using the overall company database the statisticians back in headquarters isolated three factors they said drove the low ratings. These three factors were tools and training to do the job, speed/accuracy/honesty of performance feedback, and clarity of performance expectations. The statisticians told us that these three factors accounted for 62 percent of the low ratings. Not being statisticians ourselves, we accepted their word and went to work to fix these issues.

Bob established three major initiatives. First, he insisted that everyone in his area, beginning with himself, establish monthly performance agreements with their internal staff and their external customers. (We will talk about these agreements more extensively later.) Then he insisted that all employees, including himself, receive monthly feedback from customers evaluating their delivery against the performance agreements. Last, he employed a consulting firm to help associates identify their training needs and deliver any required training.

It was tough sledding at first. Very few people believed Bob was serious. It sounded like another "flavor of the month" program. That attitude shifted when Bob published his first customer feedback scores, averaging a very poor 2.6 out of 7. Even his boss, the division controller, stood up and paid attention. His publication of his "recovery plan" also made a great impact. After three months all but a handful of his staff were making agreements, posting their evaluations and participating in some self-designed educational activity. Bob doubled his associate satisfaction scores that year. He also greatly increased productivity.

The next year, Bob's associate satisfaction scores were the best in the finance department, which was the best in the division and one of the five best in the entire company. Bob's unit won the "Outstanding Productivity and Customer Satisfaction" award from the corporate CFO. Maybe, just maybe, those statisticians were right. You can create customer success when the associates know what creates customer success, have the tools and training to deliver that success and know when they do (or don't) deliver it.

Note how Bob took charge and made a difference. He could have waffled, using the "I'm only a small cog in this big machine" argument like so many of his colleagues. He could have hidden behind the bureaucratic "I have to get approval" syndrome. He could have taken any one of the number of convenient, socially acceptable, face-saving, rear-end-covering actions we've all seen too many others take. Not Bob! He took responsibility for improving his own capabilities, making himself more valuable to his customers and his associates. His Christmas card comments to us last year say it all, "I've never had as much fun and enjoyed myself as much as I have this year." He recently got a big promotion. Obviously his employer also thinks he's pretty good. Bob created success for all of his interconnected customers—including himself and his family—by taking responsibility and being a Phoenix leader using the "create success for everyone" mentality.

Give People an Opportunity to Make a Difference— And They Will

People want to make a difference. Very few people we know walk through the door every morning and say, "How can I screw up today?" Almost everyone wants, desperately, to make a difference in their world. A successful organization enables system members to make that difference in two ways: surfacing and dealing with issues and sharing decision making.

Share the Power and Multiply the Wealth

Ed Lawler's made it his profession and life's work to demonstrate how sharing decision making with associates delivers better results. In his book *High-Involvement Management: Participative Strategies for Improving Organizational Performance,* Lawler shows that firms that share power and decision making have 4 percent higher returns on sales, 2.2 percent higher returns on assets, 5.6 percent higher returns on investment and 6.2 percent higher returns on equity. Why share decision making with associates? It just pays, that's all.

Sharing decision making helps associates control their working environment. It gives associates the feeling that "I make a difference around here." We've seen it work over and over. In one division of AT&T, GBCS, we involved every associate in a series of meetings. At those meetings we shared the marketplace trends and realities and asked: "In order for us to succeed in the market, what are we doing that we should keep doing? What are we doing that we should stop doing? And what aren't we doing that we should start doing?"

We listened to their suggestions. We dealt straight with the associates in those meetings. You can't ever do everything that needs doing. There just aren't enough resources to go around. There's never enough money in the budget. Doesn't matter who you are: the United States government, Ross Perot or your own personal bank account. Prioritization is a way of life. We listened to the associates' suggestions, prioritized them and told them what we could do right away and what we'd do later. We set up continuous communication loops so that everyone could know when their idea would be accomplished.

We did all this in the heat of a restructuring and downsizing. We did it in a strong union climate. Associate satisfaction doubled and the division reported a profit for the first time in nine years. Why? People participated in dealing with the business issues confronting their organization. They had the opportunity to make a difference, and they rose to the occasion.

People Power Doesn't Necessarily Cost Extra

None of the three drivers of associate success costs money. It doesn't cost a dime to give associates line of sight to customers. It doesn't cost additional cents-per-hour wage increases to get associates to participate in decision making about their working environment. It doesn't mean extra holiday pay to get associates the tools and training they need to create success for their customers—and themselves.

Very little of this is widely practiced, despite the fact that much of what we've written about has been known for years. Nearly forty years old, Frederick Herzberg's writings about motivators and demotivators bear a striking similarity to what we've said in the last few pages. More than sixty years ago the Hawthorne studies proved that people turned out more work in dim moonlight than they were turning out in full daylight when they felt that they had a stake in the action.

The first component in the Success Equation mentality is simple: provide a line of sight to customers, give people tools and training to meet their customers' demands and provide people with the opportunity to make a difference. Do these three activities and you will be on your way to implanting the first part of the "create success for all customers" Phoenix mentality imprint.

MENTALITY IN THE MARKETPLACE: DRIVERS OF END-USER CUSTOMER SUCCESS

Creating end-user customer success is the second strand in the self-renewing Phoenix mentality. The soaring Phoenix imprints the "create customer success" behavior on everything it does. Its mentality continually poses the question "How does this policy/action/plan/strategy help to create customer success?"

The Phoenix's "create success for all customers" mentality produces behaviors that answer positively the following two questions: "Will my solution solve my end-user's problem?" and "Is my solution the best deal my end-user customer can get?" Creating end-user customer success begins with developing your capability to solve your customers' problems. Solutions to your customers' problems are your added value. The second driver of customer success is the value of the solution you provide. Customers always ask, "Is this the best deal for me?" To get and keep their business you'd better be able to answer with a resounding "Yes!" The self-renewing Phoenix mentality produces behaviors that create customer success. Those behaviors develop both

PHOENIX WORKSHOP

1. WHO ARE MY CURRENT CUSTOMERS? WHAT DO I DO THAT THEY PARTICULARLY VALUE?

CURRENT
CUSTOMERS   VALUE

_____   _____

_____   _____

2. WHO ARE MY CURRENT NONCUSTOMERS? WHAT DO I DO THAT THEY MIGHT PARTICULARLY VALUE?

NONCUSTOMERS   VALUE

_____   _____

_____   _____

3. WHO ARE MY FUTURE CUSTOMERS? WHAT COULD I DO THAT THEY MIGHT PARTICULARLY VALUE?

FUTURE CUSTOMERS   VALUE

_____   _____

_____   _____

4. HOW CAN I DEVELOP LINE OF SIGHT TO MY CURRENT, NONCURRENT AND FUTURE CUSTOMERS SO I MIGHT BEST ANSWER THESE QUESTIONS?

_____   _____

_____   _____

5. WHAT TOOLS AND TRAINING DO I NEED TO MORE EFFECTIVELY CREATE SUCCESS FOR MY CUSTOMERS?

_____   _____

_____   _____

6. HOW CAN I INVOLVE OTHERS IN MY INTERCONNECTED NETWORK WORLD IN BETTER CREATING SUCCESS FOR OUR MUTUAL CUSTOMERS?

_____   _____

_____   _____

problem-solving competence and understanding of the customer's view of what the "best" solution really is.

Learn and Master the Secret Language of "Customerese"

Begin by defining customer success in the customer's terms. Customers always talk price, and decide on value. Most often value is a mix of time, convenience, availability and, oh by the way, also price. 7-Eleven, and the many other convenience stores, built a $32 billion business on the simple premise that customers will trade dollars for time. Convenience store prices average 23 percent higher than supermarket prices. But customers spend ten times the amount of time in a supermarket than in a convenience store. For the loaf of bread, carton of milk or six-pack of beer, the faster and pricier C-store is the shopping place of choice.

Learn to talk "customerese"—the language of your customers. Value almost never means price alone. Our cousin provides a good example of this in practice. He and his wife drive a moving van for a living. They see the country, compliments of Allied Van Moving.

In a recent conversation he told us, "I got a great deal on this new van."

"Low price?" we asked.

"I don't even know what the price was," he said, shrugging his shoulders. "The dealer gave me what he called a per-mile deal. I pay him so much per mile for every mile I run the truck. He pays for all the headaches: maintenance, insurance, etc. I pay him as I use the truck, with a guaranteed minimum. It's great because I pay him the same way I get paid, per mile hauling stuff. And, if the truck goes down, he gets me another one to use while he fixes this one. What a deal!"

Our cousin wins big. He'll likely pay a lot more for his truck this way than if he bought it outright. But he pays it as he earns it, without all the risk of downtime, maintenance time and so forth. He's now free to focus on filling his truck; which, by the way, he's doing so successfully that he's building a new house.

The dealer also wins big. He'll make more money from our cousin's truck than the others he'll sell outright. He benefits not only from the higher truck margins, but also from the income

generated by the additional services he's selling, such as maintenance and insurance. He takes more risk, for which he earns a
higher margin. Through dealing with our cousin, the dealer discovered that there are lots of other independent truck operators
out there with similar problems that he can solve—at a hand-
some profit. He's now going after that large market.

The dealer had been in business for twenty-seven years at the
same location, doing business in the same old way. The business
changed, though. He recognized the need to renew himself, to become a Phoenix. He and our cousin were old hunting buddies.
He'd read about this new mileage pricing and proposed it to our
cousin in a blind one morning waiting for the ducks to appear. Our
cousin trusted the dealer, having bought four vehicles from him in
the past. "Sure," he said. "Let's talk about it after we bag a few."

The dealer won because he saw the world through his customer's financial eyes. He looked at the situation through our
cousin's financial glasses and, through those glasses, saw a big
new opportunity for both himself and his customer. He anticipated how much our cousin could make with mileage pricing—
and how much he could make selling that deal. Understanding
our cousin's financial situation, both present and future, helped
him sell the deal and create customer success. His Phoenix mentality helped him create success for his customer—and himself.

Benchmark Performance Using the Customer's Success Measures

Customers are always comparing. BMWs are always being compared with Mercedes and Lexus and Cadillac and Lincoln. IBM is
always being compared with DEC and Compaq and Sun and
Gateway. Winners are those who compare favorably in the eyes
of the customers.

But who is the competition? People ask, "Who am I playing
against? Who do I need to outperform? Am I winning? And how
will I know when I am winning?" Ay, that's the rub. In today's
world there's a competitor hiding under every rock and behind
every door.

Take the venerable newspaper business, for instance. We recall riding the subway to work in New York as young professionals. On the crowded D train there was a sea of newspapers. We learned how to hold on to the strap with one hand and fold the newspaper with the other. We bought the *New York Times* on the way into work every morning and the *New York Post* back home every night. We rode the same D train a few years ago and the sea of newspapers had disappeared, replaced by Walkmans and Discmans. All across America and the world you can't find a major newspaper that hasn't lost readership share in the last ten years. Worse, they've suffered major losses in advertising share, as local Pennysavers and direct mail cut dramatically into newspaper advertising expenditures.

Who are the newspaper's competitors? To whom does a customer compare the newspaper? Seen from the customer's viewpoint, the competition goes beyond other major-market newspapers. It's not about the *L.A. Times* moving into the San Diego market. The competition goes beyond the national newspaper *USA Today* versus the *San Diego Union Tribune*. In the customer's mind, the real competition for news and information is Rush Limbaugh, the radio, the television and, for us at least, America Online. We're early birds, up by 5:00 A.M. The newspaper doesn't come until 7:00 A.M. By the time it arrives we're already well "newsed" by our online computer service. And don't forget those Walkmans and Discmans. They are also competitors for time and mind share.

Viewed from the customer's point of view, the daily newspaper is in the information and entertainment business. Competitors come from those industries, because those are the basis for comparisons in the customer's mind. No wonder newspapers are slipping. Which would you rather watch, the color and action of TV or the blandness of a newspaper? Even if you prefer to read rather than listen, wouldn't you rather have the color and choice of a computer online service rather than the weight and ponderousness of the newspaper? And you don't get newsprint all over your hands and clothing. Customers define competitors, like most everything else. Use your customers' glasses so you can benchmark yourself against the competitors that really count to your customers.

Do whatever it takes to find out what your customers value and against whom they compare your products and services. Technology helps. Wal-Mart made a fortune using technology to better understand customers, and deliver what their customers really

tion) be without suppliers? In tough shape, that's where. The "create success for all customers" mentality must create supplier success much as it needs to create customer and associate success. That Phoenix mentality leads to activities that share objectives, measures and rewards with suppliers and treat them like members of the organizational network. The Phoenix mentality consistently asks the question "Does this action/policy/plan/ strategy treat our suppliers like we want to be treated by our customers?" In other words: "Are we the customer we want our customer to be?"

Share the Risk and the Rewards: Include Suppliers in the Org Chart

Treat suppliers as part of the extended organization. Include them in strategic discussions, plans and actions. That's just what Airmax did with great success, as reported in the May 1994 issue of *Nation's Business*. Airmax is a $17 million surface transportation company providing ground freight services for their international airline customers. They own no trucks themselves, preferring instead to buy trucking services from various suppliers. Airmax worked with its suppliers to publish a supplier handbook, precisely spelling out the best-in-class service standards for handling air freight shipments. Airmax pledged its loyalty to those suppliers who signed up to live by the book they helped write. "We will not break agreements with satisfactory vendors in favor of minimal underbids," Airmax wrote in the book, and neither would they "operate trucks in competition with vendors." Fueled by their suppliers' success, Airmax today is the most profitable and fastest-growing firm in their market.

Everyone knows the Chrysler Phoenix story. It was written by Jeffrey Dyer in the July-August 1996 issue of *Harvard Business Review*. In a few short years Chrysler went from dead last, and more "dead" than "last," to the profit leader among U.S. automobile manufacturers. It's less widely known that the Phoenix "create success for all customers" mentality played a leading role in that renewal. Chrysler revolutionized its relationship with its suppliers, establishing many of them as sole-source suppliers (being the only, not one of several) for a given component (like seats or horns or lighting systems) for the life of the model (like the Jeep Wrangler or the Dodge Stratus). They worked with their single-source suppliers in design, prototyping and production, reducing inventory and development costs. Overall, Chrysler's new mentality led Chrysler to treat its suppliers as strategic partners. Splicing a new "create success for suppliers" mentality helped Chrysler to shorten product development cycles 40 percent, reduce vehicle development costs to one third to one sixth of U.S. competitors, reduce procurement costs by 30 percent and increase market share to 14.7 percent—its highest penetration in twenty-five years—and profitability double that of GM and 25 percent greater than Ford.

The Phoenix mentality involves suppliers in shared objectives, measures and rewards. Those activities help to create success for all customers: associates, end-user customers and suppliers.

PHOENIX WORKSHOP

1. WHO ARE MY MAJOR SUPPLIERS AND WHAT IS SUCCESS FOR THEM?

_____

_____

_____

2. HOW CAN I INVOLVE THEM IN SHARING MY OBJECTIVES, MEASURES AND REWARDS?

_____

_____

_____

MENTALITY ON THE BIGGER STAGE: ENABLING SUCCESS FOR OUR COMMUNITIES

Each and every one of us lives as part of many larger communities. Our success is inexorably linked to our community's success. The self-renewing Phoenix "create success for all customers" mentality produces behaviors that reflect seeing the world as an interconnected place and maximizing long-term success for community members.

The Oil Fields in Nigeria Cause Riots in Amsterdam

Royal Dutch Shell is generally a good citizen. They have a long history of developing local infrastructure and local management of the non-Dutch and English assets they own. You'd think that local good citizen activity would be enough to win you kudos on the world stage. It's just the opposite. Shell's dealing with the Nigerian military government triggered a recall of ambassadors by the United States and other Western nations and rioting by activists in Amsterdam who protested the Nigerian government's execution of an opposition politician.

Or consider Shell's run-in with Greenpeace over the Brent Spar North Sea oil platform. Shell did its scientific homework. Most scientists it consulted concluded that the best alternative was burial at sea, after a thorough cleaning. Towing these giant platforms to shore and dismantling them there was considered much more environmentally dangerous. Environmental activists at Greenpeace disagreed. They rallied public opinion and forced Shell to discontinue its plan to "deep six" the platform. Despite careful consultations and the best scientific evidence, Shell got egg all over its corporate face.

Shell is not the only organization being embarrassed in the public eye, as reported in the July 20, 1996, issue of *The Economist.* "Stop Propping Up the Killers," protest signs shouted at Unocal California gas stations, as activists sought to end Unocal's investment in an offshore oil field in Myanmar (formerly Burma). Heineken Beer withdrew from an investment in Myanmar after similar protests were threatened in Holland. RTZ-CRA found their usually staid London annual meeting disrupted by Javanese tribe people and environmental activists protesting the company's copper and gold mining activities in Irian Jaya Indonesia. ABB, the highly respected energy firm, is under attack in Germany for its participation in a hydroelectric dam being built in Malaysia. Kathie Lee Gifford came under fire for poor working conditions in a Honduras factory that produced some of her brand-new clothing. What's a poor multinational to do?

Shell's response is typical. "We want to engage, not enrage," one Shell manager stated. Shell launched a series of consultations and public hearings to engage anyone interested in the platform issue. They've even put up a Brent Spar Web site as an alternative place for public debate. All of these activities reflect the Phoenix mentality that considers the impact of any action—like sinking a platform in the North Sea—on a wider range of interconnected networks. This is but one more example of the linkage between the butterfly in Peking and the weather in New York.

The Phoenix mentality drives activities that reflect considerations of the larger picture and long-term perspectives. There are many examples of Phoenix organizations doing just that.

Malden Mills is a $400 million textile manufacturer located in Methuen, Massachusetts. They produce the popular Polarfleece material. They also are known for paying one of the highest wages in the textile business, $12.50 per hour. Demonstrating the big-picture, long-term thinking reflective of the Phoenix mentality, owner Aaron Feuerstein paid full salaries to all workers, at a cost of $1.5 million a week, when the factory burned down. "The community relies upon our payroll. We just had to do it," he said in an article in *Time* magazine that appeared on January 8, 1996. No wonder he has one of the lowest employee turnover rates and highest sales and profits per employee in the textile industry.

Reflecting that long-term and big picture, Huntington Bancshares of Columbus, Ohio, using local churches, met with minority groups to tailor a package of services for inner-city residents. To encourage church support, they donated money to the churches for every customer they signed up. The result was reported in the September 26, 1994, edition of *Business Week*. The bank booked $44 million in mortgages at market rates, some of the 165 participating churches earned up to $1,000 a month and many inner-city people now have mortgages and savings accounts they would never have had otherwise. "Everyone knew it was a win-win process with the church involved," a bank spokesperson said.

There are lots of individual self-renewing Phoenixes who use the "create success for everyone, including communities" mentality.

A former Ford executive and import-export businessman was mugged. Instead of getting revenge, as reported in the October 31, 1994, issue of *U.S. News & World Report,* he founded the $4.5 million nonprofit National Foundation for Teaching Entrepreneurism. His foundation reaches 2,650 pupils in ten cities. He personally teaches inner-city teens to be entrepreneurial. He saw the bigger interconnected picture, acted as a Phoenix leader and took responsibility, and is helping to eradicate the long-term conditions that create muggings.

Businesswoman Anita Roddick, founder of the Body Shop, put it best. She said, "[business must not only] . . . avoid hideous evil, it must actively do good . . . [Businesspeople] . . . need to act in ways big and small to bring sustainable and healthy growth across the globe. And our business practices must change. We have to take longer term views, invest in communities, and build long-lasting markets."

Many other organizations are heeding her words; witness the long list cited in Mary Scott and Howard Rothman's *Companies with a Conscience.*

The Phoenix mentality produces behaviors that align its own interests with those of its wider network of interconnected communities. The self-renewing Phoenix understands intuitively that business and personal interests are best served by healthy, politically free market-oriented economies that are actively supported by the general public. In the end, Charles Wilson, former president of General Motors and secretary of defense, got it only partially right when he said, "What's good for General Motors is good for the country." In truth, what's good for the country, long term, is good for General Motors and every other business and individual that is a part of the U.S.A.

PHOENIX WORKSHOP

WITH WHAT MAJOR COMMUNITIES AM I CURRENTLY LINKED, GLOBALLY, NATIONALLY, REGIONALLY AND LOCALLY (E.G., LA MESA, CALIFORNIA, WHERE JIM LIVES; SHANGHAI, CHINA, WHERE JERRE'S ORGANIZATION HAS A WAREHOUSE)?

	MY CONTRIBUTION TO THEIR SUCCESS (E.G., WHAT CAN I DO TO HELP THE
COMMUNITY	COMMUNITY GROW AND PROSPER?)
_____	_____
_____	_____
_____	_____
_____	_____
_____	_____

CREATING SUCCESS FOR SHAREOWNERS

In the beginning, someone puts up the money that funds every organization. Whether it's the community that invests in a hospital, or a J.P. Morgan who underwrites U.S. Steel, or your mother who lends you the money to start that print shop you've always dreamed of operating, someone steps forward, reaches into a pocket and produces the cash that starts the process. That person or persons often does so in anticipation of a return on that money. Shareholders are the last group in the Success Equation. The Phoenix "create success" mentality leads to activities that produce profitable market share growth and economic value added (EVA), and those activities produce shareholder success. The Phoenix mentality sends the signal, "Work collaboratively with associates, customers, suppliers and communities to develop an organization that consistently delivers profitable market share growth and superior EVA."

Grow or Perish: The Basic Principle of Life Is the Basic Principle of Business

Market share growth is an ultimate measure of any organization's success, much like personal growth in skills, income and happiness are ultimate measures of an individual's success. The key question is, "Do you have a larger share of the market today than you had yesterday, and will you have a larger share tomorrow than you have today?"

We're often challenged, "Is it really possible—or necessary—to keep growing? Aren't there market limits and practical limits? Is bigger always better?" Of course, there are limitations. But most of them begin—and end—in your mind. Argue for your limitations and they are yours, along with the stagnation they bring. For instance, Thomas Watson thought there might be a market for three or four computers a year. He saw limitations, and acted accordingly, diverting development dollars from computers into his traditional punch card business. It took his son's boldness and persistence to overcome Watson Sr.'s conservatism. IBM would likely not be around today if it had continued to act on the perceived limited computer market. You know what happened to IBM's punch card business? It totally disappeared.

Not so fortunately, the leaders of AT&T in the 1950s, 1960s and 1970s realized their vision of universal access to a telephone: virtually everyone who wanted a phone had one. They couldn't see selling many more phones. With that limitation in mind they worked on controlling the rate of technological change to preserve their dominant position. As a result, because Europe digitized its phone system in the 1980s while America worked on improving its older analog system, we are now paying a much higher price to convert to the bigger digital systems already in use in Europe. Many of those older AT&T leaders left in the post-1984 divestiture transition from monopoly to competition. More than a decade later, AT&T is still struggling to overcome that monopoly mentality sickness brought on by their perceived market limitations.

Most market share limitations begin in the mind. When we first came to the Honeywell Group the folks said that their objective was to maintain market share. Our response was, "Then it's all over. It's just a question of time until Emerson and our other competitors will eat us alive." Fortunately for all of us at Honeywell we developed a new growth-oriented mentality that led to significant market share growth. Growing the business begins with believing that you can—no, must—grow the business.

If You Don't Take the Business, Someone Else Will

The U.S. automobile companies had the best of all worlds throughout the 1950s, 1960s and early 1970s. They sold everything they made. They couldn't slake the thirst of the American public for faster, bigger, fancier new automobiles. The factory lines ran full out, automobile workers were among the best-paid workers in America and car dealers bought big new homes on the hill. It was too good to last. The folks in Detroit sneered when Japan first entered the market with little cars. "No one wants their tin cans," they said. No one paid attention when the tin cans got better and began to take market share. "We don't want that small car business anyway. It's not profitable enough," was the word from the twenty-second floor in Detroit. Twenty-seven market share points later, Detroit now benchmarks against those very same tin can makers. Worse, the fastest growing markets in the world now belong to those same tin can makers.

The U.S. automobile makers learned to their chagrin that losing one customer leads to losing many customers, then leads to losing one's business. Letting the competition into any part of your market is like inviting that smelly old camel to share your tent: pretty soon you are sleeping out under the stars.

How About a Hot Apple Turnover with That?
Growing Customer Wallet Share

The easiest customer to get is the customer you already have. Jack in the Box is a San Diego–grown fast food chain. Early in their growth they trained their order takers to ask after every hamburger order, "And how about some french fries today?" French fry sales zoomed, along with income. They added dessert menu items to encourage customers to finish their meal at Jack in the Box rather than visit another restaurant. "How about an apple turnover?" became the question from the squawk box. Sales continued to climb, illustrating a basic point. The easiest way to grow income is to sell more to current customers, encourage those folks already in line at the drive-thru to buy one more item.

Selling more to current customers is a necessity today in many industries. With the death of high distance rates in the telecommunications industry, for instance, in order to survive the telephone company must sell added services such as voice mail and call forwarding. Bankers rely upon fee income today to survive, rather than the interest rate spreads that filled their pockets until recently. Those fees come from providing such added services as loan processing and estate planning.

Welcome to the world in which the line blurs between products and services. In an effort to sell more to current customers, manufacturing firms offer a wide range of installation and downstream maintenance services. The truck manufacturer from whom my cousin purchased his truck, for instance, now operates a nationwide chain of service facilities. At the same time, service organizations bundle more and more products with their services. Andersen Consulting, the big consulting firm, offers its customers many data-based software products to help them continue the work begun with their consultants. All of this hyperactivity crossing borders and developing new competencies is based on the simple premise that it is cheaper, easier, faster and more profitable to sell more to current customers than continually recruit new ones—and more desirable to the customer, who can get "one-stop shopping."

Not only is it cheaper to sell more to current customers than recruit new ones, it is also much more profitable to keep customers than continually find new ones. We worked with a waste-handling firm that turned over 45 percent of their customer base each year. They calculated that it cost them $2,750 to add a new customer and fourteen months to break even. Customer churn cost them 6 percentage points on the bottom line. We'd estimate that almost every organization loses a similar amount at the bottom line as the result of losing customers. The customer for life is the most profitable customer.

Who's Not Buying from You Now and What Will It Take to Change That?

What's more, there are lots of noncustomers that you can attract. Take the no/slow growth gasoline business. Amoco's been a loser in the market share and profitability wars. Laurance Fuller, the chairman, coveted the number one industry position in profitability. With a five-year average return on equity of 11.4 percent, Amoco lagged more than 3 percentage points behind Exxon. Fuller recognized that he needed to attract new customers and grow market share in order to move up the profitability rankings. As reported in the March 13, 1995, issue of *Forbes,* he offered a different set of services to both sell more to the already gassing up customer and attract new customers who previously didn't consider visiting an Amoco station. His idea was a variation on the old gas station–convenience store theme. To its base of 9,600 gas stations, Amoco added branded fast food outlets like McDonald's and Burger King. Time-starved customers fed the kids and gassed up the car on the same stop. Fuller's strategy worked. He grew market share and profitability, demonstrating again that there are lots of noncustomers around that you just need to find the right hook to attract—even in a no/slow growth business like gasoline.

These noncustomers come from two basic categories. Some noncustomers already frequent your competitors, buying Shell not Amoco gas. These are the no-brainer noncustomers. Just outperform your industry competitors and they are yours. Not many firms own 90 percent of any market. So there's almost always lots of room to grow market share by taking customers from competitors.

The small percentage of any market that most firms currently possess creates lots of opportunity even in tough times. We remember talking with a client who said, "The economy is in tough shape, so I'm expecting my sales to go down."

"Baloney," we responded. "How much market share do you have now?"

"About 21 percent," he said.

"Great," we responded. "What will it take to get 25 percent share? A larger percentage of a shrinking market still gives you real growth." Worry about the economy only if you have 90 percent of the market. The Phoenix mentality is based on growth.

Create a New Market—And Fill It with New Customers

The second, and more challenging, noncustomer is the person who doesn't yet know that he or she needs your product or service. History is filled with the stories of firms that created new markets on their way to financial success. Wal-Mart created the "big-town assortment in the small-town location" and grew a $100 billion business. Trader Joe's invented the "fashion food retailer" industry and created the most profitable food store—sales of $1,000 per square foot double that of the typical supermarket. Mixing such exotic foods as salmon burgers, soy milk and raspberry salsa, along with some of the best buys on fine wine and cheese, Trader Joe's offers an entertainment-filled "culinary treasure hunt." They've also doubled the business in the last five years as Gary Hamel reports in the July–August, 1996, *Harvard Business Review*.

What's It All Worth? Measure Market Share—Or Forget It

One company we worked with had a 12 percent market share. Only problem, they didn't know their market share because they'd never measured it. When we asked the president about market penetration he said, "Don't really know, but I'd guess about 50 to 60 percent. We're the best known in this area. We have about all the business that's worth having out there." Under our strong urging they launched a program to find out how much of the market they really had. They shopped their competitors, paid attention to competing products their customers bought and researched total industry expenditures in their area.

"Wow!" was the president's response to the numbers. "I never knew." They even discovered a major competitor's store on the other side of their less-than-100,000-person hometown. With only 12 percent share (a far cry from the 50 to 60 percent he originally thought), they saw both great opportunities for growth and strong threats to their continued survival. Spurred by this new information, they launched a major new sales and marketing effort that doubled the business in one year. Knowing that it's possible to grow the business is a long way down the road to actually growing the business.

It's sometimes difficult to precisely measure market share. Data may not be available for a particular product or customer segment. Our experience, though, is that there are always good proxies. The basic point: get the numbers. They are out there. And use them to keep score of how well you are following your new growth mentality.

A Shareowner Axiom? Sales for Vanity—Profits for Sanity

Never separate the two words "profitable" and "growth." Growing for growth's sake alone is a one-way ticket to an unmarked grave in the corporate graveyard. Who benefits from profitless growth? The president of a very successful European-based cleaning firm once told us, "Sales for vanity. Profits for sanity. You can have the puffed-up ego. I'll take the bank account, and all that it buys."

At Square D we grew our market share and our bottom line by offering customers what they really valued, and were willing to pay for. The same occurred at AT&T/GBCS. In a business long dominated by price cutting, we grew both market share and margins by offering customers what they really needed.

Set measurable growth objectives, for both market share and profitability. Ask the questions "Are we getting a larger share of our customer's business? Are we getting a larger share of the customers out there? Are we making more money than anyone else in our market?" Then, as we will describe in a later chapter, link everybody's objectives, measures and rewards to these growth indicators.

Previous examples highlighted business organizations. Rest assured, the same rules apply to not-for-profit organizations as well. Take community hospitals, for example. There are several in our area. They rely upon patient flow. Without patients, they'd be very expensive motels with not very good food. Two hospitals we know measure their market share every week. They compare their pediatric unit's census, for instance, against those in other pediatric units. Every staff meeting devotes time to discussing ways to increase their census and their share. They are preoccupied with growth at those not-for-profit hospitals. They recognize that growth is the key to their survival.

Add Economic Value or Your Funding Sources Shrivel Up

Economic value added (EVA) is the single best measure of shareholder success. Three hundred ninety-one of the Fortune 500 companies use EVA as a measure of success. Stern Stewart and Company developed EVA. Most frequently cited champions of EVA are Coca-Cola and CSX. Not a bad group to be part of.

EVA recognizes that profit alone is not enough. Rather, the profit must be great enough to justify the total cost of the capital needed to be in that business. For example, a company in the mining business earns a profit of 4 percent. Is that enough? If it costs that company 8 percent to borrow the capital it needs to stay in business, then the obvious answer is no. Simply put, no organization will attract the new capital it needs to survive and grow if it does not show a large enough return on that capital. EVA, then, simply is after-tax operating profit, a widely used measure, minus the total annual cost of capital.

The Phoenix mentality produces activities that create shareholder value by generating profitable market share growth and economic value added. Those activities trigger cooperation across all the interconnected and interdependent systems, aligning objectives, measures and rewards to create success for associates, customers, suppliers, communities and shareholders.

PHOENIX WORKSHOP

1. HOW CAN I GROW PROFITABLY—MARKET SHARE/SALES/MARGINS/SKILLS/PERSONAL INCOME/HAPPINESS?

_____

_____

2. HOW CAN I IMPROVE MY PERSONAL ECONOMIC VALUE ADDED?_____

_____

Summary: The Self-Renewing
Phoenix Principles

What makes a successful Phoenix? There are five answers.

First, organizations and individuals are successful Phoenixes when they continually renew themselves, re-creating their future that leaves a legacy that makes a difference. Phoenixes focus on developing their competencies in creating better tomorrows for others.

Second, Phoenixes continually find new ways to satisfy the changing needs of an ever-expanding circle of interconnected customers. They see themselves as an integral part of a world of interconnected, interdependent networks.

Third, successful Phoenix organizations and individuals enjoy enduring and mutually gratifying relationships with their web of customers. They evidence the "create success for others" passion that is the heart of the Phoenix's mentality.

Fourth, successful Phoenixes are compulsive learners. They work hard in learning what customers want and how they can do an ever better job of delivering it.

Fifth, Phoenixes believe in carpe diem—seizing the moment—to take responsibility and assume the leadership for heightening their contributions and the contributions of others to the success of all customers.

Hewlett-Packard is an excellent example of a Phoenix organization. HP started their business in the 1970s making such instruments as oscilloscopes. The leaders established a small-business unit and delegated great freedom to employees within each unit to make decisions.

The exigencies of entering the computer business forced the leaders to more closely integrate business units. After all, all the components had to work together. So, in the late 1970s they created a new centralized organization. This gave them integration, but it also slowed decision making. At one point, it took nineteen signatures to change software pricing, for instance.

In the late 1980s when HP encountered difficulty, company founders William Hewlett and David Packard came back into the business. They visited customers and associates to find out what was wrong. Acting upon that feedback, they moved dramatically, abolishing committees, simplifying processes and creating product/market teams. Today, this revivoluted Phoenix is the benchmark in the computer industry. There are many examples of organizations that revivolute themselves and create a successful future, instead of living in the shadow of their past.

There are many successful individual Phoenix examples as well. The August 12, 1996, issue of *Forbes* tells the story of Kathleen Hammer, a linguistics professor who woke up one day to find her academic career inadequate to meet the needs of her family. Instead of living the life of a victim and fighting the system, she revivoluted herself into a tomorrow of her own creation. She started with what she knew, linguistics, and went back to school to learn computers.

It drove her nuts to have to transfer data from one computer language to another whenever a newer, better program became available. It also drove lots of organizations to the brink of despair, forcing them to remain with clunky and inadequate legacy programs because of the staggering cost of rewriting all of the code and data. She saw a market need born out of her own frustration.

Using her psycholinguistics background, she developed applications that translated varieties of computer programming code into one compatible, simplified language. Today, she is the chief executive and co-founder of Evolutionary Technologies International, a fast-growing Austin, Texas, high-tech firm that helps large corporations translate databases. She revivoluted her life by becoming a self-renewing Phoenix to create the successful life and career she enjoys today.

There are thousands of examples, many of them reported in the myriad of business and personal growth magazines. But in truth, the most impressive stories of individual triumph and renewal often go unrecorded and unread. Look around you and notice all the people you know in new and different jobs and careers, individuals who started out as computer specialists and wound up as golf pros, individuals who started out as stay-at-home moms who today are newspaper reporters and lawyers. To all the doubters among you we say, "Yes, Virginia, there is a Phoenix, lots of Phoenixes. Step forward. Seize the moment. Focus on creating success for employees, customers, suppliers, communities and shareholders. Be a self-renewing Phoenix. You can do it!"

Fellowship and Leadership on Your Personal Network

Our world begins and ends with people: wonderful, resourceful, honest and imperfect people. Our success is not the product of the organizations with which we are associated or the technologies we use. We owe any success we have ever achieved to the marvelous cast of thousands that fill our lives. George Burns said it well, "Our audiences made us successful."

The key questions each of us faces are, "What do I want my organization to be like? What do I want the rest of my life to be like?" Each and every one of us can make a choice. We come to today with a certain set of mentalities—our behavioral coding. These mentalities determine who and what we are, and how we behave in situations.

Organizationally, the mentalities determine whether we emphasize profit or growth, products or services, people or politics. However, we are not stuck with our current mentality. We can change and put in place a new set of signals. The self-renewing Phoenix carries a "create success for all customers" mentality. That mentality continually challenges us with the question "Does this action, policy, strategy, plan contribute to success for our interconnected and interdependent associates, end-user customers, suppliers, communities and shareholders?" The Phoenix proceeds with only those actions that meet the yes test. As such, that mentality drives an entirely new set of behaviors.

As a soaring Phoenix we are both fellows and leaders in our interconnected, interdependent networks. Fellowship means we accept the responsibility of cooperating. Leadership goes further: it means we accept the higher responsibility to help all members of our networks become ever more successful. As a Phoenix leader we take responsibility for creating success for all those with whom we are interconnected. Everyone is a leader in our networks: as everyone is a fellow. In the next section, we will look more specifically at how to become a Phoenix leader, creating success for all those in your interconnected network. How do each of us stay focused on the whole and not the small part we play? How can each person be a leader and take responsibility for creating that network alignment? First, we'll help you become a Phoenix leader. Then we'll lay out the tools a Phoenix leader uses to build the Pyramid that is the base for future success. Read on—so you, too, can be a soaring Phoenix.

PART II

PHOENIX LEADERSHIP: CREATING OTHER PHOENIXES

INTRODUCTION

Leadership: The Search for the Holy Grail That Launches a Thousand Ships

A young lady asked us a question at a recent presentation. "What's the first thing I need to do to renew myself and become a Phoenix?"

"Learn to be a self-renewing Phoenix leader," was our instant reply.

A corporate president we know called recently and asked a similar question. "I've got this failing division. What's the first thing I need to do to begin the renewal process?"

Our equally quick response, "Get a Phoenix leader."

Why is the answer so easy? Because it's clear that leaders make *the* difference. Leaders transform a collection of people into a team. Leaders organize well-meaning, good-intentioned, talented individuals into lean machines that consistently deliver great performance for their customers. Leaders cut through the clatter and chatter and focus an organization on delivering the few, strategic must dos to create success for customers. Leaders make *the* difference, that's why they are so widely sought and highly prized.

We saw the difference at AT&T/GBCS. The division had lots of highly talented individuals. They knew the telephone switch business better than anybody else. They were highly motivated and committed, working seventy-plus hours a week. Yet despite the talent and the expertise and the commitment, they were losing almost $1 million a day. Today that business is one of the stars of Lucent Technologies, an AT&T spinoff. What made the difference? Leaders like Pat Russo and Barry Karafin, who saw what needed to be done and did it. Leadership made the difference.

That's likely why we get calls . . . and calls . . . and calls. While they come from many different countries, and many different organizations, they share one thing in common: the people calling are all searching for leaders. One came from the Continent. The search committee for a very large telecommunications firm called. They needed a leader to take them into the twenty-first century. That call was followed by another from a search firm looking for a leader of a very large American telecommunications firm looking for a leader to take them into the twenty-first century. That call was followed by a call from a large missionary organization looking for a leader to take them into the twenty-first century. From our local minister, who's moving to find a more progressive congregation to help move into the new millennium, to the largest search firms looking for presidents and CEOs, everyone's looking for leaders.

We Are Fascinated with Leaders and Leadership

But not any leader will do. There are leaders and then there are LEADERS—in capital letters—and everyone's in search of that capital-letter leader. Leadership is the most researched subject in management. Despite all this interest in leadership and leaders, we know preciously little about how leaders perform their magic. We are long on academic descriptions of leadership behavior. We've added our thimbleful to that particular mix. Then there's a plethora of "here's how I did it" books out there by former (or even current) leaders like Max Dupree or Lee Iacocca. It's difficult to pin down the fruits of all this labor beyond the dead trees we've delivered. We agree with Warren Bennis: "Never have so many labored so long to say so little."

What we do know, though, is that Phoenix leaders are different.

How the Phoenix Leader Soars

Phoenix leaders make five essential contributions to the interconnected networks they lead: They *surface issues* that confront the organization; *engage the people* in resolving those issues, *prioritize/allocate resources* to address those issues, *unleash own-*

ership so everyone accepts responsibility for dealing with those issues, and *energize learning* for everyone in the network. These five contributions help everyone succeed in the interconnected, interdependent network. These contributions enable the leader and the others to build a Pyramid that provides a strong base for future success.

President Clinton's Shining Leadership Hour

One of President Clinton's shining hours as a leader came during the debate on NAFTA, the North American Free Trade Agreement. He *surfaced the issues* of free trade and political stability on our borders, issues that sharply divided the American people. He *engaged the people* and the Congress in debating the issues. He held town meetings. He gave speeches across the country and over national TV. He deputized his vice president, Al Gore, to debate NAFTA's primary public opponent, Ross Perot, on Larry King's national TV show. He focused on NAFTA in every public appearance. With the victory in Congress, he then *prioritized and allocated the resources* of his administration to implement the accords. He then *unleashed the ownership* for implementation to his staff and *energized their learning* by sending them out to see how the accords were being implemented. All his considerable talents and efforts delivered success for a large number of people on both sides of the border.

We worked to create success for everyone at AT&T/GBCS. We *surfaced the major issues* confronting the division: pricing, customer focus and internal competition. We *engaged everyone* in debating these issues. As a result of the debate, we decided to lead a price increase in the marketplace, align integrating customer-focused goals across previously independent units and integrate previously competitive separate internal selling organizations. We then *prioritized and allocated resources* to implement these decisions. We added resources to the sales administration group to support the price increase strategy. We sped up research deliverables to put new product on the street that would justify the price increase. We invested the time and money to hold goal alignment meetings throughout the organization to get everyone to understand the need for the price increase and the role each of them played in supporting the overall division's return to profitability. We put in place new goal setting and quality skills training activities that helped *unleash the ownership* for implementing the new strategies and *energized the learning* for future development.

There are Phoenix leaders at all levels in an organization. At AT&T/GBCS, for instance, the head of field support accounting, Bob, led his group of field controllers to surface the issues that confronted his group in accomplishing the price increase, returning to profitability and becoming more customer-focused. Bob's group found that field personnel have little financial know-how, low accuracy and poor timeliness of providing financial information and field controllers are held in low esteem by field personnel. Bob then engaged his group in discussing what they could do to improve their support. They decided that they would improve the quality and timeliness of the financial data, educate field personnel in reading and using the financial information, and do whatever it took to earn a seat at the field decision making table. Bob then led the prioritization and allocation of resources to implement these strategies. The team decided to press for both more accurate information transmitted from the field in a more timely manner and major system upgrades to reduce the number of manual correcting transactions that slowed down the release of field statements. They also agreed to spend more time teaching field personnel how to read and use financial statements. Then, Bob worked to unleash the ownership for the implementation of these strategies to the field controllers. He established monthly action plans and reviews of accomplishments. He then sponsored field training programs to encourage learning. He coached his field controllers, in turn, to become Phoenix leaders in their small field offices by repeating the process with their teams.

But there were lots of Phoenix leaders at AT&T/GBCS other than those who held official management positions. Sally was a field sales coordinator in a Midwestern region. She worked as part of a virtual team responsible for ensuring that the sales reps had the information necessary to support the price increase. She assumed leadership of the team, surfacing the issues confronting the team (competing time and priority pressures), engaging people in resolving those issues (involving the many different managers in resolving priority issues), prioritizing/allocating resources to implement the strategy (acquiring a small discretionary budget for support material purchases), unleashing the ownership for execution (tracking teammates' promised versus actual delivery dates) and learning herself about how to lead teams. There were many Phoenix leaders at AT&T/GBCS, both management and nonmanagement people, each of whom performed the five leadership tasks and enabled their interconnected networks to build the solid Pyramid base for future success.

Phoenix Leaders Are Known for Who They Are, Not for What They Do

Don't be misled by our stress thus far on what leaders do. What leaders do is certainly important. But the importance of what a leader does pales in comparison to what a leader is. Throughout this book we'll talk about role modeling and the importance of walking the talk. Leaders are the highly visible embodiment of what the organization stands for. They are the role model that represents the organization's Pyramid of visions, missions, values, objectives and strategies. The leader of the "best of us," the persona to which we all aspire. Leadership is about character and integrity, not about flying around in corporate jets and giving speeches.

One of our grandsons was born prematurely. He was a tiny little thing and we worried that he was too undeveloped to survive. We took turns visiting him during his extended stay in the hospital. The wise nurse in the neonatal care unit urged us to caress his tiny body with our finger encased in the latex glove all the while talking to him. "It's vital for Joshua's survival that he hears your voice and feels your touch. That will encourage him to fight for his life." Touch and talk we did, and fight he did, and he's now a healthy six-year-old. Only later did it dawn on us that the nurse's words were a perfect simile for Phoenix leadership. Joshua knew we cared about him; he knew from our words reinforced by our simultaneous actions. We walked our talk and talked our walk. Joshua heard and responded. Phoenix leaders do the same; they let their walking do their talking so the other Joshuas in the world can be encouraged to fight for the organization's life.

Phoenix Leadership Is Learnership

Great leaders are also great learners. They understand that no one knows everything they need to know to be successful in their current job. And also that no one knows everything they need to know in order to be successful in an uncertain tomorrow. Logic dictates, therefore, that our chief leadership challenge is to learn what's required to be successful both today and tomorrow and get on with developing those skills and knowledge. It seems to us that that's just common sense. Unfortunately, it is not common practice.

Beware the VIW (Very Important Work) Shield

Most people are so-o-o busy with their current activities that they have no time left over to devote to learning how to do things better or develop skills for a different tomorrow. A neighbor of ours works as an executive in a county office. She leaves before us and returns well after us. She tires us out telling us all that she's doing. At the same time she feels stymied in her job and would like to find a new one, but she doesn't have time to even look around or take some education to qualify for a different position. She is trapped in the busyness of her current job. We know the CEO of a large company that has been trying for two years to get some preliminary computer training. He's just "too busy" to get the three days away. His company slipped badly several years ago and has yet to recover. Maybe, just maybe, his company is struggling because he's "too busy" to learn.

The key point: Phoenix leadership relies on continuous learning. As leaders we have very limited powers. We don't design the product. We don't make it. We don't sell it. We don't ship it. In fact, we do little to the physical characteristics of what customers buy from us today. One of our principal contributions is helping others learn what's required to succeed and then helping them learn the requisite skills and knowledge. Learn first yourself, setting the tone and model, and then create the opportunity for others to learn by surfacing issues, engaging people in decisions, prioritizing/allocating resources and transferring ownership for implementation.

Phoenix Leadership Is a Heart Connection

We've heard it from the speaker's podium a dozen times. "They don't care how much you know, until they know how much you care—about them." It's more than a motivational speech, though, it's the heart and soul of Phoenix leadership. Spurred by such leaders as Tom Chappell of Tom's of Maine and Anita Broderick of the Body Shop, today, more than ever, leaders talk about the heart connection aspect of leadership. Herb Kelleher, CEO of successful Southwest Airlines, told the editors of *Fortune* that his airline has "a patina of spirituality." Even Jack Welch, the hard-boiled leader of General Electric, told Frances Hesselbein, in Fall 1996's *Leader to Leader,* "Ten years from now, we want magazines to write about GE as a place where people have the freedom to be creative, a place that brings out the best in everyone, an open, fair place where people have a sense that what they do matters, and where that sense of accomplishment is rewarded both in the pocketbook and the soul. That will be our report card."

Everywhere we go we build relationships. Our e-mail address book file bulges with the names of people with whom we've worked that we'd like to work with again, and who would like to work with us again. As one of our wives said, "Most executives collect corporate toys, things like trophies and plaques, and physical toys like jets and cars and motorcycles. My husband collects friends. We've run out of walls in the house to hang all the Christmas cards we get from his friends. They started out being business associates. They've become part of our extended family."

In short, Phoenix leaders do, Phoenix leaders care, Phoenix leaders learn, Phoenix leaders live their words. You can be a Phoenix leader. No, you *must* be a Phoenix leader if you want to renew yourself and create a legacy worth leaving. Read on into the chapters in this section that can help you be the Phoenix leader that builds the strong Pyramid base for your and your organization's future success.

CHAPTER 4

The Timeless Light of Phoenix Leadership: 10,000 Watts, 10,000 Facts, 10,000 Tomorrows

Phoenix leaders make five contributions to the success of their interconnected networks: they surface issues, engage people, prioritize resources, unleash ownership and energize learning. We'll focus here on the first major contribution, surfacing issues.

In a High-Heat, Low-Light World:
You Are What Happens After What Happens Next

Look around you and see uncertainty everywhere. Where to turn? What to do? Desperation screams at you from the TV, the newspaper and the radio. Tune in and listen to the debacle du jour.

Perhaps every previous generation felt it faced the greatest challenges since humankind crawled out of the primeval ooze. Perhaps every generation felt it had to create a whole new world order. Perhaps. But we know today that, regardless of what our predecessors faced, we face the reinvention challenge. We draw little comfort from knowing that previous generations have faced similar challenges. No, misery does not love company.

High Heat, Low Light, New Rules Create a Virtual Sauna

Sit in any organization and feel the stewing sauna of uncertainty. One of our clients is the director of a government social insurance agency in Europe. The agency provides health and unemployment benefits collected through employment taxes. In an effort to save money, the government is privatizing the agency. Within three years any private insurance company will be free to offer the insurance coverage this agency does in return for receiving the taxes the government collects.

The agency head figures that her agency's administrative and claims-paying costs are double those of private insurers. She calculates that she'll have to reduce her staff by 50 percent within the next three years just to be cost-competitive: "The culture shock worries me most. How can we get the 4,200 people who remain to move from paying claims to preventing claims, from administering rules to establishing partnerships with employers and physicians, from being a very powerful little king in dealing with dependent beneficiaries to being one of many possible suppliers to both clients who will now have the power of choice and powerful employers?"

We feel the heat of uncertainty rise past the 212 degree boiling point as the light seems to fade.

Lift Up Your Eyes: Look to the Phoenix Leader for Leadership

We really have no choice. We must accept the mission-impossible assignment, for *not* doing it leads to certain extinction. "I got it," you say. "I've got to reinvent the rules: revivolute. But how? To what? Who's going to show me what to do?"

That's the time for the Phoenix leader to step forward. In times of trouble we instinctively look to the head of the flock in search of direction and guidance. It's been trained into us. We go to "mommy" to solve a sibling problem. We go to "teacher" for help with a math problem. We go to "boss" with a budget problem. We look for superior wisdom. It's human nature.

Look in the Mirror: The Phoenix Leader You Seek Is Staring Back at You

Step forward and be that Phoenix leader. Do what needs to be done to create success for all those in your interconnected, interdependent network. Seize the torch and lead the parade. Power up the big beacon and light up the landscape to discover what it'll take to win in your market. How? That's the topic of this chapter.

FACTS ARE OUR FRIENDS: SURROUND YOURSELF WITH THEM

The Fact-Based Organization, the Fact-Based Life

The Phoenix leader lives on a steady diet of facts—in particular, facts that she can really *do* something about. She fearlessly pursues facts and challenges assumptions, hearsay and rumors. Whether you are looking for employment, looking for a spouse, looking for a place to live, a church, a better Caesar salad or a future of any kind—collecting facts about the situation is the first step on your journey to success. Do your homework. Be certain of your facts. Lots may be at stake.

One of our fathers died from cancer. Our sister is a well-known psychiatrist who practiced where Dad lived, so she looked after him in his later years. She secured the best-regarded oncologist in the area to treat him. The doctor diagnosed and treated Dad for lung cancer for several years. Dad was a heavy smoker, so the diagnosis had a lot of face validity. Years after Dad died she submitted his cancer samples to the NIH and was horrified to discover that he had actually died from skin cancer—which could have been treated effectively with early diagnosis. Even the best professionals make errors. Gather facts. Get second and third opinions. Don't settle for anything other than all the facts: your life—or a loved one's—could hang in the balance.

Search out the three sets of facts essential to a Phoenix leader's success. Search first for the facts concerning the future. What's coming that we need to prepare for, that we can capitalize on, that we need to defend against? Then search the hearts and minds of all the living, breathing human beings with which we are connected—those wonderful people who make up our network world. Discover their hopes and dreams, their fears and aspirations, so you can create the ultimate win-win situation: the organization that accomplishes its goals and the individual who achieves truly fulfilling success for him- or herself. Third, search out facts about your customers, what they *really* want and need, so you can help the people deliver it.

A Bridge Too Far: Can't Build to Tomorrow from Last Year's Wisdom

The Phoenix leader begins from the future and manages backward to build that bridge to tomorrow. That means beginning with what you want to create in the future—your vision, mission, values and goals. Then put in place the strategies, disciplined management systems, business processes and communications infrastructure that enable you to build that bridge to tomorrow, one brick at a time.

Too many try to build that bridge to tomorrow with the building materials of yesterday's facts. Unfortunately, it can't be done. We sat in the office of the CEO of a major Fortune 100 company not long ago. He complained about being "surprised" by the market and wound up eating millions of dollars of unsold inventory. "How could it happen?" he kept asking, shaking his head. "That one surprise cost us six cents a share last year."

"How come your competitor wasn't surprised?" we asked, noting that they reported record earnings.

"Dammed if I know," he said. "This reading the future stuff is very dicey."

"Dicey" is an understatement. The future is a million-piece puzzle; with no handy box lid picture to guide the assembly. Organizations likely achieve less than 20 percent of their future plans. That's not surprising, considering how most future plans are made. Data gathering begins in July, based on information from the first and second quarters. Preliminary plans are submitted in September, revised in October and November and finalized in December for the coming year. As a Phoenix leader you can't afford the luxury of basing tomorrow's plans on yesterday's information.

Wake Up: The Future Is All Around You

Yes, you absolutely can know what's coming by just paying attention. The following story is told about the Buddha.

> A traveler meets the Buddha on the road. Noticing his huge entourage, the traveler asks Buddha, "Are you a god?" "No," Buddha replies. "Then are you a saint?" "No," Buddha answers. "You must be a prophet, then," the traveler says. "No," Buddha replies. Frustrated, the traveler exclaims, "If you're not a god or a saint or a prophet—then why are all these people following you?" "Because I'm awake," Buddha replies.

> Leaders who are awake attract large followings—because they help everyone achieve success. They power up the light sources and focus everyone on what's really there.

This story about the Buddha (which may or may not be true, but it certainly makes our point) underlines an essential truth: most of us are asleep at the wheel of life—and wonder why we keep ending up in those ditches. The future is all around us, blaring at us through movies and television, bombarding us through print, video and the Internet. Yet we neither hear nor see.

Become Your Own Futurist

It's fun to think about the future. It's freewheeling and open-ended and everyone can play the game. There's a time and place for open-ended brainstorming, and there's also a time to be more systematic. We like to search with a discipline and look for facts and evidence rather than opinion. Our systematic searches generally involve three distinct activities: reading a lot, talking a lot and getting many people engaged in the process.

Read, Read, Read—And Then Read Some More. We are voracious readers. Together we scan more than sixty journals a month. Scanning is not reading. Obviously we are too busy to read sixty journals cover to cover. But we scan through them looking for anything of interest that may impact any of our many and varied business interests. For instance, one of us sits on the board of an entertainment company. So he looks for items that may impact entertainment organizations. One of us sits on the board of a materials supplier. He scans for articles that may impact his materials supplier company.

We scan widely, outside of our areas of immediate interest. We read such diverse journals as *George*—John Kennedy's political satire magazine, *The Economist* and *Rolling Stone*. We scan general interest publications, the *New York Times* and *Times* of London, industry journals and special-purpose business publications. The Internet is a gold mine, if you know how to search it time-efficiently. Both of us use electronic clipping services like the *Wall Street Journal's Personal Journal*. Scanning these services two or three times a week and downloading articles of interest extends our reach. Importantly, by using scanning services different eyes other than our own search the data, helping us escape the boundaries of our own biases.

Hold Talk-a-Thons in Corporate Think Tanks and Grocery Checkout Lines. We gather data everywhere we go. We stay awake flying in planes, talking to clerks in stores, visiting customers and just engaging people anywhere in conversation. Chatting with other shoppers while waiting in the checkout line, for instance, is a great way to find out what's really on customers' minds, though this seemingly disorganized search for clues belies our underlying systematic approach. But we've learned that the future is being created in the millions of organizational laboratories across the world. It's often old news by the time it gets reported in the press. We look to get ahead of the curve by discovering the clues while the experiment is still going on.

Be cautious, though; not all opinions are of equal weight. Two approaches work for us. We listen for opinion dominance. If many people have the same opinion in an industry or about a product, it's likely to come true. If everyone we speak to wants a Jeep as the new hot vehicle, Jeep production will likely increase, as will Chrysler's profits and stock price. Peter Lynch, the man who beat Wall Street at its own game, used this approach. He noticed what was successful in the market and bought those stocks. He identified the coming boom in Wal-Mart stock by shopping at the stores and noticing the big crowds. He repeated that success with Home Depot and Staples, also by noticing the stores' crowds and listening to the customers' comments as he shopped the store and stood in the checkout line. This opinion dominance approach works well with consumer products.

Many future issues are not directly product-related. What will the next new computer technology be? How will new materials change the shape of the construction industry? These are not questions that the consumer can answer today. You can't go into the mall of tomorrow and watch customer shopping patterns to discover these crucial trends. But there are a few leading-edge thinkers who work at being ahead of the pack. They are usually senior people in advanced organizations with one finger on the technology pulse in the laboratory and another in the marketplace. Barry Karafin was one such individual at AT&T/GBCS. Phil Neches was another at AT&T/NCR. We visit regularly with such folks, plumbing their ideas and sharing our experiences.

There's a gold mine of insight to be gleaned from the combination of random information bits in shopping center checkout lines and frequent discussions with technology gurus. We've learned to pay attention to anything that surprises us, stops us in our tracks and makes us wrinkle our brows. Most often those stop-us-in-our-tracks items make us feel uncomfortable because they seem out of place. But they're usually the ones that are the harbingers of an impending shift in the prevailing winds. In one of our companies we made a dye-tracing product that followed the flow of water. The nontoxic chemical product sold almost exclusively to water and sewer districts looking to trace leaks in water and sewer lines. We also discovered that one company used it to trace leaks in hydraulic equipment lines. Another used it to check the water tightness of brewing vats. Still another used it to test for cracks in car engines. These unusual uses signaled a much broader market for the product, one that we never would have recognized.

Get Many Eyes on the Future: Create Your Own Intelligence Network. The word TEAM stands for Together Everyone Achieves More. That's also true when it comes to reading the uncertain future. We engage everyone in the organization in searching out facts about the future. We exchange clipped articles monthly, meet quarterly to discuss the previous three months' learning and meet twice a year to analyze in depth the potential implications of what we've uncovered. Several thousand different pairs of eyes looking at the uncertain future, and active, open discussion of their findings, yield a clearer overall picture.

Shine the Light onto Your Customers' Bookshelf. Shine the light into your customers' minds and hearts. We talk constantly with our customers, spending three or four days a week in the field, in their offices, in their faces. We try, as best we can, to crawl inside their world and shine the light to discover what it's really like for them in there.

One of the best ways we've discovered to learn about customers is to experience the media world they experience. We ask our leading-edge customers what books and magazines they read. We read them also. We ask customers what TV shows they watch. While those shows may not be high on our list of favorites, we watch them also. We ask customers what commercials particularly appeal to them, and why. Then we watch those to see if we can pick up the appealing messages.

We do the same drill for our customers' leading-edge customers. We want to experience what our leading-edge customers and their leading-edge customers experience, so we can understand their world from their perspective. The media shape people's thoughts. Understand people's thoughts by understanding the media they experience. Gathering facts from customers is so important that we'll devote an entire section to it in this chapter.

A Window Seat to Tomorrow: Find the Facts at 30,000 Feet. Airplane trips can be wonderful fact-gathering experiences. People are trapped for hours at a time, with no place to go. And most folks love to tell their story. We sat next to a businesswoman flying from coast to coast recently. She's a sales manager for a large computer company. We asked a few open-ended questions, like "What do you do? How do you like it? Where do you live? What do you do for fun?" We asked and out poured her life story.

We also learned lots about her preferences in travel, jobs, housing and transportation. For instance, cigars and cognac are her favorite after-dinner treat when she's on the road. She confided that she likes to smoke good cigars in her hotel room, usually after eating ribs or some other "forbidden food." She brings her own cigars because few hotels have "the good ones."

We passed these insights on to the hotel management company we're working with, along with copies of advertisements showing women smoking cigars and articles in businesswomen's magazines talking about "secret pleasures on the road." All of this came as a surprise to the hotel owners and managers, but they were open to experimentation. In one hotel they launched a "Cigars and Cognac" room service promotion and added baby back ribs to their room service menu. Room service revenue immediately increased 8 percent, mostly from these special items. Both men and women ordered them. The entire chain adopted this approach, expanding room service menus to include other forbidden food and other secret pleasure promotions. Being awake at 30,000 feet pays.

Here Comes a Trend: "But Is It Big Enough to Worry About?"

Things change all the time. Businesses start up and close their doors every day. New products come on the market and others disappear every day. It rains somewhere every day. But when does a rainstorm turn into a flood? When does a new product turn into a trend? When does a new business steal your customers and threaten your continued existence? Change happens all the time. When does a change reach the "pay attention now!" level?

We struggle with this question all the time. Part of our responsibility is a state-of-the-company speech at our semiannual all-employee meeting. That speech lays out the important developments that we feel will alter our way of doing business in the future. In the past we successfully identified the sustainable development trend and were able to capitalize on it. We identified early the rise of Asia as a major economic power. Teams worked to secure local partnerships in many countries that helped us attain a shut-out-the-competitor position. We thought about lots of other trends, but rejected them as being not large enough to merit organization-changing attention.

A few years ago, the pressure to squeeze inventory costs down was emerging as a possible important trend. Retailers had played around with the issue for years, but with the exception of a few pioneers like Wal-Mart, little had changed in the grocery/supermarket/mass merchandising business. The whispers we heard about applying the same inventory reduction process in the industrial sphere got our attention. If that happened, it had the potential to dramatically change the way we service many of our customers. We suspected this might be one of those "pay attention now!" issues. So we paid close attention.

We read everything in sight; talked with consultant friends about their experiences; asked our executive friends what they knew about this development; and compiled a very short list of leading-edge companies now experimenting with some aspect of industrial inventory reduction and visited them. We never left one visit without asking for other names to contact and spoke to thirty-seven organizations before we finished. We asked everyone in our organization to share any and all anecdotes/experiences/whispers they'd heard about inventory-reduction activities in industrial companies. Those questions surfaced lots of leads. As the evidence piled up, we were convinced that industrial inventory reduction was a "pay attention now!" trend. We devoted more than half of the next presentation to that phenomenon.

The story doesn't end there, of course. Speeches alone do not transform organizations. Following up on our presentation, a team conducted a full investigation and recommended we partner with several consulting firms to offer an integrated inventory-reduction service for hazardous and toxic material. Capitalizing on that market caused us to go back to the beginning and reinvent ourselves. We used the Pyramid-building process spelled out later, beginning with vision, mission and values and moving on to goals, strategies, objectives/measures/rewards, processes and infrastructures, we built the basis for sustained future growth. That business is booming today.

Our job as the Phoenix leader: shine the light, surface the "pay attention now!" issues and engage everyone in the process of developing our collective future.

Facts Are Not Forever: Keep Your Eye on the Puck

But the present isn't forever. The great hockey player Wayne Gretzky says he always skates to where the puck *will be,* not where it is. That puck never stops moving. Like that puck, the future whizzes by at the speed of light.

Chuck Knight's an expert in shining the light to find the facts, and then shifting the focus when the world changes. His saga is recounted by Seth Lubow in the August 1, 1994, *Forbes* and by Rob Norton in the November 25, 1996, *Fortune.* He leads Emerson Electric, one of the great business success stories of the twentieth century, with an unbroken record of thirty-eight consecutive years of earnings growth. Knight focused on cost cutting for most of his more than twenty years at the helm. It had always worked. It always would. Forever and ever, amen.

In 1984, Whirlpool told Emerson that they could buy compressors for $30 from Brazil. At the same time, Knight was selling them for $40. He dispatched a team to shine the light and discover the facts. The facts they uncovered drove Knight's strategy for a decade. What their searchlight revealed was not the typical low-wage scenario. Rather, Knight's team found in Brazil the best manufacturing plant they'd ever seen. Then, they saw its mate in Korea. Chuck Knight decided "we must be the best cost producer, globally." Using his budgeting and planning system, he built strategies that drove costs down 10 percent per year. He fixed the spotlight on costs by ruthlessly benchmarking against the Japanese, the Koreans, the Brazilians and anybody else anywhere in the world who produced competitive parts. His unbroken record of earnings increases speaks for itself.

But there can be a downside to his fixation on costs. He looked at several possible strategic acquisitions, and turned many down because they didn't quite meet the cost-reduction/earnings-per-share standard. Emerson researched one particularly carefully, displaying exceptional due diligence. After much negotiation they turned the opportunity down, letting the deal go to another competitor for less than one cent a share difference. Today, that competitor is much stronger, taking market share from Emerson and costing Emerson much more than the penny a share they would have spent to acquire it. We wonder if Knight's cost obsession at the time didn't blind him to the growth opportunities the merger presented. We guess he'd make a different decision today.

The world turns, and the game changes as the environment changes. Today low cost is not sufficient; you also need growth. In 1994, Knight shined the light and discovered that he missed sales opportunities. Cost-constrained marketing and sales budgets prevented his people from searching out and creating new ways to meet customer needs. Furthermore, restricted R&D budgets focused on creating short-term bumps to the bottom line, rather than new products and services that grew tomorrow's revenue streams. Knight realized that he faced the possibility of cost cutting his way to corporate oblivion.

So he shifted gears. He now uses that same powerful budgeting process to generate cost containment and growth. Knight's new equation: reduce costs 10 percent and grow the business 20 percent. Knight uses the annual growth conference to shine the light and surface the issues of both growing the business and containing costs. Each of Emerson's divisions spends two days evaluating growth proposals for risk, market conditions, capacity issues and payback periods. Knight joins every discussion to ensure that the laser light discovers all the important issues and that they are discussed thoroughly.

Knight doesn't solve any issues. He doesn't tell his team what to do or how to do it. Knight lives the Phoenix leader's role: shining the light to surface the growth-opportunity issues that create success for us all and then asking the team, "How are we going to address this issue?"

Your Inner School Is Always in Session: The One-Page Gold Mine

Every day we write a one-page diary sheet which answers three questions: What did I accomplish today of which I can be particularly proud? What is yet to be accomplished tomorrow? What did I learn today that will help me be more effective tomorrow? We summarize these sheets every week, every month, every quarter and every year. These sheets are the gold that we've mined through a lifetime of learning. They are our single best source of data for creating our tomorrow. For the cost of a tablet you, too, can be documenting your inner accomplishments and expectations—and creating your future.

Every person in one of our businesses writes and shares widely throughout the organization a weekly "15-5 report"—a piece that takes fifteen minutes to write and five minutes to read, answering the same three questions. We store this information by topic in a "Knowledge Center" along with market and customer information.

Overcome the Organization's Learning Disability

We've seen too many organizations self-destruct because they develop an organizational learning disability. Ford was a star in the 1980s, tripling its market share. For the first time since Henry's Model T, Ford actually made more money than General Motors. They had the giant on the ropes. Then the learning disability took over. They took their eyes off the product development ball. Rather than investing in new technology and new products, Ford pumped money into Jaguar, bought its way into financial services and invested heavily in defense industries. They drank deep from the diversification cup. The results of that bender still plague the balance sheet today. Now, Ford trails General Motors, Chrysler and Toyota in most significant efficiency indices: profitability per car, time to market with new models and inventory turnover. The chairman is faced with another urgent revivolution job, as John Trudel describes in the September 1996 issue of *Upside* magazine.

The market respects no history. It worships at the altar of current value. It matters little if you've been great for fifty-two years or fifty-two nanoseconds. The market asks, "What value are you delivering today, right now?" Learning what the market values right now and how you can best deliver that is crucial to continued success. All that history is just interesting reading.

Keep learning or you die: literally and figuratively. Learn by reading, talking, sharing and learning. Develop your learning muscle by exercising it frequently and constantly reading the uncertain future.

Let's Pretend: The Moose That Isn't There

We've all been a part of Let's Pretend discussions. During a tense labor-management negotiation session, where the pickets are walking outside hurling obscene epithets at the managers inside, we talk about the weather, pretending that the six-week-old strike isn't going on and management isn't busy hiring replacements. During an annual planning session, we discuss new product features and enhancements without first investigating the factors that drive our shrinking market share and eroding margins. The reason for all of this seemingly irrational behavior: the Moose.

The Moose symbolizes avoidance. Imagine this huge animal, the Moose, standing in the middle of the conference table, where you're making important decisions. Everyone pretends the Moose isn't there. Everyone knows the Moose is there. Yet you peer around the legs of this big beast, work hard to overcome the smell, pretend it's not dropping waste products all over your papers—all the while attempting to discuss the serious issues. It's the corporate version of the children's game Let's Pretend.

The Moose That Lives in the Past Threatens Our Future. The Moose is the collection of past mind-sets and past successes and failures that are behind the door and under the table that no one wants to talk about. We've all lived with the Moose. The Moose is there when everyone around the table knows we are pursuing a flawed strategy, but no one raises the issue because the boss is the one who's pushing it. The Moose is there when we make an assumption based upon past beliefs that the easiest way to gain market share is to cut prices.

We've learned to ignore the Moose on the table. Most of us would prefer to shoot the beast and have it for dinner. But we've learned that such a challenge can be career limiting. It pays to get the Moose on the table, though. Don't waste your time in endless meetings pretending one thing is true when you know deep down in your heart that it isn't. Get the issues on the table and move on.

You Moose Out, You Miss Out. We've encountered many a Moose on many a table in our journeys. At AT&T/GBCS the biggest Moose was the "service is a cost, not a profit center"

Moose. That concept was drilled into thousands of people's heads. Once we got that Moose on the table, it was simple to help the field salespeople understand that service could be a competitive advantage and a potentially lucrative source of revenue.

The other big GBCS Moose was that "the only way to gain market share is to cut price." It took almost six months of almost constant discussion to get really smart people to recognize that Moose for the Moose it was: an avoidance of dealing with the hard issues of growing the business. Moose are very powerful. They obstruct your view of the present and destroy your future.

Power, Permission and Protection Slay the Beast. The Phoenix leader slays the Moose by providing people with *3Ps:* the *power* to search out the facts, the *protection* to spend the time and resources necessary to surface the real issues and get them on the table, and the *permission* to tell the king (or anyone for that matter) that he or she has no clothes and to make mistakes along the way from which you learn.

We slew the Moose using the 3Ps at Square D. Electrical circuit breaker boxes and panels were manufactured out of metal. It's just the way it was. A whole mystique grew up around the metal boxes. Everyone repeated the familiar mantras, "Electricians love the metal boxes. It has a solid look. Besides, plastic is unsafe." It turned out that these metal boxes were a very big Moose.

An engineer in Lexington, Kentucky, believed that he could dramatically reduce both the electrician's installation costs and Square D's manufacturing costs if the industry moved from metal to plastic boxes. His proposal triggered a heated debate. We gave the engineer the *power* to investigate the possibility. He interviewed electricians. He spoke to homeowners. He cornered builders. He shone his light into every corner of the industry. We provided him the *protection* he needed to test out his proposal, releasing him from other duties and providing a small budget so he could focus on his investigation. Lots of people thought he was crazy. Many thought we were crazy also for wasting resources on the project. But we resisted the temptation to accept the current wisdom and defended the funds in his project. We also provided the *permission* for him to present his findings to a willing-to-listen audience, including ourselves. We insisted that people listen to his evidence. It took lots of permission to sort out the facts in this case. Because of metal's long history and all the electricians who had been taught the fear of plastic, he had a lot of disproving as well as proving to do.

It turned out that the engineer was right. His light uncovered a potful of new information about our industry that no one else knew. Electricians actually hated the metal boxes. They frequently were scratched during installation, conveying a poor image of the electrician's work. Electricians frequently cut their hands on the sharp corners. The boxes were hard to fit into odd-shaped spaces. Building owners disliked the metal boxes for many of the same reasons. It turned out that no one really liked the metal boxes. Everyone used them because they thought they had to.

To see the results of the revolution he launched, look at the wall switches and boxes in your home today. The plastic decorator wall switches you see today are the product of that engineer's work. Based on the engineer's work, Square D introduced plastic boxes, launched a major education program and grew a previously stagnant business. Moose make nutritious meals as well.

Develop Your Own In-House Cassandra. Recall Cassandra? She was an ancient mythological prophet who correctly predicted the disaster of the fall of Troy, but wasn't believed by her own Trojan people. We build a Cassandra in as part of our future scanning process to ensure that we don't miss the Moose. For every major future trend we predict, we set up a group specifically designed to prove the opposite. For instance, when we foresaw the emergence of industrial inventory reduction as a major trend, the Cassandra group set out to prove that not only could hazardous and toxic waste not be handled with a just-in-time methodology but that there were more effective alternatives available. We also set up a Cassandra group to disprove that joint ventures with consultants were the most effective way to develop this new market. Cassandra groups inevitably discover opportunities overlooked by the main team. In fact, we pay them based upon the modifications and enhancements they surface.

Important point: discover and slay the Moose by proving the accepted wisdom wrong. Scientists test the null hypothesis in an effort to prove the positive. The scientific method is based on disproving the absence of a relationship to demonstrate the presence of that relationship. We do the same.

Shine the Brightest Light in the Darkest Corner to Identify the Biggest Moose: Individual Performance Deficiencies

Phoenix leaders shine the bright light of facts on individual per-formance. Phoenix leaders consistently ask not only "How are we as an organization doing? What are our sales per maintenance technician in comparison to others?" They also ask, "How is each individual doing?" Inevitably that bright light reveals the *big* Moose that's been on every organization table we've ever sat at: not everyone around that table should be sitting at that table. In every organization there are some people who not only do not pull their weight, they actually drag the boat. Noncontributors not only consume resources and misdirect efforts, they are black holes of time and energy that contributors must work around.

In a small manufacturing firm we encountered a vice president of marketing who was a clear noncontributor. She knew very lit-tle about marketing, having spent her entire career in customer service. She also had a very short fuse, exploding at virtually any-one who disagreed with her. Her loud voice dominated the meet-ings, even when she knew very little about the subject. Even the president seemed reluctant to confront her. Meetings that in-cluded her most often dissolved in a shambles of differing opin-ions. Meeting without her was impossible, since she routinely disapproved any decisions taken in her absence. She paralyzed the entire organization. Yet no one would talk about her perfor-mance, or anyone's performance for that matter. Her perfor-mance was the Moose that was sinking the boat.

Fact-Based Discussions About Performance. We helped the owner eliminate this Moose using fact-based discussions about performance. We suggested that he meet monthly with his staff to set objectives, measures and review performance against them. We sat in on the first few meetings. We helped keep everyone fo-cused on performance issues, both organizational must dos and individual will dos. The marketing VP consistently underper-formed. The owner, with our coaching, kept pushing her for per-formance. He kept asking, "What are the few most important achievements you and your department must deliver this month to help us and our customers succeed? Do your other teammates agree? Do your external customers agree? How do you know they agree? How will you know when you achieve what you set out to deliver to your internal and external customers?"

She came to us after the fourth meeting. "What's wrong? I always thought I was doing the right stuff. Now it seems that I can't do anything right. What do you suggest?" That gave us the opening we needed. Three hours later she was ready to turn it around. Turn it around she did. She's still dominating and loud. She's still very opinionated. Her personality hasn't changed much. But now she listens more and responds to internal and external customer requests. Her actions are more focused on what the team/organization needs. In fact, everyone's actions are more focused. Turns out that she was very frustrated with the lack of direction and everyone working at cross-purposes. Now that there's more sense of direction, she's more contributory. Like most painful experiences—visiting the dentist, for instance—holding fact-based performance discussions is more painful in the anticipating than in the doing.

We regularly set objectives and measures with the people with which we work. Every week we review programs with each person against those objectives. Sometimes it's in person. Sometimes it's on the phones. Sometimes it's via e-mail. But every week, like clockwork, we discuss performance with every person. There are no surprises at the end of any month, quarter or year. We're involved with our people, always focusing on the facts about their individual performance.

The Three-Phase Discipline of Phoenix Leaders: Coach, Coach, Change. Not everyone wins every time. That's a fact of life. There are very few perfect seasons in any sport. There are also very few bad people. But there are lots of good people in bad situations in which they will fail. Use the searchlight of performance facts to encourage people to face up to the realities of their own situation. And it helps to be methodical.

Craig was the vice president of operations for a large distribution company. He faced a tough situation. The western division was failing. The chairman's brother was the division head. Not unsurprisingly, Craig was reluctant to fire the chairman's brother. We urged him to shine the light on individual performance. He sat down with all of his twenty-seven division heads and set annual and monthly objectives and measures. He reviewed monthly results with each one. He asked each of them the coaching questions, "What can we do to improve results? How can I best support you?" After three months of failing reports, the chairman's brother asked to find another position. "I can't stand losing all the time," he said. He's now a very successful major accounts manager for the same firm. "I'm much better dealing with customers than I am managing people," he said. Chalk one up to fact-based performance discussions.

We spoke with the CEO of a large building supply company recently. He said, "After three years, there are only two out of the top fifteen people left. If you had come in the changes would likely have been done in a year instead of three. But it was painful and hard for me to do because I knew all these people. Besides, I had to give each a chance to prove that he or she could meet the new requirements. It took lots of coaching before we did the changing."

We responded, "You're right, and you did the right thing: coaching people to help them make it and helping them change when they don't. Think of it this way. If you hadn't coached people to make those moves, you would have gone also, along with tens of thousands of others, because your company wouldn't have made it long-term. Think about all the people you've helped: shareowners inside and outside the company, employees with good-paying jobs, suppliers with healthy customers that buy their products and pay their bills and communities with payrolls to support lots of local jobs and salaries. Your stock more than doubled in value during the last three years. Not bad for a ho-hum building materials company, is it?"

"No," he responded, "But the real kick is that all of the other thirteen landed on their feet and got good or better paying jobs. You even helped several with your contacts."

The CEO's story highlights our main point: Phoenix leaders shine the light, uncover the facts, encourage people to surface and confront performance-related issues and develop individuals' skills and capabilities that help everyone win. It takes courage. It takes savvy. It takes determination. It takes ethics. It takes Phoenix leadership.

PHOENIX WORKSHOP

1. WHAT TRENDS DO I SEE COMING THAT WILL IMPACT MY FUTURE?

_____

_____

2. WHAT CAN I *READ* TO HELP ME DISCOVER THE TRENDS BEFORE THEY IMPACT ME?

_____

_____

3. WITH WHOM CAN I *TALK* (IN OFFICES AND CHECKOUT LINES) THAT CAN HELP ME ANTICIPATE WHAT'S COMING?

_____

_____

4. HOW CAN I LIVE A DAY IN MY CUSTOMER'S WORLD?

_____

_____

5. WHAT IS THE MOOSE IN MY LIFE? HOW CAN I GET/GIVE PERMISSION, POWER AND PROTECTION TO DEAL WITH IT?

_____

_____

SHINE THE LIGHT ON HOPES AND DREAMS: SPEAK THE LANGUAGE OF ASPIRATION

Phoenix leaders articulate the hopes and dreams of people. Napoleon said, "A leader is a dealer in hope." He was right. Peter Levi, president of jeans maker Levi Strauss, said, "No hope, no action." Also true. The Phoenix leader gives voice to people's unconscious but deeply rooted yearnings to win—to be part of an exciting venture, to be part of something greater and higher—something that makes a difference. The Phoenix leader articulates the unspoken yet deeply driving aspirational forces within us all.

How do Phoenix leaders build that ultimate win-win situation? Get everyone's hopes and dreams out in the open. Help everyone see the linkage between fulfilling their hopes and dreams and contributing to the success of customers and constituents. Provide them the tools and learning environment to be effective.

Susan E. Davis, the president of the Capital Missions Company, uses this approach effectively. She's modeled her activity after a proposal of Virginia Satir, the founder of the family counseling movement.

Each meeting begins with expressions of honest individual appreciation. Second, each member at the meeting shares a concern along with a win-win proposed solution. Third, they discuss daily tactical plans, schedules, needs and recommended synergies. And finally, in each meeting, each member expresses his or her hopes and dreams. According to Davis in Jack Canfield and Jacqueline Miller's *Heart at Work,* "This level of sharing ensures that the company and its employees are usually dealing with core issues and expressing their underlying emotions. This is contrary to the traditional corporate practice of false politeness and pretending that emotional issues are best left alone." Davis credits the use of this meeting model for her company's "startling productivity."

Speak to the heart, from the heart, about the heart. That's what great Phoenix leaders do.

Search Their Hearts to Discover Hopes and Dreams

Buried inside each of us is a song, yearning to be sung. Most of us will die with our song unsung, because no one took the time to plumb the depths, find it and encourage its expression. We take the time: because it's good business and because it's the right thing to do.

We begin most meetings asking people to share something of which they are very proud. We always begin the process by sharing a personal or family achievement along with a business one. We set the tone by speaking in the language of aspiration, helping people get in touch with the things that mean the most to them as human beings. The heart connection comes first, the business connection follows.

Establishing Heart Connections with 170 Officers. One of us recently accepted a new assignment leading a large organization. As a way to establish the heart connection, we did two-hour one-on-ones with the top 170 people around the world. It was a really fun way to get to know people—really know people. In the beginning folks came in with briefing charts and overheads about team performance, and so on. They'd go on for a little bit, then we'd interrupt them and say, "Interesting stuff, but the real reason I wanted to talk with you today was to find out about you."

Most of them shot back a terrified look. No one had ever asked them *that* before.

Then we'd say, "There are really three things I want to do here today. One is to get to know you as a person and for you to get to know me. Second, I want you to tell me if you were in my shoes what are the top two or three things that you would concentrate on to make sure we're successful in the future. And three, I want you to tell me what you really want to do in the future and the one or two things I can do to help you be successful doing that."

The first several one-on-ones were very difficult. People had never thought about those questions before. This is a very, very successful company with a great financial record and it was business, business, business, as it is in so many organizations. Initially, many people responded to the third question (what do you want to be and how can I help you?), "Gosh, I don't know. I've never thought about that. It never crossed my mind that I could ask you to do anything for me."

That's all changed now, of course. The informal communication network did its usual effective job. Quickly after the first round of interviews, every officer knew the drill. So the overheads disappeared, replaced by slicker answers to the questions. We pushed hard, however, to get past the canned, politically correct answers such as, "I want to move up to division president someday."

Once you get past the sparring, where they check you out to be certain that you're for real, people know exactly what they want to do and where they want to go in the future. One woman said she wanted to become CEO for a company back in her hometown. Initially she was a little shy about sharing her aspiration to hold a position outside the company. We acknowledged and encouraged her suggesting that she needed some board-level experience, which we'd arrange, as well as some rounding experience over the next several years in finance and sales. She left flying high. She passed on her experience to the other officers. That opened up the floodgates for more honest communication about real aspirations.

Now when we hold our weekly and monthly performance chats with her we start by asking how she's doing with her aspirational activities. After that, we ask about last week's sales and competitor activities. We get all the business stuff we need, but we've completely changed the dynamics of the discussion. Now it's two people working together creating mutual success, company success and individual success, rather than two officers doing a job. The heart connection makes the financial connection work.

Take the Time to Find the Heart Connection. Every year we take the time to share career aspirations. Since we work in every time zone on the planet, we use electronic means. We all answer three questions: "What do I really want to be doing in three to five years? What do I have to do to get there? What help do I need from others to help me get there?" We share these single-page sheets widely across the organization, asking others to comment on: "Knowing what you know about me, can I attain this position? Are my activities going to get me where I want to go? Do I need more or different help than I've identified? Can you contribute to my plan?" More than 15,000 e-mails stream across the electronic frontiers responding to these questions. These aspirations wind up reflected in each person's personal learning plan, completion of which is a prerequisite for receiving a bonus.

Opera Singers and Rock Stars Sign Up Right Here. Your career goal needn't be within the company. Mark's one of our associates in another business. He plays with a rock band. They're pretty good, having earned three gold records thus far. He still works with us (we're his safe day job he says). He is one of the top money earners in the company, indicating that his team values his contribution. All 4,800 people in the company know of his aspirations to go full-time into music. All of us are ready with a big farewell party when he decides that he can pursue his dream. We will miss him if he leaves. His customers will miss him. And we're thankful for the years he's given us. During his eleven years he's created joy for millions of people who have listened to his music. He's helped make the planet safer for his customers and all humankind. And he's put a few shekels in all of our pockets as well. We are glad to have helped him live his dream.

Mark's not alone. There's Jane who wants to become an opera singer. There's Sam who wants to be a painter. There's Jose studying to be a lawyer because he wants to be a politician. There's Koi studying anthropology. And the list goes on and on. People don't work with us forever. They share themselves with us for a time. Our challenge is to help them achieve their goals, while we achieve ours during the time they share the road with us.

You Can't Hire a Hand, You Hire a Whole Family. We usually work in high-margin businesses, where there's lots of opportunity to try innovative activities. One of our wives used to say, "If you really want to prove your system, try it in a hotel." We did: we are: and it's sobering. The hotel business is a twenty-four-hours-a-day, seven-days-a-week, fifty-two-weeks-a-year activity. The misery of the low wages is exceeded only by the misery of the working hours and the working conditions. As a result, it's tough to hire people. It's hard to find housekeepers, bus people, bell hops and dish-washers. None of these jobs is high on anybody's career wish list. Not only is it hard to find these people, given the over 200 percent turnover, you have to constantly keep finding these folks. Compounding this personnel challenge is the fact that English is not the mother tongue for most of the people working in these service jobs. At one large hotel there are twelve languages spoken by the staff, in addition to English. Needless to say, finding and keeping good employees is a major challenge for most hoteliers.

We helped the leaders of one hotel chain think about this "problem" in a whole new light—and solve it by speaking to employees in the language of their hopes and dreams. Very few of us are natives of this land. Beyond a small number of Native American Indians, all the rest of us are immigrants. Our forefathers came to this land, some a long time ago, some more recently, but all for the same reason: to make a better life for their families.

One of our great-grandparents came from Poland and traveled across the country in the mid-1800s looking for a place to settle. We have a photograph of him and his family standing in front of their first house in Kansas. It was made of mud, with no floors or windows. The entire family worked from sunup to sunset, and beyond. My great-grandfather's proudest accomplishment was his son's college education. He was no different than the Irish policeman in Boston saving for his daughter's dowry, or the Jewish tailor working twelve hours in the sweatshop to save for the little house that his family could own in the "country," or our dad working three jobs so he could buy the family the car we needed to get around. All worked hard to make a better life for their families.

That story is repeated today by folks coming from Haiti and Vietnam and Nigeria and Bosnia and Romania. They come to America seeking a better life for themselves and a better future for their families. So we urged the leaders of one hotel chain not to hire just a hand to wash dishes or make beds, but to hire an entire family who aspires to a better life. They agreed to view personnel recruitment as an exercise in speaking to the hopes and dreams of an entire family, not just the time and talents of the specific person to be hired.

The hotel chain picked one hotel property to offer a package of "family benefits" designed to help the entire family improve their future. There's free instruction in English for both the employee and the entire family, offered partially on company time. There's Saturday morning story hour for the employee's children run by staff members from a local library. Hotel facilities, such as health clubs, workout rooms and pools, are open to employees' families during certain hours of the day. Because they're primarily a business hotel, the facilities are usually deserted in the afternoons after school, so employee family usage doesn't interfere with the paying guests' experience. Child care is provided, as is personal grooming instruction. The turnover at this hotel fell like a stone to less than 30 percent. Why? Because they didn't just hire a hand, they spoke to the hopes and aspirations of the entire family.

Spurred by the success of the first property, the chain extended this family benefits program to three other properties. It worked very well in one, and failed miserably in the other two. The difference: leadership at the property level. At the one hotel where it's working well, the leader makes it his business to personally talk with every new employee.

He's there at five o'clock in the morning when the shift starts to talk to newly hired kitchen folks. He personally conducts the one-day orientation for the newly hired people and their families. He shows up at Saturday story hour and stops by to visit with employees' families working out in the gym or swimming in the pool. He opens and closes the English classes, personally handing out the diplomas. He demonstrates his commitment to help his employees and their families accomplish their dreams and aspirations. With his actions he speaks the language of their dreams and aspirations. And when he does, he makes that heart connection with them that is the essential ingredient of successful Phoenix leadership.

Align Organizational and Individual Goals

The business of business is business. It takes place from 8:00 to 6:00 or 8:00 to 8:00, and then you go home. Right? No, wrong. No, impossible. You never hire a hand. You always hire a whole person, with hopes and dreams, fears and doubts. In fact, as we've just pointed out, you really hire a whole family, not just a pair of hands to move product from point A to point B.

Talking with one of our employees last week, he mentioned that he had a real balance problem between home and work. He added quickly, "Of course that's not your issue."

We responded, "Of course it's our issue. If you're not a balanced, excited person, pleased with what's going on in your total life, you will not contribute as much as you are capable of contributing."

"Never thought of it that way," he said.

We continued, "And to be real selfish for a minute, the better balanced you are in life, the more valuable you are to all of us here at the company and, most importantly, to your family and yourself. So, we have a vital interest in your sense of balance. Now, how can we help you to redress the imbalance?"

Think about your leadership responsibilities in human terms, and you will get payback fifty times over. Norman Vincent Peale, the great minister and speaker, was fond of saying, "I speak to people's hearts. Whether they are funeral directors or prisoners, everyone has a heart, and I speak to that part of the human soul that is universal and eternal." So does every successful Phoenix leader.

Align Individual Hearts and Organizational Heads Around Strategic Financial Goals

Merge personal hopes and dreams with the organization's strategic and financial goals. Articulate them together using the following process: Each person shares his or her personal career goals and aspirations. Simultaneously, the team (with input from its many customers) defines the team/organizational objectives for the coming period. Team objectives lay the foundation for individual objectives set by the team in conjunction with the individual and his customers. Air the following questions throughout the process: "What are your hopes and dreams? What do your customers and teammates need from you to help them succeed? How will doing those activities for the organization and your customers help you achieve your personal goals and aspirations?" Listen hard to the responses. Create the circumstances where doing the organization's work also satisfies the individual's goals and aspirations.

Vince Lombardi understood that building an effective team required aligning individual and organizational goals. He understood that the complex game of professional football was won or lost at the level of individual performance, the three-second block. If you don't make three-second blocks you don't win games. Doesn't matter how fast the running backs are, doesn't matter how good your passer is, if everyone doesn't make three-second blocks, you don't post Ws. How do you get running backs to throw three-second blocks? You help them see that their three-second blocks for the quarterback will encourage others to throw three-second blocks when they're carrying the ball, and those blocks will help them win the rushing title. What's true in professional football is also true in any other organization. Speak the language of aspiration. Line up the individual's aspirations with those of the team and organization.

Know the song buried in each person's heart so you can build the stage for its performance. Only then can you truly create success for all those with whom you are connected: customers, employees, stockholders, suppliers and communities. Know people's hearts and speak to them. That's what being a successful Phoenix leader is all about.

PHOENIX WORKSHOP

THE IMPORTANT PEOPLE IN MY NETWORK	WHAT ARE THEIR DREAMS AND ASPIRATIONS?	HOW CAN I HELP THEM REALIZE THEIR DREAMS AND ASPIRATIONS WHILE CONTRIBUTING TO MY NETWORK'S SUCCESS?
_____	_____	_____
_____	_____	_____
_____	_____	_____
_____	_____	_____
_____	_____	_____

CONDUCT A SEARCH-AND-DISCOVERY MISSION WITH YOUR CUSTOMERS

Shine the Light on Your Customers' Rich Fields of Fact

Customers have rich fields of facts. Keep the searchlights trained on them continuously. Make certain that you build regular and frequent customer feedback into your activities. Continue to find out what customers *really* want and need. Some of the most important "facts" concern their aspirations, so shine the light on their hopes and dreams.

Customers Are Great Reality Checks. Customers are the best reality checks on our assumptions. For example, a big debate raged within one of our companies. Several executives argued strongly for establishing a global customer account management program. Several others resisted, arguing that it would only confuse customers and the field sales force and add to the overhead burden. We suggested that we let the customer decide.

At the next trade show we surveyed our largest customers. All seventeen strongly wanted a global customer account management program, leaving us to wonder what else we could have asked.

Get the Real Customer to Respond. We worked with a computer manufacturer and asked the salespeople if they talked regularly with customers. Everyone enthusiastically nodded their heads. When we asked who they'd talked with almost everyone said, "The sales folks in the stores." "How many of your computers did those folks buy?" we asked. The obvious answer was, "Very few." Who's the manufacturer's real customer? Not those in-stores sales folks. This manufacturer's target market is the small-business/home-office customer. You've got to reach those folks—the people who actually turn on and use the machine, after they've reached into their pocket and parted with their cash. Otherwise, you're not listening to the real customer. The salespeople did just that, and sales soared more than 18 percent.

Internal Measures of External Activities Do Not a Success Make

In another situation we led one of the most successful organizations in its market. The entire staff focused well on facts and valued customer input. But even here, we got trapped by the siren song of internally focused measures.

We set the customer delight objectives we wanted five years in the future. Then we identified the goals we'd achieve in each of the four years running up to the final objective. We dispatched teams to visit customers to determine the most important activities to them and solicited input from both current and future customers. Customers identified areas that needed improvement. We did all the right outside-in fact-gathering activities.

Then we set internal measurements to make certain that we met customers' standards. For instance, turnaround time was important to customers. So we tracked time from order placement to order shipment. Response time was important to customers. So we tracked the number of times the phone rang before answering, the amount of time it took to handle a customer issue on the phone and the number of repeat customer calls regarding the same issue. They were all great measures, but they were all internally based.

We got caught up in the exercise along with everyone else. At the very end it hit us. We could hit the top of each measure, and still not delight our customers. Rather than seeking the customers' viewpoint on whether they were satisfied with our response time, we were focusing on hitting the response time standards. Maybe answering the phone in three rings is less important to the customer than the competence of the answerer. Just possibly customer satisfaction with the order is more important than shipping it out on time. We focused on our delivery success, not our customer's receipt success. We had another example of this with another company where the distribution people measured shipping time, not receipt time, and shipment accuracy, rather than customer receipt accuracy.

Avoid the trap of measuring the measurable, regardless of its relevance. Internal activities are most easily measured. It's easy to track phone rings and shipment dates. But do these matter to customers, really matter to them? Will a customer leave if the phone rings four times before it's answered? Six times? On the other hand how many times will a customer put up with incompetent people on the phone?

See the measures from the customer's point of view. Define winning with the customer's definition of success. Rely upon frequent personal interaction with customers to hear their definition of success and their reactions to your efforts to help them succeed. That means frequent customer surveys on both paper and in person. That's why we now track customer delight scores reported by the customer, as the principal measurement for the attainment of our customer delight goal.

Beware: What the Customer Wanted Then Is Not Necessarily What the Customer Wants Now

Most organizations move at glacial speed. They make turtles look like speed demons. There are meetings, and meetings, and more meetings; followed by even more meetings. It often takes months to get the simplest decision made. In many markets, however, three to six months is a lifetime. And customers move at an even faster speed. In fact, most customers move at the speed of the last competitor they've seen.

We were in the highly competitive specialty ink business. Colors were the name of the game. If some competitor had a certain color, and a customer wanted it, you had to have it or you lost the immediate sale. If that happened too many times, you lost the customer. It typically took twelve to sixteen months to develop a new ink color. It didn't take a genius to figure out that we'd never win the keep-up-with-the-Joneses game. We were dead if we didn't have either an early-warning system or the color on the shelf.

We circled the wagons and held a confab to plumb the best ideas. The folks erected an early-warning system combined with longer-term contracts with customers guaranteeing them short-stroke delivery of desired colors. R&D generated eighteen color platform formulas that facilitated new color variations in weeks rather than months. The salespeople set up customer councils that met quarterly to review ink demands, including anticipating what colors customers would want. Those council meetings were a key part of our early-warning system. They gave us a window into customers' developing thinking and enabled us to anticipate customer needs and reduce the number of surprises. The early-warning system combined with the new R&D procedures enabled us to supply customers' new ink requirements in weeks. We could supply new colors faster than any other competitor. As a result, we grew market share and earned higher margins.

Imagine if we had been measuring customer satisfaction with the inks we were providing. Customers would give us high marks for what we provided, but we would be going out of business because we weren't providing what they needed. The same applies to most service measures. It takes a while to develop and install customer service measures; many months usually. It took one firm eight months to install a customer service measurement program. Problem: how customers measured service eight months ago may not be how they measure service today. In fact, it likely isn't. The number of rings before answering was an important service measure some time ago. Today, with voice mail and call centers, it's a nonissue. In addition, customers have come to expect connection in two to four rings, so the difference between answering in two rings as opposed to four rings may be insignificant. Customers' measures and standards change over time. You don't want to be like the opponents of the great fighter Joe Louis. Louis said, "I get people to punch where I used to be." Too many customer feedback systems report what the customer used to want and value and expect, not what they want, value and expect today. Learn to move at customer time, not organizational time.

The message doesn't change: stay plugged into your customers.

There's no substitute for frequent, direct, face-to-face conversations with customers about their hopes and dreams, their criteria for success, their future plans. Become an expert in your customers and you will be a successful self-renewing Phoenix leader.

PHOENIX WORKSHOP

SEARCH-AND-DISCOVERY MISSION WITH YOUR CUSTOMERS

MY MOST IMPORTANT CUSTOMERS	WHAT ARE THEIR FUTURE PLANS/NEEDS?	WHAT ARE THEIR CRITERIA FOR SUCCESS, TODAY AND TOMORROW?	WHAT ARE THE BEST CUSTOMER-BASED MEASURES?

STAND IN THE LIGHT: CAST YOUR SHADOW: BE A STERLING EXAMPLE

The Phoenix Leader: 10,000 Watt Light Source for the Organization

You can't help it. You *are* the light source. You *are* a role model. People will watch you and imitate what you do. That's just the way it is. It *is* your responsibility. Children watch their parents to discover how to be an adult. Teammates watch their leader to see how to handle authority. We all learned how to be who we are by watching and imitating others that we admired, respected and wanted to be like. Learn to use your role-modeling responsibility to live your new Phoenix leader life.

Like Father, Like Son. It's a sobering experience to hear your own words coming out of your child's mouth. Many times we've grimaced at our eldest son's way of talking to his son; too loud, too authoritarian, too demanding we think. Then, tumbling out of his mouth are very familiar words, words we've heard from our own mouths. Could it be that we treated him as he now treats his son? Absolutely. We were the only father he ever knew. Everything he knows about parenting he learned from us: all the good things, like caring for people, and all the not so good things, like being loud and demanding. Yes, he is his father's son and we only wish we could have known as much when we were raising our first son as we knew when we were raising the others. He might be less loud and demanding, as we learned to be as we grew older and more experienced.

Like Boss, Like Supervisor. It's the same way at the office. Early in our careers we worked with a direct mail firm. The owner, Milt, was a brilliant statistician. He designed the market research projects that were the bread and butter of his firm. We consulted with him to improve the efficiency of list compilation and mailing activities. He loved his research design activities and dealing with customers. But he loathed his employees and had very low opinions of his production workers. His attitude showed, not only in his behavior, but in everyone else's as well.

Executives treated employees with disrespect. They called them "fodder," "brainless" and "monkeys." "Got to hire a few more monkeys today," the production manager told us one day. We frequently worked after hours laying out processes with the executives. Over cold cuts and beer you learn a lot about people. Milt's executives completely reflected his disrespecting attitudes toward employees. They looked for every way to control them, even going to the extent of drilling peep holes in the toilets to make certain that employees weren't stealing the merchandise coupons they handled.

Like Boss, Like Employee. For their part, employees worked hard to not work hard. They'd take long breaks and lunch hours and looked for every opportunity to stop working. For instance, if a name was out of alphabetical order, they'd shut down the machine and call the supervisor over to have him place the name in the proper sequence. They'd stand around until a supervisor came to their machine, sometimes as much as an hour, to move a single name one place.

We even found ourselves picking up Milt's language and attitude. We told a story at home once referring to the "monkeys" and got severely questioned by the family. We then worked hard not to be contaminated by Milt. The job couldn't be over soon enough as far as we were concerned. We soon turned down a request for a follow-on project. It was just too much work to avoid catching a bad case of values flu.

We ran into Milt several years later at a professional meeting. He'd subcontracted his entire business, except the research design part. "I really love what I do. It's a much smaller company now, and at first, that bothered me. But I'm so much more relaxed now. I even teach an evening class at the university and take regular vacations. You may not have realized it, but you helped me see what I was becoming, and I didn't like what I saw. I couldn't figure out what to do. I changed managers several times, but the employee problems never went away. I subcontracted out a piece at a time, first the mailing part, then the couponing part and finally the list compilation part. Now there's only Margaret and myself, and it's great."

After he left we kicked ourselves for not speaking up sooner. Who knows, we might have saved him and all of his people all those years of mutual agony. We left the Moose on the table, and cost people pieces of their stomachs because we didn't have the courage to speak up.

The Leader Casts a Long Shadow. Make Certain It's the Right Shadow. Counterbalancing Milt, our first boss was a prince. Matt trusted people, and it showed. He went out of his way to give us opportunities to shine. He took us along with him to meetings. Here we were young kids, just out of school. We were still trying to find the bathroom, and he was taking us to staff meetings with the vice president. "Need them here," he'd say. "In case something happens to me they can always pick up." He was as honest as the summer's day is long. He'd turn in receipts for coffee on the road, rather than just adding a few dollars to the dinner to cover the incidentals as the accounting clerk suggested. He'd not claim reimbursement if he couldn't produce a receipt. He went out of his way for others. He arranged for a company loan, for in-

stance, for a production employee to buy a house, the first time
that had ever been done in the company.

Not that Matt was soft, because he wasn't. He was tough on
work assignments. He expected completed staff work, and accepted nothing less than that. He expected projects to be turned
in on time, and let us know when he wasn't pleased with the
work. Early in our career we did a training project for the company. We hired an outside consultant to handle the actual instruction and thought it went pretty well. Matt got some strong
negative feedback from his boss, Boyd. He called us in and told
us what he'd heard.

He was very direct. "Boyd isn't happy with the results of the
training. Fix it. I'd be happy to help if you need. But this is your
project." We shook in our boots for several hours, sucked it in
and called Boyd. He was unhappy that some parts of the program
misled people into thinking they should be risk-averse when he
wanted them to be more risk-taking. We called the outside consultant, passed on Boyd's feedback, and arranged for him to meet
with Boyd. The consultant came back for two additional no-
charge sessions to clarify the misunderstanding. Matt coached
and supported from the sidelines, but kept making it clear that it
was our responsibility to satisfy Boyd.

Matt cast a long shadow over our career and leadership behavior. He bent the twig. We were blessed with excellent leadership
role models, like Matt, early in our careers. In many ways, our
leadership styles today reflect Matt's long shadow.

Many students ask for our career advice, particularly about
their first job. Many are surprised by what we tell them. "Find the
best person to work for and learn from," we urge. "Your future
business behavior will most likely reflect your first boss, so
choose as your first boss someone you want to be like." At any
career stage, choose your boss more carefully than you choose
anything else. Remember that long shadow.

Sometimes you can't choose your boss. He or she gets chosen
for you, and it's not a choice you'd make on your own. That happens a lot. When that happens, be a responsibility-taking Phoenix
leader and choose not to stand in your boss's shadow. Instead,
choose someone else's shadow to stand in. Choose another mentor from whom you can learn and after whom you can pattern
yourself.

We learned a long time ago that if things aren't going the way we want, the first place to look is in the mirror. For better or worse, the organization is a reflection of the leader. That's good news, because as the leader you then get to choose what your organization will look like and perform like.

Revivolute Yourself to Cast the Right Shadow for the Times

Times change. Successful leaders continually revivolute themselves to ensure they are relevant to the times. As the head honcho the leader climbs up into the corporate crow's nest, peers off into the swirling mists of uncertainty and sets the direction for the corporate ship of state. There are no guarantees, no certainties. Just the certainty that staying put will result in a disaster beyond your imagination. No leader wants to preside over the dismantling of his empire. Recognize the responsibility. The buck does stop right here in your mirror.

The Three Revivolutions of Jack Welch. Take Jack Welch, for instance. In fifteen years at the helm of General Electric, Welch has lived three distinct lives. His first incarnation was as "Neutron Jack." He went through GE like Grant went through Georgia, cutting factories and divisions, shrinking employment in the company by almost 50 percent. His tough tactics foreshadowed the reeingineering craze that swept industry. Then came the hard-nosed "improve what we do" approach. "Be number one or number two, or be gone," he preached. GE developed the work-out process, and it became the de rigueur drill throughout the company. That Welch revivolution produced the most valuable company in the world, with total market capitalization at the end of 1996 of $157 billion, and America's most profitable company in 1996.

Times change and Welch is revivoluting again, as described in the October 28, 1996, issue of *Business Week*. His goal: build the first $70 billion growth company. His twin strategies: build quality into every product that brings billions down to the bottom line, and sell high-margin services to create competitive advantage in the marketplace. Using groundbreaking service contracts with such diverse companies as Columbia Hospitals and British Airways, he's pushing old-line manufacturing and engineering units to find creative ways to tie continuing services into product sales.

Jack Welch is clearly *the* man for *the* season. He looks out, decides what *the* season is and becomes *the* man for that season. His actions cast a long shadow over the face of his almost $100 billion organization.

Cast your shadow. Do what you want others to do. Be what others aspire to be.

PHOENIX WORKSHOP

1. WHAT BEHAVIOR DO I WANT FROM OTHERS?

_____

_____

2. HOW CAN I BEST MODEL THE BEHAVIOR I WANT OTHERS TO DEMONSTRATE?

_____

_____

Summary: *Power Up the Searchlight*

The world turns. The environment changes. What worked yesterday does not work today. That which got us to where we are will not get us to where we need to go. What are the few most important facts that will shape our future? "Just the facts, ma'am," as Sergeant Joe Friday used to say in the popular TV show *Dragnet* years ago.

Joe Friday's not alone. Every leader is searching for the facts that will shape her organization's future. Finding the right facts is the survival challenge that lands squarely on every leader's desk. That challenge faces the occupant of the Oval Office where the fate of 260 million Americans and 6 billion humans souls rests on his decisions. It also faces the individual who sits alone in the quiet of her own home office where only her fate rides on the decisions.

Phoenix Sightings: Follow the Phoenix Leader

We all face the questions "Where do we go? How do we get there? Who do we go with?" From visionary to nuts and bolts facilitator, Phoenix leaders do it all: dream the big dream and clean the toilets when necessary. There are many Phoenix leaders to show us the way.

Tom the Magic Toothpaste Man. You find Phoenix leaders in out-of-the-way places. Try a plain red-brick abandoned shoe factory in Kennebunk, Maine, home to Tom Chappell's successful business, Tom's of Maine, which was described in the January 1997 issue of *Preservation* magazine. He's inside busy creating success for his employees, customers and communities. Chappell does more than just produce the natural personal care products that we use. He's also involved in local recycling programs, the preservation of historical sites and the education of the entire population to a more natural lifestyle. Chappell shined his light on the issues in his marketplace, his business, his community and society. He demonstrates the values and makes the heart connection with people in his organization, as well as the many systems and people they interconnect with and serve.

Velda the Door-to-Door Principal. Velda Correa is principal of the new Rico Elementary School in Weslaco, Texas. Her story is told in the January 1997 *Reader's Digest*. Velda didn't sit around and wait for the issues to surface. She went out and searched them out. She cranked up the watts and shined the light out on the community issues she served. She went door to door, asking residents a simple question: "What can your school do for you?"

She surfaced issues that needed resolving and made new rules for the new realities of public education in Weslaco in the latter half of the 1990s. She holds school on Saturdays to help students from migrant families catch up with studies. She recruited volunteers to help students sharpen English language skills. She created a special task force team called Project Saturn to provide additional support for struggling students. It should come as no surprise that her school's test scores are high and attendance is well above the state average of 90 percent.

Sister Mary Rose McGeady, Shining a Phoenix Light in the Dark Corners. Sister Mary Rose McGeady shines her purest of lights in the darkest corners of our society, as we read in the December 1996 *Good Housekeeping.* She serves the truly needy: the homeless, runaways and drug-addicted young people. Her Covenant House's national "Nine Line," 800-999-9999, is scrawled on the walls of every slum in America. It's the last hope for thousands of society's young throwaways. Her vans roam the streets and back alleys frequented by the down-and-outers from 9:30 P.M. until the early hours of the morning, offering food, drink, clothes, shelter and hope to the lost youth of our world.

Her shelters in ten U.S. cities and four foreign countries offer counseling, residential and health services and substance abuse programs. Their mission: do everything possible to get their "customers"—the young people—to believe in themselves and redirect themselves toward meaningful, productive lives. How? By training them for jobs, placing them in healthy environments and by radiating light into their young lives—powerful spiritual values grounded in the bedrock of reality.

Sister Mary Rose is a 10,000 watt beacon light that leads an organization that ignites thousands of beacons lights. Beacon lights like Father Steve Siniari, who works in the Van Outreach Program, where he touches lives and leads kids back to sanity and wholeness, with the ultimate goal of reuniting them with their families. "We see some kids we wouldn't take bets on," says Sister Mary Rose. "But once they begin to believe in themselves, it's amazing what they can do."

Phoenix leaders create more Phoenix leaders, turning everyone into a 10,000 watt beacon light, fueling the continuous circle of revivolution that grows and spirals ever upward.

We know only one way to cut through the shroud of uncertainty that shields sight of the future from us. Find the brightest searchlight, connect it to the power source of facts and then use it to surface the issues we must conquer. Once we surface the issues, we absolutely believe that together we can resolve them.

CHAPTER 5

Engage the People:
Blood, Sweat and Trust

THE PHOENIX LEADERSHIP MOMENT

Welcome to the Tennis Match Filled with Phoenix Leadership Moments

They'd been hard at it for several hours, so involved that the scheduled break time came and went with hardly a movement of the chairs. The walls were plastered with butcher paper on which were scrawled "Opportunities," "Threats," "Possibilities," the product of all those hours of brainstorming and heated discussion. Now stillness filled the room. Seven pairs of eyes turned toward the slight man who sat at one corner of the note- and cup-strewn walnut table. The question hung like putrid cigarette smoke in a bar: "All right George, what do we do?"

Well, there it is, the fuzzy little ball so deftly rapped into George's court. He sees it bounce toward him in slow motion. Now what? Welcome to the *Phoenix leadership moment*. We midwifed the unfolding drama. George's electronic components business rang up $7 million in sales last year, up from $2 million three years ago. He saw lots of opportunity to grow to $12 million this coming year and $50 million within five years. George saw what he had to do. He hired several new managers, expanded his facilities and set a vision for aggressive growth.

He issued flashlights and shovels to his seven-member management team and sent them out to forage in the forest of the future. They came back with many exotic flora and fauna: a huge bouquet of appealing opportunities and the pungent odor of competitive threats clinging to their clothing. All seven members of the management team eagerly awaited the meeting as the launching of their new venture/adventure.

By lunchtime the table groaned under the weight of all the opportunities they'd uncovered. The day was consumed with continuous volleys from court to court. The to do agenda couldn't have been accomplished in even a billion-dollar organization. There was clearly too much on George's small company's plate. Having surfaced the opportunities and threats, the seven members of the management team turned to George to decide which opportunity they'd pursue. George knew the match would be a series of classic *leadership moments,* each preceded by the question "Now what do we do, boss?"

The "What Do You Think?" Bobby Riggs Response. We anticipated this moment. It happens many times a day in the life of most leaders. The ball ends up in your court. Everyone watches carefully to see whether you make the decision or engage others in making it. It's the classic play that reveals your view of your role in this very serious team sport. It's a test. It's the Phoenix leadership moment.

We use the Bobby Riggs lob approach in these Phoenix leadership moments. Bobby Riggs built a very successful tennis career by mastering the art of the lob. Rather than trying to overpower his opponent with the speed of his serve or the power of his backhand (both of which were very ordinary), Riggs lobbed the ball back to his opponent and let him make the unforced error. He won lots of games with that strategy. So we often default to the Bobby Riggs approach when confronted with a Phoenix leadership moment. It's simpler to lob the ball back to the questioner.

George knew about this Bobby Riggs approach. He was ready for the question he knew would come. He paused, allowing the silence to clear the air and set the stage for his words. Turning to his comptroller, the most junior member of the staff, he asked,

"Melly, what do you think are the most important items for us to pursue?"

The awkward stillness was broken only by the shuffling of feet and the shifting of chairs. After what seemed like an eternity—but likely was only forty-five seconds—Melinora artfully lobbed the ball back to George, "I don't know, George. You know this business better than any of us. What do you think we ought to do?"

Bap. The racket made contact. George was steadfast. "Anybody want to help Melly decide? How about you, Jack?" George asked turning to his executive vice president. Not being the shy and retiring type, Jack rushed the net. Bap. The room sprang alive with conversation. Lunchtime came and went unnoticed. The to do list shrank to more manageable size.

Engage People in the Business of the Business. The lesson: Phoenix leaders engage people in weighing alternatives and making tough decisions. Opportunities always outnumber resources. There's always more to do than there's time to do it in. Phoenix leaders aren't the only ones making tough choices; they engage others in making tough choices as well. Phoenix leadership is not a Lone Ranger activity. The picture painted in the headlines in *Business Week* and *Fortune* is just plain wrong. We know. Many times a day people present us with the opportunity to decide or engage them in the decision process. These are the Phoenix leadership moments. Our job: engage people in the business of the business.

Phoenix leadership—engaging people—comes from anywhere in the organization. You don't have to be the CEO. Sure, the CEO engages from the top. Still, every single individual from the shop floor or the back office can engage people in the business of the business. Phoenix leadership is a matter of spirit, not title.

Avoid the Either-Or Trap. Recently we attended a worldwide meeting of one of our organizations. We discussed values at the meeting. The comptroller of one of the national companies posed the following issue.

"Our contacts call for thirty-day payment. Yet we pay in fifty-eight days. The extra twenty-eight days of float contributes significantly to our bottom line. Are you saying that we should take the earnings hit and honor our contracts to pay in thirty days?"

We immediately recognized another Phoenix leadership moment. We asked a set of questions: "What's industry practice? Isn't it sixty days? Does the supplier really expect payment in thirty days, particularly when industry practice is double that? What do you think are the relationship issues here between us and the supplier that cause a perfectly rational organization to sign a contract they don't intend to live with? Does the supplier really trust us? How can we help the supplier accomplish its goals and still preserve the fifty-eight-day payment schedule?" The comptroller left the fifteen-minute conversation with the assignment to talk to the supplier and identify the win-win relationship on payment terms. What began as a request for an executive answer evolved into an engagement by the questioner in improving a supplier-customer relationship.

It's More than *Just* Questions. Make no mistake, Phoenix leaders don't *just* ask questions. Phoenix leadership is not a passive activity. We knew the answer to the comptroller's question. Only it would be our answer, not his. We've been down this road a thousand times. The comptroller would listen politely (after all, we are the boss), and then, just as politely, find a dozen reasons why he couldn't execute our answer. We want flawless execution, not multiple excuses. Engagement is the antidote to the epidemic of excuses.

George was in the same position. He knew his marketplace. He saw what he thought were the best opportunities. But he wanted more knowledge on the table to make the best decision. Remember the 10,000 watts to surface 10,000 facts to create 10,000 tomorrows by 10,000 leaders? George knew that their decision would be more enthusiastically executed than his decision. He'd read the book. He knew the drill. Engage the people or suffer the consequences of poor implementation.

What else do Phoenix leaders do, besides ask questions? Read on for the answer.

Beyond Courteous Involvement to Gut-Level Engagement

Don't confuse the typical "employee-involvement" activity with this gut-level engagement process. On the surface, you may not see much difference between the two terms, but there are light years of difference between the character and quality of the actions they generate.

The mayor of our city asked us to lead a community-building activity. One of the city council members suggested that we do a town hall meeting similar to the one used in a nearby city. The city council and/or other institutional officials (such as the school superintendent and police chief) run the town hall meeting. Any community member may speak about the problems and issues confronting the community and suggest solutions. The town hall maximizes the breadth of possible inputs, but the decision clearly remains with the officials. Town halls are information-gathering meetings. Most individuals leave the town hall with the feeling, "I'm pleased to have had the opportunity to tell those folks what needs to be done. Now it's up to them to do it." Classic involvement activity.

We suggested the future search process instead. In this process, representatives of community interest groups, numbering often in the several hundreds, spend several intensive days agreeing upon the future they wish to create in the community, the steps necessary to create that future and the accountabilities for those steps. Individuals most often leave those meetings with the feeling, "I've got a lot of work to do to make this place into what I want it to be." Classic engagement.

The difference between "I've told them and they have to fix it" and "I have a lot of work to do to create what I want" is the difference between involvement and engagement. Involvement results in providing input where the responsibility for action rests elsewhere. Engagement results in personal responsibility for action.

Many excellent programs fail because they confuse these two terms. Quality circles, for instance, were a great idea, doomed to failure from their inception because they were involvement and recommendation groups rather than engagement and action groups. A shift foreman shared with us a particularly disastrous example of employee involvement in her company. Quality problems plagued the department. The manager called a special meeting of the entire 475-person production group announcing the appointment of several quality improvement task forces. The groups made their recommendations within thirty days. Six months passed before he implemented three of the minor recommendations. The rest just disappeared into that great management black hole, "We're still studying the recommendations." She's got her résumé on the street. "Got to get out before the roof falls in—which it will any day now," she says.

Get past involvement. Engage people in dealing with the gut-level issues that confront them and their organization.

Blood, Sweat and Trust: Paramedics and the Power of Engagement. Watch paramedics and relief workers operate in the midst of human crises and disasters. These teams/organizations engage hearts, minds, souls and bodies in a seamless, fluid collection of talent and energy all designed for one purpose: to save human life. Once on the scene of an emergency, paramedics scramble and use their best judgment, applying the learning that springs from all of their collective prior experiences. They operate in fast-forward mode, fully engaging the brains and hearts of every member of the team. Individual commitment to "customers" and each other converges with the organization's mission near the ambulance. This is where trust and teamwork jump off the wall posters and mastheads and into real life. Watch it in action and wonder, "How can I make that happen in my life, in my organization?" Watch high-tech and high-touch converge in people who are fast yet focused, intuitive yet informed, individuals yet acting together as a team. Where's the leader? Everywhere: inside of each and every one of them is a Phoenix leader—taking charge, doing what needs to be done, creating success for all those with whom he is interdependent and interconnected. Watch the paramedics in action and see the Phoenix leader at work. Are you a virtual paramedic, thinking on your feet to rescue a drowning business? How about your personal life? Do you rapidly merge your aspirations with those around you to achieve something great for everyone? Learn about engagement from paramedics.

Phoenix leaders at all levels help people discover the convergence point between organizational and personal purpose. At that magical convergence point, engagement happens and beliefs become behavior. Phoenix leaders point the way to tomorrow. People build the great suspension bridge that gets everyone there.

Engagement is built with blood, sweat and trust!

AVOID THE MOSES MIND-SET TRAP: IT'S ABOUT US—AS A PEOPLE

We've surfaced the issues. Now comes engaging the people in a way that energizes them. Personalize the dangers, risks, rewards, challenges and adventure of creating our tomorrow together. The key word: together. It's not like Moses going up the mountain, hearing God talk and receiving a vision. *It's about us, as a people.* Fall into the Moses trap, believing that it's all up to someone else, and you guarantee failure. Phoenix leadership "of, by, and for the people" works.

Farewell Superstar, Hello Dream Team

If you believe you're going to play the superstar and run the whole show—doling out pieces to others, then don't even start. You'll fail. It doesn't matter how bright you are or how energetic you are. It doesn't even matter how much money you're getting. You'll fail. Because no one can do it alone. Even Moses came to realize that he couldn't do it all himself. The ancient Israelites wouldn't have survived had not his sagacious father-in-law, Jethro, helped Moses see the reality of his own limitations. Moses saw Jethro's wisdom and divided up the work of leadership among key people: dream teams will produce the wins. Look at the network of people at hand. Engage them! That's the way to the Promised Land.

But First Get Out of Your Own Way

A high-profile CEO asked us to stop by for a chat. The daily business press was chronicling his difficulties and disappointments in gory detail. "It's a much tougher slog than I thought. This group of folks just don't move fast. They discuss and discuss and discuss some more. Our market position continues to deteriorate faster than I can react. We've got lots of cash for the short term, but . . ." His voice trailed off as he stood looking out at the foggy morning.

"Any stars on whom you can depend?" we asked.

"Stars?" he exploded. "Never seen anything like these people—they're like store mannequins. I've got to do everything. If I don't do it, it doesn't get done. Strategy is a foreign word around here. Responsibility is unknown. People talk, but don't execute—and no one cares. I'm no introvert, as you know, but even my temper tantrums don't move them. I'm at my wit's end for what to do. Any suggestions?"

"Polish up your résumé?" we said, smiling.

"Right," he said with a grimace. "And who'd take me after I've presided over the demise of one of the premier names in our business? Nope, I've got to make this one go. Let me try again. Any suggestions?"

We spent the next two hours scoping out several ways he might engage the several thousand people still in the business. Our parting words to him summarized our theme: "At the end of the day, though, all of these activities will only work if you stop trying to do everything yourself. You need to get out of your own way.

"As long as everyone looks to you—and you believe that you've got to do it by yourself—you're creating the best short-selling opportunity in the market today—and you can't even capitalize on it." Can the leopard change his spots? As they used to say at the Saturday afternoon serials we watched as kids, "Come back next week and find out."

Then Unlearn, to Learn Anew

Mort Meyerson thought he knew all there was to know about leadership. After all, he'd had one of the best teachers, Ross Perot, and a very successful track record building EDS into the power it is today. He had his priorities straight. Work came first, second and third; family, community and other obligations came after that—if there was time and energy. His leadership system worked. EDS grew at a phenomenal rate and created thousands of employee millionaires. He'd found the mother lode. What could be better?

There were a few bumps along the way. Employees often

dropped like flies from working seventy to eighty hours a week. Customers often got short shrift. The hyperfocus on short-term results often hurt the organization long-term. But the dollars kept rolling in and the stock price kept going up, so it was easy to ignore these issues.

When Meyerson became CEO at Perot Systems, looking from the outside he saw the corrosive impact of the emphasis on profit and loss to the exclusion of other values. In the April–May 1996 issue of *Fast Company*, he wrote that everything he thought he knew about leadership was wrong, so he embarked on a new Phoenix leadership strategy. He engaged the people in an extensive information-gathering process. These initial discussions led to vision-and-values forums in which everyone came together to talk and argue over the future of their enterprise. Meyerson played chief facilitator and prodder in these sessions, encouraging everyone to speak their minds and hearts. Together, the employees at Perot Systems agreed upon a new company focus and direction.

In this process Meyerson discovered that, through engaging people, the leader must make sure that the organization knows itself. The leader must embody the values, and that has to do with human relationships and the obligation of the organization to its individual members and customers.

Meyerson discovered that he had to engage people as a coach, not an executive. Rather than telling them what to do he'd encourage them to look in the mirror and look to themselves and each other, rather than to him as the leader. Only by not stepping in all the time, as he had previously learned to do, could he create a collaborative environment where people can succeed through teamwork.

He also learned that he needs to be accessible. Meyerson replies to thousands of e-mail messages a month. He found that e-mail was the single most important tool he had to break through the old organization and the old mind-set. Through e-mail he could be an instant participant in any part of the organization.

Meyerson learned a new Phoenix approach to leadership: engaging people by giving up the flowing robes and long white beard of a Moses.

Get Others to Step Forward—And Bite Your Tongue

It's one thing to decide to engage others. It's quite another thing to do it. It's tough for the leopard to change its spots. We know. It eats at our innards frequently. We recently presided over the first worldwide executive management meeting of a company. Several hundred faces eagerly awaited "the word" from the new leader. Were they disappointed! The word came from the head of a special task force responsible for engaging associates in our new vision and values.

He gave the presentation—not us. He answered questions—not us. We bit our tongues a couple of times when we didn't necessarily agree with a particular statement, but it was important to make certain that everyone understood *he* was the point person who'd lead that process. We'd take the little corrective action when we do the one-on-ones with him later.

The Agile, Amphibious Phoenix Leader Working Above and Below the Waterline. Don't let us mislead you. Phoenix leadership does not require a vow of silence. Far from it. Be engaged. We are. But the key word is engage, not control. In a crisis, a team of paramedics is more valuable than the solo virtuosity of the world's greatest surgeon.

When do you control and when do you contribute? When do you decide and when do you question? The high-visibility waterline is the dividing line between these two approaches. Participate in topics and issues that are above the waterline, like hiring or shifting budget items. Mistakes here cause embarrassment, but they are not fatal to the organization. Below-the-waterline decisions, however—like pricing for major accounts or mergers—are cats of a different color. You still want others to make these below-the-waterline decisions, but you can't afford to allow a mistake here. People might drown.

On above-the-waterline decisions we question, question, question; get out the spotlights and spades and work to make the decision as fact-based as possible. But at the end of the day, like George, we move aside on any above-the-waterline decisions. We use the same questioning and searching activities for below-the-waterline decisions. Only there, we redouble our surfacing efforts, because we know that if the group comes up with what we believe to be a wrong decision, we will have to intervene. So we work the surfacing process long and hard.

It's not an easy call. When do you play the trump card? It'll take the trick, but it doesn't win the game. We lose every time we have to trump someone else's decision. Yet we can also lose when we take the high road. It takes lots of patience and education to bring out the leadership talents of others. During that learning process, the casualties can be high.

For instance, in one business we worked hard to narrow the product focus from twenty industries to something smaller. We believed that three was the magic number. Try as we might, we could not get the group to narrow to any less than six. We bought off on six, hoping that we could come back next year and narrow it again. Only this time, there was no next year. Heavy losses forced us to abandon major portions of the company's activities. The new leaders of the next corporate reinvention narrowed to a three-product focus. Our right answer came too late for us. There are risks in this engagement game.

In another situation we moved too quickly. In our specialty chemical venture the management group wanted to invest heavily in a new product venture. We weren't convinced that there was a market for the new products, so we vetoed the proposal after long and heated discussions. A competitor launched exactly the same product and swept the market, costing us multiple points of market share.

The unspoken "We told you so" hung around like a bad penny for a long time. It's a judgment call. You win most and lose some.

"Mea Culpas" Clear the Air and Reinforce the Heart Connection. When you do lose—and we all do—call the folks together and declare your fallibility. Apologize for the error, figure out how you can do better next time and move on. We did that with the specialty chemical management team. They accepted our apology and we figured out how to counter the new product with some innovative ideas of our own. Everyone knows that no one, not even a Phoenix leader, is perfect. It helps to reinforce the heart connection when you remind people of your own fallibility.

Phoenix leaders at all levels can stand up and admit a mistake. In fact, sometimes it may be better if you are not the boss. *Sports Illustrated,* in their September 7, 1992, issue, reported the turning point for the Washington Redskins in the early 1990s. It oc-

curred when pass receiver Art Monk, a usually quiet member of
the team, stood up and called a mandatory team meeting. A
player calling a team meeting was unheard of, but it led to a turnaround in performance.

The team was in a slump and struggling when Monk stood before the whole group. Addressing them in dead earnest, he looked
around at the attentive faces. No one could believe Monk was actually talking. A hush fell as the wide receiver told them that
everyone can play a lot better—including himself—and that he
was rededicating himself to doing better right now.

That simple but powerful admission coming from a star receiver made all the difference. The Redskins beat the Dolphins
42–20 the next day—and won all but one game on the way to the
playoffs. Winning seasons followed.

Admitting Mistakes: There Are No Perfect Parents. A guided
missile is a powerful force. It locks on to a target and flies toward
it at top speed. As the missile travels, it adjusts its direction to
home in on the target with precision—until it hits. In our personal lives, the same is true. We're always making mid-course
corrections. A mistake is no more than a mid-course correction.

This applies to our personal lives. No man or woman is the perfect parent. Especially with the firstborn child—who, more often
than not, is the experimental pilot project for the children who
follow. As we raise our families, we learn from our mistakes in
guiding each successive child. After about ten or twelve offspring,
they say a parent gets pretty good. We don't know. One thing is
certain. We make mistakes and admit them when they happen.
Admitting personal mistakes reinforces to our families a very important message: that it is okay to make mistakes. Everyone does.
Not admitting them or learning from them is the real mistake.

Do you want to hear about mistakes we've made in raising our
children? How much time do you have? It's not only undesirable,
but suicidal to pretend you are infallible. You can't romanticize
your record—you've made mistakes and witnesses were present.
May as well admit it. Or hear about it at an awkward moment
from an unexpected source!

Enroll, Don't Roll Out. Recall the phrase "Let's roll out the program!" We've all heard it many times in our careers. We've likely
even said it a number of times. When we hear the words "roll

out" the picture that comes to mind is a Sherman tank rolling over the landscape, crushing objects in its path. Is that the mental picture we want to paint? The Sherman tank of the program crunching objects and objections in its path?

Obviously not. That image may have worked in the past. It doesn't work with intelligent, articulate, sought-after-by-the-competition people.

Phoenix leadership requires followership. People stand up and say "I want to follow you" because of who you are or where you are going. Phoenix leaders make it appealing to follow them. Help others win through following you, and they will line up to enroll as your follower.

Words Are Prophetic: Paint the "Us" Picture

Words paint a picture. There's a galaxy-wide difference between the words "girl" and "woman." One describes an immature, dependent female. The other describes an independent, mature female. Which word picture would you prefer if you were a thirty-seven-year-old CFO of a Fortune 20 company? A woman we know described the following personal experience.

She's earned an M.D. and a Ph.D.—and is the president of a start-up company looking for venture capital funding. The venture capitalists are due at 2:00 P.M. She's pacing the entry hall anxiously awaiting their arrival. At 2:05 the three male venture capitalists hurry through the door, led by the senior partner. He takes off his coat, gives it to her and says, "Here, girl, please tell Dr. Smyth that we're here. And I'd like some coffee, black with one sugar."

She hangs up the man's coat, prepares the coffee as requested and offers it to him with the words, "Here you are, boy. Dr. Smyth at your service."

"Maybe it was his guilt or something, but it was the easiest $7 million we ever raised," Dr. Smyth told us.

Words paint a picture. Be certain they paint the picture you want.

UP FRONT AND PERSONAL: PLEASE MOTHER, I'VE GOT TO DO IT MYSELF

Phoenix Leadership Is an Eyeball-to-Eyeball Business

Percy Barnevak, former CEO of the Swedish-Swiss energy company Asea Brown Boveria, spent five days a week, forty-eight weeks a year, on the road. For Barnevak, there was no substitute for direct involvement. He personally met with every employee of his $39 billion enterprise and looked each of them in the eye and explained his view of how his radically decentralized organization had to operate. It must have worked. For three years in a row under his leadership his firm was the most admired in Europe.

Jack Welch, chairman of highly successful GE, said, "This is an eyeball-to-eyeball business. Leadership is a personal encounter business."

We know. Phoenix leadership is about our bods, in front of associates and customers, talking about the issues. That's why we spend so much time on the road. Every customer we visit is an opportunity to demonstrate our seriousness of intent to customers and associates alike. That's what the Juice with Jerres are all about—and the quarterly videos, the JerreLine and the host of other ways we look to to get up close and personal with associates. We're not alone. Other leaders do it as well: Knight at Emerson, for instance, and T. J. Rogers at Cypress Semiconductor.

Make the Hatchet Work Personal

Firing people ranks high on the list of jobs to avoid, right above visiting your friendly dentist or proctologist. Most executives avoid terminations like the plague. "Give it to the HR person. She's the expert in doing these things." Can't do that anymore. Bite the bullet and stand tall. Termination time is when the heart connection counts most of all.

William Peace faced a difficult decision. How he handled it was reported by Thomas Teal in the November–December 1996 issue of *Harvard Business Review*. He ran Westinghouse's Synthetic Fuels division in the early 1980s. The future was clear: find a buyer or liquidate. Costs had to be trimmed to pretty up the division for possible sale. In a small division—130 people—it's hard to cut jobs, because every job comes with a face and a human being attached. So it was particularly difficult to decide whom to cut. It took a tough day-long meeting to reach agreement on the fifteen jobs/people to go. Rather than send a memo, or another manager to tell the fifteen, Pearce decided to do it himself. He felt that he owed that personal touch to the people involved.

The meetings were the most difficult Pearce had ever experienced. It was like watching your own funeral on the silver screen. People cried, shouted, pleaded and threatened. Pearce sympathized, listened and responded to every question as openly as he could, taking all the criticism they wanted to send his way. By the time he shook their hands and wished them well, most people had come to a grudging acceptance of the need to sacrifice a few in order to save the many.

Months later Pearce looked to rehire those folks. The division had been sold and the new owner invested to grow the business. Every one of the fifteen came back, several leaving good-paying other jobs they'd found in the meantime. The reason: Bill Peace's personal engagement. By handling the difficult situation himself, and not delegating it to someone else, Peace demonstrated his personal interest and heart connection with each and every person.

Pay Attention to Personal Details

People love to be acknowledged and recognized. Personal acknowledgment notes go a long way toward building that heart connection we've talked about. We send notes out with copies of articles we've read or in response to notes others have sent us. We religiously return voice mails within hours and promise to respond to e-mails by the next day.

All of that personal contact continues to reinforce the relationship between us. Without that kind of relationship all you ever get is public compliance and private defiance. People say to your face what they think you want to hear, and then go back and do just what they want anyway.

This is not a fluff-happy public relations activity. Assistants don't write personal notes for the boss. You lead a serious organization—a family, a department, a division. You're part of many overlapping, interdependent, interconnected networks, filled with people who depend upon you. They want to know—no, they need to know—that you truly care about them as a human being. Each of us yearns to be recognized and valued. Take the moment—we do—to recognize the humanness and value of each of your network companions.

Stand in Front of the Room so That the Dedicated Troops Can See Your Dedication

We received a call from the head of one of the armed services. He wanted help in eliminating overlapping jurisdictions and departmental duplications. "We need to simplify our processes and our lines of reporting. I know, for instance, that we have four bases repairing planes. We only need one. We have R&D going on in seven different locations. We'd get more R&D done and save tons of money if we consolidated it into one location. We'd likely save billions if we could eliminate layers of reporting and at least three commands. I'd really like to have you come in and help us do this."

"Love to, sir," we replied. "But we're the wrong folks for the job. These tough decisions need to be made by the people who are going to execute them when they're done. If not, you'll just get lots of pretty words and darn little action. Everyone around that table knows that you're out of here in less than three years. They figure they can dance around the issues for that time period and outwait you. They've seen their predecessors do it to your predecessors, so they know it works. The know the situation better than anyone. If they decide to stonewall you, you're lost. You'll get lots of study committee reports—and not much else.

"You, sir, must sit in front of the room, at the head of the table, thus sending the unmistakable message that you're dead serious about reaching agreement and executing that agreement before you retire. Hire us to do that job for you and you water down your impact and diminish your ability to get the job done."

The awkward silence hung heavy on the phone. Finally he said, "You know, you're right. You're absolutely right. I've got to step up to the line and do it. I know these people and they know me. We've moved together through the chairs, fought the wars, saved each other from death. We are bonded at the heart. It's time we sat down, as professionals and citizens, and do what's right for the country and our service. If I don't do that, I shirk my duty as a leader." We could have reached through the phone and hugged him. Made us proud to be an American.

It's not that he'll make all the decisions, because he won't. Far from it. He'll engage, cajole, prod and maybe even use a little pressure. But at the end of the meeting it will be *their* decision and *their* responsibility to execute. They'll do it for him. It will be *his* meeting. The people around the table will be *his* people, people with whom he forged a heart connection on the battlefields of death. They'll do it for him because he personally called each of them on their mutually linked heart line. They'll do it for him because of the personal connection between him and them, and not because he's the chairman. They'll do it for him because he's the Phoenix leader.

The Real Classroom Is the One Your Whole Family Lives In

The same principle is true on the personal level as well. Never hand over your personal responsibilities to outsiders. For example, education is your responsibility, not the schools' or teachers'. Don't drop off the kid at the local school and let someone else worry about educating him or her. We've learned the opposite is true. Disaster waits just around the corner when you let schools do all the educating.

Spend time doing homework with your children, help them and participate with them in their education. Engage the whole family in the education process. Take the leadership role and don't expect someone else to do it for you.

The real classroom is the one your family lives in—and you are standing at the blackboard. After all, it's your class. It's your family. It's your life, and you are the Phoenix leader.

NARROW THE FOCUS:
CONVERT CAN DOS INTO MUST DOS INTO WILL DOS

The Weight of the Future Makes for a Groaning Table of Opportunity

George, our electronics company Bobby Riggs, faced it. We face it every day. So does everyone. There are too many opportunities out there and too few resources to capitalize on them. The leader's task: engage people in prioritizing the opportunities, and choosing the few best ones to pursue. It's not easy because the siren call of opportunity lures many organizational sailors to their watery graves.

The world is full of activities that we can do. Today, for instance, we can do lots of things: run, work out in the gym, drive a grandson to school because it's raining, read that novel we've been wanting to read, scan our monthly magazines to identify future trends, respond to the twenty-seven e-mails we received this morning, handle the eleven voice mails in the mailbox this morning, pay last week's bills, prepare next week's presentation, prepare for and participate in the weekly management committee conference call, call three merger candidates to discuss possibilities, talk with two candidates for our CIO position, respond to the urgent incoming mail and write this chapter.

We narrowed the can dos into a smaller list of must dos. These must-do activities were: run, drive grandson to school, respond to the e-mails and voice mails and urgent incoming mail, prepare and participate in the management committee meeting, interview the two CIO candidates and write this chapter.

From that narrower list of must dos we choose the following activities that we will do today: run, respond to the e-mails and voice mails and urgent incoming mail, talk to the two CIO candidates and, here we are, writing this chapter.

Our decision rule for making these narrowing choices has roots in the stable organizational and personal Pyramids of vision, mission, values, goals and strategies we can create as the product and legacy of our Phoenix leadership activities. Running is a personal health priority. Family and driving grandson in the rain are other important personal priorities. Responding promptly to the various mails (electronic, voice and paper) is an integrity issue for us. Selection of new senior staff is an important priority, as we see this as an opportunity to both upgrade organizational capabilities as well as send a highly visible message about our seriousness.

In the inevitable time crunch, we skipped the management committee meeting to facilitate the development of the other committee members. We put off several of the other items—program preparation, novel reading and magazine scanning—for our upcoming trip across the country. This coming Saturday looked like a great bill-paying day. We constantly search for the highest and best use of our time.

The Lure of Distant Opportunity Dilutes Current Activities. One of our closest friends runs a very successful $200 million business. Historically he's booked six times the net profit of his nearest competitor, in a commodity business. It's unbelievable. He faces so much opportunity, it's staggering—but he's de-focusing his people. He's in a $5 billion market, growing at double digits. Yet he's realized single-digit growth in the last several years—with declining margins, partially due to rising raw material costs, but also traceable to overhead growth. As he puts it, "There's way too many cars in our parking lot."

What's happened? Our friend's business suffers from a disease called over-opportunitis. They are gagging on too much opportunity. They made their money with a suite of niche products. In an effort to expand, they developed a whole line of new products, using a completely different technology aimed at different markets. They also set up an information-based consulting service to sell services to distributor customers. They extended their core products into two new markets, both requiring completely different distribution systems and sales forces. They expanded into four global markets. For a small company, they had a lot on their corporate plate.

When we came in to visit, within minutes it was clear: everyone was drowning in opportunity—and had taken their eye off their core product ball. Everyone was focused on the $2, $6, and $8 million deals, which are rounding errors in a $200 million company—but ones that consume a disproportionate amount of executive time and energy. By lunchtime we met with our friend and gave him our feedback.

"I was afraid of that," he said. "And it's all my fault. I wanted to grow the business fast, and thought that introducing new products, expanding globally and marketing services was the way to go. I just moved too fast for the people. Now it's time to go back to basics and plumb our primary market. With less than 5 percent of the total market, there's lots of growth opportunity there. We don't have to look elsewhere to find gold in the streets. We'll just take our good people and refocus them on our core products and markets."

This guy is great. We love his willingness to step up to the line, admit his mistakes and go forward to correct them. We admire his ability, courage and forthrightness. We'd wager that's why he's so successful.

Done It Before, Will Do It Again: Focus, Focus and Focus. We sold sixteen businesses at Square D during the first two years we led that organization. Why? We didn't need the cash. It was a focus issue. We had a great franchise in factory automation, power equipment and electrical distribution. Prior leaders diversified into electronics, and bought a lot of pretty good companies. The management team was dying trying to cover so many different areas. For instance, we were number two in the world in copper foil. Yet that business did not contribute to our core focus. People kept saying, "That's a great business. We make a lot of money in it. Why don't we just keep it and milk it." We responded, "That's right. It is a great business, and we do make a lot of money in it. But is it going to help us be successful in the future?" Since the answer always was, "No, but . . ." we sold it for $360 million.

Narrow the Focus Among Family Members. Let's look at helping members of our household—or our extended household. They come seeking answers, and we provide questions: questions that help them narrow their focus. It's a tall order helping kids choose a career. There are 20,000 official occupations to choose from. What can a parent do when you see your kids struggling?

One of our kids graduated from high school magna cum laude—sixth in a very large class. He won a full college scholarship. Things looked great. However, after three quarters as a freshman, majoring in computer science, he dropped out, on the verge of flunking. What went wrong? He couldn't focus. Classes were dull. He liked lots of out-of-classroom activities. He wanted out of academia and into the working world. What would he do? We presented him with several alternatives—and surfaced all the hard issues.

We all sat down and talked through several possibilities. We narrowed the focus to his personal interests and he came up with a potential solution. He decided to go to work for a friend in the business of Internet services—where he could use his love of science and computers to launch a career—and complete school later when he was mature enough to understand his career goals. Today, he loves his job and looks forward to going to school part-time. Surfacing the issues and narrowing the focus made the difference.

Surfacing the issues also surfaces a lot of opportunity. Engage people in narrowing the range of choices. Drive to a conclusion, pick the few best opportunities and kill the rest. Ration your time and energy resources in both organizational and individual settings.

CREATE DISCIPLES: TRUE BELIEVERS WHO SPREAD THE WORD

Raise a Family of Phoenix Envoys

You can't be everywhere. No one has that kind of time or energy. Yet you need to engage everyone throughout the organization. That's not difficult if your organization is your family that all lives under one roof. You see each other virtually every day and interact frequently. It's a whole different perspective if your organization functions in seventy-two countries and has 46,000 associates. You could travel ever day of the year and never get to see them all. What to do? Multiply yourself by enlisting disciples.

A disciple is a true believer who actively engages others in the crusade. Every renewal effort needs disciples who carry the message to distant and sometimes hostile lands to engage the heathen. Christ had eleven disciples who spread his word. Other leaders chose a similar path, in such organizations as Metropolitan Life Insurance, Boeing, Supervalu, GTE and the Atlanta Committee for the Olympic Games. In each of these organizations, the leader saw clearly the new tomorrow that needed to be created. They saw what had to be done, but couldn't reach out across their vast organizations to personally engage everyone in the task of doing it. So they created extensions of themselves—disciples—who worked throughout their far-flung organizations to engage people in creating their mutually beneficial new tomorrow.

Commission Exemplars and Teachers. Disciples perform two crucial tasks. First, they represent the new way of life. When anyone asks, "What does this new mentality look like in my area?" we point to the disciples and say, "Watch them to see how the new mentality works." They are the visible role models. Second, disciples teach and support others in living the new behavior. Disciples are both exemplars and teachers of the new way of life.

In one situation, we advertised in the company newspaper, asking for volunteers willing to work on engaging people in living the new vision, values and strategies. More than 15 percent of the 450-person workforce volunteered. Each wrote a short paragraph explaining why they wanted to volunteer. A small committee composed of ourselves, the human resource director and the operations director read every submission and selected forty-one individuals, based both upon the words they wrote and their past record. We looked for shining examples of the new vision, values and strategies as well as people with high integrity and instant recognition for their outstanding performance. The "tiger team" vowed to be the living examples of the new approach. They created an all-employee training program, selected and trained the trainers, and staffed a hot line providing answers to questions about the new approach. They were truly both exemplars and teachers.

Get a New Life at MetLife. CEO Harry Kamen faced a challenge: reinvent Metropolitan Life quickly or watch an old franchise sink into oblivion on his watch. His efforts were reported by Edith

Howle, Gary Neilson and David Ortiz in the Fourth Quarter 1996 edition of *Strategy and Business*. He knighted three senior executives as his chief disciples. They, in turn, commissioned five subleaders and fifty full-time disciples. He charged them with aligning the organization around the company's new vision and amplifying and focusing energy throughout the organization on the process redesign necessary to accomplish that new vision. CEO Kamen personally devoted four to five days a month to working with his disciples, and he asked all of his senior officers for the same commitment.

The disciples went to work examining the full range of current MetLife activities. They involved wide groups of employees in crafting recommendations for such significant changes as centralizing services in what had been a very decentralized environment and creating two new customer-focused business units. The disciples then supported the implementation of these dramatic changes with training and communication linkages.

The senior management staff met regularly with the disciple group. They agreed upon specific expectations such as a 70 percent increase in pretax earnings over a three-year period. The disciples transferred ownership for specific process improvement results to line managers. Their "estimates" became management "commitments." The result: MetLife exceeded its own targets. Harry Kamen rescued the franchise.

Disciples Represent the Best of the Rest of the Organization. In one organization with which we worked we asked the senior management team to recommend the disciple group. The first cut surfaced nine people from the headquarters location and two from the major cross-country distribution center. "Hold on," we said. "We've got to have all geographies represented." The next cut surfaced one Canadian, three Europeans, two from Asia/Pacific, one from Latin America, two from headquarters and two each from the two major distribution centers. "That's more like it," we said, "but we're not done yet. Does the group represent all functions and levels throughout the organization?"

"Well no," came the halting answer. "Why is that important?"

We recognized another Phoenix leadership moment, and we replied, "Remember, this group has two goals. First, to be an on-site, ever-present, local representation of what the new behavior looks like, a living example of the new way at the next desk or next machine—right before everyone's eyes every day of the week. Second, to be easily available as coaches, teachers and supporters of the new behavior. If anyone has a question of whether a certain practice or policy is in keeping with the new behavior, they can go to one of these team members for an authoritative answer. Given those two goals, how can we choose people who will best help the group meet these two goals?"

"Guess we'd have to have people from every area at most important locations. Annika in Holland can't go to California—nine hours, eight thousand miles and two cultures away—to see what the new behavior looks like. We also need local people to answer questions about a certain policy's congruence with the new approach," was the quick response.

"Right on," was our even quicker response. "Now go find those excellent people at all those locations who can carry the banner, play the part and teach their fellow associates."

In other words, put together a disciple group that looks like the rest of—and the best of—your organization.

Tap the Rich Vein of Volunteers. The slight man shifted awkwardly from foot to foot waiting for the crowd of airline mechanics to assemble. Most of the folks stood, still in their grease-spotted work uniforms. There was no need for chairs, since the talk was billed as a five-minute end-of-shift presentation. When he spoke it was clear that the language was not his native tongue. He stumbled and searched for words frequently, creating painful pauses in his presentation. His sincerity shone through, though. His message was clear: help me make a difference for our customers.

Everyone in that room carried a union card, and in this seemingly hostile environment, he asked for volunteers to help him improve the airline. He read a few customer complaint letters each followed by his words, "We are better than this." He asked for a commitment of one day a month to help him reestablish the airline's reputation, and gave them a mailbox to contact him. He then thanked them for listening and their support of their customers, and said goodbye. It took just under five minutes.

Approximately 4 percent of the mechanics took him up on the challenge. He met with them and asked them to research ways to improve on-time arrivals and departures and shorten out-of-service time for maintenance, promising help if they needed it.

Eight months later they came back with their recommendations. He asked them to prove their recommendations. Tested in the crucible of daily experience, seven months later he announced the new procedures. The volunteers, who had swollen to almost 10 percent of the workforce by now, became the disciples of the new ways. They led the revolution that brought the airline to Airline of the Year. The lesson: tap the rich vein of volunteer talent in your organization.

Keep the Blood Flowing Through the Heart Connections with Your Disciples

Spend personal time with your disciples. Steep them deeply in your philosophy. Commit them strongly to the new way. Establish and exercise that heart connection.

We call each person who's nominated to be a disciple—personally—to congratulate them and lay out the challenge/opportunity ahead of us. We're careful to point out what we need them to do. It's an extra effort, but as the personal role model it's worth every second. Once you get done with those personal calls, they're ready to kill for you.

We spend intensive time together with the disciples. The first half day or so we share experiences and lay out what we are going to do and how we are going to do it. Usually after lunch we work through question and response. Then we leave and they go to work identifying their goals, obstacles and ways around them. We come back at the end of the next day, respond to more questions, help each one set specific action plans and give them their charge.

But those two launch days aren't the end of the personal engagement. It's only the beginning. Twice a month we meet with the disciples and just listen. We look forward to these sessions. We pick up things we need to tweak, what things aren't happening as well as what is working well. More importantly, we pick up things we never even thought about that need fixing. Helps us remember why no one of us is as smart as all of us.

Help the disciples become the communications hub. Charge them with collecting questions from associates, researching the information needed and responding to the associate. Encourage them to publish a newsletter—both in print and on the e-mail— which includes questions and answers and success stories. In one of our companies the disciple group brought us their first newsletter for approval. With trembling hands they asked, "Is this okay for us to send out?" Without looking at the papers, we said, "If it's from you, we don't need to look at it. It's yours. If you want to send it—just send it out." Everyone knew that we had passed another Phoenix leadership moment test. The old command-and-control culture was dead. We meant what we said about being customer- and associate-focused.

Stay in Touch Anywhere, Anytime. Provide continuing support for disciples in the field. It's lonely out there for them on their own. In one situation we did daily half-hour 6:30 A.M. phone calls. We'd share developments, hits, runs, errors and learnings. After a few weeks we dropped back to every other day, then twice a week and finally, after the third canceled call for lack of interest, we dropped it altogether. Having served its purpose, the phone call passed into oblivion.

We've also used a help line as a way to provide continuing personal social support. There always needs to be someone a lost disciple can call. Like in AA—reach for the phone and call your sponsor before you reach for a drink and call a friend—have someone there disciples can call.

Oftentimes the help line serves as a father confessor. There on the firing line disciples are always wondering, "Did I just blow it? What do I do now?" Watch a good football coach handle a receiver who drops a pass and you'll see how to handle the "Boy, did I just make a mess now" problem. The receiver who drops a pass goes back to the sidelines carrying his head in a wheelbarrow because it's so low. A good coach goes up to that receiver, puts his arm around him and gives him a word of encouragement. The good coach knows that that guy will catch eighty passes. Don't focus on the one he didn't catch. Focus instead on the next eighty he's going to catch. Disciples out there need that kind of support. They need the continuing heart connection with the leader.

Beware the Little Chairman
Who Wants to Become a Big Chairman

Like most things in life, sometimes disciples don't work out. There's a Judas in every crowd. Move fast when you sense it. Investigate, shine the light, get all the facts you can, confront the situation quickly and move on to the next item. That's exactly what happened to us early in our career. We appointed a person from quality control to lead the disciples. He seemed like a perfect facilitator, trainer, developer, supporter and tool provider.

It turned out we blew it—big time. He used his disciple leadership position to enhance his personal power. He centralized all decision making in the disciple group—slowly at first so no one noticed. But soon he was making all the decisions, giving all the answers—all under the guise of ensuring the correctness of the response. He liked being a Big Chairman. Unfortunately, that was exactly the opposite of the managerial style we wanted to implant.

We saw the signs, but waffled, waiting for the situation to be clearer. We wanted to believe in him and kept coaching him to help him let go. After four frustrating months we finally moved on him. That side trip set us back probably eight months. We had to earn back the trust and focus that we had lost because of him. It was a hard lesson, one we've never forgotten. Watch out for people on power trips.

Set Clear Goals and Measures for the Disciples

At AT&T/NCR the new business model transition team focused on three goals: facilitation, feedback and process improvement. The transition team facilitated the training and application of the vision, mission, values, objectives and strategic pillars. They also kept continuous associate feedback flowing all the time about the new business model.

They authored a ready-reference "Transition Help Book," with over 300 pages of well-organized information explaining the transition and the new business model. NCR associates had more documentation and communication for the transition process than they had ever received in all of AT&T/NCR's one-hundred-plus-year history.

They also identified processes that either needed fixing, developing or discontinuing. Acting often on their own initiative, they developed several innovations ranging from new ways to buy supplies to answering customer requests for information on a worldwide basis. The team recommended changes in resource allocations, product program rollouts, and dozens of new processes, including objectives, measures and reward systems covering every person in the company.

Render unto Caesar What Is Caesar's, and unto God What Is God's. Keep the disciples focused on facilitating, motivating, teaching and creating the tools for future success. But keep the disciples out of owning the processes or the responsibility for delivering worldwide success. Keep the disciples as advisors and consultants, not operating people responsible for delivering results. Keep measuring, keep recording progress for Caesar in delivering dollars and the disciples in delivering souls.

Creating Disciples in the School— Don't Just Manufacture Students

The discipleship approach works well outside business organizations as well. Look at Cathedral High School in El Paso, Texas. They don't just educate kids—they create disciples. The student body of 370 is 77 percent Latino, most from working-class families. Looking around the neighborhood, one might assume the school has high dropout rates, low test scores, lax discipline and racial tensions. Wrong.

Over 60 percent of the school's graduates earn college scholarships—and 98 percent go on to attend college. The school's heroes are not the athletes—they are instead the intellectual elite. Teachers at the school understand its mission—to promote excellence in the selected competencies. They tirelessly promote excellence and serve as the disciples of that mission—and in turn create disciples of students. That's why the school is in a state of continuous revivolution. It creates students who know how to think, are responsible for their own education and are actively engaged in helping others join them.

Cathedral's clear message to all: "What you do here matters. It matters to God, to your family, to your teachers. Follow the rules and you'll leave here with not just a diploma, but a destiny."

No one has the time or energy or reach to do it all alone. Create disciples who carry the banner, engage the people, model the behavior and facilitate others being successful Phoenixes.

DEALING WITH THE NONBELIEVER

Be Paranoid—The Enemy Is in the Next Office as Well as Outside the Gates

Not everyone is going to jump up and down with joy when you announce the new tomorrow. Expect opposition. It will be there. Plan for handling the nonbeliever.

Offer to raise wages 5 percent and while most folks will say, "Thank you," a few will say, "How come not 10 percent?" How many times have we heard the comments, "That's a great idea, but . . ." Or, "We tried that five years ago and it didn't work. What makes you think it will work now?" We've heard these words too many times. The world is filled with people who've made finding problems their life's work. We recall a commentary by one sportscaster minutes after a Super Bowl victory: "The big problem they face is how to repeat next year." Give us a break. They haven't even opened the champagne yet for this year's victory. Repeating may be a March concern, but certainly not a late January issue.

Some nonbelievers surface their opposition early. Others are closet nonbelievers, pretending to be supporters for a while, but always hanging back, waiting for the right moment to voice their "concerns." Can't get mad at these folks. They're doing what they think is in the organization's best interests. Can't focus on getting

even either. That's a one-way street to disaster land. Just keep
working the agenda to get ahead.

Ignore at Your Own Peril Those Who Make
Bad Things Happen to Good People

One of our neighbors is a comptroller for a small oil distribution
company. He wanted to improve the customer retention performance of the company. We helped him lay out some steps. He
convinced the owner to announce a customer service vision. Initially everyone was enthusiastic and Jack felt good about the
progress.

At a local Christmas party he shared a difficulty he encountered with several drivers and one of the terminal operators, all
of whom felt that the additional customer service activities cost
too much and were too difficult to perform. Jack listened to their
complaints, but largely ignored them.

At next year's Christmas party Jack was particularly glum.
"The critics won," he said. "They kept complaining. I kept ignoring. The owner finally couldn't stand it anymore, so he folded his
cards and canceled the program."

The nonbelievers will not go away. Deal with them, or put your
revivolution hopes on hold.

Win Back the Renegades by
Practicing the Politics of Inclusion

The first reaction to a nonbeliever usually is to isolate the cancer.
Deal the person out of meetings. Cut the person off from communication. Send the individual to "Coventry"—the old English
version of punishment by isolation. Jack discovered that this just
doesn't work. They don't go away. In fact, excluding them from
the table only gives them more ammunition with which to attack
the process.

Better to draw the circle large enough to include them in. Even
better: give them an important job. We often do that. Take a non-

believer and give that person a compelling assignment. Suzie was a shift supervisor in a small knitting plant in North Carolina. Two of her operators were constantly complaining about their machines' performance, which had the highest downtime in the department. As much as Suzie tried to facilitate communication between the operators and the maintenance department, these two women continued to be unsatisfied. Finally Suzie asked one of them, Esmerelda, to assume maintenance liaison responsibility for the entire shift. Esmerelda jumped at the chance. Within days everyone's uptime rose dramatically. The larger circle yielded larger results.

Drown the NonBeliever in a Sea of Successes. Invest energy in helping the believers succeed, not in converting the nonbelievers. Most folks want to back a winner. Win the pennant and ticket sales soar next year. Finish last and ticket sales crater. In organizational terms most folks hang back when confronted with the need to revivolute. After all, it's new and uncomfortable. Helping the believers succeed takes the vast majority of the people off the fence. So share the believers' early successes.

That's what Alikki did. Alikki owned a small women's clothing store in downtown Hong Kong. She saw customer service, particularly for Chinese visitors, as the key to her success. She talked with her people and together they put together a program to reach out to the visitors from China and prepare custom clothing to be shipped. Three of her fourteen salespeople responded favorably. After the first month they accounted for almost all the sales under this new effort. She held a staff meeting and asked each of the three women to share their selling secrets. She gave each a special gift in recognition of their success. She converted all the secret nonbelievers within three months. The last time we visited she was expanding her shop.

Keep Focused on the Bridge to Tomorrow and Let Nonbelievers Choose to Join or Jump. We worked with a firm refocusing their sales activities from an internal to a customer focus. Two of the three sales coaches were long-termers in both the business and the industry. They liked the way things were, not so much the way things were becoming. They tried hard to cooperate, but the new methods were very different from what they'd grown up with. One of them popped pills for four months, for headaches and

other aches and pains. She consumed five aspirin during one
morning meeting. The new approach was too emotionally challenging for her. She finally left, deciding it was better to find a job
she liked and could do than to work hard to meet the new requirements.

Now everyone's much better off. She's stopped popping pills,
the firm's moving forward and it's win-win for everybody. The
president focused not on convincing the nonbelievers, but on engaging everyone in the job that needed to be done. She made the
standards of performance and the rules of the game very clear.
She welcomed everyone to play. She gave them the coaching support they needed. The choice to play was theirs.

Thanks for Your Honesty—We Agree to Disagree. We've learned
a lot from raising our kids. That's why we use them as examples
frequently in this book. Like all of us, kids need to speak up when
they disagree. At the same time the family needs a firm hand on
the wheel. The balancing act takes a great deal of patience and a
lot of love.

Last week at the dinner table one of our teenagers confided
that she couldn't stand her math teacher, who keeps losing control in the classroom. "The kids keep interrupting and she doesn't
do anything. It's the worst class I've got. I may have to go to summer school because of her."

"What are you doing to keep your summer free?" we asked.

"Come on, Dad," she replied. "Save it for the office. I don't
have time to play your game. She's a pain. You could get me
transferred."

"Whoa," we responded. "Whose job is it to get this education?
Who wants to be a doctor? Who needs this math class, anyway?"

"Dad, you just don't understand. She's a class-A loser. Couldn't
teach making ice to Eskimos. She doesn't belong in the classroom, and not in one I've got to take. How about going to see the
vice principal and getting me into John's math class?"

We saw the light. "Ah ha. So that's it. Want to be in boyfriend
John's class, eh? How about either your mother or I come by
sometime this week and check out this class? Maybe then we can
talk about what you can do to overcome her quote bad unquote
teaching."

"Just forget it, Dad," she said, getting up abruptly from the table. "Parents, they'll never understand," she said, shaking her head as she walked away.

Problem is we understand all too well. Having sat through enough therapy sessions with teenagers, we know that teens want a parent who is affectionate and listens, and then sets expectations and enforces rules. Teenagers of all ages sense inherently that caring enough to be firm is true love.

People can disagree in any setting, around a simple kitchen table or an elaborate conference table. They can voice their disagreement, in a manner consistent with the values. And so that moment at the dinner table was another leadership moment. Let it pass and instantly everybody knows the leader isn't for real.

Summary

Phoenix leadership is serious stuff—and hard work. Got to be on your toes all the time: awake, as the Buddha was awake, alert to possible opportunities and *Phoenix leadership moments*. After the issues flood onto the table the leader's task is simply stated: engage the people in the business of the business—narrowing the issues, weighing priorities, coming to decisions to which they are committed. The leader asks, cajoles, confronts, insists and continues to nourish the heart connection. He or she taps the power of people to lead, opening their eyes and ears to the leader inside each of them. Everyone is brilliant at something. The leader brings out the best in us.

This is tough stuff. As is finding and prioritizing the resources. We turn to that important contribution to leadership in the next chapter.

PHOENIX WORKSHOP

1. HOW DOES MY MIND-SET CONTRIBUTE TO THE MOSES TRAP? HOW CAN I OVERCOME THAT TRAP?

_____

_____

2. WHAT WORDS CAN I USE TO PAINT THE US PICTURE RATHER THAN THE ME PICTURE?

_____

_____

3. WHAT PERSONAL CONNECTIONS CAN I MAKE TO ENGAGE THE PEOPLE?

_____

_____

4. HOW CAN I HELP OTHERS NARROW THEIR FOCUS FROM THE CAN DOS TO THE MUST DOS TO THE WILL DOS?

_____

_____

5. WHO CAN I ATTRACT TO BE MY DISCIPLES? HOW CAN I ENGAGE THEM, GUIDE THEM AND SUPPORT THEM?

_____

_____

6. HOW CAN I INCLUDE THE NONBELIEVER?

_____

_____

CHAPTER 6

Prioritize Precious Resources: Serious Goals Require Serious Hours, People and Dollars

It's time to get serious, roll up the sleeves and get to work. We've surfaced the issues and engaged the people. Now comes the tough task of putting your money—*and your time*—where your mouth is. Back up the right words with right resources upon which all futures are built: attention measured in hours, people and dollars. Speeches alone do not transform organizations. Products get sold, produced, distributed and supported with Resources, that's Resources with a capital R.

Two threads run through this chapter. You'll read them in different forms and versions, but all the subtopics relate to the big two: focused discipline and personal engagement. These are the Phoenix yin and yang, the soft and the hard edges of the important Phoenix leadership task of prioritizing resources. The hard edge is focused discipline. Relentlessly narrow everyone's focus: choose the three or four most important strategic goals and focus all your energies and resources on them. The soft edge is establishing and maintaining the heart connection through extensive personal engagement and alignment of individual and organizational activities.

THE CHALLENGE: LINE UP THE MOST VALUABLE RESOURCES WITH THE MOST IMPORTANT GOALS

Bobby faced a daunting task. Two years ago his company reported a loss. Last year they limped to small positive earnings, but far below promises to the analysts and shareholders. This year's budget showed a return to healthy profitability, but Bobby secretly questioned the organization's ability to deliver the numbers.

"We've actually had four years of off-budget performance," he said. "We always miss on the low side. Can't seem to get the organization to deliver."

"Is everyone aware of the changes in the marketplace?" we asked naively.

"Shared all the industry data with everyone. We're in a tight competitive situation. Margins in our business traditionally are very low, less than one and a half percent net after tax. We know all the warts of the competitors. We know how they aren't really delivering those outlandish promises they're making. But they keep winning customers with those promises—and we keep screwing up our service levels, making them look good. The business is far from booming, but neither is it collapsing. We are failing, though—big time—and it just got worse.

"A Fortune 100 Godzilla just moved into our market, acquiring a weaker competitor of ours. This Godzilla carries a full line of products that complement ours. We've never carried those products, which are smothered by government regulations. Thanks to this resource-rich Godzilla, our once-weak competitor just got a whole lot stronger. It's like a deep-pockets competitor just entered our market with skills, expertise and resources that far exceed ours. That promises to rile the market, put pressure on prices and make increasing profitable sales even harder. We've got to get folks to execute what we need to do, or else . . ." His voice trailed off into silence. We all knew what he meant. They had six to twelve months before their depressed stock price made them an even more attractive takeover candidate.

Bobby's challenge is typical. Many organizations face the same problem: the engines roar, the wheels spin—and they arrive at the wrong place. Motivation may crackle like lightning in a thunderstorm. Or things may be as dull as a lazy August afternoon.

What we have found is that so often the real trouble is in one critical arena: misapplied or under-applied resources. Most organizations have sufficient resources to accomplish their goals. It's just that the most valuable resources are not spent on accomplishing their most important goals.

Busy Being Busy: Time, a Precious Resource

"Let's look at your calendar, Bobby," we asked, knowing full well what we'd find. "Let's see how much of your time—hour by hour—is devoted to the three important strategies you've laid out."

The conclusion was apparent within minutes, though we took the better part of an hour to finish the detailed analysis. Bobby spent less than 20 percent of his time on the three most important strategies he'd laid out for the organization. His calendar was filled with lots of ceremonial time: retirement lunches, customer visits, industry trade association meetings and site visits. Meetings consumed another big portion of his time. He was very busy, but not with the strategic initiatives.

"What message do you think you're sending with the ways you allocate your time?" we asked Bobby.

"I know what you want me to say. The message is that these strategies really don't count a lot. In my heart I know you're right. But I'm trapped. Should I stop going to retirement ceremonies? What will people think? That I've gotten too big for the little-people things? Should I stop visiting customers? Many of our salespeople would like me to stop, because on those visits I inevitably uncover some sewer of stuff that's not being handled to the customer's satisfaction.

"Should I stop visiting our locations? The people look forward to my visits. It brightens up their day and reenergizes them to focus on our vision. Again, many of the location managers would like me to stop coming around because people tell me about the problems that aren't being fixed to their satisfaction. What am I to do? There are only so many hours in a day. I'm already working more hours than I want."

Balance the Must Dos with the Like to Dos. "Not easy to balance the must dos with the can dos. Can't you combine both? Couldn't you push the customer initiative when visiting customers and the internal efficiency/customer service initiative when visiting locations? Meetings take up a lot of time. Can't you structure meetings to include a review of the progress on the strategic initiatives?"

"Of course. Just didn't think of it. Maybe that's the way to get more done as well."

Bobby, again, is typical. Every one of us has a full agenda. The days begin early and stretch past dark. There's not much difference in days of the week; Saturday looks a lot like Tuesday. No one suffers from blank time on the calendar. Focus and alignment are the antidotes to busyness: focus on the few most important issues and align resources around those few most important issues.

Personal time is the single most important resource. It's non-renewable—once spent it's gone forever. It's a potent signal to others about your values and intentions. It's a powerful shaper of others' priorities. How you spend your time will influence other people to spend their time in similar ways. Today is the first day of the rest of your life, and it's also the last day of your current life. Spend it carefully, it's the only today you'll ever have.

Show Us Where the Money Goes and We'll Show You Your Real Priorities. Time alone is not enough. It takes dollars to run organizations, and the things that dollars buy, like offices, warehouses, plants, computer systems, marketing programs and people. Most of the dollars spent in any organization are fixed—today's consequences of yesterday's decisions that cannot be undone, except at great expense. In most organizations discretionary spending is a small percentage of total spending.

Discretionary spending reveals the organization's true priorities. Knowing this, we said to Bobby, "Let's examine your budget and see how much of your discretionary money is being spent on your three strategic initiatives."

The results were not surprising to any of us. Sure enough, less than 1 percent of the organization's money was being spent on these strategic initiatives. Of the more than 10 percent of total spending that was discretionary, only 10 percent of that had been allocated to the important strategic initiatives. No wonder Bobby's folks weren't making any progress. He'd sent them out to do battle against the fire-breathing dragon equipped with a reed sword and a paper shield. Without sufficient resources they are bound to fail.

Look at your household budget. There are fixed costs for housing: mortgage payment or rent, gas and electric, water, telephone, utilities, food and taxes. When you've first paid those essentials, what's left over is discretionary. Out of that discretionary fund comes dining-out money, movie and entertainment money, education money, travel money and so forth. If you're like most of us, the discretionary portion of your budget is a small percentage of your total spending.

However, it's what you choose to do with the discretionary dollars that sets the stage for your future. We've asked before, "What do you want your future to be like?" Well, your future is built on time, behavior—and those dollars. They are the substance of tomorrow.

Coach, Teach, Engage People in Allocating Resources. "Okay, okay," Bobby said. "I understand. I've got to reallocate the resources to align with my strategic priorities. But there must be more. Are you telling me to just go out and do that? Don't we need to involve the folks in making these reallocations?"

"Of course," we said, a big smile crossing our faces. "Now let's look at how we do that." That's what prioritizing resources is all about. "It's not hard," we said. "It takes focused discipline, setting the right example, getting the right tools and patience to coach and teach. That doesn't sound too difficult, does it?" we said grinning.

"Easy to say," was Bobby's reply. "But difficult to do."

Jo Ann's Dream World vs. Real-World Resources. Jo Ann also knows how tough it is to line up resources with intentions. When we first met Jo Ann she was a marketing representative for Procter & Gamble. She loved her job, but realized after only two years that her 8 percent increases would never earn her enough money to accomplish her dream of putting away enough savings to take seven to ten years off to raise a family. Husband John just finished school as well, and while he had a good entry level job, he was also not earning enough to save a lot.

"I decided to go to grad school and jump into a much higher paying position," she told us during the orientation meeting. She resigned her P&G position to go full-time in order to get her MBA in a year. The combination of her savings and John's salary would get them through.

But things never go according to plan. In the first month of her MBA program, John got laid off when his company closed the local office. He took four months to find a new position that paid about as much as his former job. With money tight, Jo Ann dropped one class (now back to four) in order to take on a graduate assistant position on campus to further supplement their income. Jo Ann was now on the two-year program. When we encountered her again in one of our classes, she was resigned to taking two years and working two jobs to get through.

"Have you thought of taking out student loans rather than working?" we asked. "That'll enable you to take more classes and get through faster."

"No," Jo Ann said. "I didn't think of it seriously. Didn't want to get into debt that we'd have to pay off later."

"What kind of job do you want when you graduate?" we asked her.

"I don't know. I haven't had time to think about it, really. We've been struggling so much to make ends meet. I might be interested in consulting, though—that's a high-paying job."

We urged her to attend an orientation session sponsored by Andersen Consulting as a way to learn more about the field. She called us, despondent, after the meeting.

"I've wasted my time here," she said. "I don't have anything they're looking for. They want well-rounded people. I've been so busy supporting myself and saving for my family that I haven't had the time to be involved in extracurricular activities. My GPA is good, but they're looking for higher grades than I've been able to get carrying nine to twelve units and working the equivalent of full time. They're looking for people to be committed to their careers. That means traveling and being away a lot. My marriage is extremely important to me. I don't see how it's possible to have both a committed relationship and the kind of career commitment they're talking about. I've wasted my time. I should have stayed with P&G."

We tried to be reassuring, pointing out that employers valued people who put themselves through school. We also pointed out that Andersen in particular, and most consulting firms in general, were much more family-sensitive these days, and, for example, paid to bring families together over weekends. We asked her what she could do to make herself more attractive to a major consulting firm.

"Maybe I could do some consulting projects on my own—through classes, perhaps. Maybe I could arrange an internship. Or make contacts with current consultants and plug into the network."

"Great ideas," we said. "Go for it."

Easier said than done, of course. Now in the first semester of her last year, most classes did not provide project opportunities. She couldn't arrange her hours to do an outside internship. And it was difficult to regularly attend local networking meetings.

One of Jo Ann's fellow students, now an associate with Andersen, introduced her to several of the consultants there, including the manager of the local office. He arranged for an unpaid internship for Jo Ann during winter session. She was a finalist during the rounds of interviews, but didn't get an offer from them.

Jo Ann graduated after two and a half years, and landed a good job with Ford Credit. She came by a few days ago with little Joey in tow, a cute three-year-old. She's expecting a second child—a baby girl—any day now. She's working part-time to pay the bills and save to buy a larger house.

Jo Ann's story is all too typical. A very bright and capable person, she could never quite get her resources and dreams lined up. Things kept coming up that prevented her from doing what she really wanted to do. In hindsight it's easy to see what she could have done differently: maybe worked a year longer to save more, gotten a student loan and be done in a year, found out what high-paying jobs were out there and what they required and organized her academic program and time around fulfilling those requirements. It was easy for us to see things from our outside perspective, but not so easy for Jo Ann, who was paddling as fast as she could to make progress and bailing water all the while to keep the boat afloat. Those few of us who really get ahead of the tide learn how to line up the scarce resources to support our intentions and dreams.

The Very Best Managers Can Both Do and Teach How

It takes patience to keep focused on our real objectives. There are always two objectives: a short-term drive to solve the immediate issue—and the long-term objective of sustainable strategic improvement. Work to get the best possible short-term decision made, in a way that builds long-term relationships and develops competence, so these individuals can do it on their own. Invest as much in accomplishing the long-term purpose, building the competence and the relationship, as you do in the short-term purpose of getting the best decision made.

Develop patience by teaching people rather than deciding issues. One executive told us last week, "You're in and out on this subject, in and out on that subject, in and out on another subject. You never drill down on any one subject. You just flit, like a bee, from subject to subject." She's right. We flit like a bee, teaching people how to make effective decisions themselves. Then we come back and check again and again and again until we're certain that they've mastered the capability.

Teaching requires good note taking! We're fortunate to be able to keep good notes in our heads. Others keep good notes in a laptop or a notebook. But it's important to remember where people are in their development, the issues they've been handling and what worked and what didn't work for you and them in the past. That's where the patience comes in. Teaching, like learning, is a job that's never done. Part of our own personal discipline is to keep focused on what we're here to do—teach, not make decisions—develop relationships, not dependents.

Facts Are Our Friends: Evidence Is the Currency of Friendship. Teach by focusing on facts and evidence. Be the balance wheel—the reality check—in any discussion. Make certain that all the facts get on the table—and the Moose gets off. It's easy to overlook evidence in the heat and ambition of the moment. Who can afford to be reckless when the stakes are high? Do we really want to rush in without some ability to anticipate the outcome? We don't need to be prudish and paranoid, but we must undergird our courage with evidence.

Stewart, a member of our church, lays irrigation pipe for a living. It's been tough, recently, making a living in our area, as the amount of new construction work has dried up. Ran into him at church. "We've decided to move to Colorado," he told us. "It's a better place to raise kids, the air's cleaner and I'm certain I'll find work there."

"What makes you so certain you'll find work there?"

"I read in the paper last week how things are booming there.

The article also said that housing's cheaper there. So we're packing up and going there next week."

Butting in, we asked, "Have you thought of going there yourself first, scoping out the territory and finding out what kind of work is really available there before you pack everybody up and trek halfway across the country?"

Stewart's dour facial expression told us more than we needed to know. "Nope. We're going. It'll be just fine."

Saw Stewart in church again about six months later. "How are things in Colorado?" we asked.

"Terrible," he said. "I couldn't find any work. They use different kinds of pipe there than I'm experienced in laying. It almost meant going back to being an apprentice again. We couldn't live on those wages. Called my old boss back here. He told me about a job just north of here. I drove back for the interview and got the job. I'm driving an hour each way every day, but at least I'm working now."

How many Stewarts do you know? We know lots of folks who make life-changing decisions based upon hearsay, opinion and speculation. Stewart couldn't afford the Colorado vacation he took. A little shining of the light and finding of the facts could have saved Stewart and his family a lot of grief and expense.

Equal Opportunity Starvers: Leaders Who Can't Say No

Bobby, the executive whose story began this chapter, was right. Allocating time—matching resources to goals—is very hard to do. The difficulty is compounded, though, when the organization is feeding and funding far too many initiatives and programs and activities. Bobby—like many others—was guilty of a common leadership blind spot: starting program after program after program, never ending one before starting another. We heard Bobby once say, "We'll squeeze the time out, somehow, to do this new program." That's precisely the problem—they did squeeze out the time for the new program, mostly by starving all the other priorities. Bobby, like most executives, is an equal-opportunity starver—he starves both valuable and useless programs equally—with the result that all programs suffer.

"One of These Days": A Garageful of Unfinished Projects. Lots of people are the same way: they have resources, but are too fragmented to deliver what they promise. Gil is a neighbor. A prince of a person, always willing to help with advice, tools and sweat. He was right there filling sandbags and digging trenches when we had a flood during a huge rainstorm several years back.

Gil's garage is filled with unfinished projects. A number of years back he started building a telescope. "The kids will love to do star gazing on our frequent camping trips," he said. Worked on it for a month or so of weekends and holidays. He got all the parts, built the stand and put together the rudimentary scope. But then he ran into difficulty lining up the various mirrors, got frustrated and put it aside "for a while." The kids grew up and left the nest. He and his wife don't camp out much anymore. The partially assembled telescope is still there in the rafters of his garage.

So he decided instead to build a greenhouse to grow jojoba plants. He put away the unfinished telescope and studied up on building a greenhouse. He finished the shell, but never got around to installing the motor to run the humidifier. It's now a storage shed. Then he decided he needed an MBA to get ahead in his company. He chose an evening program and went for a year, but soon lost interest and never finished.

The world is filled with Gils: good people with good intentions who start many projects, but complete only a few. Like some business executives they are equal-opportunity starvers: they don't discriminate, they starve kids' projects along with Mom's projects along with their career projects. A lack of focus robs them of the fruits of their labor.

Focus, Focus, Focus Is the Cure for the Equal-Opportunity Starver. Focus on the few most important issues—and stick with them. At Square D the big Moose issue was the profitability of the power equipment business—or rather the lack of it. Here was a $500 million business that was marginally profitable. Prior to our arrival, management felt that power equipment doesn't really have to make money, because that's the razor you give away in order to sell the profitable blades. In this case the blades were the highly profitable circuit breakers. We shined 10,000 watts of light on that theory and found it had more holes than Swiss cheese. So the management team agreed to: 1) significantly reduce fixed cost, and 2) use every cent we took out of variable expenses to shorten cycle time to market. We built our whole pricing strategy around that model.

We took the unusual step of insisting upon temporary personal approval of any project over $100,000. We don't like doing that, as it can be misinterpreted as taking away others' accountability. We did it though to send the message that we were serious about getting the product line profitable. We also centralized approval to help people learn how to say no to customers.

It's just too easy for salespeople to agree to customer requests, so we had to put a temporary backbone in the sales force. We told customers, "We'd love to say yes to you, but we need to get our act together first, and then come back to you when we really can deliver what you really need." It was just easier for us than it was for the salespersons to say it.

Jody Gore ran that business with discipline. He drove the right behavior by focusing on those two or three things that absolutely, positively had to be done in every department. His focus helped us turn that business around within two years.

First, Focus on Getting the Costs Right: Then Take Market Share

At the Honeywell Homes and Building Group, our limit controller for residential and commercial furnaces held a dominant market share (55 percent), but lost money. The prescription: "let's grow our way out of it." We shined the big light on that particular Moose and discovered the futility of that approach. The engineers agreed to reverse-engineer our chief competitor's controller and figure out how to beat their cost month in and month out. Only then did we agree to go after market share.

It wasn't easy. Sales put on strong pressure to make "just this one exception." We kept reminding them of our agreement. We personally called two large customers to tell them, "We're sorry. You're right. We were there and told you we wanted 100 percent of your business. But we're not ready for that right now, because we're not making money on this part. Until we learn to do that, you really don't want us doing it." We took "hallway heat" for months. People whispered, "Holy cow, they've really flipped out this time." But we stuck with the focus.

To make a long story short, within a year we were well under the competitor's cost. In a game played in pennies, we ended up 11 cents below their costs. Then we went out and took market share, big time. That's how the game works: when you're the low-cost manufacturers, market share growth leverages your cost advantage, drives costs down further, and it all drops straight to the bottom line. We would never have gotten there in a million years had we not had the focus and discipline to stick with the priority.

Clarify your important goals and strategies. Get a clear picture of the tomorrow you want to create. Get a clear picture of the migration path from today to tomorrow for all the people with whom you are interdependent. Stay focused on that tomorrow and that migration path. Teach, not decide, so everyone owns that tomorrow and that migration path. Keep gathering evidence of what's working and not working. Focus, teach, gather evidence: important leadership tasks in making resource allocations.

PHOENIX WORKSHOP

ALIGN RESOURCES WITH PRIORITIES

IMPORTANT GOALS AND STRATEGIES	CURRENT RESOURCE ALLOCATIONS ($,TIME)	PREFERRED RESOURCE ALLOCATIONS ($,TIME)

CUSTOMERS SET THE AGENDA

You've heard it before from us. You'll hear it again. It all begins with Customers—with a capital C. Business is about customers, getting them and keeping them for life. Your customers are your best consultants. They'll help you make the best decisions about resource allocation—because they'll tell you exactly what they want you to deliver. Are you listening?

The McDonald's of Computer Companies: Fresh, Hot, Customer-Friendly

Ask Stan Shih, founder and chief executive officer of Acer Computers. He competes in the red-hot, change-in-a-nanosecond personal computer business. He faces a fiercely competitive market that regularly humbles the mighty, like IBM, Apple and Compaq. It is a market where fortunes are won and lost in the blink of an eye. Shih understands the need to say close to customers and deliver what they want, how they want it, right now.

He set his company up like a fast food company: by centralizing component production with close-to-the-customer assembly and immediate delivery. Like McDonald's, which centrally produces hamburger patties and other food components, he centrally produces his computer components in Taiwan. Just like McDonald's, he also does development and marketing centrally. Like McDonald's, he delivers the components to local distributors who assemble and custom-configure them into "hot and fresh" computers made right to a customer's order—including the "mayo" of Office 97, if that's the configuration a customer needs and wants.

Quality is a vital element in both computers and hamburgers. McDonald's maintains its quality through constant inspection and tight control over its franchise system. Acer controls quality—and speed of customer response—by maintaining a financial interest in all of its downstream close-to-the-customer distributors. That financial interest enables Acer to ensure that its customers receive the right computer, configured correctly, in the shortest possible time. Shih realizes that there's a zero tolerance for error in the computer business. One mistake can be one mistake too many. The customer is where it begins and ends for Shih at Acer Computers. That's why he's still in this unforgiving business.

Resuscitating a Giant: The Explosive Power of Attention to Customers

Lou Gerstner faced a huge challenge. He saw it firsthand when his managers couldn't convince the CEOs of twenty customers to meet with him shortly after he took over as IBM's new leader. IBM, who prided itself on its closeness with customers, couldn't find twenty CEOs whose organizations currently bought IBM equipment to meet with their new CEO. They had more important things to do. How low had IBM fallen?

Gerstner has turned it around—by focusing on the customer. Turns out that visiting customers is Gerstner's thing. "I came here with the view that you start the day with customers." He loves to do it. He's good at it. Still spends 40 percent of his time out in the field visiting customers. And it's paid off. When Ameritech Corporation wanted to outsource its computer business, Gerstner was the only CEO actively involved in the sales process. IBM got the job. At Procter & Gamble, Gerstner showed up with his management team to brief P&G executives on electronic commerce opportunities. It was the first time in decades that senior IBM officials visited one of their biggest customers. IBM's deeply involved in P&G's technology planning these days, and will likely get a big piece of whatever P&G buys.

Gerstner not only invested his own time in listening to customers, he modified IBM's spending priorities based on what he heard. He reacted to the customers' complaints about high-priced mainframe software by cutting prices 30 percent. He heard the customers' difficulties integrating complex computer networks, so he spent $743 million to buy Tivoli Systems to improve IBM's system management skills. Customers complained about not seeing the payoff from technology investments, so Gerstner seeded the sales and marketing force with new hires who had extensive background in the industries in which they sell, and retrained the sales force to raise their industry knowledge.

Gerstner was roundly criticized when early in his tenure he was quoted as saying, "The last thing IBM needs now is a new vision." He had it absolutely correct, though. IBM didn't need a "new vision." What it needed was to return to its old customer-focused vision.

Lou Gerstner redirected the giant's resources, beginning with his own time, and created one of the outstanding success stories of the mid-1990s. With the stock triple its low before he took over, he's made himself and a lot of investors very happy.

Win the Worship of Your Toughest Customer

Everything's running just fine. You've got great products. Customers just love them. You've got good margins. The stock price keeps rising. Heads snap as you walk across a room. Everyone wants to meet you and work for you. The best of times? Watch out. Success is the enemy. Those same customers that love you today may find a new love tomorrow. Customers are notoriously fickle. Some sexy new product comes along—and they're gone. We've learned the hard way: maintain peripheral vision at all times. How? Cultivate your most demanding leading-edge customers. They'll keep you honest.

We were relatively new in the hazardous-waste-handling business at the time. Tough business. Lots of government regulations. Several stiff competitors. Many demanding customers. One customer in particular was known in the trade as a tough cookie. They were always demanding better than government minimums, shortened delivery cycles, incessantly beating on prices, insisting upon perfect execution. They chewed up two of our competitors. They approached us, asking if we wanted to do business with them, as they were getting ready to make a move.

Not many people in the organization were anxious to take them on. They were afraid that we'd work like blazes and never make a dime. But they were the big bully in their segment of the business. Lots of other, smaller firms followed their lead. If we could crack them, we could win a big slug of market share. We decided to follow the Nike slogan and "Just Do It!"

Told them we didn't want a contract. That stopped them in their tracks. Instead, we wanted a business partnership. We'd handle their hazardous toxins at cost, if they'd agree to sharing the savings from lowering the costs of handling and disposal. They couldn't believe their ears. The CFO asked incredulously, "You mean to tell me that you're willing to handle our wastes for cost and take your profits out of any savings?"

"That's right," we replied. "We know of many ways to improve performance and we're willing to gamble on our ability to do that. We want only one small agreement on your side. You need to be willing to cooperate to allow us to do what we know must be done. There'll be no contract, and either side can cancel on sixty days' notice. If it doesn't work for both of us, it won't work for either of us."

"Done," he said, smiling, counting the immediate savings to his bottom line.

"Great," we said, smiling also, figuring that this was our big opportunity. We'd never signed a performance contract like that before. We'd always pitched performance payments, and actually gotten them in some places, but most firms were reluctant to take on partners. We didn't sleep well for the first several months, wondering if things were really going to work out.

The contract worked out in spades. We lowered handling costs 50 percent within six months, reduced the amount of toxins they processed by more than 40 percent. Made more money on that deal that year than on any other in our organization. More important, we demonstrated our ability to a large segment of an industry and more than doubled our market share in a year. And the important lesson? Corral the market leader and the rest fall like dominos. The other lesson: Hang out with the best and most demanding customers to stay on top of your industry.

Touch the Body, Touch the Soul and Build a Business

Bonnie is our massage therapist, one of the best we know. She's also struggled to make ends meet because of lots of competitors, hard-to-find customers and lots of traveling (Bonnie does at-home massages). Figuring that we know something about business, she asked us one day for advice.

"Who are your customers and why do they use you rather than any one of the hundreds of other massage therapists out there?"

Bonnie thought for a while and replied, "I'm practiced in Oriental massage. It's the most relaxing and therapeutic kind. Also, I do more than massage. The music, the conversation—all contribute to a total cleansing experience. I help people move through the difficult times in their lives. Also, I do a lot of movement work, helping groups of people loosen up and feel better about themselves. I really help heal the soul as well as the body."

We nodded, recalling Bonnie's knowing, caring hands and thoughts. "How do you find customers?"

"It's random," she responded. "Many come from the exercise classes I do at various gyms. I get some referrals. I tried advertising in the holistic magazines, but that didn't work. I just don't really know how to get customers. This is my problem. People love me when they use me. But how do I get more people to use me? My dance card is pretty lonely."

"Ever thought of talking to your customers, like you're talking to us now? Maybe enlist their assistance in finding you more folks like themselves?"

"Great idea," she said. "I'll do it and tell you how it works."

Before long, Bonnie's business boomed. Customers gladly referred their friends, particularly since Bonnie rewarded them with a free massage. She also deepened her soul connection with her customers, finding that many valued that part of the experience. She went back to school and took several counseling courses to sharpen her listening skills. Bonnie's calendar is now bulging. We have to make reservations weeks in advance. Having her customers set her priorities paid off for Bonnie.

Lou Gerstner is right, the day begins with customers, ends with customers, and it's customers, customers, customers the whole day long. Spend your time and your resources finding out what the best and most demanding of your customers really wants, and keep delivering it to them in spades. There's no better utilization of your time and other resources than that.

PHOENIX WORKSHOP

THE CUSTOMER'S AGENDA

LIST THE BEST (AS INDICATED BY A +) AND MOST DEMANDING (AS INDICATED BY A*) CUSTOMERS	WHAT DO THEY WANT/ DEMAND FROM ME TODAY?	WHAT WILL THEY WANT/DEMAND FROM ME IN THE FUTURE?
_____	_____	_____
_____	_____	_____
_____	_____	_____

SET PRIORITIES CLOSE TO YOUR CUSTOMERS—WITH YOUR VISION AND MISSION FLAGS FLYING HIGH

A Revolutionary Concept Imported from China: Let Those Closest to the Work Take Initiative

Think you work in a big organization? Consider working in the government of the People's Republic of China, particularly in the countryside, where three quarters of China's 1.2 billion people live. The November 2, 1996, issue of *The Economist* reports an amazing revolution taking place in China's countryside these days: it's called determining priorities at the local level . . . or, democracy. By the end of 1997, more than 95 percent of all 900,000 villages in China will have leaders elected by secret, popular vote. It's the world's largest experiment in setting priorities at the local level.

It's not that the leaders in Beijing are suddenly becoming democratic, because they're clearly not. But as one of the bureaucrats said, "Villagers have a much better notion of village talent than the higher authorities." China desperately needs to tap that local talent to improve both the productivity and the economic lot of its rural population.

Economic growth, spurred by returning farms to private family holdings in the late 1970s, leveled off in the last few years, putting more pressure on central and provincial leaders to do something. But, in truth, as the bureaucrat said, "It is impossible for the central government to do much. And the provincial government isn't of much help either." The villagers must learn to look after themselves. Hence the decision to devolve responsibility for economic development to the democratically elected village officials.

Sounds familiar, doesn't it? That thought is sprinkled throughout this book. Same theme: get the folks closest to the action to take responsibility for fixing things. Different language, perhaps, but that's all. China hopes for the same outcome: improved performance.

Vision and Values Power Resource Allocation

Imagine the president of the company saying, "We do worry about the shareholders, but we try to think of our values first." Are we standing in Tiananmen Square, Beijing? No, we're halfway around the world, in the rolling hills of Virginia, and the speaker is not Chairman Mao, but Dennis Bakke, president and co-founder of AES Corporation, a publicly traded electric power generating and distribution company. He and co-founder Roger Sant lead an organization that consistently makes decisions at the lowest possible level in the organization, decisions made with AES's vision/mission flags flying. Their story was reported in the March 1995 *CFO* and the July 3, 1995, issue of the *Wall Street Journal.*

AES's direction is best expressed in their values:

Integrity (AES acts with integrity, or "wholeness");

Fairness (AES treats fairly its people, its customers, its suppliers, its stockholders, the government and the communities in which it operates);

Fun (AES wants people to have fun in their work; their goal has been to create an environment in which each person can flourish in the use of his or her gifts and skills and thereby enjoy the time spent at AES); and

Social responsibility (AES involves itself in projects that provide social benefits, such as lower costs to customers, a high degree of safety and reliability, increased employment and a cleaner environment).

Everyone lives by these values and uses them to make daily decisions.

Typical central-office-type functions, like project financing, operations, purchasing or human resources, are handled by plant workers. There's no company treasurer. Instead, employees like Jeff Hatch, a materials handling technician, work as part of a three-person team investing the company's $33 million investment fund. There are no plant comptrollers. Rick Geiler, a storeroom employee, works as part of a five-person team that puts together the power plant's operating budget. A rotating team of cross-trained employees handles internal auditing functions, keeping their eyes and ears open for signs of trouble.

Rather than leave recruiting and applicant screening to human resources, teams of a dozen or more workers, ranging from welders to accountants, interview and select new employees. AES also takes seriously its value of social responsibility. A team of plant workers at the Montville generating plant decided that the best way to create a cleaner environment was to plant trees that offset the carbon dioxide emissions from the plant. So in the late 1980s they donated $2 million to CARE to plant more than 50 million trees in Guatemala. That contribution represented the company's entire annual profits that year.

To ensure fairness all company books are open to everyone. There are no secret files, except for personnel information. As a result, all employees are considered insiders by the SEC.

Making low-level decisions that fly the vision/mission flags pays off for AES. The company has grown at the average annual compound rate of 23 percent a year since its founding fifteen years ago. It's increased its bottom line sixfold since 1990. It now operates in ten countries and employs more than 1,500 people. This approach pays off for many other organizations as well.

Salvation Army Interiors Enable Designer Customer Solutions

One of our organizations glories in its policy, "Never, ever, ever buy anything new." Does it sound strange—particularly since it's the employees who decided upon that policy? Not really. Their vision—creating success for everyone—focuses us outward toward the teammates, customers, suppliers and communities we serve. As one of the team members put it, "Can't see how a fancy, high-dollar desk creates success for any of my customers or a single kid in my community. I sure don't need it, since I'm not at it very often. Some old, beat-up, secondhand desk with character works fine for me."

Everyone flies coach, stays at Motel 6 and rents subcompacts. Again, fancy hotels and big cars don't help customers win. People know that—those who are close to the customer. Maybe, just maybe, the reward system has something to do with this seemingly aberrant behavior. Everyone works on a 50/50 profit sharing plan, where half of the net margins are shared with the team.

That means that 50 cents of every $1 spent on fancy desks and first-class air fare comes out of the teammates' pockets.

Given the choice, teammates choose to keep the cash and make do with Salvation Army furnishings. They make decisions that fly the vision/mission flags. In the next part of this book we'll look in greater detail at how the objective-measurement reward system indelibly shapes those choices.

Kids, Kids, Kids: What's the Matter with Kids Today?

That line from the Broadway musical *Bye Bye Birdie* runs through our heads when we think about raising children. It's difficult to get children to think longer term than the next minute and a half. Trying to get teenagers to think about the consequences of their nonstudying, irresponsible behavior is like trying to climb a sheer glass wall with slippery sneakers: it's impossible—or so it seems. Moreover, other parents' kids always seem to be smarter, more committed and better behaved than ours. Makes us wonder, "How do they get their kids to behave that way? Did we miss it at PET (Parent Effectiveness Training)?"

While it's far from perfect, we've found that weekly family discussions help keep kids—and parents—reminded about our mutual commitment. Every week we talk about what we've accomplished toward our objectives. We also share the week's errors and dropped passes, things we didn't accomplish that we said we would. We take the time to acknowledge ourselves and each other for the actions that supported our values of which we're particularly proud. Everyone has chores, and we review how everyone's done on their list. Leadership of the family group rotates every week, with every member from age ten on up taking a turn.

As we said, it isn't perfect. There are still kids' toys in the living room, the music is still too loud, the dishes still pile up in the sink and the trash baskets still don't get emptied. But last week our grandson offered his $500 savings account—his life's savings—to a family friend who got socked with an unexpected $800 tax bill that he couldn't pay. Wow. Talk about unselfish. Maybe, just maybe, all those household conferences really do pay off.

People will not always automatically know how to make decisions that reflect the vision/mission. In fact, most folks will show up at the organization's door and *not* know how to do it, having been well trained in other organizations *not* to make decisions at all but to pass them off to somebody else. Your job: teach and train people to use vision, mission, values and goals to make decisions.

Getting people throughout the organization to live, live, live the vision, mission and values really pays off. Ask the folks at AES, one of the 900 million farmers in China or . . . members of our families.

PHOENIX WORKSHOP

WHO MAKES THE RESOURCE PRIORITIZATION DECISIONS?

MY MOST IMPORTANT DECISIONS ABOUT RESOURCE ALLOCATION	WHAT IS THE RELATIONSHIP OF THIS DECISION TO MY VISION?	WHO NOW MAKES/ SHOULD MAKE THE PRIORITIZATION DECISION?
_____	_____	_____
_____	_____	_____
_____	_____	_____
_____	_____	_____

LEVERAGE YOUR MOST PRECIOUS RESOURCE: PEOPLE'S LEARNING

Numbers, numbers, numbers. That's all people talk about these days. Profit margins, growth rates, market share. If it moves, people measure it. If they measure it, they report it. If they report it, someone looks at it and makes future projections based on it. Call it economic numerology.

With all the focus on numbers, it's easy to lose sight of what drives the numbers. It's people who create the numbers, make them appear, as if by magic, on income statements. It's people who produce boxes that go on shelves. It's people who move boxes from shelf to shelf. It's people who move boxes off shelves.

It's people first, second, third and always. Great people make great organizations—the great numbers follow.

Want a great organization? Get or create great people. It's as simple as that.

Always keep the priorities straight. When rationing scarce resources it's people first, second and third. Cut training and you limit your future. Cut hiring of new blood and you flash-freeze the organization in the past. Create tomorrow—and invest in people—because only people will take you there!

Big Events, Big Results: Grow the Business by Growing People

XBS (Xerox Business Systems) is growing rapidly: from 3,000 people in 1981 to 15,000 in 1995 to an anticipated 30,000 in 2000; from $1 billion in 1995 to $2 billion in 1997 to a projected $5 billion in 1999. How do you grow a business so rapidly? Answer: as described in the October–November 1996 issue of *Fast Company*, by growing people first.

Chris Turner is XBS's "learning person," responsible for helping 15,000 XBSers, located at more than 20,000 customer sites, continue to grow themselves and the business. Her challenge: help people be expert in the businesses they serve, learn from each other and develop their own unique set of skills. Her goal: "create a community of inquirers and learners."

Her strategy: big learning events for 400 people, a network of smaller thirty-person subgroups, drawn from the 400, to continue to spread the learning throughout the organization, an annual four-day Camp Lur'ning for 300 (which increases to over 1,000 as the campers set up local Camp Lur'nings) and three learning centers that offer continuing education options.

Chris points out that every manager has a choice to either be the last of the old generation of managers or the first of the new generation. She's determined that she and all other XBS managers will be the first of the new breed, not the last of the old. Right on, Chris.

Develop the Explosive Power of People or Watch Your Organization Implode

XBS, like most organizations, is not without lots of strong competitors. Lots of companies offer supplies and equipment, just like XBS. What distinguishes XBS? It's people. People are the only sustainable competitive edge.

You think computer chips are powerful? Look at your people—specifically, the brains they bring to work every day. Dr. Ralph Merkle of Xerox Palo Alta Research Center has shown that the human brain stores about 10 to the 18th power bits of information—or a billion billion bits. The brain processes these bits at 10 to the 16th power bits per second. A chip to replace the human brain today would be the size of an office building.

Datamation in its February 15, 1994, issue reports that the human memory is a huge database that operates at the speed of light. Learn to harness and direct the astonishing power of people. That's the real source of unstoppable, unbeatable nuclear energy. It's also a true test of your leadership.

Develop Everyone to Be a Chief Financial Officer and Help Manage the Bottom Line

The first learning challenge is to know your own business well enough to run it. After all, not only are you the CEO of your business, you're also the CFO. CFOs make important financial decisions on such matters as pricing, buying and investments. At XBS everyone goes through profit-and-loss training, in order to understand what drives profitability for an account. In the past, the question was, "Do you need to know the financial data?" Now everyone needs to know, and to be able to interpret and use the financial data to make decisions.

Close friend Ralph Stayer, CEO of Johnsonville Foods, trains all his "members" in reading and understanding financial statements. After all, teams of plant members make purchasing and investment decisions. Teams of sales members manage their own inventory and selling expenses. Everyone at Johnsonville needs to understand financial flow and how the business works, so they can do a better job of serving their customers.

At AES, the energy company we discussed earlier in this chapter, plant employees plan budgets, do internal auditing, manage the investment pool and raise investment capital for building projects. All employees go through an extensive training program in financial analysis, supplemented by monthly review meetings.

Teach everyone to be an "insider," knowing how and where the business makes, and loses, money. Develop everyone to be the CFO and manage the organization's and their own bottom line.

Develop People to Know the Customer's Business Better than They Know It Themselves

We work hard to amaze our customers with our knowledge of their business. In every contact we strive to leave our customers with one piece of new insight or information. We count our successes in the "Gee whiz, we didn't know that! How did you find out?" comments.

XBS works hard to understand their customers. At the Boeing account, for instance, XBSers work right alongside Boeing employees in designing and building aircraft. At a major law firm, Chris Turner won a significant piece of business for her company. Her presentation had little to do with the equipment and supplies XBS would provide. Instead, she researched the law firm and discovered that they faced significant change issues. So her presentation was all about how XBS was building a "learning community" in order to stay ahead of change. The law firm decided to buy from XBS so they could learn from Chris how to build a learning community of their own. Chris's knowledge of the customer won the business.

The December 9, 1996 issue of *Business Week* reports how Lou Gerstner at IBM is building a customer-knowledgeable sales force. He recognizes that knowledge of the customer's business is the price of admission into the playing field these days in computer sales. To fill that gap, he's both hiring newcomers who already possess such knowledge as well as providing extensive education about the industries in which they sell to the current staff. For instance, he hired Sean Rush to run the higher-education unit. Rush came from twelve years heading up Coopers & Lybrand's higher-ed practice. One university president said, "Rush knows as much about running this institution as I do." He may even buy from IBM now, even though he had a bad experience with them several years ago.

As someone once said, "Knock your customers' socks off" with your knowledge of their business. That's the way to get them to trust you with their business.

Get 5,000 Cutting-Edge Thinkers and Doers Working on Your Customer's Problem

One of our businesses employs more than 5,000 people, operating in every time zone on the planet. Most of these folks work at the customer's site, so we're virtually a virtual organization. How do you get a person in Singapore to know that a person in Frankfurt has just the expertise she needs to solve her customer's problem? That's our challenge. In the best of all worlds you want to bring the full force and talent of the entire organization to bear to solve every single customer's problem. To most ordinary people that sounds like an impossible task.

Not so for these folks. They've built a "Knowledge Center," a software program that includes, among other features, a Personnel Information System, which lists each person's skills and areas of expertise. For instance, here's one partial profile:

Frances Kao - Singapore

Education   - electrical engineer (microelectronics) and
               MBA
Experience   - 4½ years—electrical engineer in chip design
               and fab
             - 4 years—ran chip fabrication plant in Thailand
             - 3 years—independent chip fabrication plant
               and equipment designer
Skills   - chip fabrication manufacturing processes for
               both silicon and gallium arsenide [including a

list of twenty-two processes with which the
employee is familiar]

- chip fabrication plant design and construction, including all utilities and services
- chip fabrication equipment design and construction [a list of seventeen different kinds of equipment]
- familiar with industry applications for chips [she listed fourteen industries]

Languages - Chinese (several dialects), Thai, most common Indo dialects, Malay, German, Spanish, Farsi

Experience - [She listed here all her assignments in the company along with a contact person for further information.]

This data is then indexed by skill and language, so that anyone looking for a person skilled in fab etching processes would look up "fab etching" and surface everyone in the organization who knew something about it. Knowing who can help you do almost anything a customer needs is only a few keystrokes away.

In addition, there are ongoing electronic conferences and chat activities in each technical specialty. People dial in all over the world, at any time of the day or night, and share their latest insights and experiences. Each month a team of experts in each specialty summarizes the learnings from the month's chats and posts it in the Knowledge Center. This helps every person with that technical specialty keep his or her knowledge fresh and new.

The Knowledge Center also invites technical experts from outside the company to participate in chats and contribute their latest papers. In many technical areas the teams have developed a reputation that attracts the leading thinkers to participate and contribute.

Our Knowledge Center is a combination of approaches used by Bell Labs and Hewlett-Packard. Bell Labs does weekly brown bag lunches where individuals come together to share and learn. Hewlett-Packard leaves work on the desk so engineers passing by can share ideas.

Being able to harness the talents of many people and learn from the best in their field is one of the biggest advantages of being part of a large organization. Work hard to make that advantage real for everyone.

Develop Each Person's Individual Skill Set

Each person in the organization needs a different skill set to best help their customers win.

Jose needs coaching skills, for instance, and Brad needs setup skills for the Cincinnati milling machine. Each person needs to identify the skills he or she needs—and then develop a plan to develop them.

Each person completes a semiannual learning plan with their teammates and customers. That plan specifies the skills they intend to develop, the development plan and the measures for delivery of that plan. We take learning seriously. Access to the bonus pool is conditioned upon successful completion of this plan. There's just not room in any of our businesses for people who aren't learning and growing.

On the following page is a sample of a learning plan developed by Michelle Garre, a financial analyst partner in the Barcelona, Spain, office. Note how she's working to improve her basic financial management skills by learning more about currency transfers, upgrade her financial skills by becoming the cash flow expert for the entire company, develop a new skill (benchmarking, making comparisons of business processes and performance between organizations), and work more closely with her customer service partners helping to create success for customers.

Our approach is no different than the one utilized by George Fisher at Kodak, as reported by Linda Grant in *Fortune*'s January 13, 1997, issue.

Fisher recognized the need to redefine the social contract with his cutback-ravaged folks. He offered a minimum of forty hours of training to meet each employee's specific developmental goals, in return for employees agreeing to give 100 percent of their effort to better understand both Kodak's business and their customer's business and be willing to adapt and change. To make certain that the learning really happens, Fisher made part of the managers' bonuses conditional upon the employees achieving their development plans.

Learning Plan

MICHELLE GARRE   SIX MONTHS ENDING: June 1996

Partner—financial analyst

SKILLS/ KNOWLEDGE TO MASTER	ACTIONS/TIME FRAME	MEASURE
ACQUIRE KNOWLEDGE OF CURRENCY TRANSFER REGULATIONS IN CHILE, ARGENTINA, BRAZIL, PERU AND COLOMBIA.	-2/96: LOCATE BOOKS/ COURSES/EXPERTS IN CURRENCY TRANSFERS. -COMPLETE 6/96.	-PARTNERS CALL ME FOR EXPERT ADVICE. -WE NO LONGER USE TRANSFER CONSUL- TANTS.
DEVELOP AND TEACH CASH FLOW AS A MEASUREMENT TOOL TO ALL PARTNERS, SO THEY CAN TEACH IT AND USE IT WITH THEIR CUSTOMERS.	-LEARN CONCEPT BY 3/96. -DEVELOP PARTNER EDUCATION PLAN 3/15/96. GET APPROVED BY 4/14/96.	-EACH PARTNER IS USING THE CONCEPT TO MANAGE THEIR OWN BUSINESS AND HAS AT LEAST ONE CUSTOMER USING IT AS WELL.
BECOME THE LOCAL BENCHMARKING EXPERT.	-LEARN THE BENCH- MARKING PROCESS FROM AT&T AND AQP BY 4/96. -ESTABLISH COACHING RELATIONSHIPS WITH AT LEAST TWO BENCHMARKING EXECUTIVES BY 3/96.	-SECURE AT LEAST TWO BENCHMARKING PROJECTS WITH CUSTOMERS. (TBC IN SECOND HALF OF '96) -OTHER BENCHMARK- ING EXECUTIVES VALUE MY ADVICE.

Go Ahead, Get Personal: Support Individual as Well as Career Development

People don't only live to eat, sleep, breathe, work and make a living. They work to create a meaningful life. Help people do that by supporting their personal and career development, even if it doesn't directly contribute to the current job assignment. We talked about the heart connection. Here it is. Michelle is more than a financial analyst. She's also a mother, an opera devotee and a devout Catholic. Her development plan follows. Sounds like a lot of time devoted to learning, doesn't it? It is a lot of time. But Michelle works a full schedule and has a very active family and community life. She says, "I need to spend more time in learning, developing myself." If you think education is expensive, try the price of ignorance. By the way, it's just as important that she learn to live her life as well as she learns to do her job. So completion of this development plan is also a precondition for access to the bonus pool.

Development Plan

MICHELLE GARRE   SIX MONTHS ENDING: June 1996

Partner—financial analyst

KNOWLEDGE TO MASTER	ACTIONS/TIME FRAME	MEASURE
LEARN PARENT EFFECTIVENESS TRAINING SKILLS TO TEACH OTHER PARENTS IN MY CHURCH PARENT SUPPORT GROUP.	-TAKE TEACHER TRAINING COURSE BY 1/96. -TEACH AT LEAST TWO FULL COURSES BY 6/96.	-MY OWN PARENTING SKILLS IMPROVE (THE BEST WAY TO LEARN IS TO TEACH). -THE PARENTS IN THE CLASS REPORT HOW THEY'VE IMPROVED THEIR PARENTING SKILLS IN FOLLOW-UP SESSIONS.
PARTICIPATE IN ONE OPERA AS A MEMBER OF THE CHORUS. CONTINUE TO DEVELOP MY VOICE RANGE.	-CONTINUE TWICE-WEEKLY VOICE LESSONS ADDING AT LEAST ONE NEW HIGH NOTE TO MY RANGE.	-LAND A CHORUS ROLE IN ONE OF THE TWO OPERAS THIS SEASON. -INDEPENDENT VOICE APPRAISAL REPORTS PROGRESS FROM LAST YEAR AND ADDITION OF TWO NOTES TO RANGE.
LEAD A SUCCESSFUL WEDNESDAY PRE-SCHOOL BIBLE PROGRAM FOR OUR CHURCH.	-DEVELOP PRESCHOOL BIBLE CURRICULUM WITH FATHER JOSE AND SISTER MARIA BY 2/96. -RECRUIT AND ORIENT TEACHERS FOR THE PROGRAM (I PLAN TO COVER TWO OF THE SESSIONS MYSELF) BY 3/96. -CONDUCT THE FIRST SERIES, FINISHING BY 6/96.	-FATHER JOSE AND SISTER MARIA APPROVE THE PRO-GRAM. -WE HAVE TO TURN AWAY QUALIFIED TEACHERS. -THE KIDS LOVE THE PROGRAM,WANT TO SIGN UP AGAIN, AND WE HAVE OVEREN-ROLLMENT FOR THE NEXT SERIES.

Learning is such an important issue that we devote an entire chapter to it. The key point here: great people make great organizations and training helps great people become great. That's why learning is a major priority investment.

RECALL SOLOMON—A LOT IS RIDING ON THE BABY

The biblical King Solomon built magnificent cities, a colossal temple, and reigned over a lasting peace while amassing unbelievable economic resources that benefited the citizens of a great national organization. But his reputation was launched with one momentous and highly publicized decision: a dispute over a baby. Remember how Solomon resolved the dispute between two mothers who each claimed the same baby? He had to make a difficult, highly public choice. He worked to find out who the real mother of the baby was, so he could decide in favor of that mother. He surfaced the facts by threatening to kill the baby, thus encouraging the real mother to give up the child rather than see it die.

Solomon surfaced faces and used them to make a prioritization decision.

Make no mistake, the buck stops at our desks. Just like King Solomon, there are times when we must make the monumental, high-visibility decision. Not often, but how we do it influences many future actions.

The water is clearest at the top of the aquarium. Everyone else can see what the few folks at the top decide and how they decided it. There are times when you must play Solomon. The job requires it. Your responsibility to the other interdependent and interconnected people requires it. Exercise your wisdom so that the baby survives. Remember, the king who killed babies was Herod—who died defeated, hated and insane. Be a wise and respected Solomon. Everything is riding on what you do about that baby in front of you—whether it's one person or a whole organization.

Solomon Plays the Leading Role but Also Knows When to Co-Star

Earlier in this chapter we reported how we took the highly un-usual action of requiring our personal approval for all expendi-tures over $100,000. We did that to send a message, to make a point that we were serious about focusing everyone's effort on re-ducing costs in the power equipment business. We modeled the behavior we wanted from everyone else: an extraordinary focus on the power equipment product line.

In another setting, we did just the opposite. We said, "We never want to see anything unless it meets one of two criteria: the issue has to go to the board and as chairman it needs my approval, or one of you has to come in and talk about it because you are not feeling comfortable." That one statement, and backing it up with consistent action, changed the whole mind-set right away. We replaced a very top-down, want-to-be-involved-in-everything leader. Our style is 180 degrees from his. So it took a lot of get-ting used to by the other officers.

Now our president comes in probably five times a month with: "This is a big one. Here's what I'm thinking. Let's kick it around." He's approved three of them and sent two back for more facts-are-our-friends evidence. Make no mistake, though. He knows he's accountable: he knows it and loves it.

That same pattern is now cascading throughout the organiza-tion. The drill now is, "I know it's my responsibility, but I'm feel-ing a little uncomfortable. Can we talk?" Everyone knows that you can talk to your coach, your coach's coach or us. Just call if you want to bounce it around.

But at the end of the day, you will make the decision. Our role modeling of the let's-talk-but-you-decide behavior set the pattern and standard for everyone.

The Solemn Solomon Vow: Seek Out Truth, Act on Evidence

We learned that there's one key leverage point we have when mov-ing into a new organization: the approval list. That's one place we get down into the details and go into it with the rest of the staff. Set-ting approval levels sends clear messages. Tell people who manage multimillion-dollar facilities that they can only approve $10,000 in expenditures, and you send an unmistakable "we don't trust you" message. Give your people an approval level based on either standard guidelines or preapproved projects (rather than dollar limits) and you send a very different "you are responsible" message.

We happened upon the president and CFO working on the approval policy one night about 7:30. They immediately began to play the answer-in-back-of-the-book game, assuming that we had the answer and their job was to try to wheedle it out of us. They were working on the director approval levels. These are the 126 top people in the $15 billion company.

We volleyed for about twenty minutes, until they realized that we didn't have a predetermined answer and were deadly serious about them coming up with the recommendation. We just kept asking questions, searching for evidence. Within an hour they had an answer that they were comfortable with, and one that we felt good about as well. We kept the focus on facts and evidence. They stewed, thrashed and wrestled with the difficult issue. At the end the recommendation wasn't, "This is what the boss wants," but, "This is what we think it should be."

We did the tough, tenacious fact finding. We let them make the decision.

Our Solomon vow: keep asking the tough questions; keep searching out the little known facts; keep everyone focused on the evidence in the case, not opinion; and use these facts to make the decision.

THEY WON'T BUILD TOMORROW WITH CARDBOARD AND TAPE—PROVIDE THE TOOLS

As a Phoenix leader you need the right tools to allocate resources. On the following pages we'll review some of the principal tools you might use.

Give People the Best Information or Watch Margins Swirl Down the Drain

We decentralized at one organization and gave the account teams responsibility to make pricing decisions. It was not a good move, we discovered. Why? The teams lacked a basic tool—complete and accurate information upon which to make sound pricing decisions. Good people wanted to make good decisions, but they were frustrated by their lack of a supporting information infrastructure.

The teams had access to internal transfer prices from manufacturing and some data about direct selling expenses. But they had no access to any of the indirect selling costs, like technical support. Turned out that manufacturing's transfer prices were too low to cover all of their full-stream costs, including research and development and downstream product support. And there was no mechanism to track per customer costs for indirect selling expenses like technical services. So the teams flew blind. They were good people, well intentioned—but they couldn't do the job they so desperately wanted to do.

They learned their lesson, though. If you visit their telesales people today, they can tell you by product, by hour, their cost, their margins and average margins for the day, both for their products and their competitors' products.

People need the facts—the evidence—complete and accurate information—to make good decisions. Build the information tools that get the facts to everyone who needs to make those good decisions. They'll realize how precious those resources are—and act more effectively.

Pay People Right for the Right Decisions

We'll talk in greater depth later about the objective-measure reward systems that are so essential to success. In one situation, we thought we'd handled the objective-measure reward issues. We paid the teams on margin, thinking that would work. We never realized that there were seventeen different definitions of "margin" in the company, none of which represented full-stream costs. The teams spent more of their time negotiating internally about cost charges than they did externally serving their customers. The compensation system caused the team structure to crash and burn.

We've put this experience to good use elsewhere. We talked to a Japanese company last week about how we manage inventory, and explained that we do it by paying purchasing people based on fill rates, days of owned inventory and accounts payable. The goal is zero days inventory owned, 98.2 percent fill rate and fifty-seven days payable. The Japanese were surprised that we didn't pay purchasing people for inventory turns or amount saved on purchased parts over last year.

Given the strong information infrastructure, the purchasing person can balance at every order decision point the three factors—owned inventory, fill rates and amount owed that vendor. That enables us to take advantage of buying opportunities that produce immediate revenue and turn our inventory faster, getting us better overall margins. The purchasing folks get rewarded then, for directly contributing to both our customer delight and our earnings goals.

Furthermore, not paying purchasing people for beating suppliers down on price encourages more supplier partnerships. Paying folks to wring the last penny out in price reductions is just not conducive to forming productive partnerships. You can talk about supplier partnerships until you're blue in the face. Until you change the objective-measure reward system for purchasing people, you just won't get it.

The right objective-measurement reward system will help allocate resources to the priority strategic issues confronting the organization. The wrong objective-measurement reward system will ruin your day. Chapter 11 will lay out "right" and "wrong" systems in greater detail.

Just remember that when you give people small parts to manage and pay them for managing those small parts, they will manage the heck out of those parts and not only forget about the whole, but likely damage it as well. Reward people for strategically effective decisions and behavior.

Training Is the Ultimate Tool Because
Competency Is the Ultimate Weapon

Training isn't an expense, it's an investment. It's the best investment you can make in your future. Ask Bob Galvin at Motorola.
About twenty years ago he set up Motorola University. He said,
"We're going to spend X on this university training our people in
quality, strategy and other vital skills that will help us succeed in
the future. I don't care what kind of year we're having. I don't care
what's going on in the marketplace or in our company. We will
spend X per year teaching these important topics." The folks at
Motorola have stuck to Bob Galvin's injunction, and it's helped
them immeasurably.

Unfortunately, too many training and development dollars are
not spent as wisely. In fact, most T&D investments are wasted because they aren't focused around either specific individual development needs or organizational needs. Focus T&D expenditures
by specifying behavioral outcomes the organization needs and
can accomplish given available resources. Within that context
help people make decisions about the specific development they
believe is important for them. It's another example of focused discipline and the heart connection.

PHOENIX WORKSHOP

1. HOW CAN I GET PEOPLE THE RIGHT TOOLS—THE
INFORMATION, SYSTEMS AND TRAINING THEY NEED TO MAKE
THE PRIORITIZING DECISIONS?

_____

_____

_____

_____

Summary: A Tale of Two Leaders

John's Experience: All the King's Horses and All the King's Men

It's not easy being a leader. There are lots of casualties. Ask John. He led one of the world's largest companies. He learned that leadership is more than expensive Italian suits, fast private jets, chauffeured limos at 7:00 A.M. to the office every day, a ballroom-sized office and endless meetings. We know John very well. We were personal friends, even godparents to one of his children. We talked frequently during his difficult times. He saw what needed to be done. His company had drifted. Spoiled by success, it had become inward-dwelling and disconnected from its customers. John knew that. He just didn't know how to fix it.

He spent his days and nights in meetings, almost all with his senior staff. They endlessly debated program options and approaches. His wife complained that he worked harder now than ever before in his life. "Give it up and go back to selling," she'd often tell him when he came through the door at 10:00 in the evening after another fifteen-hour day. But John wasn't a quitter. He had to see it through.

John wrote memos, held meetings, ordered the Year of the Customer, put 15 percent more people on the street to get in front of those customers, and launched three major culture change programs. Yet somehow he could never get sufficient resources devoted to make any of his programs work.

John was stuck. When the first set of meetings didn't work, he held a second, longer round. When they didn't work he tried a third even longer round. He moved the meetings to other sites, away from headquarters, hoping that that would change the outcome. It didn't. The same old people in a different geographic setting were still the same old people. There were still the same old debates, the same old arguments, the same old promises and the same old less-than-satisfactory results.

To us outsiders the problems were obvious. John had risen through the hierarchy, moved through the chairs. He believed he had to work through the established order. So he rarely if ever dealt directly with associates. "We have to preserve the chain of command, or else we'll lose direction and focus," he said frequently. And the same restriction kept him from visiting customers. He likely visited fewer than ten customers during his seven years in office—except, of course, for the high-level social/political contacts during U.S. Chamber of Commerce Executive Round Table meetings or company-sponsored golf tournaments. Again, John said, "I don't want to send mixed messages to either the sales force or the customers. The sales force needs to maintain that relationship with the customer. I don't want to muddy up the waters with my presence."

John also knew all the folks in his senior staff and had risen with them. He just couldn't confront them over their consistently poor performance. One person in particular ran one of the biggest pieces of the company and hadn't shown a profit in years. John couldn't bring himself to move the person, always hoping things would get better as promised.

Nothing seemed to stem the tide. Vicious e-mails circulated throughout the company that found their way into the public press. Sales continued to grow, but at a slower rate, and margins continued to decline. Finally, the market gave up on John's stewardship, wiping out more than 80 percent of the company's market value. The board couldn't take it anymore either and asked John to leave.

Staring out the window of his comfortable home, John knows now he should have personally reached beyond his office into the laboratories, sales offices and factories of his former company. He knows that he spent too much time in meetings and not enough time with customers. He knows that he needed to confront those poor performers and make certain that the resources were allocated to fund the important priorities.

"It's like turning around a huge ocean liner in a narrow canal. It takes lots of time and lots of resources. I could never get all the noses in the same direction, singing off the same hymn sheet, spending their money on the same priorities. It was tough, real tough."

Camilla's Experience: Cinderella to City Council

Camilla worked hard, long hours as a waitress. She had two kids, no husband and a burning desire to make something of herself, so that her two daughters wouldn't end up like her. She wanted to go to college and become a lawyer. For a high school dropout that's a noble, and seemingly impossible, dream. But not for Camilla.

She often took her youngsters to night school with her, getting her high school equivalency diploma. Taking four classes a term, summer and winter sessions, she got through college in six years. Neighbors, friends and family baby-sat the kids. Camilla worked her network of interconnected, interdependent people, trading baby-sitting for special meals (Camilla was a great cook) or outings for neighborhood kids. For instance, Camilla took all the neighborhood kids to the park during the Super Bowl, allowing the other moms and dads to enjoy the game without interruption.

Camilla quit her waitressing job, and took a law clerk's position with a large law firm. Working her network magic again, she convinced them to help her go to law school, paying part of the tuition and arranging her hours to permit time off to go to school. By now the kids were old enough that they attended many classes with Camilla, thus easing the baby-sitting burden. They got to be real good at doing their homework during Mom's classes.

Camilla graduated in four years, in the upper half of the class. She received lots of job offers, but stuck with the firm that hired and supported her. She's now a partner in the firm. Still working her network, she's now running for city council. And her daughters are doing very well: one's at Berkeley studying (you guessed it) law and the other's at Northwestern majoring in business.

Difference between Camilla and John? John knew what needed to be done and could neither get the resources to do it nor the people lined up behind him to accomplish it. Camilla knew what she wanted, didn't know exactly what she needed to do to get it, but she personally engaged her network to scrape together the resources to accomplish what she wanted. She established strong heart connections with everyone. Camilla successfully led her own company, Me, Inc. John was not so successful.

Hindsight is 20-20, and worth about a cup of coffee in today's currency. But foresight is worth millions. Be awake, like the enlightened Buddha, to future developments that are already all around you. And use wisdom, like the great Solomon. Engage your interconnected, interdependent network in surfacing the critical issues that confront us all.

Then use focused discipline and the heart connection to line up the dollars with the words. Get the team moving in the same direction. Then unleash the ownership. Make certain that the person to whom you've passed the ball actually runs with it in the right direction.

CHAPTER 7

Unleash the Power of Ownership and Curb Victimitis, the Disorder You Give Yourself

Surface the issues, engage the people, get the resources: three important leadership tasks, whether you're leading a 300,000-person organization or your own interconnected, interdependent network. But they're not enough. Grand plans and golden words will not create success. Soul-stirring locker room speeches to "Win one for the Gipper" do not make three-second blocks—or put Ws on the board. At the end of the day, the tackle needs to see it as his responsibility to make that block and the running back needs to see it as his responsibility to hit that hole fast. Thirty coaches stand in front of their teams during the dog days of August and their hot, sweaty, exhausted players: "We're going to win the Super Bowl." Come January, only one team celebrates.

OWNERS WIN—VICTIMS WHINE

Ownership is the major difference between the Super Bowl winner and the other twenty-nine teams. Ownership is willful behavior. It springs from the heart and mind of the individual, and is exercised—vigorously. Your will to win is based on the strong belief that doing the job—whatever that job is, whether it's making blocks, moving product or soldering wires—is truly in your personal best interest. Ownership is best expressed in the words "I do it because I want to." In this chapter we'll show you how to create that "I do it because I want to" ownership.

You Can't "Transfer" Ownership: The Folks Already Have It

Please note: we're not talking about "transferring" ownership. Why? The people at the cutting edge of the organization *already have* the responsibility and ownership. Jack Welch, GE's CEO, talks about "pushing decision making down to the lowest possible level." Check it out, Jack: the folks down there already make decisions—maybe not the ones you want them to make—or in ways you want them to make them—but they are already doing it. If they waited for you—or any boss—to tell them what to do, nothing would get done. Give people at the lowest level the power to make decisions? Nonsense, they already have it!

Many leaders miss this important distinction. We did for the longest time, talking about "transferring ownership" rather than "unleashing ownership." Could never figure out why people thought that transferring ownership meant giving responsibility away to others so that they didn't have to own it themselves anymore.

In one organization, too many managers interpreted their job as coach and cheerleader on a superficial level. They failed to see they were also play-callers and team-focusers. Such shallow leadership definitions miss the whole point. In most cases, the people doing the work know best what needs to be done. It's our leadership job to make certain that people have the right tools, training and information to unleash their abilities to make—and own—their decisions.

Create the opportunity for people to make good decisions that affect them and their future. Create proactive, interconnected, interdependent owners in your network, not dependent employees waiting for instructions. Provide the tools, training and information that unleash ownership behavior.

Don't Steal Other People's Ownership—And Their Pride in Accomplishment. Matt was one of our first bosses. He helped us learn a lot about unleashing ownership—namely, our own. After about six months on the job, he asked us to research and recommend a new hourly wage compensation plan. He asked us what we needed to know, who we needed access to in the corporate office and what policy guidance we needed. After that, we owned the project. We tried several times to shuffle part of the responsibility back to Matt, claiming that it was too difficult to get to people in the corporate office or we couldn't find wage data. Matt listened sympathetically, made a few door-opening phone calls, but refused our best efforts to get him to assume ownership for the project.

We worked hard. It was like a college term paper: lots of data to sort through and analyze. Only this paper *really* counted. It was our first big, visible assignment. We wanted to impress Matt and the other readers in the corporate office. We figured it was a career opportunity and we didn't want to blow it. When we were just about finished, we asked Matt to review the draft. He asked us, "Is this your best work?"

"Well, it's still preliminary. We'd like your opinion before we turn it in," we said.

"I'll read your best shot—but only your best shot. This is your work. Again, is this your best work?"

We stammered and shuffled our feet and took back the draft. Matt made his point. We had the responsibility to turn in the best project. Three days later we dropped off the final copy at his desk. He passed it on upstairs. The corporate office asked us to present to the senior compensation committee. Imagine our pride when the VP of compensation called our report the best he'd ever seen.

Matt taught us an important lesson about ownership: ownership creates pride. We knew it was our work—not Matt's. That's why we could—and did—feel great pride in the compliment. All too often "help" robs people of that sense of accomplishment and pride. The Phoenix leader unleashes the power of ownership—and in the long run it proves its worth.

The Mirror Has Two Faces: John and John. Examine two different pictures. Picture one occurs at 10:25 A.M. in a noisy, dirty factory setting. John stands around waiting. He's been waiting for forty-five minutes as the parts pile up in front of his idle machine. "Don't touch that machine," he calls out to one of his mates at the next machine. "The foreman said he'd can you for messing with it again. He'll be here soon enough. Let him fix it." About thirty-five minutes later three people stand around, waiting, while more parts pile up. "Give anything for a smoke," John says out loud. Typical victim behavior, you'd say. Waiting for somebody else to fix a problem.

Fast-forward to picture two, twelve hours later, at 11:00 P.M. that evening. In a neat, carefully arranged garage a big man carefully nails highly polished trim on the deck of a partially constructed boat. His cheerful humming breaks the silence. His wife comes to the door and calls to him, "It's late, dear. When are you coming to bed?"

"Soon," the big man replies, pausing only a fraction of a second to look at her before returning to his work. "Want to get this trim in tonight and varnish it one more time, so it can dry during the day tomorrow, so that tomorrow night I can top-coat the entire deck. About another forty-five minutes or so." Typical pride-in-ownership behavior you'd say. Proactively planning today's activities to create a better future.

Funny thing: it's the same person. The victim/person standing around waiting for the boss and craving a smoke is the same owner/person who twelve hours later can't quit until he creates tomorrow's work. "If only we could get John to bring that commitment to work with him," many executives say to us. "It's really not that difficult," we reply. "Just create the ownership environment."

The "They Should" of Victimship Versus the "I Must" of Ownership

The grease-spattered mechanic leans into the clean-shaven face of the crisp, poised militarily buffed man with the eagle on his shoulder. The mechanic says in a stern voice, "Colonel, don't break my plane."

Four hours later, the same mechanic, with lots more grease and reeking from the sweat of a hard day in the hot sun, looks up from the sheath of computer papers he's been studying, leans across the table, raises his voice, points his finger at the same man and says in an insistent voice, "Colonel, I told you not to do that. Why did you do it?"

Sure, taxpayers may have paid for the aircraft with tax dollars.

The air force may have developed the specs and purchased the plane. But this twenty-nine-year-old mechanic, a sergeant, is responsible for maintaining it. He *really* owns it. The pilots who fly it only use it. The mechanic who works under the hood like a surgeon knows the plane so well he calls it by name—and fusses over it like a mother hen. He looks at this government-funded utility vehicle as his personal accountability. He sees the gigantic $30 million machine in the hangar—and says from the heart, "It's mine, all mine."

The Team That Takes a Loss as a Lesson in Winning. The tired, perspiring women file into the locker room. It was a grueling basketball game. They lost by three points. The room is deathly quiet. The female coach quietly closes the door behind her, so as not to disturb the thoughtful silence. She waits until every eye is fixed on her. "What did we learn here tonight?" she asks softly.

The tall center breaks the uncomfortable silence first. "I've got to roll down more. They must have had five or six easy baskets because I wasn't down there to stuff the lane."

One of the smaller women pipes up, "Got to do a better job of passing. I threw away four balls we should have scored on."

The words flow from around the room, softly, respectfully, always sounding the same theme, "I've got to get better." Not a single "they" or an accusative, "How come you didn't . . ." No one whines: "They cheated . . . the refs blew the call . . . the crowd was too loud . . ." None of the self-victimizing pseudo-bravado and blaming that we have come to expect from a losing team in a big game. Just old-fashioned taking of *personal responsibility*. No wonder this coach's team ranked in the top ten in her division every year for the past decade.

The Victimship Mantra: "If Only 'They'd' Do Their Job . . ." Contrast those experiences and responses with ones we recently observed at an executive retreat for a large organization. The chairmen led off with the speech that sounded the theme: "We've dropped the ball too many times this past year. Sales fell short. Operations didn't deliver. Overhead got out of control. We've got to fix it."

The balance of the two days was filled with recriminations, accusations and blame shifting. The typical hallway comment was, "We'd get our job done if only those guys in (fill in the blank) would just do their jobs." The final to do lists were filled with activities for the "other guys" to fix. We sold the stock the next day. That leadership team had a one-way ticket on the express train to disaster.

Unfortunately, there are too many people on the vintage "whine list"—and far too few looking toward the next big win. We live in a victim-creating society. And yet victimitis is the disease you give yourself. People blame others for their situation without asking, "What can I do to help myself?" A group of teenagers scale an eight-foot barbed wire fence and break into a locked switching station. After one falls into a generator and dies, the parents sue and win an $18 million judgment from the electric and gas company, who was found to be at fault for having an "attractive nuisance." Go figure.

We met with a president a while back. His opening question was "Why do so few people step up to the line and take responsibility anymore?" How many times have you asked yourself that question?

Victimitis Stalks Young Members of the Family. The seventeen-year-old looks forlornly across the table at his stern-looking dad. The kid's in trouble and he knows it. He promised to finish his algebra before going off to play basketball with his friends. He didn't, and the teacher's note indicates that he's seriously behind in his assignments.

"Didn't we agree that you'd get the math done before you left?" the father asks.

Silence from the teenager, just some uncomfortable shifting of the feet.

"Answer me," the father firmly insists.

"Yeah, but . . ." His voice trails off. "I thought I could catch up before class, but it was too hard. The teacher never explains things. And I didn't understand the assignment. Besides, I thought it was due next week. As far as being behind, I've done the assignments, I just can't find them. I must have lost them or something. I searched my room, but . . ." Again the voice trails off.

"What's the consequence we've agreed upon for not getting your homework done?" Dad wearily asks.

Silence again, as the teenager squirms some more in the seat. "Ahh, Dad, do I have to? I'll make it up. I promise."

"Nope. We've been down this road too many times, son. You've promised and not kept your word too many times. You're grounded until you catch up," says the exasperated father.

The teenager slumps in the chair, mutters something under his breath, stands up abruptly and stomps out. Another day in the life of raising teenagers. The father sighs deeply, feeling a hundred hairs turn gray.

Does that teenager own the responsibility for getting the homework done? Absolutely not. He'll only do the minimum to keep out of trouble. It's a familiar game: one played in offices, factories and homes across the globe. It's called "Catch me if you can as I minimize the work, not maximize the opportunity." Nonowners play it all the time.

An Eye-Opening Lesson from the Good Old Days. It wasn't always that way. Once upon a time, people stepped up to a hearty challenge.

In 1910 the following small advertisement ran in the leading London newspaper.

WANTED

Volunteers for a hazardous journey. Small wages. Bitter cold. Long months of complete darkness. Constant danger. Safe return doubtful. Honor and recognition in case of success.

There were more than 10,000 responses for the twenty positions. A five-hundred-to-one applicant ratio—for a trip to the South Pole. Those were the days.

These Are the Good Old Days for Many. Things are still that way in some places. There are still innumerable applicants for every expedition to Antarctica, where the temperature falls to −60 degrees Celsius, the wind often reaches 190 knots per hour and the combination of cold and dryness shatters steel.

How do you get that kind of responsibility taking? That is the 2:00 A.M. cold-sweat, knot-in-the-stomach issue these days. The answer is relatively simple: get people to think and act like owners rather than employees.

Help them see, in fact, that they truly own—not only the organization—but their own lives. And that the two are profoundly intertwined.

PHOENIX WORKSHOP

1. WHAT VICTIMITIS WORDS/THOUGHTS DO I EXPRESS?

_____

_____

_____

2. HOW CAN I CHANGE MY THOUGHTS/WORDS/AND ACTIONS
TO MORE REFLECT OWNERSHIP?

_____

_____

_____

WITH A CLEAR PURPOSE, OWNERS CREATE THEIR FUTURE

Clarity equals power. It's been said a thousand times: if you don't know where you're going, you'll likely never get there. We've heard all the shibboleths, catchy phrases from the podium. They energize us—for the moment. However, organizations don't run on catchy phrases. They run on hard work, focused work, sweaty palms and tough choices. The messages that work best are delivered eye-to-eye, face-to-face, and heart-to-heart. No more color by numbers—go for heart excellence—paint a Rembrandt. Unleash the power of ownership by shining the light of clarity.

Life's Musical Question: What Are You All About, Alfie?

Do you have a clear picture of what you want to create over the next five years for yourself? Your organization? Your children? Your spouse? Your friends? What do you want to accomplish _today_ that will help you realize that five-years-from-now dream at work? At home? In the neighborhood?

We once heard a very powerful speaker ask, "What do you want written on your headstone? What do you want the eulogist to say about you at your funeral? What if that funeral was tomorrow? Next month? Next year? Could that person say the words you want them to say?" She then peered intently into the audience, seemingly fixing everyone in the audience in her gaze, and asked, "What can you do *today* to make those words come true?" Her words caused us to stop, think and change our agenda.

Ask most leaders about five years from now and you get blank stares, followed by lots of stammering and glittering generalities. Not so with the folks whose stories we chronicle below.

High-Profile, Five-Star Clarity: Defend and Protect. We work with the leader of the Air National Guard. He has a clear vision of the "Cyber-Guard" of the future. Ask him about the future and he'll whip out his overheads and give you an instant presentation. More impressively, virtually any state commander can do the same, because he's presented the vision at every quarterly commanders' conference, mentions it in every written communication, and talks about it in virtually every informal communication opportunity. We counted seventy-two mentions during the half day we spent with the general.

We visited an air force base to check the clarity of the vision at the operational level of the organization. Everyone on base could repeat the words. More importantly, they continually challenged each other to live the vision. At the base their daily contribution to the mission was clear: defend our country's airspace and protect us from attack. Every one of the members on the base knows what he and she shows up to do every day: "Get the planes off and back safely with their mission accomplished." They do it seven days a week, fifty-two weeks a year, year in and year out. We all sleep a little more comfortably knowing they are vigilant—defending and protecting us.

A Coach's Clarity: Put the Ball in the Hoop. Sit in the locker room of the most successful women's basketball team in this decade. Their mission is very clear: put the ball in their opponent's hoop, prevent the other team from putting the ball in theirs and earn Ws in the standings. Any questions?

Everyone understands what they show up to do every game day and every practice session. The coach keeps reminding them. Repetition of the message encourages repetition of the action. Go, go, go—do it, do it, do it. Now that's complete clarity.

Admiral to Crew: We Are the Forward Strike Deterrent. We supplied Admiral Hyman Rickover's nuclear navy. Their mission was incredibly clear: deploy the swiftest, most powerful underwater forward strike force to deter any enemy attack on U.S. soil. Every sailor, every supplier, every civilian in the program understood the mission. The admiral made certain we did.

He made that mission clear in every meeting, every conversation, and every memo. Not ten minutes passed without him reminding everyone in earshot or eyesight about our purpose and mission. He was an obsessed, driven man, who created the circumstances where thousands of people owned the responsibility to build a great service of which they could be (and were) very proud.

A Child Goes for the Global Gold. We spoke to one of the early morning skaters at the Ice Palace, a nine-year-old girl. She's been skating for three years and already won several peewee titles. She talked nonstop about her skating activities, her upcoming competitions and her dream of winning a gold medal at the Olympics in 2006. All this excitement at seven in the morning during a break in her two-hour workout with her demanding coach. Now that's clarity of purpose.

Mom was also excited about her daughter's prospects, but she had a more sobering view of the future. They'd recently moved here to work with this coach, renting a small apartment near the skating rink. Her husband was still back home, commuting cross-country every weekend. She calculated it will take between $15,000 and $20,000 a year in coaching, travel, equipment and entrance fees over ten years for Shawna to qualify for the Olympics. "It's a big commitment," she said. "But, isn't she graceful? And she so wants to do it." Talk about ownership.

Make Certain That Everyone Knows the Purpose. All too often we set sail with a full head of steam, believing that everyone is on board, only to discover later that most folks are still standing on the dock. That's what happened to the CEO of the distribution company. All his managers agreed to a very aggressive sales campaign—or so he thought.

Piles of uncompleted action plans later, he discovered that no one really believed they could deliver the aggressive goals. When we asked, "Why didn't you speak up sooner?" one of the senior managers whined: "He wanted it so much that I didn't want to be the discouraging voice." Later, after a flood of red ink, the CEO swallowed the plan and substituted one put together by the managers that represented 30 percent (rather than 150 percent) sales growth.

As a Phoenix leader, capture everyone's undivided attention on day one—and cover the room, halls and building with the Way We Will Create the Future, Together. Get everyone to raise their right hands and take the oath, a covenant, a personal commitment signed in blood, so everyone knows that this is something jointly created and owned. Make things clear from the beginning, so that everyone sees the future—and creates it.

Pay Close Attention to the Victimship Symptoms. How do you really know that everyone is on board? Pay close, close attention. As Yogi Berra said, "You can observe a lot by just watching." We chuckle at his obvious redundancy—but the point is clear.

"The warning signs were all there," one of the senior managers recalled. "The body language, the absence of affirming statements, the early missed plans. We were so distracted by our own adrenaline that we failed to read the signposts."

How right she is. Learn to watch the avoidance body language: the shifting in the chair, counting ceiling tiles, nonsmiling smiles. Note the "enthusiasm index" in the responses. On a scale of one to ten, you may see a nonverbal lukewarm two rating: "Okay." Or an enthusiastic ten: "Great!" Pay particular attention to the early indicators of acceptance and ownership. Enthusiasm is the highest at the beginning of any project—thus, missed *early* deadlines signal incomplete commitment.

"Pay me 89 cents now to maintain your engine—or pay me 800 dollars later to fix it," the advertisement trumpeted. It is also true in building ownership. Take the time up front to build commitment to common goals, or you'll spend a lot of time later changing them.

It's What's Up Front That Counts: Clarify Individual Contributions

Phoenix leaders get agreement on individual contributions as well. How many times have you heard, "Oh, I thought she was going to do that. I didn't know that I was responsible for it." Outline accountabilities clearly in advance—down to the details. Or each detail will pop up later—like a cactus on a tender backside.

It's a good idea to put things in writing. There's nothing magic about documenting individual commitments—and no one will lose time trying to recall what was said.

Chapter 11 looks at several good ways to gain up-front understanding and commitment. We'll cover some more approaches in the following pages.

Clarity in the Mansion. The plush meeting room was still. All seventeen pairs of eyes focused on the sleek, good-looking woman at the head of the table. She studied the five bullet points written on the white board behind her. She turned and said, "Are you certain that those are the five most important items you want me to address? I'm surprised at several of them. Why do you want me to negotiate with the governor about these jurisdiction items? Are they that important to us as a department that you want me to spend some of our political capital securing them? Will they really help us do a better job of serving our clients?"

A spirited conversation filled the room for the next twenty-five minutes—discussing her questions. At the end, the group agreed that she had two other higher priorities than ones they listed. They dropped the "negotiate with the governor" item. One of the participants said leaving the meeting, "This was the first time I ever knew the department head's priorities and responsibilities— and I've been here eighteen years. Our discussion helps me now frame my priority responsibilities and those of my section. It was one of the best meetings we've ever had in this department." Clarity is comforting.

Samantha was new in the job. She inherited a dispirited, discredited group. Annual turnover soared past the 50 percent mark in the few months prior to her selection. She knew she had to move quickly both to right the listing ship and get it actively supporting the governor's direction. She also knew from her due diligence prior to accepting the position about the rampant infighting and backstabbing that characterized the group.

Samantha asked her direct reports to meet and draft her priority responsibilities for the balance of the year. They initially didn't believe the assignment, so they ignored it. Samantha's request for a date for their joint meeting to review their recommendations spurred them to action. They took the morning to meet among themselves and then arrange to meet with her beginning with a quick lunch.

The entire conversation took more than six hours. Hot words ebbed and flowed around the table. Establishing the department heads' priority responsibilities exposed all of the conflicting section priorities. Many unresolved issues went to the "parking lot" for additional investigation. At the end of the grueling meeting Samantha told us, "This was hard. There's a strong undercurrent of distrust and conflicting goals. I'm glad we took the time.

"However, my most important priority did not get listed today, though we spent six hours talking about it: it's getting these folks to work together cooperatively to support the governor's initiatives. That's my big challenge. Today we took the first step. At the next meeting we'll set each of their priority responsibilities, and that will be another step. Then we'll make certain that everyone repeats the priority-responsibility-setting process throughout his or her section. This first round will likely take several months, but it will bring a clarity that this department has lacked forever. It's a big job."

We would add to Samantha's comments—"and an essential one."

Lose the Tin Whistle: Be a Coach, Not a Referee

Our job is not to wear the pinstripes and enforce rules. Tin whistles do not a Phoenix leader make. Nor do we sit in the locker room, reviewing films and grading players' performances. As Phoenix leaders, we belong out there on the field—making a real-time contribution to the team's success. Coaches sweat, share the hurt and the ecstasy—and get dirty fingernails.

Hearing that they are now "coaches," many managers often withdraw themselves from the team's activities and let the team stew, fuss and do what they want to do. They become referees, more interested in enforcing the rules. They ask: "Was your foot on the line or wasn't it? Were you offside or weren't you?" This will get you nowhere.

When coaches stop coaching and start refereeing, they withdraw one of the most valuable assets of the team: the coach's experience and knowledge. As a coach, share your experience, your knowledge, your insight, so everyone knows what needs to be accomplished and what each must contribute.

Focus on the Purpose, Not the Procedure

Coaches stay focused on fundamental purpose. All too often folks inflate procedural rules and tactics to the full importance of a major goal. The administrative policy of where people walk on campus or the size of a business unit can become more important than the purpose of creating a positive campus environment or focusing on customers.

Many times this *suboptimization* leads to less than productive behavior: like the storeroom clerk locking up the storeroom so she can protect the company's assets and prevent theft. She's oblivious to the fact that locking the storehouse prevents technicians from doing their job for customers and eventually destroys her job there. Her behavior leads technicians to set up their own private storerooms, stashing parts under benches, in locker rooms and in trucks. They want access to the parts they need to do their job. The storeroom people perpetually argue with the technicians all because of suboptimization. Each person gets focused on his or her short-term tactic—while sabotaging the organization's long-term goal.

This misbegotten task inflation can blow up in everyone's face—and actually undermine the purposes it was established to promote.

We Could Make a Fortune—If Only We Had That Key. AT&T got it right a decade ago: organize customer-focused business units and bring bottom line responsibility to those folks who serve those customers. Their strategic business unit strategy served their customer focus goal. It was the right strategy for the time.

Somehow, though, the right strategy went wrong as it was elaborated and formalized into a set of Byzantine bureaucratic rules. We've all seen it hundreds of times: the inflated tactical rules frustrate the implementation of the strategy that leads to accomplishing the goal.

We saw it up close one day when a group of field technicians from two AT&T units, Global Business Systems (GBS) and Business Communications Systems (BCS) from southern New Jersey, asked us to come and hear some of their issues. We were absolutely astonished by what we saw. They were told that AT&T's strategy was to break up any business that grew larger than $1.5 billion. As a result, the telephone switch business (PBXs) was broken up into two parts, GBS for customers with thirty telephone lines or more and BCS for customers with fewer than thirty phone lines.

They regaled us with story after story of how they were forced to compete against each other, reducing margins for both of them and inviting other competitors into the market. The crowning example was the warehouse where the same product piece parts were in two different cages. The GBS technicians had the keys to one cage and the BCS technicians had the keys to the other. They told us of dozens of times where part A was in one cage and not in the other, and they couldn't get in to get the part and take care of their customers. These cages were locked up tighter than a bank vault!

The technicians saw clearly what they needed to accomplish. They understood the business issues. They knew what their personal contributions needed to be. They knew that if we would listen to them, they could help us turn this business around.

The BCS/GBS example gets repeated thousands of times every day all across the globe. A good strategy goes bad, undercut by the well-intentioned efforts of individuals to standardize it. Rather than creating value, the administration of the strategy destroys it.

Beware the Mighty Grass Police. Suppose you were responsible for landscaping a major university campus in the Northeast. Healthy green grass is a big priority in keeping the campus looking beautiful, one of your major responsibilities. You have two options. You might hire an industrial engineer, lay out the sidewalks that achieve the most efficient traffic patterns, post "Please Don't Walk on the Grass" signs and employ grass police officers to keep people off the grass. Or you might notice where people actually walk, relocate the walkways there, plant very hardy grass—and go on to the next priority.

We're on the advisory board of a large university. When we visited in the early spring the head landscaper was busy replanting the lawns and had snow fences around them to keep the people off the growing grass. The snow fences were still there when we returned in June. We discovered that he'd hired an industrial engineer, done the traffic study, laid out efficient paths and taken the fences down. He ran into trouble keeping the students off the grass, however, so he hired several students to patrol the lawns and give out trespassing tickets to those walking on the grass. After a firestorm of complaints, he reinstalled the snow fences to protect the grass.

Here was a classic case of the purpose being buried by the procedure. Somehow he lost sight of the goal of a beautiful campus, sacrificed to the policy of green grass at all costs. Now the green grass is obscured by the ugly snow fences that stand like Berlin Walls surrounding every lawn on campus. Policy administration runs amuck once again.

He Who Hath Ears:
Just Listen to the People and Get Clear on the Purpose

We faced a difficult situation when we returned from a European tour of duty. Honeywell's residential heating, ventilation and air-conditioning business was losing money. No one in headquarters knew what to do. We didn't know ourselves what to do, but we had a pretty good idea of who might have a good idea—the folks in the field. So we talked with and listened to the folks out in the shop and the field—doing the work—and found that they knew exactly what needed to be done.

One twenty-five-year employee in particular had a clear handle on the problem. It seemed that the company installed a new automatic environmental control system product line and never trained the people on the line to optimize it. The training assignment was tied up in a jurisdictional dispute between union and nonunion folks. While the dispute dragged on, the plant pumped out less than top-quality products at higher than budgeted costs. In other words, the losses were directly attributable to the ownership debate.

"Enough," we said, and got the facts. The best-trained trainers were the union group leaders. "Let's stop worrying about the union-nonunion line and more about getting the job done," we said, giving the training responsibility to the union group leaders.

Productivity rose 47 percent and the losses disappeared. Getting the right partner to own the responsibility really pays off—for everyone.

We noted a similar situation at the Square D facility in Cedar Rapids, Iowa, where we faced low-cost offshore labor competition, and shared the decision and the rationale for assembling a set of products at our Tijuana, Mexico, plant. Two teams of union International Brotherhood of Electrical Workers and Teamsters decided to support assembly in Tijuana by doing the plant setup and training the employees there—this, in exchange for setting up self-directed work groups in Cedar Rapids to find ways to increase the volume on the remaining, nontransferred products. Because we were able to sell the products assembled in Tijuana at a lower price, we were able to pull through many more Cedar Rapids products. By assuming ownership for the situation, we actually added jobs at Cedar Rapids.

It's all about listening to the employees and getting clear on our reason for existing—our purpose. Did we show up at the factory to fight with each other? To see who could win the arm wrestle? Or did we show up to create job security and prosperity for us all by helping customers?

It's time to refocus! We absolutely believe that almost everyone shows up to work every day wanting to do the right things. Yet most are never quite sure what the right things are. So everybody works hard, often at cross-purposes. Then everyone goes home feeling very frustrated having worked very hard, but having accomplished very little.

Listen Up and Wisen Up. You can almost hear the chorus from the students and the AT&T technicians: "Just listen to us. If you'll listen to us, you'll see we know what has to be done to help us all be successful going forward. We can do it. Just ask us and we'll tell you."

Arbitrary rules often get in the way of the purpose you're trying to accomplish. We've learned to listen to the people and help them help us stop inflated rules from sacrificing the original purpose. We get agreement on general purposes and strategies and leave the details to the individuals to execute.

PHOENIX WORKSHOP

1. HOW CAN I HELP ME AND EVERYONE ELSE GET CLEAR ON WHAT I (AND THEY) NEED TO CONTRIBUTE? (HINT: WE'LL TALK ABOUT A DETAILED PROCESS OF HOW TO CLARIFY EXPECTATIONS IN CHAPTER 12.)

_____

_____

_____

2. WHERE HAVE I (AND THOSE IN MY NETWORK) ALLOWED PROCEDURE TO OVERWHELM PURPOSE? HOW CAN I CORRECT IT?

_____

_____

_____

UNLEASH THE CYCLONE OF PERSONAL CAPABILITY

Capitalize on the capabilities that people bring to the table. None of us is good at everything, even though some of us may think we are. In professional football, centers don't throw passes and quarterbacks don't make blocks. There's a very clear division of labor. The coach's work is to develop each person's unique capabilities that will most benefit the team: for example, centers work on their blocking and quarterbacks on their passing.

A New American Folk Tale: The Albuquerque Cyclone

We unleashed a cyclone in a Honeywell plant in Albuquerque, New Mexico. That factory had a clear goal: create the world's most cost effective, most responsive commercial energy management system, and have it on distributors' shelves in nine months.

We set the goal, made it clear, provided the freedom to invent the rules they needed to achieve that goal, and then got out of their way. The wind rose rapidly and before long people and projects were spinning across the landscape.

Customers Get the Cyclone Spinning. The team began with customers, always the right place to start. They learned through listening what customers wanted and what product features best excited customers. The teams calculated price levels that would provide customers a six-month payback on the energy system. The cyclone touched down.

Working backward, the team designed the product and its cost structure. They figured out what it would take to produce what customers wanted. The teams started at the beginning—with customers. Once they had a clear picture of their future and how to get there they flew like the wind.

The Match Game: Align Capabilities with Requirements. The cross-functional teams began with a member skills and capabilities inventory that detailed people's skill sets. They posted that list in their team meeting room, so anyone could consult it at any time to find the best person to do a specific job.

Using that capabilities inventory, and the list of things to get done, the team held twice-daily fifteen-minute stand-up meetings to develop individual to do lists. The team worked to make certain that each person's to do list matched that person's highest and best contribution to the team. Each person left every meeting with a clear set of short-term objectives. They'd write each person's objectives on the big chalkboard and review them at the next meeting to make certain they were accomplished.

The teams invented a new rulebook for their operation. For instance, they designed their own incentive plan. We agreed to it in a heartbeat, because they researched it, they designed it and they owned it. We knew they'd make it work. They made it work in spades, beating the sales plan by 50 percent, the profit plan by 72 percent and all with awesome quality levels.

Albuquerque is a classic example of the results that are achievable when you unleash the cyclone of individual capabilities. Give people a clear goal. Get them the resources they need to do the job. Help them get clear on what each can best contribute. Then, get out of the path—a cyclone is about to touch down!

Respect and Value Each Other's Contributions

In addition to keeping everyone informed and focused on achieving the objectives, the fifteen-minute twice-daily stand-up meetings also helped individuals learn to respect and value each other's contribution.

In most organizations, people don't value the contributions of others nearly enough. Caustic put-downs clog up and contaminate most organization informal chat rooms. Read them and weep: "Well, what do you expect from a salesperson?" "After all, she's just an engineer!" "Those guys in quality wouldn't know a good piece if it bit them in the backside." On and on it goes. But you can't do that and build productive network relationships. Our interdependent, interconnected network world is based on respecting and valuing each other's contribution, period.

Visibility Helps Respect. It's hard to respect and value someone else's contribution when you don't see it on a regular basis. Most folks overvalue what they do, and undervalue what others do because of this visibility factor. The fifteen-minute stand-up meetings at Albuquerque provided that intimate visibility that is an essential ingredient in building mutual respect. As a Phoenix leader, ensure that you have an information infrastructure that provides visibility into ongoing activities.

We work hard to provide visibility in our family. Teenagers often devalue parents' contributions. They don't see what it takes to make a living. Money magically shows up in the bank account and the family goes out to eat. There's very little connection between eating out and working long hours.

On the other hand, parents often don't understand how difficult (or boring) a subject can be to a high schooler. Try helping your son or daughter with algebra and get one dose of reality. Read a couple of his textbooks and get another.

To enhance visibility, we take our children on office visits and business trips so they can see that it's all not just drinking coffee and staying in nice hotels. We visit their classrooms and spend a day with them in school to do our own dullness meter for a particular teacher or comprehensibility measure for a given subject. At least we all understand better each other's issues and circumstances. That helps us respect and value each other's contribution.

Draw a Line in the Sand: Insist upon Respect. All of our companies are people-centered outfits. They reflect the shadow of the leader—all of us. One in particular is very strongly people-centered. In that organization, there are only three reasons for termination: poor performance, dishonesty and disvaluing. Trash talking about anyone else is just not tolerated: not competitors, not customers, not teammates. This value got tested early in our organization's life.

We were about one hundred people strong, located throughout southern California. Lisa was our top salesperson, bringing in more than 15 percent of our business. Everyone loved Lisa. She was personable and likable. But she had one big flaw: she sold by selling against the competition. She trash-talked their code, their people and their company. We counseled with her many times. She would promise to change, but always fell off the wagon. Finally, several employees approached us to do something. They were concerned that her reputation would come back and hurt them. "Besides," they pointed out, "it's against our code."

We called an all-employee meeting—which they chose to hold on a Sunday afternoon. It was one of the touchiest meetings we've ever attended. Lisa was the best salesperson we'd ever met. She was also a great individual. We'd hate to go head-to-head with her in the marketplace. But she wasn't honoring and respecting others. If she talked competitors down to potential customers she was likely talking some of us down to her customers when things didn't go right. After six hours of wrestling and hand-wringing, the group unanimously agreed to ask Lisa to leave.

Lisa-type situations don't surface much anymore because Lisa is a legend in our company. Every one of the 5,400 people know how Lisa, our top salesperson, got fired for trash talking. The message is clear. The only way to get ahead in this organization is by valuing the positive contributions others make to all of our successes.

Unleash the cyclone of people's capabilities by focusing on what they can contribute and by valuing that contribution. Build a situation where they can contribute what they're good at doing. Marry clarity of what needs to be done with the individual's capabilities, value their contribution and acknowledge them for it. That's not so hard to do, is it?

Look Beyond the Job Title to Uncover Gems of Capability

Don't get confused by what people are paid versus what people are capable of owning and doing. It's easy to assume an inverse relationship between salary level and skill and ownership levels. Often we make the mistaken assumption that those individuals with lower salaries also have less skill and ownership potential. And the size of the office gets equated to the size of the IQ.

Not so. Take Eric, for instance, a six-foot-four, 240-pounder working part-time on the third shift in our warehouse. He responded to our e-mail request for business improvement ideas. Since he worked close by we invited him to stop in. He did. We were surprised. He's a former marine officer who has traveled to twenty-one countries. Currently a paralegal, he's finishing his degree in psychology and enrolled in an MBA program. He works the third shift so his wife and three kids can have some of the extras.

When we first mentioned his name and job assignment, several executives wrinkled their noses as if to say, "What can some part-time guy on the third shift in the warehouse teach us about improving our business?"

It's real clear to us that the answer to that unspoken question is, "A lot!" We'd bet that nine out of ten people jumped to the conclusion that this person was working in our warehouse because he was unemployable and very anxious to get any job. People likely labeled him as a person who's only capable of doing X because of his current job title and location. Just ten minutes with Eric convinced us that he is capable of doing X, Y and double Z. He wants to stay and grow with our company and is now rapidly moving up in the organization.

Facts are our friends, not stereotypes or assumptions. Shine the light of evidence on the contribution required by the job and the capabilities of the individual—not the job title or pay level. That third-shift person just might have an MBA with the answer to your pressing business issue. Think of people as bundles of skills, capabilities and ownership just yearning to burst free. Engage everyone in the business of the business, unleashing their ownership energy in creating our future.

PHOENIX WORKSHOP

HOW CAN I:
* ENSURE THAT CUSTOMER DEMANDS DRIVE THE PRIORITIES?

---

* ALIGN CAPABILITIES WITH JOB REQUIREMENTS?

---

* CREATE VISIBILITY ALL ACROSS ACTIVITIES?

---

* INSIST UPON RESPECT FOR AND VALUING OF EACH CON-
  TRIBUTION?

FEEDBACK POWERS UP OWNERSHIP

All Humanity Yearns for Continuous Feedback

Ever show up at a meeting and after a while wonder why you
came? You could have never been there and no one would have
noticed. Lots of people feel that way about most of the organizations that fill their lives. People show up at work, sweat for ten
hours, go home and wonder: did it really matter?

We all yearn for feedback. We look into our lover's eyes in
search of the answer to the question that burns a hole in our soul:
"Do you really love me?" We study carefully the facial expressions and nonverbal behavior of our boss to discern, "Does he
really approve of what I've done?" We listen carefully to our
friends' and teammates' words to find out, "Do you really like and
accept me?" We yearn for feedback. Feedback is the magic di-

vining rod that locates and brings the precious fountain of ownership gushing to the surface.

We will talk about how to provide feedback in Part 3. Ken Blanchard is right: feedback is the breakfast of champions. Use scoreboards, both group and individual, to keep people informed about their progress on agreed-upon goals.

We use our weekly family review sessions to keep us all up to date on how each of us is doing in meeting our important goals. Our grandson is quick to point out when Granddad doesn't get his dishes in the dishwasher. The 360-degree feedback helps to keep the communication flowing, and the ownership blossoming. We've noticed that that grandson, for instance, is much more likely to put his dishes in the dishwasher, knowing that that measure will be reviewed during the family discussion. He wants to look good on that score.

Feedback: The Most Important Moment of Any Mission

The flight was terrific—the F-16 flight, we mean. We learned a lot, particularly about the value and role of feedback. We spent half an hour checking out the plane, an hour in preflight briefing, an hour and a half for the mission itself and two hours of debriefing. Does the time allocation send a message? You bet it does. In the U.S. Air Force—the gold standard—feedback is the most important part of any mission.

During the feedback session, every aspect of the mission was scrupulously examined. The mechanic, crew chief and two pilots talked openly and honestly about hits, runs and errors. The crew chief examined the computerized records of the planes' performances and asked detailed questions of the pilots about their experience of the planes during flight. He took twenty-seven pages of detailed notes.

The mechanic stuck to the computerized flight records and asked very specific questions. He was most interested in performance during acceleration and deceleration—apparently he wanted to verify the maintenance record for one of the planes. The base commander colonel came in for his share of comments. The captain who flew our plane commented on the colonel's slow response to several situations. The colonel claimed radio problems that were confirmed by the maintenance report.

The colonel also admitted that he felt rusty in the plane today and promised to sign up for additional training exercises. Seems that he's missed the last two weeks of flying because of administrative duties. Everyone spoke. Everyone commented. Everyone took their share of need-to-improves. No wonder the U.S. Air Force is the world-class standard. We're sure glad these folks defend our skies.

Feedback Tools Help Owners Make Better Decisions

Owners need information to make decisions about what tomorrow to create and to identify what can be improved now. Owners also need information that enables them to see the whole picture, because the owner understands the necessity to manage the whole interrelated, interdependent, interconnected network.

Feedback information helps owners behave like owners. We work hard to make certain that our organizations possess the information infrastructure that unleashes ownership energy. Our information feedback system enables each and every person to know how good a job she is doing—right now. The feedback system helps every owner understand what he or she must do to create success for us all.

Unleashed ownership behavior ran rampant during a recent conference call. We do a worldwide conference call two weeks after the end of each month to review the financial results. Canada had a great sales month, but margins were down in comparison with a year ago.

The Canadian management team shared the sixteen different "competitive, buying and customer" factors that drove margins down on thousands of different products last month. They'd already mapped the key factors for the last two months, put action teams together to correct the situations, were already back to a day-by-day feedback system with some of the vendors and changed several pricing metrics used by our associates. The owners saw the developing problems, rolled up their sleeves and went to work fixing them. They didn't wait for approval from a boss, or advice from a staffer. They acted just like owners, seeing the problems and going right to work fixing them.

The information infrastructure unleashes the owners' energy. Every organization needs information tools that identify one-month trends at a small-enough level that concerned owners can take immediate remedial action. You also need very good feedback on competitive actions in the marketplace. For instance, we walked away from some business for the time being, slowing our growth to only 40 percent for the next couple of months, versus the 50 or 60 percent we could grow, just to send a clear signal to our competitors that we were serious about holding price levels.

That conference call was populated with owners making decisions like owners. The information infrastructure enabled them to act like owners. Be a Phoenix leader and invest the time, technology and talent to build your infrastructure to unleash the power of information and ownership.

However, realize that any infrastructure only provides you with a static picture of what is a dynamic world. Any system can only give you a snapshot of what's happening today. If it's 12:22 P.M. on Friday, the fourteenth of February—even the best information system will only give you a picture of what's true on Friday the fourteenth of February at 12:22 P.M. The picture changes at 12:23. It may be only microscopically, but the picture will change. It will change—perhaps dramatically—by March 1.

Owners recognize the need to plan and prepare for the future. Information tools help people see what happened yesterday. Owners need learning tools to anticipate what the picture will be tomorrow. That's why continuous learning is critical. We turn our attention to that topic in the pages to come.

PHOENIX WORKSHOP

WHAT TOOLS DO I (AND THOSE IN MY NETWORK) NEED TO EXERCISE OWNERSHIP? HOW CAN I GET THEM?

_____

_____

_____

Summary: Get Educated or Get Obliterated

The Great Commandment:
Know and Grow Thy Business and Personal Value

What are the key success factors in your business? Why do customers buy from you as opposed to other suppliers? What is your business model and how effective is it? Who's your major competitor today? Who will be your major competitor five years from today? What will your market look like five years from today? How will you succeed in that market? These questions eat at the innards of most owners. They are the 2:00 A.M. wake-up-in-a-cold-sweat issues. They tie stomachs in knots and nag at the consciousness.

We work with a privately held organization where the ownership mantle is shifting to the children and grandchildren of the founders, none of whom work in the family-owned business. The new owners realize they need education about the business they are coming to own: how it works, its future and the role they can/will play in it.

They've made the commitment to attend one industry show a year, join one industry association, read at least one industry publication and meet at least once a year to talk about the developments in their industry. They've also pledged to attend at least one board meeting and meet with the CEO at least twice during the year to keep up with developments in the current business—all in an effort to be educated, informed owners.

How many associate-owners in a business are informed about their business? Too few. Engage every lathe operator, secretary, designer, truck driver, engineer, manager and executive in thinking about, wrestling with and answering the questions we listed in the lead paragraph of this section.

The Whirling Clock Hands: Learn to Thrive in Net Time

The world changes rapidly: the hands on the clock whirl around. Decades ago, we talked in "automobile time"—the six to eight years it took to develop an automobile. In the 1990s that sped up to "computer time"—the year or so it took to develop a new personal computer. Now we talk in "Net time"—the month or two it takes to bring a new product to the Internet. Today, February 14 is the equivalent of March 14. We just haven't got time to delegate as we did in former days. Decisions need to be made by the person on the spot at the time. That on-the-spot person must make that right-now decision looking through the high-flying Phoenix eye of ownership—not the squint of self-inflicted victimship.

The Leader's Challenge: Grow Learning

The leader's challenge is to unleash ownership energy, mentality and competence so that the best decisions are made—ones that create success for everyone in the interconnected, interdependent network. Organizations that unleash the power of ownership and energy will survive. The rest will be interesting case studies filed in the library of forgotten examples.

We invest most of our energy in improving the value of products and services we produce. We also invest in improving the processes we use to produce our products and services. But we invest almost nothing in improving the capability of the assets that generate all our wealth and value—the intellectual capabilities of the people in our network.

Self-renewal occurs through growing the value of all the members of your network system at work and at home. As the world speeds by, like a whizzing hockey puck, the survivors and thrivers will be those few who have the learning tools in their heads that enable them to capitalize on the rapidly changing world. Learn how to learn, so you can learn how to earn. We turn to that critical dimension of leadership in the following pages.

CHAPTER 8

Energize Learners: Open Doors, Break Through Walls, Let the Future In

The following help-wanted advertisement recently appeared in *The Economist*, March 15, 1997, one of the world's leading business magazines.

LEARNING LEADERSHIP

If you are keen to move into an environment where you can play a strategic international role, pushing out the boundaries of learning development, consider this. . . . We provide leading-edge solutions to many of the world's largest institutions. . . . Our continued growth is based on an unmatched knowledge of customers' business needs—and the ability to create solutions to meet them. It's an environment that encourages the desire to grow knowledge and give of our best. And that's where you'll be chartered to realize that aim. . . . You will help us maximize the business advantage we gain from the finest minds we employ.

We've seen similar help-wanted advertisements in other leading newspapers. Headhunters tell us that their most frequently requested (and most difficult to fill) recruiting assignments are for "learning leaders." And we hear discussions about "learning" in board rooms and offices across the world.

Why this sudden interest in learning? Simple. More and more leaders recognize that their organizations sell knowledge along with their products. Doesn't Microsoft make wonderful products? Obviously lots of folks believe they do, judging from their booming sales. Do we buy their products because of the bytes and bits in their software program? No, not really. We buy their programs because of the knowledge embedded in those bytes and bits that help us do what we want to do with the computer better, faster and with more fun. Microsoft really sells knowledge (and fun) that's useful to us, the computer user. That's why Microsoft's advertising slogan is "Where do you want to go today?" Microsoft sells productivity and fun, with a pleasing graphic interface.

Microsoft is no different from GM or GE or AT&T. All of these companies sell knowledge as an integral part of their marketplace offering.

As the organization's Phoenix leader, how do you generate and focus that knowledge? You create an "environment that encourages the desire to grow knowledge and give of our best. . . . [to] maximize the business advantage we gain from the finest minds we employ." That's why the obsession with finding learning leaders.

Like Rowdy Roosters at Dawn, Learning Leaders Wake Up Everybody

How do you create a more secure future in an insecure world? Become a learning leader. What is the key to learning leadership? Let the future in! Like the Great Buddha, Be Awake! And, then, like the rowdy rooster, wake up everybody else as well.

Ever visited or lived on a farm? Early each morning, your cozy slumber ends abruptly with the brass-band-crowing of a rooster breaking the holy hush of dawn with an unholy racket. That bird's solo brass section is our wake-up call from Ma Nature. Like roosters, learning leaders send wake-up calls that resound: "Wake up! Life is fascinating. Open your eyes. Look around. Learn!" We've made a career of not letting people sleep!

Routine Miracles:
Our Quality of Life Is the Product of Human Learning

It's Saturday morning. Lingering over morning coffee, we spy the watermelon on the counter. Imagine, buying watermelon in February for 29 cents a pound. Not too many years ago we couldn't get that summer fruit in the middle of winter at any price. "It's a miracle," we think to ourselves.

All around the kitchen we see evidence of the use of knowledge to dramatically improve our life. We are amazed (and pleased) with our ancestors' ability to create stronger dishes to eat on, more efficient pans to cook in, more tasty food to consume, all the while reducing real-time costs so that we spend a constantly shrinking portion of our income in feeding ourselves. Imagine the impact on our lives of inventions like refrigeration, which brings us fresh, crisp apples in March, air transportation which brings us pineapples from Hawaii, bananas from Morocco and fresh grouper fish from Chile, and hot house hydroponic farming, which grows three crops of rich tomatoes a year regardless of rain, heat or snow. Everywhere we look there's evidence of the miracles wrought by human knowledge.

Knowledge Converts Diminishing Returns into
Increasing Prosperity

Nonetheless, there are many among us who worry that this progress is all temporary and will vanish right before our eyes, leaving us worse off than before. The economists saw the finite amount of physical material on the planet and postulated the law of diminishing returns. "We can't have both guns and butter," they lectured. "We've got to trade off and make compromises." Perhaps that's why economics is called "the dismal science"?

Of course, they're correct. There is an absolute limit on the amount of coal or oil on the planet, as well as only so much arable land. But if the doomsayers are right, why didn't the human race disappear eons ago, drowned in its own selfishness?

The simple answer: the relentless drive and human ability to learn.

Facts are our friends, and the total collection of facts show that we are better off, by almost every measure of human well-being, than any previous generation in history. Why haven't the doomsday Malthusian theories proven correct? Malthus and his followers counted mouths, and projected that the number and voraciousness of mouths would outgrow the planet's physical ability to provide the basics of food and shelter. But human beings are more than just mouths and hands, we are also brains. And our ability to use our brains is our salvation and our future hope.

Economist Paul Romer points out that resource consumption is more a product of human brain power than it is of the physical characteristics of the resource itself. For instance, the number of people at work in the production of food dropped by better than 97 percent during the twentieth century. At the same time, food production increased 2,000 percent. In economics, brain power counts for more than the resources in the ground and in the air.

The ability to convert that brain power into knowledge makes the difference. Knowledge creates new technologies, new products, new ideas and new ways to combine limited resources to create new value. The message is clear for our society and planet: improve your knowledge and you improve your capability to create value for yourself and others.

Move Away from Selling Things and Learn to Traffic in Knowledge

The same applies in business organizations as well. Look at American Airlines. They're in the airline business, right? No, wrong. American is in two businesses: the flying-seats-through-the-air business that used 92 percent of their fixed assets to generate 71 percent of their sales and 56 percent of their profits, and the information-about-flying business that used only 8 percent of their fixed assets to generate 29 percent of their sales and a whopping 44 percent of their profitability. Net margins and return on investment for the Sabre business must make Bob Crandall, American's CEO, wonder what business he'd rather be in—the cutthroat, huge-investment flying business or the high-margin, low-asset investment knowledge business. It's real clear what choice we'd make.

Virtually every business leader we meet is going into the knowledge business. We worked with a credit report company. They're the best in their business, and determined to expand beyond it. They see their future in helping financial institutions and retailers of all stripes combine their credit information with other demographic data in order to custom-tailor product offerings and credit decisions. They help retailers, for instance, customize their product promotions based upon the customer's previous purchases as chronicled in their credit files. The credit report company is now in the consulting business, selling knowledge.

Similarly, we spent some time with a large printing organization. They're one of the best in their business. Customers often give them their unqualified faith and trust. One customer said, "We've stopped proofing their material. They've become our proofing department." They've grown better than 25 percent per year for the past decade, not a bad track record in a supposedly mature commodity business.

Yet they see half their revenues (and more than half of their profits) by the year 2000 coming from the sale of services such as personalization and outsourcing. They now sell the ability to cataloguers, like Damark and L.L. Bean, to choose a subset of products from their entire catalogue and mail them to a given individual based upon his previous pattern of purchases and lifestyle considerations. For instance, they help direct marketers, like American Express, offer a special package trip to Hawaii to a couple who went there last year, along with an introduction to Amex's mortgage brokerage firm because the couple just went into escrow on a new house. Moving far afield from their printing roots, this organization seeks to double their margins through selling high-margin knowledge in addition to low-margin printing.

Jack Welch expects General Electric to earn more money from the sale of services than from the sale of products by the year 2000. His medical products division sells hospitals not only X-ray machines, but also sells them GE's famous management systems like workouts and strategic planning. The attraction is simple: knowledge today is more valuable than things.

Hardware? Software?
Learn What Wares Are Worth Most

Look at the difference between IBM and Microsoft. In 1982, *Fortune* magazine hailed IBM's Thomas Watson, Jr., as the "entrepreneur of the century," having created more wealth for more people than any other human being. In ten short years the realities of the marketplace embarrassed both the *Fortune* editors and Watson, as a third of the IBM staff along with better than 65 percent of the stock value disappeared. Just a few short years later, Microsoft passed IBM in market value, and hasn't looked back since. In 1996, Microsoft's market value exceeded a recovered IBM's value by more than $15 billion—a lot of money in anybody's ball game.

What happened? IBM focuses on producing things, like hardware, that require physical assets in excess of $17 billion. Microsoft focuses on producing knowledge-based products like Windows '97 and Internet Explorer, and therefore uses less than $1 billion in physical assets. Investors value Microsoft for its knowledge in producing new and desired software products, granting it one of the highest price-earnings ratios in the market today. In the stock market knowledge pays.

Actually, it's always been that way. Knowledge has always been the differentiator. Hannibal's knowledge of the Alps enabled him to defeat a superior Roman force. American ingenuity enabled us to defeat a far superior German force in North Africa during World War II. Better-trained Israeli pilots defeated a much larger Arab air force during the Six Day War. Superior knowledge inevitably wins.

The stories are legion. The facts are indisputable. The conclusion is inescapable. Get smarter—or get out of everyone's way. As the Phoenix leader of your interconnected, interdependent network, your chief responsibility is to grow learners, people who actively seek out opportunities to learn and grow—and use what they know for the benefit of everyone in the network.

BE THE CHIEF LEARNING OFFICER

As with everything else in your interconnected, interdependent network, it all begins with you. As the Phoenix leader you cast a long shadow. Be certain that you cast a long learning shadow! Set the standard by expecting learning to be a major part of everyone's job by making it a major part of yours. Demonstrate your commitment to learning in every way possible.

There Are No Learning Organizations, Just Learning Individuals

We've all read lots about "learning organizations." In truth, there's no such entity as a learning organization. Organizations don't learn. People learn. You can have a collection of learners in an organization, but you can't have a collection of organizations that learn. Since organizations don't learn, the question is, "How can you help people learn?"

We talked to a senior executive yesterday in a company we were visiting. "Oh yes, we're building a learning organization. It's a very important priority for us. I realize how crucial it is."

"Tell us about it," we asked, interested in seeing what we could learn from his experience.

"We're Working on It": Lukewarm, Cream-of-Wheat Commitment to Learning

"We started about eighteen months ago. We gave our quality coordinator an American Express card and told her to find out what the best practices were in learning organizations. She took six months traveling around visiting organizations and came back with a slew of recommendations. We put together a committee that designed a Knowledge Center to centralize all our information. Got about, oh I'd guess, 25 percent of our customers' information on it by now. That's a big job, taking it from several different sources. We get pretty good usage out of that center now, approximately fifty requests a day for information. I'm very pleased. We think we're on the way."

"And what have you done to foster a learning organization?" we asked.

"We sent out a memo to all 6,000 employees announcing the Knowledge Center and urging people to both use it and input into it. We created a new position, director of quality and knowledge development, and promoted the former quality coordinator to it. I scan the reports she generates and urge her to keep pushing the center's activities."

"Have you used the center at all?" we asked.

"Nope, we haven't had the need. When I do need the information they store, I certainly will dial it up, though."

"What else is going on?" we prodded.

"There's lots of discussion about forming learning teams, though not much has happened yet. We need to jump on that to push it a little. We operate such a diverse, decentralized organization that it's hard to focus people on common activities. That makes sharing knowledge tough. We need to find ways to do that more effectively."

Listen to the low level of urgency. After eighteen months, they're just getting started in putting the infrastructure together. Only fifty out of 6,000 employees access the center daily, and with their incomplete database we'd guess that few come back a second time. They're still "thinking about" teams. And there's no talk about modifying the culture. Most tellingly, the executive's personal involvement is almost nonexistent. We'd wager that he'd have a much higher level of personal involvement and urgency if his earnings dipped, wouldn't you?

Unfortunately this executive's reaction to the learning challenge is similar to that of many of his colleagues. We often hear from executives that they've: created a center, appointed a director, sent out a memo. But in almost all cases, they didn't change a single thing.

Within months this executive will be off on another "priority" and the learning organization will be one more starving activity. Is this really being the chief learning officer? Absolutely not.

Are You Serious About Getting Top Returns?
Invest in Learning

As the chief learning officer ask yourself, "Are we investing sufficiently in learning to generate the growth and return we need?" We know there's a correlation between investments in learning and shareholder returns. We had a group of graduate students research the topic, plotting long-term shareholder returns against a number of factors. They discovered that investments in training and development were the single best predictor of shareholder return, three to five years down the road. Do you want to pick the future top performing stocks? Choose those that invest the most in training and development.

We worked with a Dutch supermarket chain that invests 5 percent of its gross revenue in employee training and education. There are two unique characteristics of this organization: each one of their fifty-four stores carries a personalized-to-that-location merchandise inventory, and they guarantee that no checkout line will have more than two customers, because they guarantee that "three is free"—in other words, the third person in any checkout line gets his groceries free.

Imagine being able to know how to discover what customers in each location really want to buy, and develop the knowledge to be able to anticipate customer-flow demands so accurately that there's never more than two people in any checkout line. We thought about that last point as we spent twenty-five minutes in the checkout line at our local supermarket last week!

No wonder this innovative chain's sales per square foot are double—and their margins triple—those of their nearest competitor. Their executive vice president told us, "We work hard on helping our people all learn our proprietary methods and techniques. But we get the biggest return from people taking what we teach them and using their own native intelligence to improve it. Funny thing, the more we spend on training and development, the more improvements we develop and the more money we make. We wonder if there's any correlation there." We know there is.

Alan Greenspan hit the bull's-eye in the *Wall Street Journal*: "Human skills are subject to obsolescence at a rate perhaps unprecedented in American history." Even more apropos were these words from the March 1996 editorial page of *Money*: "Investors should stop chasing after companies that are saving money by laying off workers and start switching to firms that spend money training their employees." Those organizations that invest in learning will be tomorrow's winners.

Learning Is Much More Than Training—It's Also Coaching

Learning is not about sitting in a classroom and listening to a lecture (no matter how entertaining). The best learning occurs on the job between a coach/mentor, and a person with a burning desire to master a specific skill, behavior or thought process. Effective learners don't just show up to learn something because their boss/mother/friend thought it would be good for them. They show up to learn because they know that their life/livelihood/reputation/status depends on it.

Make learning part and parcel of every single job assignment. We recently visited several locations in the distribution company we're leading. We're probably pretty typical in that organization in the way we manage our training activities: the folks at the top decide what people need and provide it to them. That's pretty normal. The site manager, for instance, decided that his group needed to improve their teamwork. So he asked his HR manager to arrange for a teamwork training session. The HR manager canvassed his files and arranged for a local consultant to come in and offer a series of four teamwork training meetings. He then put out a sign-up sheet and got twenty-two sign-ups (out of 1,400 people at the location). This was typical top-down "we know what training you need."

We showed up and changed the landscape by asking people, "What do you need to do your job better? Is it a tool? Is it training? What kind of training, in what?" And so on. Not surprisingly, "teamwork" was not high on the list of frequently mentioned topics. Of course, everyone we asked had an answer. But like so many organizations, the initiative automatically started top-down.

We asked the production control manager what he needed to get to 100 percent guaranteed correct output while cutting turnaround time from forty-eight to twenty-four hours, because we're always looking for ways to cut time. He told us, "I really need a planning system. Don't care if it's a local system that doesn't connect up with our central computer. I just need something to do a better job of moving parts through our process. Then, as soon as I get that new planning system up and running, let me have a day with every associate that does the checkout so I can show him or her what the system can do for them. They'll tell me what else they need to know and what processes we need to change."

We wanted to hug the guy. Listen to how the education is focused around doing a better job for customers. Listen to how it's all driven from the associate out. Listen to how learning involves specific on-the-job activities. No wonder that division is tops in its activity.

Full Speed Ahead:
Be the Coach/Vehicle for Other People's Learning

"Coach" is an old French word meaning "a vehicle to transport people from one place to another." In organizations, a coach helps a person move from one capability or emotional/psychological/physical "place" to another—from one skill/performance level to another. Coaches perform a very valuable function: they help people grow. Whether it's in a family, a friendship, a neighborhood, a business or a church, great leaders are great coaches that help ordinary people do extraordinary things. Yesterday's leader asked how he or she could best exploit and mine the employee's abilities for the organization's gain. Today's coach asks, "How can I help this person learn to become more valuable to him- or herself—as well as all of us?"

Arm Wrestling for Dimes and Learning:
A Great Coach at Work

Our pastor is an extraordinary coach, particularly with young people. We watched him one day involve a particularly sullen and withdrawn teenager. The boy sat slouched in the corner, the crotch of his frayed oversized jeans and his chain-link key chain practically dragging on the floor. He'd been staring at the ceiling all during the first part of the youth group discussion, not speaking a word. At the break, Rev. Josh came up and put his arm around the boy's shoulders and said, "Tough day today, Billy."

A shoulder shrug was Billy's response.

"I need your help in this next part. I need someone who's very strong to demonstrate a point I want to make. Are you up for it?"

Another shrug, followed by some shuffling of feet.

"Seriously, Billy, I need your help. You're the strongest guy here. It'll be painless—and fun."

"Oh, okay," was the boy's reluctant reply.

"Okay, folks, let's reassemble," the Reverend said in a loud voice. "I want to demonstrate an important lesson. I've asked Billy to help me, since I need a really strong guy and we all know how strong Billy is. Billy, come on up—and thanks for helping. Now we're going to do a little arm wrestling, so let's use this table up front here. I bet you're pretty good doing this, being so strong and all."

"Not bad," Billy responds, warming to being in the spotlight.

"Now, the rules are very simple," the Reverend says. "We'll wrestle for about five minutes. And Billy, I want you to know that I can't afford to lose in front of this crowd." He glared at Billy with the most stern "I'm-going-to-win-this-game" face he could muster.

The two assumed their clasped-hands positions around the table, staring at each other. Billy easily won the first round in nothing flat, as the Reverend didn't offer any resistance. Billy looked surprised.

"Guess you won that one," the Reverend said, moving their hands to the initial clasped-hands position. "Billy, I forgot to tell you that your dad promised a dime a win." He then offered initial resistance, but went limp again after a few seconds and Billy won again. "Guess that's two dimes for you," he said, moving their hands to the original upright position. This time the Reverend offered strong resistance. Billy struggled for an instant, then a smile crossed his face and his hand went limp.

"That's right, Billy," the Reverend said, smiling. "Now you've caught on. Let's both get lots of dimes. Hey, John," he said, calling to Billy's father in the back. "Hope you brought a stash tonight." With that both Billy and the Reverend quickly moved their clasped hands back and forth in perfect unison. The audience broke out in laughter and applauded.

"Now Billy," the Reverend asked, "what's the lesson here?"

"Cooperating wins me more dimes. Dad, you owe me two and a half bucks."

Here's an example of a great coach in action. Rather than scolding Billy for his obvious inattention, he *engaged* Billy as a coequal player, praising him, both privately and publicly, for his capabilities. The Reverend set up the *expectations* for Billy's success and made him the center of attention. He created a *learn-by-doing learning situation*. His learning situation also helped the observers learn as well, though the doer (Billy) always learns more. His *light and fun approach* to a serious life lesson also made the learning more palatable for everyone. He *positively reinforced* Billy with smiles and verbal acknowledgment. He *asked questions* so that Billy (the learner) developed the answer, not the coach. The bottom line is: Billy learned a valuable life lesson and moved to a higher level of understanding.

Months later we overheard Billy talking to some other teenagers in the youth group about his arm wrestling with the Reverend and how he won "a bunch of money" by cooperating rather than competing with him. It's a pleasure to watch a master at work. We learned a lot about coaching from watching the Reverend.

Coaching Is a Two-Way Street

Coaching is a bilateral activity. It always involves two interdependent parties: a coach and someone wanting to be coached. That's an important point: people must want to move from where they are to where they want to go. Lots of folks talk about wanting to move, to learn, to grow, but only a few are truly dedicated to spend the time and energy to do so.

Ishmael was an undergraduate student of ours. He regularly stopped us after class with a plethora of questions about business opportunities. We had another class to get to, so we never had a lot of time to talk. We always suggested that he come in to talk during office hours, but somehow or other he never found the time. He stopped us in the hallway next semester to talk again about opportunities, but he was rushing off to class, so the conversation was brief. We offered to set up an appointment, but he was in too much of a hurry. Then we heard that he returned to his native country before he graduated. Guess he was too "busy" to complete the requirements.

The world is full of Ishmaels. All of us know people who talk, talk, talk about wanting to do X Y or Z but never seem to get around to doing it. These folks are not good candidates to be coached. It takes a commitment to make the journey before you can climb aboard "the coach."

Great Coaches Ask Great Questions

Here's a process we use when we coach. Notice the three steps: *thinking* about what you want to accomplish as a coach, *practicing* your coaching skills and then *reflecting* on your experience.

COACHING MODEL

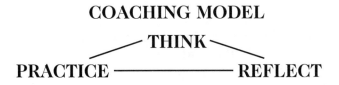

Think: What Do I as the Coach Want to Accomplish in This Coaching Session? Begin your preparation for coaching by thinking, "Why am I doing this?" Focus on your long-term and short-term goals. Thought precedes action. Think in new ways to act in new ways. Ask yourself:

1. What *long-term outcomes* do I want to create as a result of this coaching experience?

- What do I want my organization to look like, be, produce, stand for in the next one to three years?

- How do I want the coachee to perform, feel, act over the next one to three years, so she can become what she needs to be?

2. What *short-term goals* do I want to accomplish in this coaching interaction that contribute toward my long-term outcomes?

- What do *I* want to do and feel during and after this coaching interaction?
- What do I want *the coachee* to do and feel during and after this coaching interaction?

Coaches have agendas. Coaches have needs. Coaches have expectations. Articulate them so you know where you're coming from—and what you want out of the coaching experience.

Think: What Does the Coachee Want to Accomplish in This Coaching Experience? Shift your focus to the coachee. Ask yourself, "Why is she doing this?" Focus on the coachee's long-term and short-term goals. You might even ask the coachee these questions to begin the conversation. Help the coachee *think* in new ways—so she can *act* in new ways. Ask:
1. What *long-term outcomes* does the coachee want to create as a result of this coaching experience?

- What does she want her organization to look like, be, produce, stand for in the next one to three years?
- How does the coachee want to perform, feel, act, so that she can become what she needs to be?

2. What *short-term goals* does the coachee want to accomplish in this coaching interaction that contribute toward her long-term outcomes?

- What does she want to do and feel during and after this coaching interaction?
- What does she want the coach to do and feel during and after this coaching interaction?

Coachees have needs. Coachees have expectations. Coachees have agendas. Get those on the table as well. Openly share these mutual expectations up front to establish a trusting relationship.

Practice: And Pay Attention to How You're Doing. Action follows thought. So go out and play hard to win. Be an effective quarterback, though. On every play, read the situation and change the play at the line of scrimmage when necessary. Be an effective *participant-observer*. Hone the skill of reading the situation by continually asking the following questions during the coaching session:

1. Are my words and actions accomplishing my goals?

- If yes, how can I continue and strengthen my performance?
- If no, what do I need to change?

2. How is the coachee responding?

- Is she participating, or withdrawing?
- What can I do to encourage a more productive situation for her?

3. Am I listening to the coachee's feelings and expectations, or am I trying to push my own solution?

Play hard. Play smart. Play together. Encourage the coachee to ask himself the very same questions. Discuss your answers and learn together.

Reflection: Review the Game Films to Find Out How You Really Did. As with any other activity, study previous performance to improve future performance. Ask the following questions:

1. Did I accomplish my short-term goals in a way that helps me meet my long-term goals?

- What did I do that contributed to my success?
- What did I do that frustrated my success?
- How can I improve the next time?

2. Did the coachee accomplish her goals?
3. Did I help the coachee own the responsibility for his development?
4. What do I need to learn in order to be more effective?

In most coaching situations, the question is the answer. Too many people rush in with answers before they've even heard the questions—let alone think about it, gather information about it, analyze it and come up with an informed response. Answers should come from reflection, not reaction.

It's hard to be a good coach—an effective facilitator to take other people where they want to go. We've all learned to give fast answers—in classrooms, in offices, in family rooms. People look to us as "the experts" with all the "right answers." They come, as novitiates, seeking wisdom from the mystic storehouse of all wisdom. Yet we know that the best answers are those found by the individual himself.

Being a coach means enduring many painful silences when you don't answer their questions—and ask instead for their ideas. Steel yourself to survive the withering glances of disappointment and sometimes even disgust when, after someone's poured out his or her latest soap opera to you, you ask, "And what do you think would be best?"

The search for answers feeds both the coach's need to provide answers and the coachee's need for quick solutions. Many folks are bundles of answers looking for questions, like a hammer looking for a nail to hit. Just as many people carry around bundles of problems they are looking to offload on someone else — to blame, should things not work out. Use questions to keep the ownership where it belongs (remember Chapter 7), and provide the highest value coaching help.

Using Job Assignments to Stimulate Learning

Coaches do much more than ask questions, though. Coaching is an active, engaging role. We're in the business of transporting people from one place to another. Coaches are also stage-setters. Help people move toward their own objectives by providing them "stages"—called job assignments—upon which they can learn and grow.

Sabrina is a very talented process engineer working in our Frankfurt office. Her goal was to broaden her knowledge of several polyethylene production processes so she could more effectively redesign them to reduce the amount of toxic by-products. We knew several big polyethylene producers. We tapped our network and found four excellent internship projects for Sabrina.

She chose to complete all four, eventually winning two of them as redesign customers. She's now one of the organization's experts in polyethylene process redesign. We set the stage for Sabrina to develop a new talent. She seized the moment and made the most of it. One of our treasures is a framed note of thanks from her for locating those internships. Coaching has its rewards, too.

We share career and personal development objectives every year in the company. Larry, one of our Canadian leaders, listed "an Asian leadership experience" as his highest ranking career development objective for the coming year. Actually, we likely stimulated that interest during one of our visits to the Canadian facility. We asked Larry about his long-term interests and suggested both that he could use a non–North American experience and that Asia was a major expansion market for us.

So Larry asked for and got the assignment to lead our Japanese efforts. During our first visit to Larry in his new role, he wanted us to join him in visiting several potential customers and partners. On the way back to the hotel that night he said, "It's really exciting to watch you work the crowd, asking potential partners and customers how their business was going, what they did personally, what things were important to them and how they saw the business developing. I learned so much today in these conversations that I'm going to try your system tomorrow."

Next morning, Larry took the lead in asking the questions. He performed magnificently. We kept reinforcing his victories while helping him see how he might keep improving. He made copious notes and, like fine wine, got better as the day went along. Just last week he left us a long voice mail telling us how successful this question-asking process was with a prospective partner in Hong Kong.

Larry's job assignment to Japan was a major learning opportunity for him. As Phoenix leaders, we set the stage and he performed. You, too, can use the leverage of job assignments to help people move toward their individual and career development goals.

Stay Engaged: Don't Hit and Run

In the ten days after we left Larry and returned home to the
U.S., we exchanged six or seven voice mails. He'd call with an
observation and we'd volley back with both a compliment and a
suggestion. He'd call back with a report and we'd respond with
more compliments and suggestions. You've got to stay involved
in the coaching activity. Job assignments are wonderful learning
opportunities, but only if the coach continuously stimulates the
learning from the assignment.

In too many instances, a person posted overseas sees a coach
once a year. That'll never work. In fact, we were called in to help
with a very difficult, but all-too-typical situation. A major company dispatched Dwayne, one of its "high flyers," to lead a large
country organization in Europe that was in deep financial trouble. "Should take about six months to a year to straighten out,"
Dwayne was told.

Dwayne went over, took an apartment near the office, and
dove into the assignment. Meanwhile his wife and three children
remained in the States to finish out the school year, five months
away. The task proved much larger than Dwayne anticipated.
The problems were much more deeply rooted and complex.
Moreover, he wasn't prepared to deal with the European way of
managing. He couldn't just lay off people when necessary—without laborious discussion with the workers council first and huge
severance payments that made it extremely unattractive to cut
staff. He worked long hours. "After all, what else is there to do
here?" Dwayne quipped. But the harder Dwayne worked, the
deeper he got buried.

The family came over in June. Janet, his wife, found a house,
and they moved in during July. By October the family was a
shambles. The kids all wanted to go home. Janet talked incessantly about Stateside visits. Dwayne was never home as work
problems continued to escalate.

Dwayne hadn't spoken to his boss in months. Their last interaction, when he flew back to headquarters for a meeting, was
cool and unpleasant. The boss couldn't understand what was
taking Dwayne so long, and Dwayne felt isolated from his American colleagues.

The situation was too far gone in our opinion. We recommended that Dwayne be reassigned to a U.S. post and his family move back. Dwayne and his family were victims of too little coaching.

Encourage HighER Performance: Keep Raising the Bar

Imagine a first-time runner that shows up to run the mile in four minutes. Can anybody do that on the first try? Of course not. It takes lots of grueling practice, followed by more grueling practice, followed by even more grueling practice. The first time you run the mile you're lucky to do it in twenty-four minutes. A good coach doesn't beat the runner up for running the mile in twenty-four minutes. The good coach sets the initial bar at twenty minutes, then fifteen minutes, then ten minutes and so on: continually raising the bar in incremental steps until the runner reaches the world-class standard of less than four minutes. Incremental steps are the only way to achieve world-class standards. So the coach keeps raising the bar, keeps reinforcing current achievement and, as the chief learning officer, keeps creating situations where the individual can be challenged to learn and grow.

Some time ago we were in Chicago visiting a major customer where today we have a very small part of his potentially very large business. The area sales leader came along with us. She assumed that we were always going to be a small supplier, so we needed to concentrate on becoming a better and better secondary supplier. That's not a bad position, but it's not good enough. So we began by asking the owner what he thought was going to happen in the industry over the next few years and what we needed to do to help him be more successful. Twenty minutes later he told us exactly what we needed to do to become the prime supplier.

In the car going to the next appointment, our area sales leader could hardly contain herself. "I can't believe it. We've got a shot at becoming this guy's prime supplier!"

"Yep, we learned a lot in that exchange," we said. Raising the bar again, we added, "Not only did he give us several great ideas for how to win his business, he also showed us how to make a difference in a whole bunch of other customers' businesses as well—and win their business also."

She cracked a great big smile, counting the sales volume increases in her head.

In that little exchange we demonstrated another important role of the chief learning officer—CLO—continually demonstrate that you are also learning all the time. We don't have all the answers—no one does. We're not expected to have all the answers—and we don't expect anyone else to have all the answers, either. It's perfectly acceptable to say, "I don't know, but I'll go and find out."

Help People See Over Walls and Through Blind Spots

We all suffer from tunnel vision. As we live life we get to be more and more focused on fewer and fewer things. It is said that the process of education is learning more and more about less and less, until you earn a Ph.D.—and you know everything about nothing. The consequence of a narrow focus is missing important peripheral developments that may dramatically impact your future. Recall how the Buddha attracted a large following because he was awake. The CLO's responsibility is to help keep people awake to systemic developments throughout their entire interconnected, interdependent network.

Competition often comes from over the wall. We worked with a billion-dollar printing company that wants to manage their customers' digital information assets. As such, they bump up against such consulting firms as Andersen Consulting and EDS, computer distribution companies like Ingram Micro, credit reporting firms like Equifax and database companies like SAS—all of whom see the management of those same digital assets as their legitimate business turf. The printing company is tightly focused on such printing competitors as RR Donnelley and doesn't see any of these other peripheral firms as competitors.

For instance, today they are too small in these peripheral businesses to show up on Ingram Micro's radar screen. Likewise, Andersen does not show up on the printing company's competitive screen. But they are all, in fact, competing for the same management of the same customer's digital assets business.

Much like the way restaurants compete with movies and theme parks for the consumer's entertainment dollar, the printing company competes with SAS for the customer's data analysis investment dollars. The company not on your radar screen today may eat your lunch tomorrow. Aluminum did it to steel; Toyota did it to General Motors. Ask yourself, "Who is waiting in the wings to do it to me?" The CLO builds learning situations that help people see over the walls of their own specialization and functional discipline focus.

Establish Focused Training Experiences—And Follow Up on the Job. Although we've launched a major expansion into Asia, unfortunately, most of our folks have only North American experience. We commissioned the HR leader to find a practical culture training program, and he found a great culture training source right in our backyard. All of our 200-plus officers will go through the two-week program. In-house follow-ups to the program focus on applying the new cultural mind-set to our activities. In fact, we take time at every officers' meeting to discuss how each issue we cover might be viewed differently in other cultures. Those discussions reinforce learning—and encourage consistent, disciplined focus—so all can participate more effectively.

All of our non-U.S. management people go through a parallel course in U.S. culture. Most organizations have the limited view that it's only the U.S. managers that need training. But the truly global view also requires that non-U.S. managers clearly understand U.S. culture (which for them is the foreign culture). By the end of the year, the entire senior management group will have a much better mutual understanding of the cultural drivers of behavior.

Then we plan to engage the rest of the associate group in the same cultural training experience. Notice how the classroom experience is reinforced with follow-ups that focus on application and specific on-the-job activities, like the officer discussions about how different cultures view an issue. Tie in the classroom activity to business goals—global expansion, say—and specific on-the-job activities. That's the way to make classroom training pay off.

Build Assessment Centers to Help Leaders See Themselves as Others See Them. Very few of us see ourselves as others see us.

Ninety-two percent of Americans believe that they are above average. The inability to see our own strengths and weaknesses is a big blind spot. Yet as valuable as the information may be, it is also very threatening.

Working with a local university and several other companies in our area, our human resources leader set up a Center of Learning. People spend a day and a half in a series of experiences and tests to learn about themselves and their leadership style. They get feedback from their back-home associates and their fellow participants on what works and doesn't work in their leadership roles. The feedback is invaluable, both from the back-home folks and the participants. It is also valuable to benchmark that data against other leaders in other organizations.

The entire process is developmental rather than evaluative or competitive. We learned over the years that a competitive environment chills learning. When people feel threatened, they close up like morning glories at midnight.

Eventually, the top 1,000 people in the organization will go through the center. It's voluntary, but the expectation is that everyone will go. Each person gets his or her report, and it's up to them to share it or not with their associates. Virtually everyone shares the report. We talked to John, one of the sales VPs, who said he learned a lot about himself at the program, but missed the ability to talk about his learning with his coach, who hadn't gone yet. His comment signaled us to push even harder to get more people to sign up and attend.

Application Delayed Is Learning Lost. John's comment points out another vital role of the chief learning officer: making certain that people have an immediate opportunity to apply what they've learned. Too many great training programs produce little impact because the gap between learning and application is too wide.

We talked to the HR leader and he arranged for sharing sessions immediately upon return from the center. These sessions developed into a network of former participants. People used the sessions to validate their learning in the program and set specific targets and goals for their continued development. People really yearn for support in their development efforts, and these informal networks provide invaluable assistance during personal growth times.

Visit Others to Improve the View in the Mirror. Often our own record of success is a big blind spot. We believe that we know how to do things best, so we stop looking to improve. It happens to us all. We work with a hotel chain. One property was the consistent top performer, but they developed an arrogant "we know how to do things" attitude. We helped the owners launch a new marketplace-in-strategic-planning process. In the course of that planning we discovered that the high-performing hotel had actually been losing market share!

The property general manager immediately urged the staff to start investigating the competition. She set up a fund to pay for all staff members, from housekeepers to front desk people, to eat and/or stay at competitive hotels. Within weeks the staff accumulated enough data to begin redesigning their own hotel. Everyone took part. Everyone contributed. The next six-month competitive market report showed a six-point share growth. "Now they're really insufferable," one of the other GMs said. "But they've earned the right."

You can never do enough looking over the wall, seeing how others do things. Encourage everyone to do it, at all levels in the organization. The folks at our distribution company who do technical support and answer hotlines for our customers also visit each customer's back office activities, spending several days absorbing their culture. When they come back, they can answer the telephones just as if they were the customer's employees.

We've learned to work hard on continually benchmarking activities. For instance, we arranged to visit Baldridge quality award winners to help folks see quality superiority in action. Then we visited other firms, even those in tangential industries, who are doing some particular piece of business very well, so we can see how we might learn from them. Cardinal Health is an excellent example of a firm, not necessarily in our industry, that's doing a process especially well—Internet commerce. Even though they're in the health care products business, we learned lots from them. People came back from that trip saying, "They're doing this and that. I'm going to see how we can do something very similar." Seeing excellence in action helps individuals visualize how they can do it for themselves.

When we return from these benchmark site visits, we don't talk about the terrible plane ride or the lovely hotel or the great meal we had together. No, we talk about what we are going to do to capitalize on what we've learned. We create a joint action plan that becomes part of each person's weekly and monthly action objectives.

Make Learning a Part of Everything You Do

Too many people separate learning from doing. They learn in a classroom and then go out and do on the job. Learning by doing is the best way to learn. Build in learning as a part of every activity. The best people seamlessly integrate work and learning. And Phoenix leaders help everyone do it.

Start every meeting by agreeing on the principle of learning from that meeting. Take time at the end of every meeting to check whether everyone has accomplished their learning purposes. Ask this question in every conversation: "What did you learn from that activity and how are you going to apply it?" Keep the focus on learning. In so doing, you'll find you are also focusing on the real business value of every meeting and activity.

How do we do that? We take notes—in a notebook or laptop. We keep a journal. We write down what we're learning. We're voracious tearer-uppers of newspapers, journals and magazines, clipping articles that pertain to our professional and personal lives. We share those clippings with others to stimulate their learning.

Accentuate the learning dimension in every task, every meeting—and with every person you know. Work and learning are simultaneous, continuous loop activities. The coach intervenes to make certain that the learning is capitalized on and applied on the job. In fact, successful Phoenix leaders create an environment where learning is expected as part of the job. We turn to that task next.

Learning begins with you. As the chief learning officer in your interconnected, interdependent network, set the pace, build the stage and help your learners bloom. Life is a great teacher. The CLO helps us all learn its lessons.

PHOENIX WORKSHOP

1. HOW CAN I DEMONSTRATE MY PERSONAL COMMITMENT TO MY (AND OTHERS') LEARNING?

_____

_____

2. HOW CAN I IMPROVE MY SKILL IN USING THE COACHING MODEL TO HELP OTHERS LEARN?

_____

_____

3. HOW CAN I USE JOB ASSIGNMENTS TO FURTHER LEARNING?

_____

_____

4. HOW CAN I KEEP RAISING THE BAR TO HELP PEOPLE CONTINUE TO LEARN?

_____

_____

5. HOW CAN I HELP PEOPLE SEE OVER WALLS AND THROUGH THEIR BLIND SPOTS?

_____

_____

6. WHAT FOCUSED TRAINING PROGRAM CAN WE USE TO HELP US ALL LEARN?

_____

_____

BUILD THE LEARNING PLATFORM TO LAUNCH THE LEARNING ROCKET

Nothing valuable grows in an uncultivated garden—only weeds. If you want roses in your garden, it takes hard work and constant attention. You need to make certain that the roses get regular watering and spraying, plus healthy doses of fertilizer. Roses cannot be left to chance.

It's the same with learning. In theory, everyone's in favor of learning. No one we know of campaigns for ignorance. But like roses in your garden, substantive learning doesn't happen automatically. It takes hard work—lots of it—and a system that proactively facilitates the learning equivalent of regular watering, spraying and fertilization. That's what we call the "learning infrastructure."

Building Learning into the Management System

Incorporate learning into the ongoing management system, the heart of which is the objective measurement and reward systems. And remember, training isn't enough. The management system must encourage learning by doing.

Everyone Has a Learning Objective. Everyone has an annual learning objective, one of five shared across the entire organization. Each person chooses his or her own personal learning objective, in conjunction with their coach, teammates and customers. Everyone reports quarterly how they're doing against all five objectives. The bonus plan pays out in five equal shares; one fifth for attainment of each of the five objectives. We put our time and money where our heart is. Expect, measure and reward learning. Make the personal learning objective as important as the financial and market share objectives.

Share Learning Experiences with Your Intranet. Set the pace with your own personal learning objectives. This year, we chose our European board membership as the focus of our personal learning objective. Since one of our companies is expanding internationally, we promised to bring insights from this board experience back and help the senior officer staff develop a more non-U.S.-centric perspective. The board gives us a European peer group from which to learn how non-U.S. companies think and behave. As a by-product, this learning objective also gives us the chance to demonstrate again that important learning takes place outside the classroom.

Every time we return from that particular board meeting, we share via e-mail several important learning points from the meeting. In that way our learning points bounce all over and through the organization. Last time, for example, we shared that another board member, the leader of a large German organization, felt that XYZ-Deutsch is the best distribution company in Germany.

We asked, "What do we think about his recommendation—and should we consider trying to work some sort of a relationship with them? And here's a couple of the other things we discussed. What do you think about these?" We now talk about the learning from this board experience in every speech we give, at every location we visit. People get the message: we're serious about the personal development objective.

Some Personal Learning Objectives Are Very Personal. Some personal development objectives are very personal. For instance, the CFO's objective at Square D one year was to take a two-week vacation with his family, leave the office before 7:00 at night and do his Christmas cards at home with his wife instead of two nights before Christmas at the office. Another specific such objective was the sales VP at AT&T who became factory superintendent for a time as part of her learning about the manufacturing side of the business. That particular experience came in handy when she later became vice president of the entire business unit.

Throughout the years, many people have attended programs at Northwestern, Cornell or Dartmouth as part of their personal development objective. We work to keep track of them and follow up at every opportunity and make certain that they incorporate their learning into their daily practice.

Reward Learning by Recognizing Learners. Compensation is important—very important. Miss a few paychecks and you realize how important that paycheck really is. But all the research shows conclusively that compensation, while critical, usually ranks between fourth and seventh in importance to employees. Individual recognition and words of praise from high-profile people (like the coach or the leader) rank higher than raw dollars in most situations.

We do a recognition program for the folks who bring the most learning into our organization. This year we plan to use this special recognition program by rewarding those that help us learn by bringing in new and valuable outside information. Usually, forty to fifty of our best learner associates get together for a few days to share learning experiences. We've learned it pays to pay for serious learning with money, special status and personal recognition.

The "Shot-in-the-Foot" Award for Learning from Mistakes. One of our divisions initiated a Shot-in-the-Foot Award. Mistakes are a part of learning. Most times we seek to bury our mistakes. It is said that while success has many parents, failure is an orphan. This group decided to capitalize on their failures by learning from them. They arranged monthly meetings where people shared their biggest mistake from which they learned the most.

The person with the biggest mistake from which he learned the most was awarded the privileged use of a special coffee mug, labeled "Top Learner," resting in a plaster-of-paris foot with a big bullet hole in it. It was so popular many other groups copied the idea. Someone offered to compile the learning from all the groups and share it throughout the organization. That became the forerunner of our Knowledge Center. There are still groups scattered throughout the organization that use the Shot-in-the-Foot recognition scheme, though most others have moved on to other techniques to recognize and reward learning.

Build a Knowledge Center to Encourage Learning

Many organizations, like Arthur Andersen, for instance, work very hard to share their accumulated knowledge across their entire organization. Their challenge is simple. How can consultant number 30,001 access the knowledge contained in the heads of the other 30,000 Andersen consultants?

Andersen, like many other organizations, sells knowledge. But knowledge is inherently a very personal property. How do you capture and share that personal property knowledge in a meaningful way? Ask anyone who's thought about it, or worked to do it in an organization. They'll likely shake their head and say such words as, "It isn't easy." We've wrestled with this challenge for a long time. As we pointed out earlier, the Knowledge Center is a part of our answer.

Four Pillars in a Knowledge Center: CIS, PIS, MIS, MPIS. Begin by building a Knowledge Center upon four databases: the *customer* database, the *people* database, the *management information* database and the *marketplace* database. Everyone needs access to these. We use the data-warehousing and data-mining technologies, combined with data query tools, to make this knowledge available to all associates.

CIS for Customer Knowledge. Many people touch customers—help-desk folks, accounts receivable folks, truck drivers. In fact, many more people touch customers than most organization leaders realize. Install a customer information system (CIS) that's a central point where anybody in the company can go and get information about any customer.

Our CIS contains not only the typical ordering and financial information—order history, margins, turnover rates, inventory levels and payment history—but also a wealth of personal data about people in the company, including birthdays, anniversaries and favorite colors/teams/activities. Product usage data and anecdotal information about issues/problems/future prospects are also included. Everyone who contacts the customers adds a comment or two summarizing what they learned during their interaction. The database automatically categorizes each comment. For instance you can literally find out the five most frequently mentioned complaints by end-user customers about Microsoft's word processing program.

One of our distribution company customers recently asked us to help him understand his customer (the end-user) better. He wants us to gather and process the knowledge for him. He has a good-sized operation, about $450 million a year—however, in his words, we have the technology he can't afford to buy himself. With that end-user data, we can help him differentiate himself in the market. We frequently get those kinds of requests from our retail customers—for help in understanding their end-user customer. Our knowledge center is gearing up to respond to these requests.

A close friend makes a commodity meat product. He wraps his commodity meat product in a rich package of information. He approaches the supermarket meat manager with the following pitch: "Let me tell you, Mr. Supermarket Manager, how to boost your sales in the entire category, and leverage the affinity products throughout the store. Here's our market basket analysis of people who buy our branded commodity meat product. Notice all the additional affinity products they also buy. Here's the market basket analysis of the folks who buy your private label product—which we also produce for you. Notice how slim their basket of additional purchases is in comparison to the baskets of the buyers of the branded products.

"But notice also how the private-label buyers have a different pattern of purchases. Let me show you how to advertise our branded product—and then merchandise several other manufacturers' coupons with it, to attract the higher-spending brand buyers. At the same time, let me show you how to advertise your private-label products and co-advertise several other products with it to maximize your market basket from those buyers."

Unlike his big competitors who still push cents-off promotions or slotting fees, our friend sells knowledge of the customers to the supermarket manager and gets 30 cents a pound more at the wholesale level. He commands that premium because the retailer knows he'll get 75 cents to a dollar more at the retail level. Our friend uses customer information to command higher prices, margins and market share for himself and his retailer's customers.

The CIS contains a great deal of granular, microscopic information about each and every customer. Anyone can find out what Customer A ordered, what they paid for that product, what margin we earned on it, how they used that product, what they thought about it and how they saw it matching up to the competition—as well as the birthday of the chief engineer's daughter and her favorite kind of candy. That's a customer-profile gold mine.

PIS for People Knowledge. In Chapter 6 we wrote about our personal information system (PIS). Any team that needs a person with specialized knowledge of hydroflorins, and the ability to speak Mandarin Chinese, can query the database and call any of the seventeen people surfaced in the search. The PIS spells out each person's background, experience and skills.

The database automatically categorizes all personnel information and makes it easy to access people with specialized skills. Need a masseuse who speaks Polish? Look it up in the PIS— which serves as a virtual competency-on-demand gold mine.

MIS for Management Knowledge. Every organization runs on financial information. Ensure that financial information—complete and accurate—is available in granular form to all associates who need it.

Our management information system (MIS), for instance, provides detailed financial information on the price ranges, gross margins, fill rates and inventory levels for any given product for every customer on an hour-by-hour and day-by-day basis. Both selling and purchasing associates use this database regularly.

MPIS for Marketplace Knowledge. Every industry landscape is being rearranged daily by new technologies, new competitors, new products, new customers with new demands and expectations. Are you up-to-date? Are you out-of-date? Will you be obsolete tomorrow? The day after tomorrow? To answer these questions you need a fourth database: a marketplace information system (MPIS).

In our organization, we track current competitors, possible future competitors (potential competitors that we've identified from our scanning process), technological developments in our fields, technological developments in ancillary fields identified by our customers as impacting their businesses in the future, and the potential needs of new customers who may enter our markets through new applications and technological developments. Our future scanning activities develop most of the information contained in the MPIS database, supplemented by continuing input from all those who touch customers.

The Knowledge Center Is Also a Learning Lab and Networking Place. Even though the learning infrastructure is built around a computing network, it's much more than just bits and bytes. It's also a mechanism to enable and support shared learning and competency development. Our Knowledge Center includes group forums, chat sessions and user groups. It's much more than just a data access system—it's an electronic meeting place and marketplace.

All the talk about intranets and Web sites obscures their basic raison d'être: socializing knowledge throughout the organization and facilitating learning. The Knowledge Center becomes THE PLACE to find out about customers, financial results, people capabilities and marketplace developments. It also becomes THE

PLACE to find other people who share similar needs and interests. The Knowledge Center is THE PLACE to find others to learn from, to mentor, to be mentored by, to share off-the-wall ideas with. The infrastructure is knowledge- and competency-driven rather than transaction- (files, functions and operations) driven, so that it supports the anytime, anywhere access to the knowledge and the people that you need to integrate work and learning.

Customers also have access to our Knowledge Center. In a previous chapter we explained that customers are our best consultants. Why cut yourself off from your best consultants? Let 'em in! Furthermore, we include future customers (both former customers who will be customers again and never-before customers who will also become customers) in the Knowledge Center. We want access to them so we can learn from them what we can do differently.

Knowledge Centers are technologically feasible today. But they go beyond the technology to incorporate and advance the interests of the people. Information systems must be harnessed to support and grow people and competencies. Never forget their purpose: facilitate knowledge, growth and shared learning. The Knowledge Center provides the Christmas tree on which we all can hang beautiful learning ornaments.

Learning takes place on an ongoing, daily basis. It is mostly unstructured. It is mostly unfocused. It is largely random. But all of us learn. Life is learning. However, the chief learning officer builds management system and information infrastructure platforms that create focused learning opportunities that will fulfill the aspirations of both the learner and the organization.

You can't capture and share 100 percent of all learning, but you can organize more than the 1 percent that currently gets captured. Just imagine if you could capture 10 percent, you would be ten times ahead of your competition. Seize every moment to create learning platforms and then capture and share the knowledge created from them.

PHOENIX WORKSHOP

1. HOW CAN I ENSURE THAT EVERYONE (INCLUDING ME) HAS A LEARNING OBJECTIVE?

_____

_____

2. WHAT MEASUREMENT AND REWARD SYSTEM CAN I PUT IN PLACE THAT WILL ENCOURAGE LEARNING?

_____

_____

3. HOW CAN I BUILD AND ENSURE THE CONSISTENT USE OF A KNOWLEDGE CENTER?

_____

_____

MAKE KNOWLEDGE MORE POWERFUL THAN RANK

Important Decisions Require the Best Knowledge

You face an important marketing decision. To whom do you turn? The head of the marketing department, right? Maybe, maybe not. If you want to make the best decision, find the person who has the most knowledge about the marketing question you have, regardless of where that person is in the official hierarchy—and even if that person is several organizational levels removed from the head of the department. Getting the best information to make the best decision means getting the person with the best knowledge.

Larry works in one of our organizations. On his own, almost like a hobby, he learned quality improvement processes. He also studied companies like Disney to discover how they trained and developed people in ethics and value leadership.

We picked Larry to lead our worldwide Partners in Excellence effort. He's facilitating the training and implementation, enlisting cooperators (disciples) worldwide. In less than a two-month period he made it happen. Larry was a natural for the leadership spot. We knew we could count on him to learn whatever it took to be successful in this activity, as he'd learned what he needed to be successful in the past.

Encourage Knowledge Development

Why do people work hard to acquire knowledge? Some because they just love learning. Others because it's the superhighway to a bigger, better-paying job. Others because it leads to greater in-dependence. Whatever the reason, people acquire knowledge in order to satisfy some personal desire. But what happens to the motivation to learn if after investing hours or days or weeks in acquiring knowledge that knowledge is ignored or discounted by important decision makers in your life? How would you react? Ask Luanne.

Use Associates' Knowledge—Or Your Competitor Will. Luanne was a receptionist in a sales office. She handled the flow of visitors and phone calls, working to provide a positive image of the office to outsiders. She was very good at her job, but she yearned to become a sales representative. She enjoyed selling things for her church group and several volunteer organizations. "Get some education in marketing and sales," the office manager suggested.

Luanne enrolled in a certificate program at the local community college, taking seven sales and marketing classes over a three-semester period, earning an A in them all. She showed her books to the office manager, discussed her term papers with her and proudly shared her grades. During Luanne's year-and-a-half attendance at the community college the office added four new sales representatives. Luanne bided her time, not asking about a sales job until she received her certificate. When she completed her last class, she proudly framed her certificate and hung it over her desk. "I'm ready now to take on a sales position," she told the office manager.

Imagine her chagrin when she met the newest sales representative who'd been hired after she graduated and spoke with the office manager. "Thought you needed some more experience,"

the office manager said. "Be happy to consider you for the next
junior sales position that comes up."

"Why did I go to school?" Luanne asked us angrily. "They didn't
care about my education. It was just a way to put me off."

"But other people will value that education," we suggested.
"Why not look for a sales job on your own?"

Luanne wound up with five job offers, all of which at least doubled her salary. She couldn't have been happier. Her current
(soon-to-be-former) employer didn't value her education—and
lost a valuable motivated associate.

There are lots of Luannes in the world—people whose education and knowledge are ignored by their organizations. Imagine
how an engineer feels when her boss—a nontechnical person—
overrules her technical recommendation on "business grounds."
Sadly, most organizations value hierarchy status more than personal knowledge of the subject. We look to the boss/head coach
as the logical person to make a decision, rather than the person
who has the information and knowledge, regardless of where they
are in the organizational hierarchy. We think first of organizational position and only secondarily of who has the knowledge.

Put the Knowledge Holders in Charge

Words from the Chairman: "I Work for the Team Leader." We reorganized NCR into customer focused teams (CFTs), where all the
knowledge needed to serve a given customer was brought to that
customer interface. We searched for learning leaders to head the
CFTs. Of course we didn't use that term. It hadn't been invented
yet. But we looked for leaders who were models of the new Phoenix
and were deeply committed to personal learning and growth.

Ray was the casting director's/HR director's dream come true.
He was the tintype candidate to lead a CFT. He was a very successful salesperson who truly exemplified the new values and
lifestyle. He was customer-focused, associate-sensitive and
learning-committed. He fit the mold perfectly.

Ray led the biggest CFT for the biggest customer, Wal-Mart. His
team consisted of salespeople, service technicians, financial analysts, hardware engineers, software developers and a raft of other
specialists needed to help Wal-Mart win in their marketplace.

Early on the customer tested our commitment to the CFT concept. They didn't do it deliberately. It was just one more *Phoenix leadership moment* that occurs in the normal course of life. They had a big, multiyear order. Competition was fierce: IBM, HP, DEC, all deeply wanted the deal. One of us got a call from the chief information officer. "We've got a problem on this project that I think you ought to know about. We really like doing business with you. You've got great stuff. But your price is out of line. Tried to talk with Ray, but he's stuck on his price. Can't you talk some sense into him? He's new in this management business, and doesn't know when to sharpen his pencil. He sure could use some coaching. If not . . ." His voice trailed off, but we knew what he meant.

"Great to hear from you," one of us said. "Sorry, but in this case, I work for Ray. His price is my price. He knows the situation better than I do. I'll be happy to tell him you called and suggest he give you a call. But it's his decision."

The silence on the other end of the phone hung like Los Angeles smog on a bad inversion day. Finally he came back with, "Okay, have Ray call me and we'll see what we can work out."

We got the job. Ray did sharpen his pencil (a little coaching from us helped him repackage the proposal). But we sent the clear message to everyone that "The chairman says the CFTs are making the decision—and he won't overrule them. They really are in charge." Knowledge is more important than rank.

Chairman: "Get the Engineers Together and Get Me Out of the Loop." A similar situation occurred at Honeywell. We set up a number of worldwide account teams. Sam led the account team creating success for our largest customer. They came to him with a request to de-feature one of our most popular models. They wanted to reduce the controller's temperature sensitivity from plus or minus two tenths of a degree of temperature to plus or minus one degree. Doesn't sound like much, but that change would put a product on the market with our name on it that created perceived discomfort for people.

He refused to make the change, pointing out that doing so would damage our reputation as the recognized world leader in temperature control, and proposed an alternative. The same day, we received a call from the customer's president. He asked, "How can you do this? You claim to be customer-focused. We're your customer and we want this change. Your guy turned us down. Better take him out to the woodshed and explain the facts of life to him."

After he cooled down, and we listened to his side of the story, we explained that Sam was in charge. He knew the situation better than we did. His solution sounded reasonable and we urged the president to have his engineering staff work with Sam's and see if they could come up with a cost-effective way to maintain the precision temperature control. He did, and the story has a happy ending as the engineers found a win-win solution (much along the lines that Sam originally proposed). Rack up another score for knowledge being more important than rank.

Knowledge Is Power—Regardless of the Package It Comes In. It's even harder to place knowledge over rank when that knowledge comes in an unfamiliar package. We asked a young woman who'd just completed her MBA at Stanford to lead the team responsible for planning and building a new facility. Back then, young women did not carry these kinds of responsibilities.

Priscilla handled it exquisitely. She did a great job finessing the hard hats and hard heads with whom she dealt. We got a ton of phone calls from folks trying to go around "the skirt"— Phoenix leadership moments all. Each time we politely but firmly reminded them that Priscilla (not "the skirt") was in charge, her word carried weight, and we backed her 110 percent. Priscilla enabled us to demonstrate, one more time, that it doesn't matter how old you are, or what sex you are. What matters most is what you know—and how you use what you know— to create success for our customers.

Fayol Loses, Taylor and Knowledge Workers Win

There was a titanic struggle in the management field around the turn of the last century. Two giants battled it out. On the one side, Frenchman Henri Fayol urged matching authority and responsibility in a centralized, hierarchical, command-and-control organization. And on the other side stood the American Frederick Taylor. Taylor urged that knowledge was more important than position.

So he developed a concept called "functional management," where the person with the greatest knowledge about a subject exercised decision control over that subject. So, the steelworker took orders from the chief metallurgist in setting temperatures on the Bessemer furnace, and orders from the rolling mill expert in rolling the ingots into flat sheets. In fact, the same worker could have as many different "bosses" as there were different expertises needed to produce the final product. Fayol's simpler and neater "one boss" concept won the battle—then. Management theory reflects Fayol's writings and thoughts.

But times change. Old Frederick Taylor—wherever he is—must be smiling. Today, more and more business leaders practice Taylor's functional management concept, only we call it "matrix management." Increasingly, we recognize that knowledge must be more important—and more powerful—than bureaucratic rank. Those who know must be in a position to influence outcomes that fall within their area of expertise. And we must develop individuals throughout the organization who know so they can make decisions without resorting to the hierarchy. We need more Rays and Sams and Priscillas in the world who know and decide.

Creating valuable-to-customers knowledge faster than the competitors is the critical marketplace differentiator today. In fact, it's people who keep learning and creating more knowledge that are the only true sustainable competitive advantage. Recognize that knowledge is power, and give the power to those with the knowledge. Or else you discourage and negate the investment that people are willing to make in learning and applying that learning to the solution of customers' business problems.

PHOENIX WORKSHOP

HOW CAN I PUT THE KNOWLEDGE HOLDERS IN CHARGE OF IMPORTANT DECISIONS?

_____

_____

_____

MAKE YOUR UNIVERSE YOUR UNIVERSITY: MULTIPLY THE LEARNING, SQUARE THE VALUE CONTRIBUTED AND EXPONENTIALLY INCREASE YOUR PERSONAL FUTURE SECURITY

Every company we know is moving from selling things to selling knowledge. The story is the same whether you're a printer moving into managing customers' digital information assets, a credit report company selling customer profile information to retailers and banks or a turbine manufacturer selling aircraft (and engine) maintenance services. Knowledge rules. Learning is critical. And your universe is your university.

Today we revivolute organizations to make knowledge more powerful than rank, with a management system and information infrastructure that institutionalize the creation, capture, sharing and use of knowledge. It will be led by those whose principal task is to be the chief learning officer of the interconnected, interdependent network in which the organization is involved.

In tomorrow's world, knowledge will not only supersede rank, it will redefine it and redistribute it to everyone who is willing to grow. The challenge is to actuate learners in your network to enable them to fulfill the human aspirations of all those with whom they—and you—are interdependent and interconnected.

Lead the charge to learn faster, higher, deeper. Open doors. Break through walls. Let the future in!

Summary: Phoenix Leadership

Rest stop ahead! Let's pause for a moment, stretch our intellectual legs and review where we've come. The first thread of our argument screams at us from the headlines and six o'clock news every day. "The times they are a-changin'—too fast for most of us." The earthquakes rearranging our business, economic, political, technological and social landscapes force us to rapidly change ourselves and our organizations. But change is a rare bird, talked about often and seen only rarely. We've discovered that it is easier to create tomorrow than change today. Therein lies the second thread of our argument—one that speaks to us daily also, only in a softer, dulcet tone. See nature's way of change in the daily sunrise and sunset and in the changing of the seasons. Nature speaks not of change but of renewal—the renewal of the sun every day and the trees every spring. Combining these two threads is our word *revivolution—renewal through revolution (or rapid evolution that looks a lot like revolution)*. Each and every one of us, in our personal and career lives, faces the urgent need to revivolute.

Thus is born our use of the Phoenix—that mythical symbol of the continuing self-renewing life force. Throughout the pages of history the Phoenix is the ultimate symbol of optimism, representing organizations, nations and individuals that emerge, rise, soar, rebound, return, make amazing comebacks, reappear and spring eternal. The self-renewing Phoenix soars using five principles: 1) to renew by creating a future that makes a difference and leaves a legacy, 2) to recognize, honor and leverage your connections, 3) to create success for all those with whom you are interconnected and interdependent, 4) to learn more in order to contribute more to others' success, and 5) to take responsibility and become a Phoenix leader of your interconnected networks. Our challenge is to become the self-renewing Phoenix in our personal and professional lives, revivoluting to meet the ever-changing needs of all the good people with whom we are connected.

The Phoenix leader steps forward, seizes the initiative and takes responsibility to create success for all those with whom he or she is interconnected. She focuses on accomplishing two critical outcomes that perhaps sometimes sound contradictory: building heart connections with individuals and installing disciplined, fact-based processes. Both are essential to creating success for all the interconnected, interdependent people with whom she is involved. This combination of soft and hard is what distinguishes the rare species of Phoenix leaders from other more commonly found species of managers and leaders.

Self-renewing Phoenix leaders create these outcomes by: surfacing the issues facing the organization, engaging the people in defining these issues, prioritizing the resources necessary to effectively deal with these issues, unleashing the feelings and behaviors of ownership, and energizing learners and learning. Throughout all of his activities, the Phoenix leader builds heart connections with people and encourages fact-based living.

The Phoenix leader, having renewed and revived the organization, steps up to the line and takes responsibility for leading his or her connected people by then creating the symbol of stability: the Pyramid, the solid base for future success. In the Pyramid the Phoenix leader lays out a systematically constructed, perfectly aligned vision, mission, values, goals and strategies, disciplined management systems, business processes and communications infrastructures that build upon Phoenix leadership to create the base for a successful future. The Pyramid becomes the Phoenix leader's enduring legacy and symbol of the organization's renewal, creativity and success. In the next section we'll show you how the Phoenix leader leads the construction of the Pyramid. Although more hard work is straight ahead, a successful future is within our grasp.

PART III

CREATING YOUR FUTURE

INTRODUCTION

It is time. What started as a trickle now seems like a thirty-foot tsunami. Coming from every which way across your network-linked world, the zillion ERROR messages all sound a similar theme.

Yesterday's e-mail from the big boss still gives you shivers. Buried amid the myriad of announcements that fill your mailbox, he wrote, "Ran into Hein from Frankfurt. He told me that their system still isn't operating properly. Thought it was fixed. What's the story? He's pretty unhappy. We can't afford to lose his business. (He is our biggest customer, you know.) Keep me posted." You thought it was fixed also. ERROR message.

Stan just left your desk. He stopped by for "just a minute"— forty-five minutes ago. Serious political problems on the Johnson front. The folks in finance seem to be gunning for you on that project. They've got some data about overruns that doesn't look good. "Got to look into that," you make a mental note. Protect your flank. ERROR message.

Team Blue, one of the four development teams on which you are a member, is four weeks behind schedule. You can't get the folks to play together. Each is still protecting their own turf. If you can't get it ironed out—soon—it'll be a black mark on your career. "I know what to do," you tell yourself. "I just need the time to sit with the three big mouths and help them see how Blue is in their interest. Next week, maybe." ERROR message.

The guilt-reading pile grows higher on your desk. You need to get to that latest technical report buried somewhere in that pile. Shauna in St. Paul is waiting for your reaction to it. Is it something we ought to be working on? She left a voice mail last Tuesday. She would like some input so she can make up next year's budget. "Where did the day go?" you ask yourself as darkness falls. You search through the pile for the report so you can take it home with you. "Maybe I'll get a chance to read it tonight," you say hopefully to yourself. "Oh sure. Right. At 2:00 A.M. maybe," the cynical response flashes across your mind-screen. ERROR message.

Things are no better on the home front. You and your husband seem to be competing for who can come to bed later and be more tired. You are winning. ERROR message. You can't remember the last time you and he had a date, just the two of you. ERROR message. Your twelve-year-old daughter's face floats across your consciousness. "You'd have been proud of me," she said last night. "Scored a goal. Sorry you weren't there." Her baleful eyes burn a hole in your stomach. ERROR message.

Just threw away the weekly newsletter from church. The minister's letter lingers in your mind. He reported the results of his visit with several members of the congregation to the Costa Rica project. You wanted to go on that nine-day trip. "Life is more than just this stuff. Got to give back," you remind yourself. "I'll write a bigger check next Sunday. Go next year, maybe." ERROR message.

Have we been spying on you, reading your mail, snooping through your subconscious? How do we know about all of this? We know because we've been there, done that; gotten all these ERROR messages from our own Internet-like overlapping systems. All the ERROR messages from all the interlocked interdependent systems of which you are a part lead to one inescapable conclusion: now is the time to begin building the foundation of a better tomorrow.

I know that my world is not isolated. Like the Internet, I am connected to everything and everybody, in some way. I impact others; others impact me. Basic question: how do I create a new, more effective me?

The Pyramid:
Strong Base for Future Success Built by the Phoenix Leader

The Phoenix leader, relying upon the five Phoenix principles, builds a Pyramid as a strong base for future success. The Pyramid follows from the Phoenix's vision, mission, values, goals and strategies, disciplined management systems, business processes and communications infrastructure.

When David graduated from college it was tough finding a job. What can a sociology major do anyway? He finally hooked up with a large discount retailer as assistant manager. After two years of moving from store to store, he finally got his own store as the soft goods department manager. Eighteen months into his assignment David can barely get himself up to go to work.

"I hate it," he told me. "This is the sixth major reorg I've been through in three and a half years. They've eliminated all my part-time help, so I wind up straightening up the floor all the time. To save money, and make the quarterlies look good, the policy's just come down that we can't replace anyone who leaves. I'm losing two of my eight people who are going back to school. I can't run the department with six people. It's not possible. It's so frustrating. The store manager and the regional guy just shrug their shoulders. 'Corporate policy,' they mutter and change the subject.

"My wife's expecting in three months. That'll crowd our one-bedroom apartment. I've been answering ads for months now trying to change jobs. Only other retailers reply. A headhunter told me last week, 'You're tagged as a retail person. It's hard to escape that.' I'm trapped. What do I do?"

We worked with David, helping him become a Phoenix leader taking responsibility for building his Pyramid base for his future success. In the following chapters we'll share how others, like David, put together their integrated and aligned vision, mission, values, goals and strategies, disciplined management systems, business processes and communications infrastructures. In those chapters we'll also include the experiences of several organizations with which we've been involved in the renewal and foundation-building process.

CHAPTER 9

Focus, Alignment and Integration— By Design: Vision, Mission and Values

Tomorrow arrives all too soon. The time for renewal is upon you. The message is clear: revivolute now! However, revivolute to what? What will the new organization—or the new you—look like? Stand for? Do? What products and services will you/it market? To whom? How? Deciding to revivolute is the first step, but only the first step. It's a long way between deciding to renew and being renewed.

Deciding to step up to the line and become a responsibility-taking Phoenix leader is a giant second step along the highway to the future. It gets you to the starting gate. But the race isn't over yet. Notice, though, that the crowd of runners has thinned considerably. There are lots of wannabes in the stands, people who want to be successful but who haven't taken the responsibility to be a Phoenix leader and get down on the field and spend all those early morning training hours. Look closer, though; this race to the future will not be a cakewalk. There are a number of strong contenders. Besides, the ground may shift and the rules may change without notice. You have your work cut out for you.

Here are the tools you will need to create your future success. As a Phoenix leader you take responsibility for creating the systematically constructed and perfectly integrated Pyramid that will form the base for your future success.

THE PYRAMID: ENDURING THE HOT DESERT WINDS

The Phoenix Perched on the Pyramid: Renewal That Creates Stability

Why a Pyramid? An ancient mosaic found in a Middle Eastern temple shows the mythical Phoenix bird perched upon a stone pyramid. The Phoenix soars beyond the sun and is the symbol of the constantly renewing life force. The pyramid is a symbol of success and stability (just try to knock one over)!

Travel out of Cairo on the hot and dusty road to the south and there, rising like majestic mirages in the desert, stand the pyramids, built of millions of individual blocks that fit smoothly together with a mathematical exactitude that amazes our most advanced mathematicians. Those blocks have stood on that ground for thousands of years. During those millennia, great empires rose and fell, great armies marched by, plundering thieves carved passageways into them in search of royal treasures, desert storms raged. The pyramids prevailed through it all. Stand in awe, as Napoleon did two hundred years ago, at the perfect construction of the pyramid.

Look at the pyramid on the dollar bill. It's an integral part of the Great Seal of the United States. All points come together at the top in the all-seeing eye—where vision originates. The thirteen ranges on the pyramid correspond not only to the thirteen original colonies, but also to the number of transformations and rebirths in numerology. Coincidence? Perhaps. Perhaps not.

The ancient picture of the phoenix perched on the pyramid illustrates the linking of two great archetypes: the endlessly renewing Phoenix and the perfectly engineered and aligned Pyramid. As the Phoenix renews itself it creates a new future by constructing a perfectly aligned and integrated Pyramid that forms the base from which it can soar. The Phoenix builds the Pyramid of its future life and then uses it as its home "airport." To us, the Pyramid symbolizes success, strength and longevity. Whatever it symbolizes for you, we have found the Pyramid a useful tool for describing and creating new futures for ourselves and the organizations with which we are associated.

The Pyramid: Your Practical Template for the Future

Like a protractor in the practice of architecture, the Pyramid displays the lines and angles necessary to create future success for yourself and all those with whom you are interconnected. The Pyramid also helps you create focus. It beats drifting along in a visionless half pursuit of the Next Big Thing.

THE PYRAMID

The Pyramid helps us think systematically about the future we want to create and integrate all of the essential ingredients of that future together. It all begins with *vision*, a raison d'être for existence. A vision focuses on where you are going. From that visionary direction springs a *mission* of what you must do to realize the vision. A mission is a set of binoculars that brings the vision up close and personal. Vision is a desired state. Mission is how you'll get there. Then there are *values*. Values shape be-haviors, words and decisions. Values establish standards of right and wrong. They are the common bond that shapes all personal interactions.

Synchronized vision, mission and values establish the context for your goals, strategies, objectives, measures and rewards. You establish *goals* and *strategies* that implement your vision, mis-sion and values. Then you establish *disciplined management systems* that encourage behavior necessary to accomplish those goals and strategies. Supporting *business processes* and *com-munications infrastructure* provides the necessary context for the right behavior.

The Pyramid begins with vision, mission and values. These en-during convictions define and characterize us. They suggest the ringing words in the Declaration of Independence, "We hold these truths to be self-evident . . ." They serve as beacons, binoculars and compasses on our trip to tomorrow.

But fine words alone will not create a success. Vision is no so-lution; execution is everything. We translate the inspiring words of the vision, mission and values into concrete actions with dis-ciplined management systems, business processes and commu-nications infrastructures.

All the Pyramid elements follow a systematic format. Begin at the beginning with vision. Don't start in the middle by reengi-neering business processes. It hasn't worked for others and it won't work for you. You can't build a house beginning with the second floor. If you don't follow the systematic blueprint, at the end of the day all you'll have is a pile of stones.

The Pyramid:
Let the Voice of the Customer Resound in Every Block

We've said it before, and we'll say it again. Your successful future begins and ends with customers. We believe it. We practice it. Practically that means that the voice of the customer must re-sound in every block of the pyramid you construct. The Summer 1996 issue of *Sloan Management Review* reported how Sonoma Investment Capital lost their way when they forgot that funda-

mental principle. Sonoma was a very successful investment
bank in the 1980s. It grew rapidly from fifteen to 350 people in
less than seven years. The firm's informal vision statement,
"Make gobs of money," worked well for a while. Eventually,
though, making money wasn't enough. Good people left to work
elsewhere. Someone wrote in an e-mail memo: "Well, I need a
more important purpose than that to justify the hard work and
commitment I put into this place." Leadership got the message,
and launched a vision-producing process. It started with lots of
fanfare. Then after three months, it stalled. Three years of hard
labor later there still wasn't a vision. Why?

The belly button fixation is the answer. Too many organizations and individuals begin the visioning process by focusing internally. They go off together to a mountaintop and wait for the
lightning to strike. They do internal employee surveys asking for
ideas. They poll the management. They do a SWOT analysis
(strengths, weaknesses, opportunities and threats). They hire vision experts and consultants to engage them in visualization,
creative games, daydreams and imaginative dialogues. They do
everything except the right thing: ask their customers.

Begin thinking about your business the way your customers
think about it. Talk to them. Think, see and feel yourself through
the eyes and minds of your customers—all of your customers.
Understand what is important to all of the customers in your interconnected, interdependent world. Think about how you can
help people meet their aspirations. Vision will answer the customers' question, "What does this do for me?"

Think about customers in the future tense as well. That's exactly what pioneering business consultant Mary Parker Follett
did as reported *Executive Excellence* in its November 1995
issue. When asked to help a floundering window shade company,
she pressed the managers to get beyond their narrow business
definition of producing window shades. She helped them see
that they were really in the light control business. That broader
definition sprang from their customers' concern for controlling
the amount of light coming through their windows. Using this
new customer-based lens, the managers saw new opportunities
to control light—and new businesses to enter and products to
produce and sell.

Stanley Magic Door made automatic garage doors. Based on
customer input they envisioned themselves in the business of

"facilitating and controlling the access of people and things through buildings." That vision, based upon meeting future customer needs, opened up new product and business vistas.

Most organizations have vision, mission and values statements. Check out any corporate Web site and you'll usually find them in a prominent location. Boeing, the aircraft manufacturer, aspires "To be the number one aerospace company in the world and among the premier industrial concerns in terms of quality, profitability and growth." Boeing also spells out "goals and objectives" with values interwoven. Merck, a highly admired pharmaceutical company, aspires to "Build our business by better serving society." They separately identify mission and values. Johnson & Johnson Company, a premier health care supply manufacturer (Band-Aids and Tylenol), has its famous "Credo" that integrates its vision, mission and values in one sweeping statement.

Most individuals have vision, mission and values statements, though these are often unspoken and unwritten. David, from the Part Three introduction, wants to succeed (a value), but not at the expense of his family life (another value). He sees himself as a manager/leader of people (his vision) and wants to grow that management competence in another industry (a part of his mission).

Each of us has a vision, mission and values statement that guides our behavioral choices. Is it the right statement? Will it create success? Will it create success for others? Read on and discover how to design your new Pyramid.

VISION: THE BEACON THAT LIGHTS THE ROAD AHEAD

The Unending Pursuit of the "Vision Thing"

Preoccupation with the "vision thing" goes back a long way. The Bible reads, "Without vision, the people shall perish" (Proverbs). In ancient Greece, Aristotle wrote, "The mind never thinks without a vision or picture." IBM's Thomas Watson, Sr., wrote to his son in college: "The three primary qualities of the ideal business leader are vision, character and pride in record." From the beginning of time, vision's been "the thing."

Here are the vision statements for the four organizations with which we've built Pyramids over the past few years.

AT&T/NCR (manufacturer of computers, software and services): Together, always delighting our customers.

AT&T/GBCS (manufacturer of telecommunications switches, PBXs): The Partner of Choice: Dedicated to Quality, Committed to Your Success.

Supply Company (distribution company): Doing whatever it takes to create success for our customers.

Legent Corporation (developer of middleware software products and services): Together, always creating success for our customers.

What's a Vision Really Worth, Anyway?

What's a vision worth? In a few words: a lot. Mark Lipton reported in his Summer 1996 *Sloan Management Review* article that, over a sixty-year period, eighteen visionary organizations showed 700 percent higher returns on investment than nonvisionary competitors in the same industries. Harvard professors John Kotter and James Heskett found that firms with a strong vision outperformed nonvision competitors by a huge margin. Strong vision firms grew revenues four times faster, jobs eight times faster and stock value twelve times faster. Two Stanford professors discovered that strong vision companies showed more than fifteen times the shareholder returns of the overall stock market. In short, vision pays off for everyone—employees, shareholders, suppliers, communities and customers.

History is full of examples where a strong vision created not only a great company, but also changed an entire society. At the turn of the century, Sears defined its vision as being "the informed buyer for the American family." The Sears catalogue set the fashion and value standards for several generations of Americans. The catalogue was the TV of its generation. What Sears sold became America's standard.

Across the pond, another retailer, Marks and Spencer, defined a vision that drove its success and changed England. They envisioned themselves as "the change agent in British society by becoming the first classless retailer." They tapped into the strong anti-class feelings that swept England around the turn of the century. Their stores were paragons of classless organizations, where everyone ate in the same lunchrooms and used the same bathrooms. Such equality was unheard of at the time. Marks and Spencer created a classless society within their organization, which became the model for the classless society.

Moreover, Marks and Spencer believed they understood their customers better than their suppliers and manufacturers did. That was heresy in those days, as manufacturers told retailers what to stock and what to sell it for. Marks and Spencer focused employees on learning what customers wanted. Using that customer data, they pioneered the St. Michael label, one of the first retailer private labels. They understood exactly what customers wanted and built their vision around delivering it.

Similarly, AT&T defined their vision as "universal access to telephone service." By providing universal telephone service, AT&T fundamentally changed American society and business. Much of America's success today in computers and telecommunications is the direct result of AT&T's infrastructure.

Hear the words of the Phoenix resound through the AT&T, Marks and Spencer and Sears stories: create the future by taking charge and boldly contributing to the success of all your interconnected customers. Imagine, think and aspire to outrageous world-class accomplishment.

Successful visions feature one of four dimensions: aspiration, competence, differentiation and inspiration. Many visions are rooted in *aspiration* where the people aspire to accomplish certain objectives in order to create success for themselves and their customers. AT&T's vision of universal access to telephones is an example. Other visions are based on *competence*, using a premier skill set to outperform competitors. McDonald's is the premier service and logistics firm in the fast food business. They leverage their competencies to dominate their business. Some visions are based on *differentiation* of the organization from others in the marketplace. Such firms create futures of distinct and memorable originality. The Disney organization is a classic example of using differentiation as a vision. Disney positions itself as the creator of fantasies where everyone can enjoy being a child again in a family values setting. Finally, there are organizations and individuals who are motivated primarily by *inspiration* to create a better quality of life for others. Various religious organizations and individuals—witness Mother Teresa—feel impelled by a higher calling.

Vision As Aspiration: The Dream Becomes the Destiny

The root word for "aspire" is to breathe. Life is aspiration. We either aspire—or expire. The Phoenix vision reflects our future aspirations for ourselves and for our entire interconnected customer network. And, like everything else in the Phoenix world, it all begins with customers.

For example, hear the aspiration in NCR's vision: "Together, always delighting our customers." The vision certainly did not reflect the current reality at NCR. Age and deterioration showed everywhere throughout NCR's vast system of international offices and facilities. NCR responded slowly to customer demands as the fragmented organization tripped over itself frequently, trying to coordinate the efforts of 46,000 associates in 130 countries selling hundreds of complex products and services. Navigation of NCR's complex system required multiple Rolodexes and a fat binderful of organization charts. One sales associate described it, "Checking an order status is like wrestling with a giant octopus." Customers described NCR as very hard to do business with.

The vision set a clear level: customer delight. Satisfaction wasn't sufficient. For an organization with most customers in the lukewarm "I guess things are okay" category, setting delight as the vision standard is pure aspiration.

Find aspiration in the word "together" as well. Internally, the vision aspired to end the ongoing war between sales, engineering and manufacturing. As one long-time NCRer put it, "We have 270 persons deciding internal transfer allocations, and 46,000 others fighting about them." "Together" also aspired to create cooperation with other units of AT&T, software suppliers, systems integrators and the whole panoply of computer resellers.

We frequently ask class members to participate in a career-planning activity. One of our students told us, "My vision is to start my own software company. I've got an idea for how to use object-oriented programming to design multimedia programs. I'd like to grow that business and use it to fund my retirement." Eleven years later we ran into him at a meeting. He'd founded his company, grown it and sold it for $125 million and had retired—at thirty-two. We kicked ourselves all the way home that night for not investing in his start-up when it went public four years ago. Shame on us. Good for him for living his aspiration-based vision, finding a product customers needed and then becoming a Phoenix leader, taking charge of his life.

Vision reflects our aspirations. It announces our dreams and hopes to our network world and encourages others to join us in building the future Pyramid.

Vision As Competence: Building Destiny from Expertise

"Build on strength" is an old truth. Leverage your strengths to soar into the future with the Phoenix. Ask yourself, "Which skills and talents will help create success for customers? What competencies will help suppliers and communities succeed, or help shareholders get a better return? What skills and capabilities do you bring to the table?" Really understand yourself and your business.

McDonald's vision is "to dominate the global food service industry. Global dominance means setting the performance standards for customer satisfaction while increasing market share and profitability through convenience, value and execution strategies." And dominate they do. As many as three new McDonald's open every twenty-four hours somewhere in the world. Chances are good that within a year each of them will gross about $1.7 million. Despite predictions that McDonald's "was doomed to become a lumbering cash cow in a mature industry," McDonald's used its competencies to become the most profitable retail business in American history.

Visions are usually multidimensional. AT&T/GBCS's was. GBCS was formed by the consolidation of two separate—and competing—business units. Both companies were in the telecommunications equipment business. They were originally divided by the size of their telephone installation. Customers with fewer than thirty phone lines were handled by GBS, General Business Systems. Customers with thirty lines and above were handled by BCS, Business Communications Systems. Both were losing money, accumulating losses of better than $8 billion over an eight-year period.

Listen to the multiple dimensions in the vision statement, "The Partner of Choice: Dedicated to Quality, Committed to Your Success." GBCS *aspired* to be the customers' "partner of choice." When they announced that vision, GBCS was one of many telecommunication equipment suppliers, far removed from being a partner.

"Partner" was another aspirational word, since the new unit merged two former competitors. These units needed to think and operate in partnership terms, not only with each other, but with the entire combined network of customers.

The words "dedicated to quality" represented the *competency* dimension of the vision statement. Both divisions committed early to quality as a process goal. Both enjoyed fine reputations in the marketplace for quality products. So the vision built on that reputation.

The phrase "committed to your success" extended the focus beyond customer satisfaction to an active engagement in the customer's business success. That approach was absolutely novel in the market at that time, and was intended to *differentiate* AT&T from its competitors, who were focused on selling more equipment and not creating customer success.

Base personal vision on competence, not wishes. It would be foolish for us to envision ourselves becoming brain surgeons at this stage in our lives. No one is going to invest eight years in training these fifty- and sixty-year-olds. We're certain that we couldn't master the science required, let alone the hand-eye coordination demanded of a surgeon. Instead, our personal vision is to "Help others develop their competence, and then to help them develop confidence in that competence so they can use it for the benefit of humankind." That vision is based upon a demonstrated coaching competency built up through many years of skill development.

Vision As Differentiator: Organizations in a Class by Themselves

Vision differentiates us in a sea of swarming look-alike competitors. Supply Company's vision is "Doing whatever it takes to create customer success." "Doing whatever it takes" represents a powerful thought. They intended to be not just one more distribution company, concerned with putting product on retailers' shelves. Rather, they focused on the owners' concerns about business issues such as hiring, training, marketing, financial controls and taxes. They saw themselves as business partners with their customers, rather than as a traditional distributor.

This vision moved the company from being a distributor, much like every other distributor competitor, to providing a wide range of business-related services. Their vision told their customers, "We are *not* focused on selling you more product. We *are* focused on helping you get more customers, generate more revenues, motivate your people better and relieve you of your payroll and tax problems. We will handle your business concerns, so you can focus on being the best merchandiser and businessperson." That differentiating vision doubled the business in a few short years—and then doubled it again.

The new Phoenix Square D vision was, "We respond." Very simple. But it was a real differentiator in the stodgy old electrical equipment business. The giants in the business, GE, Westinghouse and Siemens, acted like entrenched dinosaurs. They took forever to respond to customers' needs. Three- and four-month lead times were the industry standard. Using their vision, Square D cut delivery times by 75 percent—and took market share as a result.

Customers didn't want to wait. That vision—and the actions that backed up that vision—differentiated Square D from its competitors in the marketplace.

Vision As Inspiration: Improving the Quality of Life

Vision appeals to the heart, not the mind or the pocketbook. Vision appeals to emotion. It activates quality-of-soul feelings. Some companies realize this and have leveraged it to the fullest.

At Legent, the middleware software and service company, we used inspiration as part of our vision. Prior to 1994, customers perceived Legent as piecemealing them to death. They thought Legent sold them random applications to fix isolated problems, then walked away. Legent brought out new product releases that were incompatible with previous versions, forcing customers to rewrite existing application codes. This strategy maximized short-term sales for Legent while maximizing short-term costs for the customers and sacrificing long-term relationships. Customers felt that Legent wasn't listening to them or focused on creating success for them, but on creating success for themselves, often at the customer's expense.

We designed the vision "Together, always creating success for our customers" to inspire customers to trust Legent to help them through future product migrations. The word "together" was particularly important, used to inspire associates to work more closely with customers and each other across previously impervious organizational boundaries. "Together" was also intended to inspire work with suppliers of open platforms and a broader range of third-party distributors. Legent's vision inspired everyone to provide integrated solutions across many platforms and distributed in ways that suited the customer, not Legent.

Legent addressed a wide number of different customer sets, reflecting its "create success" mentality. Suppliers benefited from Legent's expanded platform scope. End-users benefited from increased compatibility and flexibility. Internal employees were more successful through their enhanced line of sight to customers. Communities were more successful as Legent expanded into other areas and grew employment. Shareholders were more successful as the $19 stock soared to $47 when Computer Associates recognized the value Legent was creating and purchased the organization.

The power of ideas, not impersonal organization, attracts people. People are drawn by visions that touch their souls, that promise the opportunity to make a difference. Check the Internet and you will find the vision of a church in Salina, Kansas: "We are Trinity United Methodist Church, accepting God's love, united in Christ, living in faith, hope and love which empowers us to live and teach a life of service without boundaries." That vision inspires not just on a Sunday morning, but also on a Tuesday morning, and Thursday night. The vision fills us with inspiration not necessarily to be what we are, but what we'd like to be, and need to be in order to fulfill our purpose in life.

Jeff Blake dreamed of being an NFL quarterback. His dad, a former Canadian Football League running back, ran football clinics over dinner every night, nourishing Jeff's dream as well as his body and mind. Based on his college team's 11-1 senior season, the New York Jets chose him in the sixth round of the 1992 draft.

The Jet experience ended two years later with precious little playing time to his credit. He'd never gotten the opportunity to prove what he could do in the NFL. Though the winds of disappointment blew strong, Jeff held on to his vision. Cincinnati picked him up as a third-string quarterback. When both quarterbacks ahead of him were injured, Blake got his chance to show everyone what he could do. Almost beating the champion Dallas Cowboys, he followed with two consecutive wins. He became the starting quarterback for the Bengals and one of the better-rated quarterbacks in the NFL. He continued to be inspired by his vision, and he got the opportunity to live it every Sunday on the playing field.

Beware: What Works Here May Not Work Everywhere

Get real, though. Just because it worked in one place and time does not mean that the same approach will work everywhere and every time. It didn't for Marks and Spencer. They tried to establish their egalitarian stores in India—and failed miserably. After two and a half years they withdrew from India, defeated by the more deeply entrenched Indian class structure.

Bottom line: begin building the strong Pyramid base for your future success by creating a vision that will serve as a beacon light for all of your activities. Begin creating tomorrow by talking to your customers. Identify what you will do to create success for others. Focus on how you can enhance the value of your contribution. And then be a Phoenix leader and take charge!

PHOENIX WORKSHOP

1. WHAT ARE THE DEMANDS/OPPORTUNITIES IN THE COMING FIVE YEARS UPON WHICH I CAN CAPITALIZE IN THE MARKETPLACE:

- FOR MY CURRENT CUSTOMERS?_____

_____

- FOR MY CURRENT NONCUSTOMERS?_____

_____

- FOR MY FUTURE CUSTOMERS?_____

_____

2. GIVEN MY THOUGHTS ABOUT THE OPPORTUNITIES/ DEMANDS IN THE FUTURE:

- WHAT DO I SEE AS MY MAJOR OPPORTUNITIES TO CREATE SUCCESS FOR MY NETWORK OF CUSTOMERS?_____

_____

- WHAT *COMPETENCIES* DO I NOW POSSESS OR WILL I DE-VELOP THAT WILL ENABLE ME TO CAPITALIZE ON THESE OPPORTUNITIES?_____

_____

- HOW WILL I *DIFFERENTIATE* MYSELF FROM ALL OF MY COMPETITORS IN CAPITALIZING ON THESE OPPORTUNI-TIES?_____

_____

- WHAT WILL *INSPIRE* ME AND THOSE UPON WHOM I DE-PEND FOR SUPPORT TO CONTRIBUTE TO ME IN CAPITAL-IZING ON THESE OPPORTUNITIES?_____

_____

- WHAT DO I AND THOSE IMPORTANT TO ME *ASPIRE* TO BE THAT WILL HELP ME CAPITALIZE ON THESE OPPORTUNI-TIES?_____

_____

3. GIVEN ALL THAT I'VE WRITTEN AND THOUGHT THUS FAR, WHAT ARE THE FEW BEST WORDS THAT DESCRIBE MY VISION FOR MYSELF OVER THE NEXT FIVE YEARS?_____

_____

MISSION: BINOCULARS THAT
FOCUS OUR FIELD OF DREAMS

Do I Really Need Both Vision and Mission?
Absolutely! It's Not Either/Or

Vision defines a future end state. It reflects what we want to be. Mission defines the high-level actions we will take to achieve that vision. If vision is 30,000 feet, then mission is 10,000 feet. But mission is still general. It doesn't spell out what you will do today. It does, however, narrow the focus. That's why mission is the binoculars for your future Pyramid. Mission lays out the general course of action you will follow in creating your new tomorrow.

Mission defines a transcending and solution-based description of what the organization will be and why it will exist. It is task-related and action-oriented. It's based on verbs, not nouns. Mission is the proactive, problem-solving job description that will help you set priorities and allocate resources that best meet customer needs. In short, mission defines the general tasks we perform, how we will get the job done to solve the customer's problem and improve the quality of life for everyone.

Dell Computers is one of this decade's major success stories. Starting in his college dorm room, Michael Dell grew a multibillion-dollar business—and made the front cover of *Fortune* along the way. He had a clear differentiating vision: supply inexpensive computers directly to the home. Bypass inexperienced retail clerks and send the computer ready to start out of the box to the home. Problem was he lacked a clear mission. So his organization floundered around, trying first this and then that. He copied Compaq, trying to become a technology leader in notebooks—and failed. He experimented with retail distribution—and flopped miserably. Then Mort Topfer came on board as vice chairman. Together, Dell and Topfer established a clear mission. They said: "We will refocus on the direct channel for distribution that we essentially created for personal computers when Dell was founded in 1984—and which best suits our integrated, build-to-order, customer-focused business model—with its emphasis on service and support." That focusing righted the ship and got it back on its success course.

Missions include three dimensions: defining customers to be served, identifying products and services and competencies you will deliver that will create success for all customers, and describing your position in the marketplace. Sound mission statements focus attention and provide criteria for prioritizing resources and making resource allocation decisions. Here are the four organization examples of mission statements we've developed and used:

AT&T/GBCS: To be the worldwide leader in providing the highest-quality business communications products, services and solutions.

AT&T/NCR: To be the world's best at bringing computing and communication solutions together to provide people easy access to information and to each other—anytime, anywhere.

Legent: To be the global leader in delivering integrated product and service solutions to help customers manage information technology resources . . . today and tomorrow.

Supply Company: To provide the most appropriate distribution, marketing, business and financial services that enable our targeted customers to achieve their personal and professional goals.

Creating Success for the Right Customers

Mission focuses, like a good pair of binoculars, on providing exceptional value for all your interconnected, interdependent customers. The mission binoculars focuses activities on providing the right products and services to the right set of customers.

Often the right customer is the customer's customer. David Sheppard, a Fleet Services executive, told a group of AT&T/NCR account managers, "I want you at AT&T to bring all of your resources to bear on *my* products and services. But this is not about your company designing a product or solution for Fleet. It's about NCR and Fleet together designing solutions for Fleet's customers. Together, we must think about their business like she or he would. Together, we must ask ourselves what his/her issues are and how we can make a difference."

The Supply Company mission focused the organization's attention on "targeted customers." The retail market divides into several different segments; ranging from a large number of very small stores to the very small number of very large stores often operating multisite locations. Each segment of the market has a different set of needs that mandate a different approach. The small operator usually is not concerned with hiring or marketing assistance, but is focused on convenient supply and financial assistance. The larger stores, on the other hand, worry a lot about personnel matters and marketing but typically have professional financial assistance so that that service is less attractive to them. The mission focuses on customizing offerings for specific customers.

Maximizing Technologies and Competencies Providing the Right Products/Services

Mission clearly identifies the competencies we will bring to bear to solve specified kinds of problems for specific customers. The mission spells out the technologies and competencies we will use to live our "create success for everyone" mentality.

Xerox's mission is: "By helping our customers navigate and manage the world of documents, we can help them improve their productivity and grow their businesses." Xerox focuses on making a difference in their customers' business performance. They're not in the entertainment business, making life fun. They're in the document business, helping people move information more effectively. That's focus on the technologies they will provide to create that form of customer success.

Oracle Corporation is the world's largest independent provider of software and services for managing information. Their mission statement, taken right from their Web site, is: "Oracle is committed to be a single source for enterprise-wide systems and development software, technology leadership and integration, robust business functionality, and a vast array of implementation services that focus on helping our customers streamline business transactions, optimize day-to-day productivity, maintain the highest possible levels of service, and prepare for the future." Oracle is clearly using their technological competencies to help customers succeed.

Battelle Laboratories is a technology developer. Over the years they've developed such technologies as CD technology, alternative fuels, xerography, holograms and high-performance toothbrushes. With 8,000 technical, management and support professionals, they are a leader in applied technology. Their vision is: "Developing high-quality products and reducing time-to-market for our clients." Their mission is: "We insert technology into systems and processes to turn problems into opportunities for manufacturers, trade associations, pharmaceutical and agrochemical industries and government agencies supporting the environment, health, national security and transportation." That's a clear binocular focus on using technology to solve customer problems. The mission also limits the customer focus. They don't serve petrochemical customers, for instance.

Mission statements also focus on new competencies to develop. Notice the use of the word "solutions." AT&T/GBCS talked about "business communications . . . solutions." NCR talked about "computing and communications solutions." Legent's mission emphasized "integrated product and service solutions." In all cases "solutions" added an additional competence to previously traditional products and service offerings.

NCR's mission emphasized another competency to develop: the integration of products and services. This required developing partnerships across the vast AT&T organization as well as NCR's external partners and suppliers.

Similarly, Legent's mission identified the competency it needed to develop in order to meet the number one customer problem: "manage information technology resources . . . today and tomorrow." The information technology arena is a zoo, a collection of rapidly appearing and vanishing products and services that dazzle, deliver and die within months. Legent recognized the need to develop the competency of delivering "integrated solutions" that provided forward and backward compatibility and interoperability. In that way "solutions" created success today and tomorrow.

The Supply Company recognized the need to develop consulting competencies in financial, marketing and business services.

While they had accumulated considerable expertise in distribution, they recognized the need to extend that competency into new methods of distribution.

Mission narrows the focus and helps to identify the competencies we currently possess and those we will need to develop to create success for our entire customer network.

Describing Our Place in the Market

Successful organizations and individuals differentiate themselves in the marketplace by creating a unique position that sets them apart from all the other look-alike competitors. The mission statements for the four organizations with which we've worked over the past few years all established a differentiating marketplace positioning. NCR capitalized on the coming together of communications and computing by promising easy access to people, information and services anytime, anywhere. Their relationship with AT&T gave NCR a decidedly different place in customers' minds.

For AT&T/GBCS, providing "solutions" was the differentiating marketplace position. Product and service offerings dominated the marketplace at the time.

Legent differentiated itself in the market by helping "customers manage information technology resources . . . today and tomorrow." Few, if any, of their competitors offered a way that their customers could move from yesterday's technology to tomorrow's. By offering a migration path, Legent aimed to create a significantly different place in the market for itself.

Supply Company's service-supplying mission carved out a clearly differentiated position in the marketplace. They were the first distributor to supply professional services in that marketplace.

Mission provides the binoculars that narrows the focus of the vision to specific customers receiving specified products and services within a defined marketplace. No one individual or organization can be all things to all people. The mission statement helps sharpen the focus of the soaring Phoenix, in order to lay a few more rows of brick on our Pyramid that will form the basis for our future success.

PHOENIX WORKSHOP

FOLLOWING MY VISION STATEMENT, WHAT ARE THE
CHARACTERISTICS OF MY MISSION:

1. WHAT CUSTOMERS WILL I SERVE?

_____

_____

2. WHAT PRODUCTS AND SERVICES WILL I DELIVER?

_____

_____

3. WHAT CHANNELS WILL I UTILIZE TO DELIVER MY
PRODUCTS AND SERVICES?

_____

_____

4. WHAT COMPETENCIES AND TECHNOLOGIES WILL I
EMPLOY?

_____

_____

VALUES: THE COMPASS THAT GUIDES US TO ALWAYS DO THE RIGHT THING

Values Are the Internal Compass That Point Us True North

Values drive behavior. They are the unseen, often unconscious, compass that guides us through the rocks and shoals of everyday life. In millions of little ways we are challenged to make decisions that call upon our values. Do I go to visit clients today, or do I clear my desk of the ever-increasing stacks of paper? Do I stop and chat with associates on the way to the office, or do I head directly to my desk and get on with my work? Do I stay in the office and finish this important, the-boss-is-waiting-for-it project, or do I go home and see my daughter's soccer game? Do I listen any further to the very angry employee that's accosted me in the hallway, or do I send her off to HR to handle the problem? Each decision, standing alone, seems innocuous. Taken together, though, your actions reveal the values compass that guides your behavior.

Values are deeply held beliefs of right and wrong. They specify in broad terms how we will treat others in achieving our vision and mission. They describe correct day-to-day behavior in general terms. The Ten Commandments are value statements, for instance.

Values help us set direction. As with the compass needle always pointing true north, values always point us in the direction of doing the right thing.

Vision is the dream of what we want to be. Mission is the focus on who we serve and what we serve them. Values determine how we deal with all our interconnected people. Vision is dream; mission is focus; values are behavior.

Clear vision alone of what you want to create is not enough. The clarity of mission, spelling out in general terms who you will serve and what you will serve them with, is not enough. Your Pyramid must include several rows of bricks labeled "core values" that will guide your everyday behavior.

Values Answer the Question: What's Worth Dying For?

Stand to sing the national anthem at a football game and feel the pride and emotion surge through you. "This is my country, and I'm proud to be an American." These are values at work. Hear someone attack the product your plant makes and feel the flash of anger. "People I work with made that product. We're good folks. How dare you criticize us and our work." Values at work again.

Values surface in stark and harsh situations. Like war. Watch CNN nightly and see the compelling images of young men and women taking up arms and risking their lives to right some wrong, to throw out some invader, to gain independence. See values at work in concentration camps. Recall Victor Frankl's account of concentration camp life. When all else is stripped away,

personal values surface to fill the gaps. One Vietnam POW recounted how he set out to recall and write the Bible in the sand
of his cell floor. His desire to continue the task kept him going
through days of torture and months of starvation. Other prisoners recounted Bible stories like Daniel's courage in the lion's
den, the three devoted men who survived the fiery furnace un-
scathed, the selfless suffering of the crucifixion. Values surface
and guide us in the harshest of circumstances.

Choose Your Compass Carefully

The list of values usually includes the following: achievement,
community, control, customers, efficiency, equality, excellence,
family, fun, growth, harmony, innovation, integrity, leadership,
learning, profitability, quality, safety, teamwork and tradition.
Which will be most important to you in your new Phoenix life?
When asked that question, the senior editors at the *Pittsburgh
Post Gazette*, as reported in their March 12, 1995, editorial,
ranked excellence first, followed by quality, integrity, community and achievement. Here's a group of people very concerned
about the work they produce. They ranked profitability and efficiency very low, possibly putting them in conflict with the newspaper's owners, who might rank those values higher.

Here are the value statements for the four organizations we
have been tracking:

AT&T/GBCS: Customer satisfaction, integrity, teamwork, accountability, excellence.

AT&T/NCR: Respect for the individual, dedication to our customers, highest standards of integrity, innovation, teamwork.

Legent: Respect for the individual, teamwork, integrity, accountability, excellence.

Supply Company: Teamwork, excellence, integrity, caring.

Look Inside Your Heart to Find the Values That Drive Your Behavior

There are no perfect and absolute value statements for all organizations. You may like NCR's or Supply Company's—or some combination of all of them. Any of the statements above may be good statements for someone. But are they the right statements for you? Which of those words will you choose to establish true north for your personal compass during the days, weeks, months and years ahead? Only you can answer these questions, for values are inherently personal.

For the answers, look deep inside yourself. Values must reflect what you truly believe. Put each of the twenty words we've listed above (or any words you'd like to consider) on a separate 3x5 card. Then rank them in either descending order, beginning with the most important one first, or ascending order, beginning with the least important one first. Expect to make several passes and spend many hours thinking about the exercise, particularly if you include other members of your interdependent world.

The last time we did this exercise was shortly after our youngest son got married. We did it during one of our regular family gatherings, taking the better part of an afternoon. Though we'd done the exercise many times in the past, each time a new component is introduced (like our new daughter-in-law) the dynamics change. We get new thought and information input into our system and the system changes, particularly when we discuss something as personal as values.

HP founders Bill Hewlett and David Packard made respect for the individual a value because they believed it was the right thing to do. They passed up growth and profit opportunities by turning down big government contracts that would have forced them into a pattern of on-again/off-again hire-and-fire employment. They looked into their hearts, decided what they wanted their organization to be, and followed what they saw there, not their pocketbook. That heart decision also paid off in dollars, as Hewlett-Packard is one of the most successful and admired companies in the world.

Values Disagreements: Static on Our Network Line

Values bind us to others. They establish the ground rules and boundaries of acceptable and desirable behavior. They tell us: these are your agreements, honor them. The absence of common values leads to breakdowns.

Sam is the administrative assistant to one of our clients. His daughter is an excellent ballet dancer, having won many national awards. She received an invitation to visit Moscow and practice with a famous ballet group there. Sam and his wife organized a family trip to Moscow to accompany her. Unfortunately the dates for that trip coincided with the deadline for submission of the final budget.

Sam knew that he had primary responsibility to get the budget submitted on time, so he worked hard to prepare the papers and get everything ready before he left. Had the process gone according to plan, everything would have been fine. But, as usual, things did not go according to plan. There was a dramatic last-minute funding shift that resulted in a serious revenue shortfall, which meant that all the budget numbers had to be redone. Worse, someone had to coordinate getting the revised budget numbers from reluctant department heads who had to cut their allocations. Had Sam been on site that would have been a difficult task. From more than 8,000 miles away it was a horror.

Several department heads complained about Sam's absence. Oh sure, everyone paid lip service to the value of "balance" and the importance of "family." But this was an emergency. Sam's co-workers experienced his absence as a serious violation of their teamwork value.

That perceived values violation produced many angry intercontinental phone calls and bitter exchanges. Sam spent innumerable hours on the phone with each department head reviewing the numbers and hashing over and rehashing performance schedules. And every hour spent on the phone was matched by many additional hours poring over faxed (and barely readable) budget sheets. About the only part of Moscow that Sam saw was his hotel room and two of his daughter's practices.

Everyone—Sam, his wife, his daughter, his colleagues—was emotionally drained by the experience, not to mention the financial drain of supporting the telephone company. It wasn't until afterward that everyone realized what was going on. They patched it up eventually, but it would have been infinitely easier on the heart and the pocketbook had everyone clarified their values early. In short, values enable the interconnected systems to work together. Without common values it is difficult to maintain equilibrium across interdependent systems.

Alignment of Values Creates Power

Sam's experience reinforces a great truth: values are profoundly important, yet must be aligned to be valuable. Individual values must be aligned within a team. Individual values must be aligned between individuals and the organization. And, obviously, individual values must be aligned within a family.

We took great pains at the Supply Company to ensure alignment of values within the working teams of the organization and between the individual and the organization. First the leadership team met to clarify their values, both organizationally and individually. Once they agreed upon a set of organizational values aligned with their individual values, they then met with groups of employees to discuss their individual values and the organization's values. The purpose of these meetings was very simple: align the individual's values and the organization's values. Some meetings lasted only an hour or so. One took a whole day plus an evening. It didn't matter because the leadership team was committed to doing whatever it took (part of their vision statement) to live their values of "caring" and "teamwork." Each working team also met to discuss and align their values.

Alignment does not necessarily mean consistency. Values are inherently personal. People can have different values and still work together. Muslims work in peace with Jews and Christians. Each worships a different God, in a different way, on a different day. But each can respect the other's values and align their personal values with the organizational value of "respect" or "teamwork."

Corporate values shared across dozens of countries, cultures and languages bring unity in the essentials and allow for variations in nonessentials. They don't force everyone into a mold, but liberate people within the established values context. For example, NCR's value of "respect for the individual" meant in the U.S. that men and women would be very careful about touching or any affectionate gestures. While in Scandinavian countries, a pat on the back or even a greeting with a kiss on the cheek was considered not only acceptable but respectful.

Establishing common values does not mean setting up a KGB-style monitoring system. Discover the values of all those who share your world and align those values around the common visions and missions of your Pyramid. It will pay off. Personal lives of managers whose personal values are consistent with their organization's values are more optimistic and have lower stress levels.

Values Set the Points on the Compass

Values lay out the points on the compass. First, values establish standards of behavior. They spell out what's right and wrong, good and bad. Second, values live the vision and the mission. They translate the fine words of the first two parts of the Pyramid into day-to-day actions. Third, values are not for sale. They are a bedrock for behavior, a not-to-be-violated standard.

Values Set Standards of Behavior for You, Me and Us

Values will set our priorities. They will determine where we spend our time, with whom, doing what. Do we sleep in or go jogging? Do we watch television or attend a self-improvement class? Do we take center stage or do we share the glory? Do we talk about "I" all the time or is it mostly "we"?

Behavior reveals values. We know too many executives who talk the game of customers but haven't seen one in years except at company-sponsored golf tournaments. So much for the value of dedication to customers. We all know senior executives who talk about the value of their "employee assets," and cut training and development expenditures at the first sign of a budget slippage. Say goodbye to valuing employees. Business life is filled with examples of contradictions between those values stated on the wall in bold four-color posters and those practiced day to day in the organization.

Our research with more than 27,000 executives worldwide discovered a huge gap between stated and practiced values. We discovered that the most frequently stated values are (in order of importance): long-term market success, customer satisfaction and employee respect. The most frequently practiced values are (again, in order of importance): short-term financial results, sales/market growth and new product development. Notice the vast difference between the stated human values revolving around customers and employees and the practiced financial values. Notice also the difference in the time frame. Stated values emphasize a more long-term approach to both financial and human issues, while short-term perspectives dominate actual practice.

We determined long ago to narrow the gap between stated and practiced values in our organizations. At AT&T/NCR, the senior leadership team, and then the entire associate population, agreed that listening to customers was important, so we could discover their needs and satisfy them. Hence the value of dedication to customers. We completely reorganized the company to focus more on customers. We launched customer focus teams to deal directly with them, finding out what they needed and assuming responsibility for satisfying those needs.

We simplified the reporting structure, bringing the customer focus teams closer to the senior management. Each senior manager "adopted" several customers and became their "sponsor" and "spokesperson" throughout the organization. Following that dedication to customer value we personally spent three to four days a week in the field working with customers. We chose highly visible customers to visit, and then shared the results of these meetings with all associates through e-mail, so that everyone could see a living example of our valuing dedication to customers.

Similarly, we took the teamwork value seriously at AT&T/ GBCS. That value was particularly important since GBCS was stitched together from two formerly competing organizations. We established joint customer teams comprised of members of the two previously separate organizations. We gave them common objectives, measures and rewards as an incentive to work together. We changed the leadership positions so that representatives from both organizations wound up heading significant pieces of the business. Shining the light of personal attention on those living the teamwork value, the senior leadership team made frequent visits to integrated groups, recognizing teamwork across previously competitive boundaries.

The GBCS and NCR experiences reflect a hard lesson we've learned. Values begin with us. Others in the organization will watch what we do, and follow. They will ignore what we say, in either speeches or formal memos. But they will study assiduously what we do. They will assume, rightly so, that our actions reflect our true feelings, priorities and values. It's only natural. Sons are a lot like their fathers. We learned by watching our dads handle life's situations. We then "taught" our sons as they watched us. We inevitably hear our words coming from the mouths of our sons. Daughters are a lot like their mothers for the very same reasons. Behavioral psychologists call the process "behavioral modeling." It is the principal way we learn. Model the values you want others to live.

Be a visible role model of your values. You can't hide in a closet, or a magnificent office on the hundredth floor, and have the kind of organization you want. Ask Mr. Sun, from Taiwan, and Mr. Tu, from Shanghai. They founded Kingston Technology and based their business on Asian family values, deciding that employees and customers would be treated as members of the family. They live their values, and get incredible business results.

Kingston Technology is the second largest manufacturer of add-on memory modules for personal computers. They run the business based upon the family values of ethics and trust. Most of the firm's multimillion-dollar supply deals are done on a handshake. There are no written contracts. Kingston pays ahead of schedule and never cancels an order. Because of that, in this business where component supply is critical, they're always at the top of the deliver-to list. They get their parts first. Applying their Asian family values to their employees, Kingston pays above-average wages, and sweetens the pot with a generous profit-sharing plan.

As reported in the November 19, 1994, issue of *The Economist*, the values proposition worked in spades. Sales doubled every year. Revenues topped $800 million. In 1994, each of the 300 employees accounted for $2.7 million in sales. That compares with Intel's $354,000 sales per employee. Kingston's overhead is the lowest in the business, and they turn their inventory an unheard of three times a day!

IKEA is another interesting story of how values, modeled by the senior officers, result in extraordinary business results. The same issue of *The Economist* reports how IKEA also uses family values to excel in the retail assemble-it-yourself furniture business. As modeled by their Swedish founder (who set up a Dutch foundation to own the business) IKEA treats its associates and customers as members of the family. People don't get fired, but counseled. There are family days off and child care at every store, for both employees and customers. They emphasize education, for both customers and employees. They pay above-average full-time wages, in a business characterized by part-time minimum wages.

It also works in spades. On the financial side, growth averages 35 percent a year, at margins double those of anyone else in the business. Employee turnover is a remarkable 2 percent a year, in a business characterized by closer to 200 percent.

Values Are Not for Sale:
Doing the Right Thing for the Wrong Reason Is Still Wrong

Tough times reveal core values. We relearned that lesson, big time, several years ago. One of our enterprises operates extensively in the Pacific Rim, using self-directed customer-focused work teams. These teams do all the typical managerial functions including hiring, firing and training.

We all agreed that integrity is a basic value in our organization. Operating in many parts of the world where bribery is customary, we also agreed that our value of integrity prohibits the paying of bribes for any reason. We walk away from business if paying a bribe is the price of obtaining that business. While we've lost business as a result of that value, we stick with it because we strongly believe that it is the right thing to do.

One successful team works with a huge refinery in a Pacific Rim country. The project involves sixty-eight people and generates $47 million of profit each year. One of our young teammates needed a parts shipment from the U.S. to fix a serious customer downtime situation. The parts sat in customs for several days, waiting for the paperwork. Meanwhile, the entire refinery sat idle waiting for this repair to be completed. Being a native, the teammate understood that a monetary "gift" often motivates underpaid customs officials to speed up the paperwork. She reached into her own pocket and paid a $5,000 bribe. The paperwork got completed, the parts were delivered and the customer was delighted. She lived our vision of creating success for customers.

She later informed the team. The team discussed possible actions to take. They concluded that she did the wrong thing in paying the bribe, but she used her own money, not the organization's money, and she did it for the right reason, creating success for her customer. After much debate, the team excused her behavior.

But the incident came to light. These behaviors always do. People find out, whether it's years later or minutes later. A huge uproar erupted. As the leader, we had to defend the right values. Besides, we found the action repugnant to our personal values. We traveled to meet the team in their country.

We told the team, "Look at our values and her behavior. If this happened in another team, what action would you recommend? We leave it up to you. But understand, if you decide not to take an action that supports our values, we will terminate this activity. We will either give you the opportunity to buy it from us and operate it as your own, or we will give the customer notice that we plan to exit the business and give them time to find somebody else to replace us. We understand how you feel and why you did what you did. As an organization—and as individuals— we choose not to be associated with those kinds of activities." We caught the next plane home. The team wrestled with the issue for two days, finally deciding, "We will live within the organization's values." They terminated the woman.

Two months later the woman appeared at our organization-wide business meeting, having asked for, and received, fifteen minutes of scheduled platform time. She told the 2,000 assembled people, "I did the wrong thing in paying that bribe. I personally apologize if I did anything that embarrassed any of you. I learned my lesson. I'll never do it again. Thank you for giving me the opportunity to work with you all these years and come back today and tell you how I feel." Then she left.

The group unanimously recommended to the team that they rehire her. The team did rehire her, and today she's one of our best contributors. The toughest times reveal your most basic values. She helped all of us reconnect with what we truly valued. She taught us the value of living our values even in the toughest of times.

Values are not for sale. They are a not-to-be-violated touchstone for behavior.

PHOENIX WORKSHOP

LIST EACH OF THE FOLLOWING VALUES ON A SEPARATE 3X5 CARD: ACHIEVEMENT, COMMUNITY, CONTROL, CUSTOMERS, EFFICIENCY, EQUALITY, EXCELLENCE, FAMILY, FUN, GROWTH, HARMONY, INNOVATION, INTEGRITY, LEADERSHIP, LEARNING, PROFITABILITY, QUALITY, SAFETY, TEAMWORK, TRADITION.

BEGINNING WITH THE LEAST IMPORTANT VALUE TURN DOWN THE 3X5 CARDS. WHEN YOU GET THE FIVE MOST IMPORTANT VALUES, DIVIDE THEM INTO TWO GROUPS OF THE THREE MOST IMPORTANT AND THE TWO LESSER IMPORTANT.

TAKE THE TOP THREE CARDS AND BEGIN AGAIN WITH THE LEAST IMPORTANT AND SORT UNTIL YOU GET THE MOST IMPORTANT.

TAKE THE SECOND- AND THIRD-RANKED CARDS AND PUT THEM TOGETHER WITH CARD NUMBERS FOUR AND FIVE AND RE-SORT THE FOUR CARDS AGAIN FROM THE LEAST IMPORTANT TO THE MOST IMPORTANT.

COMPARE THE CARD YOU CHOOSE AS MOST IMPORTANT NOW WITH THE NEW (MAYBE?) NUMBERS TWO AND THREE AND BE CERTAIN THAT IT STILL IS YOUR MOST IMPORTANT VALUE.

WHAT ARE MY MOST IMPORTANT VALUES AND WHAT DO EACH MEAN TO ME?

VALUE_____ MEANING_____

VALUE_____ MEANING_____

VALUE_____ MEANING_____

Summary: Vision, Mission, Values

What will the renewed *you* look like? Stand for? Be willing to die for? What will your renewed organization provide? To whom? The Pyramid is the solid structure from which the future is built. It all begins with vision: the dream and hope of what we want to become. Vision is the beacon light shining through the fog of to-morrow's uncertainty. That gives rise to a mission that tells us what products and services will provide to which customers. The mission binoculars narrows our focus and lays down broad conceptual tracks. And then Values establish standards for behavior. Values are our compass that guides us on our mission following our vision.

Be a Phoenix leader and seize the time now to lay rows of bricks in your Pyramid. Create a whole new interconnected world and way of life. Henry Ford envisioned everyone owning a car and founded the modern automobile industry. Charles Merrill believed everyone should own stock. His company today manages more private money than the gross national product of all but a handful of countries. McDonald's founder Ray Kroc felt everyone should get a quick sandwich. Nine thousand stores later, you can get a Big Mac anywhere from Beijing to Moscow to Great Falls. Bill Gates saw a personal computer in every home. Almost half of U.S. homes now have a personal computer, and the number grows daily.

What do you believe in? What do you want to commit your life to do? To prove? To accomplish? Success is inevitably the result of a sincere and other-centered commitment to something greater than one's self, the desire to leave a footprint, leave a legacy. The vision, mission and values portion of the Pyramid begins to translate that desire into more concrete thoughts and actions. And the next chapter will bring us closer to the day-to-day. We will look at the general goals that provide a framework for thinking about strategies—and then, specific objectives, measures and rewards.

Get the mortar ready. There are more bricks to lay.

CHAPTER 10

Getting There Means Getting Real: Creating Workable Goals and Strategies

Moving Toward the Peak Calls Us to Action

The partially completed Pyramid rises in the windblown landscape. The beacon light of your *vision* illuminates your future destination. The binoculars of your *mission* narrows the focus of your passion to how you will achieve your vision. The compass of your core *values,* those beliefs worth fighting and dying for, will guide your behavior as you work toward that vision. Now we move to more granular considerations that call us to action. What are your goals and strategies? How will we move from thought to action, from dreams to realization? The real world and its challenges looms over us like a mountain. What's next?

Answer: set goals. When climbing a mountain, you move upward from plateau to plateau: each is a vantage point on the way to the peak. Look up a few hundred feet, and see your next vantage point. Climb one rock, one crag at a time. Those goals are your calls to action. The vision is the peak. Your goals are the plateaus and steps on your way to the top. Goals are set, met and reset as you move toward the peak.

Getting Real Means Creating Workable Goals and Strategies

Setting goals means thinking things through and coming up with a workable plan. One's business goal might be creating a national chain of retail toy store outlets in major metropolitan areas, or becoming proficient in Spanish. The national retail toy store chain is one *goal* toward achieving a *vision* of helping children learn while having fun. That vision led to the *mission* of providing retail educational play-and-learn products. You decided that dedication to creating better-educated children and parents was an important *value*. Thus, opening a chain of retail toy stores across the country is one logical goal that creates success for both your customers and your shareholders. Being the recognized educational resource for play-and-learn activities might be another goal that creates success for your communities.

Developing proficiency in Spanish is a sensible *goal* toward achieving a personal *vision* of being in the export/import business. That vision led to the *mission* of focusing on South America for two-way import/export trade in soft goods (textiles/clothing). One of your core *values* is to contribute to the economic and social development in South America. Therefore, learning Spanish is a logical goal in creating success for your teammate associates, making you a more valuable contributor.

Developing business contacts with people currently doing business in South America is another goal that creates success for those South American communities you want to help. It clearly integrates with the other Pyramid stones you've been laying of vision, mission and values.

With your goals established, you then need *strategies* that lay out the general ways you will accomplish your goals. Strategies are your road map to reaching the goals, driving the mission and fulfilling vision. They cascade from and support your goals. For example, strategies for the toy store might include:

- sequentially blanket in-depth concentration in specific metro areas (like Chicago), opening sufficient stores to deeply penetrate a market before moving to the next one;
- employ full-time personnel (rather than the industry standard part-time pattern), paying above-average wages and providing substantial training in the use of games and toys as learning tools;

- sell only top-quality, proven, leading-edge hardware and software that helps children and parents learn;
- develop partnerships with toy and game providers to help them create and build software and hardware that helps children and parents learn;
- build a customer-focused organization.

Strategies for mastering Spanish might include:

- identifying your best learning mode (tape, video, classes);
- locating the best educational vehicle (community college, specific language school, adult education classes, private tutor);
- scheduling time to study and develop mastery.

Think in terms of altitude. If the vision is at the level of 30,000 feet, and missions are at 10,000 feet, goals and strategies are much closer to the ground—1,000 feet. They are more granular, though still far removed from the individually hand-tooled stones necessary to integrate the Pyramid. Objectives, measures and rewards bring us even closer to ground level, five or ten feet.

This chapter will provide a framework for laying the goals and strategies blocks in your Pyramid. The next chapter will lay out how to build the objectives, measures and rewards portions. The chapters after that will show you how to design the final rows of your Pyramid.

GOALS: THE DREAM DELIVERABLES

Beyond Wishful Thinking: Real Goals Have Due Dates

In *Through the Looking-Glass* the White Rabbit tells Alice, "If you don't know where you are going, any road will take you there." That applies to goals. If you don't have clear and measurable goals, how are you going to know when you achieve them?

Goals are not wishes on paper. They are deliverables with due dates. You can't achieve your vision dream without achieving in-

termediate targets first. So setting goals is the next step after setting vision, mission and values. Goals are macro targets that
shape your course and direction. Without them, the greatest vision and mission are like a Rolls-Royce without wheels.

Goal Setting in Several Settings

Goals create success for all members of the system. Here are the
actual goals we established for the four business case studies
we've tracked in this book.

AT&T/GBCS

Associate Value: A positive work environment as indicated by
62 percent "satisfied" and "very satisfied" responses on the associate satisfaction survey to the question "Considering everything, how satisfied are you in your job at GBCS?"

Customer Value: A willingness on the customer's part to continue to do business with GBCS. Indicated by 82 percent customer responses of 5, 6 and 7 (on a 1 to 7 scale) to the question
on the annual customer satisfaction survey, "Please indicate
your willingness to repurchase again from AT&T/GBCS."

Profitable Growth: Division operating profit of $1.00. The divi-
sion had lost money for all nine years of its existence.

Shareholder Value: Positive economic value added. Having lost
money for nine consecutive years, the division had a negative
impact on AT&T's EVA.

AT&T/NCR

Associate Delight: 61.7 percent of associates mark either 6 or
7 on the annual associate satisfaction survey to the question
"Considering everything, how satisfied are you in your job at
AT&T/NCR?"

Customer Delight: 49 percent of customers respond either 6 or
7 on the annual customer satisfaction survey to the question,
"Considering everything, how satisfied are you with AT&T/
NCR?"

Profitable growth: Annual revenue of $7.7 billion with division operating profit of $466 million, growing to sales of $10 billion within two years and profits of $1 billion.

Shareholder Delight: Profitability of $466 million (up from $206 million last year) and EVA of $157 million.

Legent

World-Class Associate Delight: Exceeding 79 percent responses of 6 and 7 (out of 7) on the annual associate satisfaction survey.

World-Class Customer Delight: Exceeding 82 percent responses of 6 and 7 on the annual customer satisfaction survey.

Profitable Growth: Number one in market share in every segment and product family. Earnings of $2.00 per share.

Shareholder Delight: A price/earnings multiple that brings a stock price of $50.

World-Class Process Infrastructure: Compared for such processes as order entry, on-time delivery and accounts payable against the best-in-class.

Supply Company

All associates have a learning plan and accomplish the plan to the satisfaction of teammates, coaches and customers.

50 percent of market share in the target geographic market.

100 percent of wallet share of targeted customers.

Perceived as a "valuable business partner" by 75 percent of customers as indicated by responses of 5 or 6 on a 6-point scale.

Logistics performance, as measured by inventory turns, days in supply chain and back orders, that equals or exceeds best-in-class.

Set Customer-Led Externally Focused Goals

Everything, including goal setting, starts with customers. Find out what your customers need to be successful. Look at key interdependencies. The fresh air and sunlight come from outside, not basements or attics. The marketplace and the customers always provide the direction.

It was clear what our customers wanted from us at Legent. It was equally clear that we needed to do a much better job of delivering what they wanted. As we pointed out earlier, customers perceived Legent as piecemealing them to death. We had a lot of work to do to build credibility with our customer base.

Legent needed to fix several internal barriers as well. Battles among departments drained off energy and diluted focus on meeting customer needs. Legent also often battled with suppliers, treating them as adversaries, rather than partners. The goal of achieving number one market share focused everyone on providing integrated solutions across many platforms and distributed in ways that suited the customer. Everyone knew that fixing the internal issues and building trust with external customers were absolutely essential to achieving that lofty position.

In the examples cited, the goals reflect the "create success for all customers" mentality: associates, end-user customers and shareholders are all recipients of specifically targeted goals. And, in all cases, goals tie closely with vision, mission and values.

Internal Goals: Murky Phantoms from the Dark Lagoon of Assumption

Phantom assumptions arise and dominate the collective mind-set and actions when goals are not set from the customer in. Even talented and capable people get sidetracked when they get locked on the wrong target. Yes: bad goals happen to good people in good companies. That was exactly the story when we first encountered AT&T/GBCS.

Based upon an internal focus, their basic assumption was: "We've got to drive prices down to gain market share." GBCS was the big gorilla in the market with the largest market share. Their decision to keep driving prices down forced everyone in the market to follow suit. The result: continuing price wars and large losses for GBCS. Senior management decided to divide the organization into two separate organizational units: sales and manufacturing/R&D. These two organizational units negotiated internal transfer sales prices between themselves in an effort to drive costs down. Everyone in the business bought the assumption that GBCS had a cost problem not a sales problem.

Open warfare erupted among the internal organizations negotiating transfer prices. Manufacturing worked to minimize product variations, so they charged high transfer prices for nonstandard items. Sales wanted low transfer prices to encourage customization. Under the internal transfer price approach one unit could win, but the whole company could lose. Somehow the customer got completely lost in all of the brouhaha about transfer pricing. GBCS had very good people, trapped by insidious, internal goals driving unhealthy business behavior.

The Minister Listens to His Customers and Makes a Difference

Our minister is a social activist, like many in our faith. He spends time with the homeless and less fortunate, finding out how he and his congregation can help. Food shortages plague those with whom he speaks. "Help us get more and better food to feed ourselves and our families," they tell him.

Listening to his less-fortunate customers, and blending those needs with his congregation's interest in expanding the membership, he launched a food drive with a twist. Once a month parishioners bring five cans of food to Sunday service. The twist is you must collect the cans from neighbors, rather than simply reaching into your own cupboard. This encouraged parishioners to engage their neighbors in both the food solicitation and the work of the church. This helped spread the word about the church in the local area and expand the membership. Not only does the church collect thousands of cans of food each month, but church membership has soared. A single individual, our minister, set two customer-led goals—feed the hungry and grow the membership. This butterfly flapped its wings and changed the world for us all.

Set Goals That Beat the Best and Amaze the Rest

Set stretch objectives that beat the best. Stretch goals result in great performance for our customers. Always go for the gold. Why aim low? Who wins? Only your competitors. Grow your value and contribution to your network by delivering great performance and watch your security grow.

Setting stretch goals is a hallmark of our kind of activity. Imagine the surprise at AT&T/GBCS when we suggested that the shareholder goal might be to make a buck, a measly single dollar. The great people at GBCS had been shell-shocked by a string of huge losses, $390 million the previous year, $800 million the year before and likely more than $8 billion since divestiture. They had already stretched to come up with a budget for only a $190 million loss. They hadn't the foggiest notion of where they might find another $190 million in operating profit, plus that one buck in profit.

The folks at GBCS thought about it, came up with ways to increase margins, and went to work executing them. We didn't make that buck that year. We did lose a lot less than the $190 million we'd been scheduled to lose. Most importantly, we changed the mind-set in the division, which set the stage for it to become one of the most profitable parts of Lucent Technologies, one of the AT&T spin-offs.

Our stretch goals at Legent had a more immediate payoff. It was certainly a stretch to attain world-class status as the goal for associate and customer delight, particularly since the current scores were 20 to 30 percent below those levels. Similarly, there was lots of stretch in the goal of "world-class process infrastructure" as well. Legent was thirteen separate companies in search of a common infrastructure. The people around that planning table that day all agreed that it would take lots and lots of very hard work to move the needle toward those stretch goals.

But they went to work. Legent began to improve almost immediately. In fact, they were quickly spotted by Computer Associates as a prime acquisition candidate. Legent was on the threshold of exponential success, and success attracts offers. Zap! The stock price doubled, achieving the year 2000 price level in 1995. Lots of new millionaires debuted at their local bank.

Best Margins Will Survive the Inevitable Downturn

Ford Motor Company was the success story in the late 1980s and early 1990s. They came back from serious trouble early in the 1980s with their "Quality Is Job One" vision. They redesigned the Taurus to become the biggest-selling car in America and it drove significant profit for the company. Still, Ford trailed Chrysler in profit-per-car sold: Chrysler earned $828 per vehicle; Ford, $323. It's also true that General Motors lost $189 on every car and truck it produced that year, but that did little to help Ford delight shareholders or prepare for the future. Ford understood that as a smaller producer, it needed to earn more per car to survive any downturn in the very cyclical auto business. So the chairman established the goal to achieve the highest profit per vehicle in the industry. Talk about stretch.

The highly centralized and extensive financial control system was a major cost at Ford. Years ago, Robert McNamara and his "Whiz Kids" put that centralized system together. It had served Ford well over the years, but no longer.

S.L. Mintz, in the March 1995 edition of *CFO,* reports how comptroller (and Phoenix leader) Larry Reichenstein went to work laying stones for his Pyramid. He put in place a new decentralized vision for McNamara's crown jewel, putting controls in the hands of people who develop, manufacture, sell and service the product. His new mission and values reflected his new vision. He put his financial people out in the five major vehicle centers, working alongside designers, engineers, manufacturing and marketing folks, to help operating managers make better financial decisions. He moved 90 percent of his staff out of headquarters and into the field. This dramatic revivolution was designed to help Ford meet the stretch goal of achieving the highest per-vehicle profit in the industry—a goal the company has not yet reached.

Stretch Goals Grow EVA

CSX was a $9.5 billion railroad and shipping company on the slow track to nowhere. In most of the last ten years, its return on capital was far below its 10 percent cost of capital. CEO Jack Snow saw that the bridge was out on the track bed up ahead. To change the railroad's course, he donned his Phoenix leadership gloves and began excavating for a new Pyramid. In addition to his new vision, mission and values he established the stretch goal that within two years CSX's earnings would exceed their 10 percent cost of capital. His story is reported in *Fortune*'s November 14, 1994, edition.

Very few CSXers believed that it was possible. "I thought the objectives were impossible, but without them we would have gotten comfortable and kept using railcars like they were free," said Dave Sharp, the new coal division president. To meet the stretch targets, Sharp took on headquarters, where many of the car-scheduling issues were created. He prevailed over the bureaucrats. His group surpassed its stretch target, cutting 1,000 of 5,000 railcars—that's 20 percent—and 25 of 100 locomotives—that's 25 percent. The reduction in rolling stock cut depreciation and operating costs, which led to a 63 percent increase in profit. Reduced capital costs combined with these higher margins produced a dramatically higher return on capital.

Pete Carpenter, the head of CSX's railroad business, decentralized run scheduling, sales, maintenance and other functions. Last year, Carpenter sent five volunteers from Jacksonville, Florida, to tiny Cumberland, Maryland. There, they set up an independent profit center to haul coal for customers in western Maryland. Carpenter set the stretch goal that the region was to go from break even to substantial profit within a year, and eliminate 800 of its 5,000 coal haulers at the same time. The stretch goal worked.

In eliminating so much of its rolling stock inventory, CSX shrunk its capital expenditures from $825 million to $625 million, a reduction of more than 25 percent. It achieved a positive EVA for the first time in a decade, and then added to its performance in the next year. Stretch goals generate new behaviors, at CSX and elsewhere.

Stretching for Growth in Hard Times

We're currently working with a large medical distribution company. They're going through some tough times. They took a big acquisition and suffered indigestion. They reported consecutive quarterly losses for the first time in a hundred years.

In working on their next year's goals they said, "Well, we can probably get a 5 percent sales increase." We responded. "Five percent increase? Over this year, down from last year, which won't even get us back to where we were three years ago? Which won't even match the growth in the marketplace? Five percent? That's not worth getting up in the morning for. What kind of sales increase do we really want to have? The stock price used to be $25. Today it's $10. What kind of earnings do we need to get the stock price back to $25? How much of a sales increase do we need to achieve that earnings level and stock price?"

Thinking that way, the numbers come out very differently. It'll take a 23 percent sales increase to achieve the earnings and stock price goals.

"Twenty-five percent is what it must be," the CEO said.

It's easy to think incrementally. But it takes passion and determination to set and meet stretch goals. Never think small: small is hardly worth living for. If we are going to engage people in achieving great things, don't ask them for anything less.

Keep It Simple: Fewer Is Better

Most of us respond best to clear targets. "Take that hill!" "Score the touchdown!" "Get the order!" All of those are clear and easy to understand.

We've learned that four or five clearly stated goals is plenty. Notice that all of the four case studies have few goals, two have four goals and two have five. We've found that fewer is better in goal setting.

We met Georgeanna at a workshop. She was a nurse-practitioner working as part of a change team in a local hospital. She liked nursing but loved what she was doing in introducing change. "The project is coming to an end," she told us. "I've got to make a decision. Do I go back to my floor job—which I thought I loved until I did this job—or do I take a voluntary reduction in force and get tooled up to enter a whole new career. What do you think?"

We responded, "Imagine yourself five years from today. Describe the perfect day, what are you doing, where are you doing it, and so on."

After twenty minutes or so it was clear that she was captivated with the change opportunities. "Okay," we said. "Let's set some specific goals for you over the next year that will help you move into your new field. Think about your customers, what they want and what you can provide that others can't." Twenty-five minutes later we had the following goals: Become a skilled group facilitator. Secure at least one health care client for a change project. Become a recognized expert in the change facilitation process. Secure a part-time faculty position teaching change-related subjects. Take a two-week family trip to establish closer relationships with her two children. These goals focused Georgeanna on what her customers needed and how she could address their needs. She's off and running, streaking toward the goal line of her new Phoenix career.

In short, integrate customer-led goals across the entire network. All too often, we measure ourselves against a budget, an aging plan filled with internal phantom assumptions and political compromises. But goals mean nothing unless they deliver on the dream by moving everyone closer to the vision. We turn to the next step along the way—developing strategies.

PHOENIX WORKSHOP

WHAT ARE THE FEW MOST IMPORTANT GOALS I NEED TO ACCOMPLISH IN ORDER TO LIVE MY VISION, MISSION AND VALUES? (BE CERTAIN THAT THESE FEW GOALS REPRESENT WHAT CUSTOMERS REALLY VALUE AND WILL SET THE STANDARD IN YOUR AREA.)

GOAL_____

GOAL_____

GOAL_____

STRATEGIES: ROAD MAPS TO FUTURE SUCCESS

Goals are wonderful, but how will we achieve them? Strategies answer that question. Strategies support goals, values, mission and vision. They are road maps to the future where success happens for everyone with whom you're connected.

Strategies have three key attributes. First, they are created and played out on the field. So they begin with customers. Second, they involve everyone in formulating them, particularly those people in direct contact with the customers and the market. Third, they must be aligned with vision, mission, values and goals.

Learning from Experience

Let's follow along with the strategies at the four companies we are using as business cases. We report here the strategic headlines. In the summary at the end of the chapter we spell out all of the detailed thinking that went into these strategies.

AT&T/GBCS

1. Make people a key priority.
2. Win customers for life.
3. Utilize the TQM total quality management approach.
4. Lead in customer-led applications of technology.
5. Rapidly and profitably globalize.
6. Be the best-value supplier.

AT&T/NCR

1. Be market- and customer-led in providing complete, integrated solutions to selected industries worldwide.
2. Provide customer information solutions that help companies help their customers and prospects by more effectively getting, moving and using customer information.
3. Execute through the value equation.
4. Use the customer-focused business model.
5. Apply technology to develop solutions for customers.
6. Take advantage of AT&T synergy.

Legent

1. Deliver integrated product and service solutions.
2. View customer relationships as long-term, win-win partnerships.

3. Develop a worldwide direct and indirect channel strategy that is driven by the customer.
4. Organize business systems and practices to make Legent associates highly efficient.
5. Provide the best total solutions for customers.
6. Form third-party alliances and partnerships, which are essential to satisfying customers.

Supply Company

1. Develop consulting and professional services for retail owners.
2. Hone logistics skills in warehouse management, distribution and Electronic Data Interchange.
3. Build long-term business partnerships with customers and manufacturers.
4. Implement the customer-focused business model, using the Interlock system (discussed in Chapter 11) to coordinate customer-focused activities.

Strategy Begins in the Field with Customers

Strategies are created and played out on the field. So begin with those people on the field, your customers and field-contact associates, who are closer to the ground. At that level we are able to see the more granular landscape, a horizon dotted with obstacles but also opportunities.

We realize that earthquakes frequently come and rearrange everything. Customers' needs and interests will change. We need to stay alert and be able to adapt at a moment's notice as conditions warrant.

Customers are your best ground-level strategists. They know what's happening. They also are a reality check for strategies you develop. Customers are great business consultants. They will give you advice you can take to the bank, because they need and want you to get it right! They have an obvious business stake in your success.

Strategy 101: Lessons from Professor Pericles

The term "strategy" derives from the ancient Athenian title "Strategos," denoting a commander of the Athenian armed forces. That term itself was created from the two words, "stratos," or army, and "agein," or lead. For the Athenians the strategist led the army in the defense of the city.

Pericles led the golden age of Athens. He presided over the great expansion of Athenian culture and art, best represented by the Parthenon on the Acropolis. He was a great orator and a great strategist. He knew that strategy was won or lost on the battlefield. So his strategists were his army field commanders, those people out there on the battlefield who knew what was going on and could (and did) make on-the-spot strategic decisions. Pericles would never approve of the recent tendency to centralize strategy at the executive level and the hiring of business-school-trained MBA strategic analysts.

Why? Pericles knew that strategy took place on the field, and was best performed by field personnel. It's only on the field, dealing directly with customers and competitors, that you know what you're up against. Learn Professor Pericles' lesson well: go to the field and ask your customers and field-contact associates.

Leverage the Best Business Strategists in Your Network— Your Customers

We spend the first month of any new assignment mostly out with customers and associates who have direct field contact. When we first moved into AT&T/NCR we spent four days a week for several months with customers. Many people complained that we weren't available back at headquarters to handle all of the important strategic decisions that needed to be made. "We are available to make the important strategic decisions facing our company," we countered, "out here in the field, where those important decisions are best made." Talk about sending a message.

In all four of the case studies, we began formulating the strategic imperatives by actively and extensively visiting customers. Then we solicited input from front-line, customer-contact associates. Then we met with the senior executive staff. Our behavior sent the message that customers and field people were going to be actively involved in formulating strategy.

Too many people rely upon learning what's happening in their field from secondary sources, such as industry publications or popular business journals. There is no substitute for direct, face-to-face, nose-to-nose, belly-to-belly unvarnished, unscrambled facts that come directly from those actively playing in the field. In the biblical sense, "arise and go" to the land of your customers and field associates. Do your own research. Interview and inquire until you have the landscape mapped out. Strategy is about "taking charge," one of the key attributes of becoming a Phoenix leader, as well as understanding and taking charge of your customers' best interests.

Sam is a student of ours. He was interested in starting up a real estate information business. He'd been reading the business press about the need for more accurate and timely real estate data. Sam's a good programmer, so he figured he could write a program in a few months that would sell well. We urged him to talk directly with several real estate agents about their interest in such a program. We also urged him to visit at least two of the major real estate franchising groups to test their interest.

He followed the advice and came back a chastened man. "They're both already testing a program just like the one I was going to create. Man, I would have absolutely wasted my time sweating that code. Also, all the real estate agents I spoke with are deeply opposed to any computerization. I never saw such an old-fashioned, stick-in-the-mud group. But I think I've found a niche. Both franchising companies need a field training component for their rollout. Neither had even thought about it. They both were very interested in my thoughts on how it could be done. I think I've found a way to take my interest and knowledge about real estate and combine it with my computer skills to make a viable business. I'm going back next week to talk with the two franchisers. Thanks for the great advice. You sure saved me a ton of wasted time." Nothing beats real-time data from the field.

Pericles was correct. Craft the stones that you'll lay in the rows marked "Strategy" in the *field*—with customers and field-contact associates.

Involve Everyone or No One Has a Future

Involve everyone in the bottom-up, organization-wide, intensive strategic-planning activity. Listening to and communicating with people about strategies is one of the best uses of your time. Get input from every person. Ask about the current state of the business, the environment, customers' issues and challenges, where they think we need to be. Then solicit input on strategies. Develop the five or six key strategic pillars from that.

Georgeanna, the nurse-practitioner turned change agent, went home that very same day and talked to her husband and children. They actively supported her new career goals. She laid out a plan to contact several change-agent consultants in the health care field and learn from them what she needed to do. Each of them recommended someone else for her to contact. By the time she completed her strategic investigations she had spoken with more than forty people.

Finally, she fixed on the following: attend two change-facilitator workshops and get certified as a facilitator, write and publish two articles in professional journals, appear at at least two professional meetings to present change-related papers, meet deans and presidents of local universities and community colleges to secure part-time teaching opportunities, join and become active in several health care administrator associations to identify possible clients, and book a two-week Hawaiian family vacation. Georgeanna got lots of help in identifying what she needed to do to launch her new Phoenix career. She became a Phoenix leader, took charge of her life and focused on improving her capabilities in creating success for others.

Get Lots of Eyes Looking for Tomorrow Other than Your Own

We are often asked, "Aren't you at risk if you really are led by your customers? Most customers don't know what they really need in the long run—only what they want in the short term." We also hear comments like, "Most innovations occur from outside the industry. For instance, some of the most unique computing devices weren't designed by commercial computer manufacturers."

These comments are absolutely accurate. Most customers think short-term. They have a problem that needs fixing today. It's also true that most innovations occur from outside an industry. George Eastman, who invented the affordable, easy-to-use camera, was a watchmaker, for instance. Computers came from the calculator industry. But, and it's a big but, everyone must take responsibility for planning the future, and responsibility is usually a product of involvement. The challenge is how we accomplish involvement while still thinking out of the short-term, "this is how we do it now" box.

Most customers think short-term, because they live short-term. In every industry in which we've ever been involved, however, there have always been a few leading-edge customers. We make it our business to connect with and cultivate these. Wal-Mart is one of these leading-edge customers in the retail business. That's why at AT&T/NCR we cultivated close strategic relationships with their CIO and senior management staff. Similarly, there are almost always leading-edge suppliers, like Intel with AT&T/NCR, with whom it's possible to share strategic thinking.

Associates are also great forward-thinking resources. We've always discovered leading-edge thinkers right down the hall. Phil Neches is one such individual. He helped create and shape the data warehouse field through his work at Teradata. Phil anticipated customer needs and educated the rest of us neophytes (including customers) to understand what that technology could do to create success for us all.

Often industry gurus, people who work for various research organizations, have leading-edge thoughts and observations. The world does not suffer from a lack of people who think out of the box. We mostly suffer by either ignoring their message when it comes from outside the organization, or repressing it when it comes from inside. We organize frequent exposure to these leading-edge thinkers, customers, suppliers, internal and external gurus. We're intent on not being surprised by tomorrow. As the Phoenix leader keep your eyes on the future—while you still have your hands on the present. The eyes on the future may not be your own eyes, but rather someone you trust and believe in.

Behind Every Great Strategy Is Line of Sight to the Vision

Align strategies, goals, values, mission and vision. That's key to strategic discipline. Take the Legent situation. Our vision was "Together, always creating success for our customers." You can absolutely measure that. Customers wanted long-term win-win relationships. Our mission "to be the global leader in delivering integrated product and service solutions to help customers manage information technology resources . . . today and tomorrow" suggested continuing relationships and linked clearly to customer long-term win-win partnerships. With those words we drew a line around that ballpark, saying, "We're going to stay in that integrated product and service solutions ballpark."

PHOENIX WORKSHOP

1. GIVEN MY GOALS, I'LL USE THE FOLLOWING STRATEGIES:

GOAL   STRATEGY

_____   _____

_____   _____

_____   _____

2. HOW CAN I ENSURE THAT THE GOALS AND STRATEGIES BEGIN WITH CUSTOMERS?

_____

_____

3. HOW CAN I MAKE CERTAIN THAT THE PEOPLE IN DIRECT CONTACT WITH THE CUSTOMERS AND THE MARKET FORMULATE THE STRATEGY?

_____

_____

4. HOW CAN I MAKE CERTAIN THAT THE STRATEGIES ALIGN WITH VISION, MISSION AND VALUES?

_____

_____

The values were clearly linked to the strategy as well. For instance, the value of teamwork implies continuous partnerships and winning together. Goals also were aligned. The goals of world-class associate delight, world-class infrastructure, world-class customer delight and shareholder delight all tied back to the "create success" mentality.

STRATEGIES HELP GET US THERE

Establishing a vision was the easy part. From the 30,000-foot view, the obstacles are barely discernible. Down here on the solid ground where we must begin, the rocks, crags and ridges now fill our view. It is easy to lose motivation as we get closer to harsh reality. It's fun—and easy—to dream about what might be. It's a lot harder to scramble up the cliff with rope and picks in hand. But breathing the rarified air of the mountain peak requires hard climbing.

Goals help us focus our efforts on specific, measurable outcomes. They show us the next crag and rock. They challenge us to climb higher. They raise the questions: "What do we really want to achieve? Where do we need to be? How will we know when we've done it?" Goals help us stand a little taller.

Strategies help us move toward our goals. They are enablers. More subtle, perhaps, than the more concrete objectives we'll talk about in the next chapter. And not as exciting, perhaps, as the vision we talked about in the last chapter. They are critical linking pins, though, between the mountaintop words of the vision and the down-to-earth nuts and bolts of the objectives. There are important bridges to cross and highways to traverse.

Having established workable goals and strategies, we will now proceed to an even more granular view. Roll up your sleeves. More rows of stones to lay. Hard work ahead.

Summary: Customer-Focused Strategies

Here's the thinking that went into the development of the strategies of the four companies we've been tracking.

AT&T/GBCS

1. Make people a key priority.

GBCS had a plethora of very good people; Bell Labs folks and so on. The division's grinding losses de-motivated and unfocused these people. We needed to reconnect with the people, rekindle their enthusiasm for the business and their commitment to the organization and its customers. Despite the fact that this was a high-technology business, we saw our competitive advantage lying in the capability of the people throughout the organization to establish close relationships with customers. Tapping and focusing the talents of the people was an essential first step to realizing the vision and mission.

2. Win customers for life.

As in any commodity business, it is easy to focus on the transaction: get the business, make the sale and move on to the next opportunity. However, there are a limited set of potential customers in the marketplace. And downstream maintenance income represents much of the long-term profitability in the business. Furthermore, we saw the need to escape the bid mentality among customers and generate a sole-source relationship. We set this customer-for-life strategy as a way to focus everyone in the organization on external customers rather than internal competitors.

3. Utilize the TQM total quality management approach.

AT&T pushed hard for use of the quality management approaches. The senior management believed in the quality approach as they saw great strides in divisions like Universal Card. There were a number of quality programs throughout the division. None had been successful, largely because of top management focus on the deficit. We used the emphasis on the quality approach as a way to send the signal that we were permanently committed to improving—not selling—the division. We intended this as a signal of top management's commitment to the long-term success of the division.

4. Lead in customer-led applications of technology.

Much of AT&T's history was spent as a monopoly telling customers what equipment to order. The monopoly mind-set is especially difficult to change—for both external customers and internal associates. This strategy was intended to reemphasize the external customer focus and the need to work cooperatively across units that previously were competitors. This strategy was also intended to reach into the R&D organization and enlist their active cooperation in the new customer focus. All too often Bell Labs–trained people developed a technical arrogance toward customers that prevented them from hearing customer needs and then designing equipment to meet those needs.

5. Rapidly and profitably globalize.

Until divestiture, AT&T was limited to servicing American customers only. The great growth in the telecommunications business occurred outside the U.S. The opportunity to capture some of that business was a driving force in AT&T's agreement to the 1984 divestiture. However, nine years after divestiture, less than 5 percent of the division's business came from overseas. We saw these global markets as the single biggest growth opportunity, and the best way to move from red ink to black ink in the profit column.

6. Be the best-value supplier.

We deliberately emphasized value, not low price. Coming out of the commodity mentality, which emphasized price cutting as the way to gain market share, we saw the urgent need to focus the entire organization on providing greater value to customers: value for which we could charge a higher price. We intended to give the sales force an entire series of sales and marketing tools to help them sell value rather than price.

AT&T/NCR

1. Be market- and customer-led in providing complete, integrated solutions to selected industries worldwide.

This strategy meant that we would listen to customers and understand what they needed and wanted. We focused on producing products for those solutions that aligned with customer requirements, concentrating R&D activities on creating new ways to provide innovation. We also aligned with the best external partners to produce the best solutions.

For example, where we previously sold only ATMs to a bank, we proposed a broader set of products and services that added up to complete solutions. We aimed to address a financial institution's broader need to provide solutions to its customers. The team serving the account combined all products into a customer-specific solution, involving ATMs, processors and other systems with software, services, media, training and network technology, all designed to fulfill the customer's need.

2. Provide customer information solutions that help companies help their customers and prospects by more effectively getting, moving and using customer information.

Our competencies had always been in transaction-intensive industries. We knew that. So we capitalized on it. Together with customers and partners, we established a product and service linkage that articulated our competencies in a logical pattern:

"GET IT" capabilities included capturing information about the characteristics, buying patterns, preferences and service requirements of customers and prospects. We leveraged our background as a recognized leader in data collection at the point of customer contact with point-of-sale terminals, ATMs, scanners, PCs and telephones.

"MOVE IT" capabilities referred to transporting information between locations and individuals with a need for or interest in it. The "move it" piece really gets at the issue of connectivity and communications. Who better than AT&T to provide capabilities in terms of networking?

"USE IT" capabilities referred to computer analysis of the information for making decisions on how the organization seeks or serves it customers. The solution supports decision making in many places: a centralized location, the point of customer contact or at distributed company locations. Our leadership in massively parallel processing, our client-server systems and partnerships with relational database companies, as well as our media solutions, enhanced our capabilities.

We saw that the market was ready for these solutions. Our customers told us that they needed them. We intended to assume market leadership by "helping our customers better understand and serve their customers."

3. Execution through the value equation.

The value equation was the mentality, the cellular heart, of our plan. The four key components of this equation were: delighted associates, delighted customers, profitable growth and delighted shareholders.

4. Use the customer-focused business model.

We talked about this model in Chapter 3. We reorganized resources to promote cross-functional partnering with the customer to provide complete solutions.

5. Apply technology to develop solutions for customers.

The marketing team identified customers' requirements and set priorities for the development of new technologies. This strategy helped us focus our research-and-development activities in client server technology, middleware, object-oriented technology, mobile and wireless and pen-based technologies, system security technologies.

6. Take advantage of AT&T synergy.

NCR remained independent since the time of the AT&T-NCR merger. There was little effort to leverage the strength of both organizations. We knew this wouldn't work going forward. We focused on enabling AT&T to lead in bringing together computing and telecommunications, helping AT&T globalize, aligning more closely with other AT&T businesses to create synergies and leveraging the AT&T image and brand.

The first example of this synergy was a jointly developed product released in 1993, the AT&T personal video system Model 70. This hardware and software telemedia connection allowed PC videoconferencing. This strategy took us a step closer to our mission by "bringing computing and communication solutions together to provide people easy access to information and to each other."

Legent

1. Deliver integrated product and service solutions.

We intended to become the single partner for software and services to manage customer information technology infrastructures. Earlier we talked about the need to integrate our offerings, breaking down internal barriers so customers could receive seamless services from us. This strategy implements those vision and mission statements.

2. View customer relationships as long-term, win-win partnerships.

The thinking behind this strategy is similar to that for the customer-for-life of AT&T/GBCS.

3. Develop a worldwide direct and indirect channel strategy that is driven by the customer.

Global opportunities drive this statement, much like at AT&T/GBCS. Legent also needed to develop the indirect channel. Legent emphasized the direct sales channel, employing its own sales force calling on customers. This is a high-cost, limited-customer-contact approach. Many customers neither need nor desire a direct sales call, preferring to order by phone or from local distributors. In addition, third-party channels reach a much wider customer net.

4. Organize business systems and practices to make Legent associates highly responsive.

This statement derives directly from the goal to have a world-class infrastructure. Recall the infrastructure difficulties in knitting together the thirteen acquisitions that comprised Legent.

5. Provide the best total solutions for customers.

This strategy sounds a familiar refrain. It closely parallels strategies at AT&T/GBCS and AT&T/NCR.

6. Form third-party alliances and partnerships which are essential to satisfying customers.

Legent needed third-party alliances with software and hardware partners in order to provide the integrated product and service solutions referred to in strategy number one. In the past, Legent dragged its feet in forming technology partnerships. This strategy refocused Legent's activities.

Supply Company

1. Develop consulting and professional services for retail owners.

Traditionally the Supply Company was in the distribution business. The vision, mission and goals of the company required it to develop an entirely new set of consulting capabilities in financial management, tax, marketing and human resource management.

2. Hone logistics skills in warehouse management, distribution and Electronic Data Interchange.

Supply Company already possessed a strong set of logistics skills. They were the best in their business. But they needed to enhance their electronic linkage both with stores (very few small stores had any electronic capability) and manufacturers.

3. Build long-term business partnerships with customers and manufacturers.

This strategy complements strategy number one and implements the goals, vision and mission.

4. Implement the customer-focused business model, using the Interlock system (discussed in Chapter 12) to coordinate customer-focused activities.

Supply Company adopted the customer-focused business model, like AT&T/NCR. They reorganized into customer-focused sales and distribution teams. Then they adopted the system we will discuss in Chapter 11.

CHAPTER 11

Getting It Done in the Trenches: Disciplined Management Systems

Get It Done in the Trenches: Where Real People Help Real People

It's time to get down to earth and turn your attention to making it all work. At ground level, Phoenix leaders take risks, dodge bullets and help real people. A lot is at stake—people's lives and tomorrows! Step up and face the challenges. Think fast, connect the dots, make a plan and go for it. How will you execute the strategies that take you to your goals? What are your objectives? How will you know when you've reached those objectives? How will you reward people to motivate them to do even greater things?

There's plenty of heat at ground level—like the surface of Venus. Creating and acting on objectives, measures and rewards is not for the faint of heart. What are you made of? You're going to find out soon. Time to make some choices. Get your hands and feet and collar dirty. And do it fast—everyone's waiting!

Align the Stones for a Stronger Base for Future Success

Think in terms of altitude. Recall that the vision is at the level of 30,000 feet, the mission is at 10,000 feet, and that goals and strategies are much closer to the ground at 1,000 feet. They are more granular, though still far removed from the individually carved stones necessary to build the Pyramid. That's where *objectives*, *measures* and *rewards* bring us even closer to ground level—five or ten feet. The following brief explanation will help you see how objectives, measures and rewards align with the rest of the stones in the Pyramid.

Objectives are granular, individual outcomes. They give rise to precise measures—the meters, inches and minutes by which we indicate our progress through life. These lead to equally precise rewards—our due for achieving (or the consequences for not achieving) the objectives.

For example, in the toy store venture we discussed earlier, annual *objectives* for the area manager might be to:

- open four stores in the Chicago area exceeding both opening and operating budget and time expectations;
- achieve a 5 percent local market penetration within six months of store opening;
- achieve 15 percent of customer spending within targeted customer segments;
- develop strategic partnerships with at least 30 percent of the leadership of the educational institutions in the local store area;
- coach store managers to develop effective customer-focused, learning-based associate teams at each location.

Measures might include:

- comparison of budget performance and opening dates against expectation;
- market share data;
- share of customer spending data for targeted customer segments;
- number of educational leaders who participate in formal partnership meetings;
- feedback from associate satisfaction scores (particularly in response to questions dealing with the availability of tools and training, customer focus in the store, teamwork and coaching ability of the store manager).

The *reward* might be a bonus plan that paid one fifth of a profit-sharing bonus based upon attainment of each of the specific objectives.

For the goal of mastering Spanish in the earlier example, objectives might include:

- signing up for the educational experience and completing it within nine months (before September 30);
- participating successfully in one business transaction that requires proficiency in Spanish.

Measures might include:

- a specific grade in the class (B, say) or passing the final examination;
- personal feeling of comfort in effectively participating in the Spanish language business discussion;
- feedback from the other participants that they understood you and believed that you understood them;
- being invited to participate in other future Spanish business discussions.

Rewards might include:

- a personal sense of accomplishment and satisfaction;
- business contacts that produce import-export business in South America;
- profit on the Spanish business transaction.

The components of the Pyramid for the toy store model fit together like building blocks. *Vision* (helping children learn while having fun) interlocks with *mission* (providing retail educational play-and-learn products). These interlock with *values* (dedication to creating better-educated children and parents) that interlock with *goals* (opening a chain of retail toy stores across the country).

Those goals interlock with *strategies* (sequentially blanketing in-depth concentration in specific metro areas, such as Chicago). The vision, mission, values, goals and strategies translate into specific individual *objectives* (opening four stores in the Chicago area this year, exceeding both opening and operating budget and time expectations), *measures* (comparison of budget performance and opening dates against expectation) and *rewards* (a bonus plan that pays one fifth of a profit-sharing bonus based upon attainment of each of the specific objectives). In this instance, the Pyramid forms a strong base for future success because it is constructed of internally aligned and perfectly integrated building blocks.

OBJECTIVES: THE HARD WORK CONNECTING THE MILLION DOTS

We are finally at ground level, at the action point, where the rubber meets the road. We all live in the world of objectives, the ubiquitous to do list. Here's where we join the huddled masses of humanity striving for that next step ahead, that next score.

Go into any organization—of five people or 500,000—and you'd likely make a huge, quantum improvement in performance if you did nothing but eliminate all the conflicting internal objectives. More than 70 percent of business problems start with conflicting and confusing objectives. Link objectives clearly and explicitly to vision, mission, values, goals and strategies in order to bring sanity and efficiency into any organization.

Objectives share many characteristics with goals. We will just briefly review the similarities before moving into greater depth about objectives.

Objectives and Goals: The Three Similar Attributes

Like goals, set objectives *from the customer in.* Set individual and team objectives with both internal and external customers. Look to your current interdependent, interconnected network and determine what you must do to create success for them all, while living your vision, mission, values, goals and strategies. Ask the question "What are the few most important contributions we/I make to creating success for our customers?"

Second, *set stretch objectives*. Think about what customers really want and need, unconstrained by what you feel is possible or doable. Stretch to be the best for your customers. That's the way to enhance your personal security. Measure your performance in miles and meters, not inches and centimeters. Set stretch objectives that contribute to achieving the vision, mission, values, goals and strategies.

Lastly, *keep objectives simple*. Objectives need to be simple, just like goals. Start with a set of four or five goals for the company, four or five objectives for your team and four or five objectives for yourself. No more than that. They should be easy to understand, so anyone could repeat them. Remember, a million micromeasurements do not one macro make. The key is simplicity. Complicated objectives breed excuses and errors.

Objectives Differ from Goals: We *and* I

Unlike goals, set both team and individual objectives. At the Supply Company, the finance department needs objectives that will create success for its customers. The accounts payable manager and the payroll clerk also need objectives that spell out their contributions to creating customer success. Individual objectives contribute to team objectives that contribute to customer success.

Unlike Goals, Objectives Are Shared and Interlocked so Everyone Is Joined at the Heart and Wallet

Share and interlock objectives across your entire network. Set objectives systemically with associates, customers, suppliers, communities and shareholders. The objectives from the finance team at the Supply Company example cited just above were all shared and interlocked with their customers—internal associates and external store operators—and their suppliers—the manufacturers.

Interlocking objectives connect all the dots. They get everyone to play the same game, perform from the same musical score and work toward the same goals. As a Phoenix leader, take charge of your own life and set objectives that enhance your ability to create success for others by interlocking your objectives and activities with theirs, thus contributing to your and their personal value and worth.

Otherwise, people get jaded. Conflicting objectives breed cynicism. Hardworking, well-intentioned people crash into each other. First they laugh. Then they think. Then they cry. It's a comedy of errors and a tragedy of terrors. People fear for their jobs. "How long can this go on?" they silently ask themselves. How successful are teams with players who have different ideas about how to play and win the game? Not very.

Interlock is especially critical since no unit, no single person, is an island, unto itself alone. Everyone is connected to everyone. Your objectives and my objectives and her objectives must add up to a win for all of us, and for all our customers, suppliers, communities and shareowners. Empowerment is not about everybody working independent objectives. People must come together and really think about how their work impacts others. Let's look at what happens when objectives are not shared.

Objectives Are Not Flat: Like the World, They Are Three-Dimensional

Objectives have three purposes. First is *performance*. Each of us gets paid to do and/or deliver something: sell the product, close the deal, work within the budget, solve the problem, meet the quota, design a thing, schedule a blah blah, build a gizmo, test a thingamajig, develop a whozy and so forth. Deliver something that helps someone else achieve their success.

Mike David of the Supply Company promised to take actions that would deliver the following performances: "to achieve 100 percent wallet share with targeted customers; to coach the management team to prepare the logistics plan; to improve teamwork; and to reduce back orders." His performance objectives ranged from very quantitive (sales and back order numbers) to much more qualitative deliverables (shorter meetings).

Second, *build relationships*. Look around you: people as far as you can see all crying out to be part of your network. No one flies solo. Recall the great Lone Eagle, Charles Lindbergh. He was part of a twenty-seven-person team that built and flew that *Spirit of St. Louis* on the first ever nonstop airplane ride across the Atlantic. Even the Lone Eagle didn't fly solo. Grow relationships with every objective. Use objectives to contribute to building a stronger, deeper understanding with customers, teammates, suppliers, stockholders and community members.

For instance, Mike also promised to deliver the following improved relationships: "better business partnerships with customers; improved coaching relationships with sales reps; closer working relationships with the management team; closer relationships between myself and each of the management team members; and improved relationships with suppliers so they plan with the company's needs in mind." Notice that Mike's relationship objectives included building relationships with customers, suppliers, his management team and sales associates.

Third, *learn and help others learn*. Life is a great teacher, if only we'd be open to learn its lessons. Look to learn in everything you do, because learning enhances your value to others and deepens your security. Similarly, help others learn so they can do the same.

Mike's learning objectives included: "to better understand customer needs; to improve coaching skills; to learn new distribution systems, methods of delivery and EDI technologies; to improve coaching techniques; to coach the development of individual and working-together capability; and to learn more about suppliers' needs." Notice that Mike's learning objectives involved both *his* learning and those of associates.

Every objective contributes to three important outcomes: delivering something of value to someone else, building relationships and learning for yourself and others.

Relate Objectives Back to Values

Values are the behavioral component of the vision, mission and values triangle. Objectives are necessary to begin the translation of well-intentioned words into day-to-day actions. So link the two tightly together.

Virtually everyone wants to do the right thing and wants others to do the same. Four-color value statements with all the right words decorate most corporate walls and fill many corporate wallets. Yet despite all the public pronouncements, we face a values crisis. We all face the challenge to get others to live the values we value.

How can you get everyone to live the values? The answer is surprisingly simple. People do what they are expected and paid to do. Most people want to do the right thing. Usually the right thing is what pleases the boss. People know what pleases the boss. In most organizations today we merely expect and pay people to sell products, cut costs and make margins. We neither seriously expect nor do we pay people also to live the values.

At AT&T/NCR we changed the ground rules and expected, measured and rewarded associates for living the values. Here's how: AT&T's common bond values are: respect for the individual, dedication to customers, integrity, innovation and teamwork. Every AT&T/NCR associate had two sets of objectives: organization/team objectives and personal objectives. As you recall, the leadership team set four business goals: associate delight, customer delight, profitable growth and shareholder value. Each unit/team then set its own objectives jointly with their customers, associates, operating partners and suppliers. These objectives were based upon the answer to the question "What must we do to contribute to the overall business objectives?" Common bond values served as the framework. For instance, a marketing group's goals were (in part), "to maximize leverage of marketing programs into sales motions and successful customer implementation, using the common bond values of innovation, teamwork, respect for the individual, and dedication to customers." Increasingly specific team objectives cascaded throughout the organization that interlocked organizational units and teams together in achieving business goals while living the common bond values.

Every associate also set personal objectives based upon the

common bond. These goals were set using upward or lateral feed-back. Team members wrote goals for each other answering the question "What can you do, using the common bond values, to help our team be successful?" The chairman's direct supports put together his personal objectives. He then shared them with all the associates through his daily publication. His were (in part):

Respect for the Individual: To coach associates to raise personal expectations beyond current performance levels, striving to be all that we can be. To coach associates to develop additional capabilities, to claim personal ownership of objectives and to exceed increased expectations. To teach others how to coach in raising expectations and developing capabilities.

Dedication to Customers: To be a role model of customer-focused behavior. To continue to actively visit and communicate with customers and share the learning from visits with all associates. To encourage all associates to be actively engaged with and learn from customers.

Integrity: To be a role model of candid-disclosure behavior. To modify individual behavior to support the new business model.

Innovation: To be a spokesperson to focus on and raise the value of innovation to be equal to or greater than the values of quality and cost.

Teamwork: To coach, teach and demonstrate the new collaborative business model, coaching and encouraging associates to effectively work together where no single individual has control.

Three sets of data also indicate "living the values" behavior. Every coach annually participated in an upward leadership values feedback (LVF) process, the common bond values forming the basis of the LVF instrument. For example, one of the chairman's measures for his respect for individuals objective was "results of the Chairman's LVF report." In addition, everyone participated in an annual associate satisfaction survey. So a measure for the chairman's teamwork objective was, "Specific score on our associate satisfaction survey which indicates associates'

belief in the widespread use of teamwork." There were also behavioral indicators such as the measure for the chairman's dedication to customer objective, "The number of activities canceled
because they do not add value to our customers." Every associate used similar measures.

You won't get value-driven behavior unless you pay for it. Like
most organizations, AT&T/NCR had both incentive payments and
merit adjustment, both depending upon living the values. Incentive payments were based upon achievement of the four business
goals. Achieving the associate and customer delight goals directly
depended upon living the common bond values, particularly
given the high visibility of the commitment to these values in
both the customer and the associate communities. Merit increases were based exclusively upon achievement of the personal
common bond objectives. So salary improvement was absolutely
dependent upon living the common bond values.

Tie objectives, measures and rewards to living the values. Set
objectives that reinforce success-producing behaviors, like living
the values, delivering what others value, building relationships
and enhancing your own ability.

MEASURES: KEEP SCORE, LEARN MORE, DO MORE

Yes, You Can Measure Your Way to Success

A venerable old company with a proud tradition had fallen on
hard times. It was drowning in a sea of red ink. Its customers
were leaving in droves. Most importantly, no one seemed to know
what to do. Employees threw up their hands. "What can we do?"
they said. "Management won't let us act." Executives worked long
hours, held extended meetings and announced frequent reorga-
nizations. Asked how things were going, they usually maintained
the approved PR stance: "Everything is improving. Customers
seem satisfied. We are holding our own."

Yet market share continued to erode, the return on capital was
substantially lower than the cost of capital and margins contin-

ued to shrink. Clearly, it was time to polish up résumés and acti-
vate the buddy network. Soon, the case study writers would compose this company's epitaph so future generations of Harvard
students could pick through the remains, looking for valuable
lessons to avoid a similar fate.

Anxious to avoid the bankruptcy staring them in the face like
an express train barreling toward them down a one-way track,
the board hired a new president. He talked to customers. He visited employees. He watched operations. He measured internal
operations and discovered a few simple, but powerful, facts. Deliveries were late 45 percent of the time. Customers' bills were
wrong 25 percent of the time. Customers returned 27 percent of
the company's product because it didn't meet specifications.
Downtime averaged 41 percent, with more than 25 percent of the
equipment out of service at any one time. A very profitable service business obscured the losses in every other product line.

Then the new president looked outside the organization at
competitive benchmarks. The company had been working on a
presumption of 88 percent customer satisfaction. That was above
average for the industry. But that rating included scores of 4, 5, 6
and 7 on a seven-point scale. Counting only the 7s reduced the
figure to 21 percent. Counting 6s and 7s, it was 42 percent. Competitors who counted only 6s and 7s had consumer satisfaction
scores of 85 percent. The revised, more realistic figures put the
company more than 40 points behind. A little more investigation
found that the company ranked dead last in virtually every
financial measure: sales per employee, profit per employee, general and administration expense percentage and sales and marketing expense per employee. Most worrisome, market share was
slipping rapidly. Competitors were growing rapidly while this
company grew hardly at all. Furthermore, the entire industry
share of its customers' business was slipping as another industry
bustled in to redefine them right out of the market.

The board was stunned. Conditions were far worse than they
knew. The bankruptcy train was closer and moving faster than
they had imagined.

The president launched four initiatives, all based on measurement of objectives. First, he established a simple customer-based
goal: be the supplier, employer and investment of choice for customers, employees and investors. He left no doubt about the
identity of the important customers. When asked, "What are we

supposed to do?" his answer was simply, "Whatever it takes to be the choice of all three!"

Second, he asked people to identify their major contributions to achieving the goals. Everyone was asked to answer the question, "What are the most important things I do to help us be the supplier, employer, investment of choice?" People shared their answers across the entire organization, using e-mail.

The president saw that a cross-functional, cross-organizational team was the only way to serve customers effectively, so he asked two interdependency questions: "What do you need from others? What do they need from you?" Answers filled the e-mail system. Individuals and teams reached agreements on individual/team contributions across internal and external interdependencies. Everyone reviewed these as they became available on the e-mail.

Third, each person was asked to agree with his customers on the best measurements of both internal financial and external competitive results, specifying no more than four measures. Everyone shared these measures on the e-mail.

Then the president insisted that everyone plan and execute against the agreed-upon objectives and report progress using the agreed-upon measures. People shared their actions on e-mail. The president reported his actions to his staff, reviewed their actions with them and insisted that everyone else do the same, throughout the organization.

The result: within nine months, the train had reversed direction and was heading the other way. Within two years, the organization had the highest return on investment in its industry and was growing at 22 percent per year.

The important lessons to learn from this experience are: First, lay out a clear, customer-focused goal. Second: measure, measure, measure, both internal financials and external competitive analogs, and report the results. There is no substitute for a scoreboard to get and keep people's attention. Just make sure it's the customers' scoreboard as well. Third, hold people accountable for delivering what they promise. The monthly meetings made performance visible. They forced everyone to get agreement, in advance, from customers and from people upon whom they were dependent, on what they needed to deliver. Then they had to measure performance every step of the way. No wonder people accuse us of being measurement freaks.

Like Objectives, There Are Three Types of Measures

There are three types of measures. Use any or all of these to answer the question "Did we achieve our objective?" *Performance*
is the first type of measurement: Did you deliver on time and
within the budget? Does the software work? Did you make the
sale? Did your behavior meet expectations? This ties back most
directly to the performance purpose of objectives.

Look at Mike's performance measures at Supply Company: "to
achieve 100 percent wallet share from targeted customers; to establish business partnerships with customers who sign up for
business services; to make sure the upgraded logistics plan is implemented by the management team; the achievement of business plan goals; reduced back orders; and modification of our
programs to better incorporate supplier needs." Performance
measurements are typically statistical evaluations—financial results usually—or deliverables like partnerships established or an
implemented strategic plan.

Feedback is the second type of measurement. Gather feedback
from both customers and teammates. How satisfied/delighted are
your customers with what you delivered? How much do they
value your coaching? What is their rating of your competence?
How much do people trust you? Do people see you living the vision, mission and values? These measurements tie back most
closely to the relationship-building purpose of objectives, though
they can also be related to the learning purposes.

Look at Mike's feedback measures: "Sales representatives report that they feel more comfortable in selling business partnerships; I feel more knowledgeable about customer requirements
for business consulting; sales reps report I was an effective coach;
team members give me high scores on my coaching ability; management team reports on the monthly reports that they work
more effectively together and more effectively with me; better
coaching scores on my monthly report."

Behavior is the third type of measurement. Watch people's
nonverbal reactions and you can tell a ton about what they are
feeling and what they will likely do in the future. Listen to people's tone of voice and inflection on the telephone and you can
tell how satisfied they are with the interaction. Notice the enthusiasm—or lack of enthusiasm—and you can tell how involved
and committed people are to any given activity and project. The

number of times people call you for advice speaks volumes about the value they place on it. These measurements tie in most directly to the relationship-building and learning purposes.

Look at Mike's use of the behavior measurement: "Team works together more effectively and effortlessly in producing plan; I feel more comfortable with the logistics area; managers identify strategic consequences of their daily actions before they act and modify their actions accordingly; better teamwork as evidenced by shorter, more productive meetings and supplier plans including our needs." He measures his own feelings and behavior and that of his teammates, associates, customers and suppliers.

Here is Mike's example with the completed measurement portions.

MIKE DAVID   1995

PRESIDENT & CEO   SUPPLY COMPANY

OBJECTIVE	PURPOSE	MEASUREMENT
No. 1: Coach and lead, growing the wallet share and market share for Supply Company. Teach sales reps to sell value, not products. Expand our sale of services.	*Performance*: Achieve 100% wallet share with targeted customers. *Relationship*: Build business partnership relationship with customers so they sign up for business service. Build coaching relationships with sales reps. *Learning*: Better understand customer needs. Improve coaching skills.	*Performance*: Achieve 100% wallet share from targeted customers (performance). *Relationship*: Establish business partnerships with customers who sign up for business services (performance). Sales representatives report that they feel more comfortable in selling business partnerships (feedback). *Learning*: I feel more knowledgeable about customer requirements for business consulting (feedback). Sales reps report I was an effective coach (feedback).

OBJECTIVE	PURPOSE	MEASUREMENT
No. 2: Coach the upgrade of logistics system to world-class status.	*Performance*: Coach the management team to prepare the logistics plan. *Relationship*: Develop closer working relationships with the management team. *Learning*: Learn about new distribution systems, methods of delivery and EDI technologies. Improve coaching techniques.	*Performance*: Upgraded logistics plan is implemented by management team (performance). *Relationship*: Team works together more effectively and effortlessly (behavior). *Learning*: I feel more comfortable with the logistics area (behavior). Team members give me high scores on my coaching ability (feedback).
No. 3: Coach management team in strategic thinking and teamwork to help them develop their management/leadership skills.	*Performance:* Improved teamwork, with each member helping the others achieve their individual objectives. Individual managers are better able to see the strategic consequences of their actions so that their actions contribute more directly to strategic goals. *Relationship*: Build closer relationships among the management team and between myself and each of them individually. *Learning*: Learn how to coach the development of their individual and teamwork (working together) capability.	*Performance*: Achievement of business plan goals (performance). Managers identify strategic consequences of their daily actions before they act and modify their actions accordingly (behavior). Better teamwork as evidenced by shorter, more productive meetings (behavior). *Relationship*: Management team reports on the monthly reports that they work more effectively together and more effectively with me (feedback). *Learning*: I receive high scores on my coaching ability on the monthly report (feedback).

OBJECTIVE	PURPOSE	MEASUREMENT
No. 4: Coach improvement in relationship with major supplier to reduce/eliminate back orders.	*Performance:* Reduce back orders. *Relationship:* Improve relationship with supplier so they plan with our needs in mind. *Learning:* Improve coaching skills. Learn more about supplier's needs so we can be more congruent with their programs.	*Performance:* Reduced back orders (performance). *Relationship:* Supplier plans include our needs (behavior). *Learning:* Better coaching scores on my monthly report (feedback). We modify our programs to better incorporate their needs (performance).

Scoreboards Lead to Ws

If you're not keeping a scoreboard you're not playing the game. And how you keep the scoreboard will determine how you play— or if you win—the game.

Red Auerbach, the winningest coach in pro basketball history, understood the fundamental truth in the above statements. He avidly tracked his players' performance. For instance, when Bill Walton played for the Celtics, Auerbach valued his defensive play. So he measured the number of times Walton rolled down to prevent an easy layup on a fast break as well as the number of block outs under the basket. It was perfectly okay with the coach if Walton only scored five or six points a game.

Coach Auerbach kept the right numbers on the scoreboard. He talked with each player about his unique contribution and agreed-upon performance measures—roll downs, blocked shots, shooting percentage or assists. He used this scoreboard to focus the player's attention.

Red Auerbach is a great management teacher. In too many situations, performance standards are not clear because measurements have very little to do with performance. For instance, everyone wants profitability. But measuring profitability in business is like measuring wins in basketball. It's obviously important—but will knowing it help you win tomorrow?

What really contributes to profitability? We know. In every

market, customer delight with our efforts to help them succeed is the prerequisite to long-term margins and market share. And employee delight with their learning and ability to make things really happen for their customers is a prerequisite to customer delight. The evidence is overwhelming. That's why we include those factors in the success equation. Employee delight in their ability to make a difference for customers is as much a predictor of financial success in business as blocked shots and assists predict success on the basketball court.

It's a trite truism that "All businesses are people businesses." But how often—and how well—do we measure a coach's people performance? In most cases the answer is a shrug of the shoulders. "I agree with you," one president recently told us. "We should measure our associate delight, but how can we do that without denuding the rain forests and turning our people into survey completers rather than workers?"

We've worked out a way both to get good associate feedback and save the rain forests. We set a performance contract each month with our fellow associates. Every week we solicit verbal feedback from our associates on how we're doing against their expectations, which often change from week to week, causing us to frequently modify our behavior. Every month they give us written feedback (using a simple five- or six-item questionnaire we've designed together) which reports our performance against our agreed-upon understanding. For instance, if we agreed to coach one employee to handle a particularly difficult customer situation, she'd tell us how well we coached her to handle that situation. That upward feedback helps us learn what works and what doesn't work and helps us improve our leadership behavior.

Customer delight in our efforts to solve their problems and contribute to their success is the second most important predictor of future economic success. We use two different but interrelated measures of that vital predictor on our scoreboard. Each person sets monthly goals and measures with customers—both internal and external. Each month each person uses the measures to review his or her customers' satisfaction. One of our goals with an external customer last month, for example, was to complete an organizational audit as the first step in a major systems integration project. We agreed that acceptance of the audit report by the CEO would be the measure of success. By the end of the month the CEO had accepted the audit report. We scored

100 percent on that measure. Individualized feedback on personal customer performance agreements is one important customer feedback entry on the scoreboard.

Customer evaluation of overall organizational performance is another vital scoreboard entry. Every month we send 7 percent of our customer base a twenty-four-item questionnaire which asks their satisfaction with both specific functions, such as billing and the help desk, as well as general issues such as willingness to recommend us to others. The answer to the "Would you recommend" question becomes part of the scoreboard.

At AT&T/NCR we installed a "one-up" entry on the scoreboard. The plant manager in San Diego, California, tracks both the scoreboard measures for his plant and those for the next level up in the organization, the entire product and supply division. This one-up entry focuses people on working together to create overall organizational success as well as individual/team success. Use the scoreboard just like Red Auerbach—as a trigger and focus to ongoing dialogue about performance. The scoreboard focuses everyone on the truly important factors that put Ws in the books. Peter Drucker said, "Measure it—or forget it." We'd amend that to read, "Measure the right stuff—or forget it."

Learning from the Open Book

Measures help us learn. Jack Stack shows us one way. He's president of Springfield Remanufacturing Company. His book *The Great Game of Business* shows how he used a technique called "open book management" to take a "broken-down" company, literally on the steps of bankruptcy, and turn it into a very productive, successful organization. Stack opened the company's financial books to everyone. He taught people how to read the books, how to read a balance sheet, how to understand what costs are, how to understand what drives costs, and how to lower costs. It helped people evaluate their impact on the organization's performance.

By making everyone knowledgeable about their impact on the overall cost structure of the company, Stack transformed Springfield Remanufacturing from a big loser to a big winner. He used measurements to teach people how to be more effective. Lots of other firms jumped on the open book management bandwagon. There's even an association of open book management organizations, where folks get together to swap war stories and learn even more about how to use measurements to promote learning and better performance.

One Last Word: There Are No Excuses—Measurement Data Is Easy to Get

Today, we have no excuse for not measuring. Information is more accessible than ever before. It's abundant. In previous times, people operated like the monks, spending a lifetime copying a single manuscript. But it's not like that anymore. Computers give you access to virtually any kind of information at any level of granularity anywhere in the world.

The data and measurement tools are available. The entrance to the digital highway is there at your desk. You can measure anything, and share that information to quickly improve performance. We are measurement fanatics because we know measurement makes a big difference and we know it can be done.

REWARDS: ENCOURAGING REPEAT PERFORMANCES

Want to learn about motivation? Watch the rat run the maze to get the cheese at the other end. Watch the pigeon press the bar to get the pellet of food. Watch the verbal pirouettes and slick power point presentations at most management meetings, with every eye glued to the person at the head of the table. Want to motivate behavior? Just hang out the right reward. It works with rats, pigeons and human beings. The catch? It must be the *right* reward, or else it doesn't work. Remove the cheese and the rat rapidly loses interest in the maze. Stop delivering pellets and the pigeon immediately finds something else to occupy its attention. Have no boss at the meeting and watch the meeting dissolve.

The principle of reward is elegantly simple: reward the right behavior with the reward the person values. That's it. That's all. Zillions of words and thousands of books all boil down to that very simple statement. Ah, but the statement is not as simple as it looks. What is the "valued" reward? What is the "right" behavior? How can you closely link that "right" behavior and the "valued" reward?

The Pyramid reward equation is equally simple. Reward the person with the reward she values for creating success for everyone in your interconnected, interdependent network. Simple to say. Very difficult to execute. It is amazing how much difficulty most organizations and individuals have in executing that very simple concept. Yet the proper reward is a vital ingredient in your new Pyramid.

Today's Wage Systems Were Designed for Another World

Why do so many reward systems fail? Because they are based on either long since discredited concepts or long dead requirements. Most of the compensation plans in place today trace their parentage back to the War Labor Board of World War II. During the war, in order to control wages and prices, the board established a systematic method of justifying pay scales. They insisted upon job descriptions, job analyses and an industry or geographic wage survey as the basis for any wage adjustment.

Until that point in time, there weren't systematic compensation systems. Pay was usually a matter of boss discretion, which produced tons of variations and discriminations. Most people received either a straight salary or a wage per hour. Incentive pay was limited to salespeople and a few production people. Unions rationalized the pay system in those places they organized, paying everyone the same flat rate. Sixty years later, the same compensation systems dominate the landscape. There are job descriptions, job analyses and area/industry wage surveys. Not much change in sixty years, even though the original reason for the approach long since died and the circumstances certainly changed radically.

The Pyramid Formula: Reward Creating a Successful Tomorrow for Everyone

There are three fundamental Pyramid reward principles.

First, *link rewards with behavior that accomplishes the objectives* that, in turn, contribute to the strategies, goals, values, mission and vision. The Pyramid is tightly integrated and precisely designed. Rewards play an important role as the completer of the objectives-measures-rewards triangle. One executive put it best. She said, "The vision, mission, values and strategies, etc. are important. They're the car. But the gas in the car—the power that makes things happen—is the reward system. Put leaded gasoline in your fine new Cadillac and all you have is some very expensive scrap metal."

Second, provide *extraordinary rewards for extraordinary performance*. The truly great companies pay their best salesperson better than they pay anybody else, because that great salesperson has created more success with her activities than anybody else. Caps on incentive systems never made any sense to us. Why send the message to your sales force "Don't sell too much"? Flat salaries with annual 4 percent "merit" adjustments never turned us on either. Imagine the de-motivational effect of the message "Work hard and we'll give you just about enough to stay even with inflation." We love approving profit-sharing checks for millions of dollars, because that means that the company put tens of millions of dollars in its pocket also. Pay for performance. That's simple enough.

Third, reward is a *coffee cup with many handles*. A long time ago Sly and the Family Stone sang the line, "Different strokes for different folks." Different rewards turn on different people. Pay turns on good salespeople. They're in it for the money, and will endure rejection after rejection to score the big prize. Some people thrive on additional responsibility. They seek out opportunities to take on bigger and bigger projects and challenges. Still others value personal contact and friendships. For them, work is a social experience. Don't talk to them about telecommuting. Discover the "strokes" that turn on your "folks" if you want your reward system to strengthen the Pyramid.

Pay for the Right Target—Or Forget About It

Link objectives, measures and rewards. Rewards go together with objectives and measures, like coffee and cream, ham and eggs, day and night. First, set the right customer-focused, create-tomorrow targets, then establish the best measures of those targets, then pay off.

What's in It for Me Must Be in It for Everybody

You've heard about the power of WIIFM—What's in it for Me? WIIFM drives the world. It is the universal power source, the optimal reward system. We'd change WIIFM to WIIFE—What's in It for Everybody? That small, but very significant, modification is one of the cornerstones of the Pyramid.

Take BMW. They were a typical sales-oriented car company. They knew how to run profitable dealerships. They had the model. It was simple. Pay salespeople to move cars. Put parts folks in a different organization and pay them to make money moving parts. Put the service mechanics in a separate organization and pay them on the basis of meeting service standards. If the standard is eighty-two minutes on a brake job, pay the mechanic a bonus if he gets it done sooner or dock him if it takes longer. Everyone's on incentive pay. If everyone does their job, the whole dealership prospers. Right? No, wrong!

The salespeople are paid to sell cars, so they push cars even to bad credit risks or at less-than-the-best margins. Because they are only paid to sell cars, when the sale is done, so are they. Kiss the client goodbye and hope he never calls you again, because you don't have time for him since you're looking for new people to sell cars to. The parts folks get paid to sell parts, so they look to replace parts before their useful life is over, thus running up the client's repair bill. Furthermore, since parts are expensive and slow-moving, one way to increase inventory turns and profitability is to short-stock. That forces the client to wait for parts and lengthens the repair cycle. Mechanics work a very tight clock. They haven't got time to schmooze with the customer or check out what else may be wrong. You get the picture. The compensation system drives behavior at the dealership that could result in every department succeeding and the entire dealership failing. Worse, the customer gets short-shrifted at every turn. Charge more for repairs that take longer and may not solve the real problem, and there's no one to talk to because everyone is focused on their little piece of the pie.

In the late 1980s BMW saw plummeting markets and eroding margins. They called us in to help. We helped them turn it around. Today, BMW sells more cars than Mercedes in the U.S. They're the only German car manufacturer that's actually growing sales beyond pre-1987 levels. What's the magic? WIIFE.

We created a new reward system that changed the basis of incentive pay for the people at BMW. Everybody, at both the dealer and the BMW support organization, was paid on the basis of customer satisfaction and dealer profitability. We stopped rewarding the sales department for just selling cars, the parts department for showing a profit on moving parts and the service department for meeting service standards. Instead, everyone shared the two goals of satisfying customers and making the overall dealership profitable. Rather than focusing on "What's in It for Me?", everyone focused on "What's in It for Everyone?"—including customers.

The result?

Notice the increasing number of BMWs on the road.

The BMW lesson is clear. Set clear, customer-focused, shared and interlocked stretch goals and objectives that create success for everyone. Use appropriate measures of those goals. Base rewards on attaining the goals. It's neither hard nor complex. It doesn't take a sophisticated compensation formula, with twenty-seven what-if scenarios. It really doesn't take hours of meetings to decide. Get the customer-focused, create-tomorrow criteria straight—create success for everyone—and go for it. Divert everyone from asking, "What's in this for me?" to asking, "What's in this for *all of us?*"

The Gates to Reward Heaven

Use gates to tie rewards so that behavior supports the other elements of the Pyramid (vision, mission, values, goals and strategies). Gates are just what the name implies: doors through which people pass on their way to receiving their reward. The Supply

Company organization, for instance, set gates to focus associates on living the Pyramid elements. Their gates were:

Customer satisfaction: Customer satisfaction scores of 5.5 or better. Reinforces the *vision* (doing whatever it takes to create success for our customers), *mission* (enable customers to achieve their goals) and *goals* (perceived as a valuable business partner).

Measured by a six-item, seven-point scale questionnaire completed every six months asking such questions as, "How successful were we in helping you create personal and business success?" This was measured at the unit/group/team level.

Profitability: Achievement of 90 percent of unit profitability level (if one was established). Enables all the rest of the vision, mission, goals and strategies to occur.

Measured by monthly actual versus budget performance. Operations and salespeople had profit budgets. Overall organizational profit was the gate for the administrative people who did not have a unit profit goal.

Fulfillment of monthly objectives set with customers: Delivering the objectives set each month with internal and external customers. Reinforces the vision (doing whatever it takes to create success for customers), goals (creating success for customers) and objectives.

Measured by monthly performance agreement reports filed electronically each month.

Attainment of personal learning plan: Each associate sets a semiannual learning plan in conjunction with customers and teammates. Reinforces the vision (doing whatever it takes to create success for customers), mission (enable our targeted customers to achieve their goals) and goals.

Measured by learning plan filed electronically as agreed upon and then updated monthly.

As you can see, these gates help ensure alignment and integration of all the Pyramid elements.

Reward Epic Performance with Epic Pay:
Those Who Do It Big, Get It Big

Pay a ton to those who produce the most. Why is that simple premise so difficult to understand or accept? Some years ago, Honeywell put in a new incentive program. One salesman booked a big job with a large university in Pennsylvania. He earned $112,000 incentive pay. In 1970. The branch general manager thought it was way too generous. "We'll pay that much to a single salesperson only over my dead body," he was quoted as saying. The regional vice president had a different perspective. As related in Mark Honeywell's book, *The Restless Spirit,* he approved the payment. Unfortunately, the entire program crashed and burned leaving lots of corpses on the corporate battlefield. The general manager harbored bad feelings for a long time about the incident. He never moved beyond his branch manager level. The regional vice president left the organization a few years later to seek his fortune in a more accommodating climate. Perhaps recognizing the threat from his very disaffected branch manager, the salesperson took his money, left Honeywell and started his own competing firm. For years he kicked Honeywell's tail in the market. Doing the right thing—paying extraordinary rewards for extraordinary performance—is clearly the right thing to do.

In one of our businesses, we hired an outside salesperson and put him on a steep incentive plan. We wanted him to really bust his hump getting us on the map. He did. By year three he was earning more than we were. Think we were overjoyed at his and our success? Think again. Our partner was furious. "How can we afford to pay him so much?" he kept asking. We kept answering, "Why not pay him so much? After all, for every dollar we pay him we put six dollars in our own pocket. Not a bad deal." Our partner finally won out. We fired the salesperson and saved his big salary. Of course we also lost ten times his salary in sales. Who really won? Our competition, that's who.

Pay for Performance, but Determine the Performance You Want First

Paying for performance is hot. *Business Week* in its November 14, 1994, issue, reported that nearly two thirds of mid-sized and large companies have some form of incentive pay for nonexecutives. That's up from 50 percent four years ago. The consulting firm Towers Perrin reports that increased pay for higher performance programs increased by 40 percent in the last two years alone, and that average bonus payments in 1998 will exceed 7 percent of base pay.

GTE Corporation made customer satisfaction a key component of its incentive plan. They took regular surveys of their customers and paid employees based on the results. GTE believed that customer service drove their business results, so they paid for it.

The Black Box Corporation, a Pittsburgh-based marketer of computer networks and other communications devices, uses skill-based pay. By learning new skills Black Box workers can double their pay without changing jobs. For example, order entry clerks earn between $17,000 and $20,000 a year. As they increase their product knowledge, their pay can go to about $28,000. If they add skills, such as learning a foreign language, they can make up to $35,000. And at each stage, they earn a profit-sharing bonus in addition. The company provides formal training, but each employee decides whether to sign up.

Another communications company, XEL Communications of Aurora, California, uses incentive pay to encourage people to join production teams. Each XEL team shares a bonus on meeting a quarterly goal, such as improving on-time delivery from the team to its customers. Top teams can earn up to 10 percent. Teams that don't meet their goal get nothing. The average reward is 4.5 percent of payroll and the payoff for XEL is extraordinary. Average production time fell from thirty days to three days, and waste was cut in half.

Pay the Right Person for the Right Performance: Don't Overfeed the Top Cats

In one of our companies we allowed our marketing vice president to reward the wrong person and that message reverberated negatively throughout the entire organization. We'd recently purchased a high-flyer company with some hot new technology. When the time came to add several new high-level marketing jobs to integrate the two companies' product offerings, the VP ignored the marketing folks from the new acquisition. Being a member of the traditional good old boy system, he surrounded himself with people from the acquiring company. The new company people felt disenfranchised and disempowered. Many left and the rest spent most of their time sharing horror stories of how their old customers were being mistreated by the new teams.

Reward the wrong people, send the wrong message and your ship develops a leak that threatens to send everyone to Davy Jones's locker. Everyone knows who's performing and who isn't. Reward the wrong people and you kill the incentivizing effect of reward. One of our corporate president friends put it best, "I have the simplest reward system imaginable—and the most effective. Those that do—get it. Those that do big—get it big. Those that don't do it—get gone."

Reward Is a Coffee Cup with Many Handles

There are lots of ways to reward people, as many ways as there are people. Everyone talks about monetary rewards, but those aren't the only handle on the coffee cup. There are also incentive benefits rewards, such as additional insurance or retirement, that go beyond the usual salary and bonus arrangements.

There's a wide range of performance recognition awards. Research demonstrates that people value recognition above money. Recognition is a very great driver of positive response. And on the reverse side, the lack of recognition demoralizes people.

Reward High Performance with Autonomy: Nice Work if You Can Get It

Autonomy is a powerful reward. It loosens the creative juices. It puts people in charge of their own situation. It takes the hand-cuffs off and lets them fly free.

Square D's biggest U.S. plant was in Lexington, Kentucky. When we took over the company, they had a foreman for every nine people on the factory floor. We couldn't afford that kind of overhead in a competitive industry. We visited the plant and met with the people and explained the marketplace situation. We told the people it was up to them. We made the goals and objectives very clear, and rewarded those who met them.

That plant improved productivity beyond anything we could have imagined. People took the autonomy and ran with it. Within two years they had organized themselves so that five facilitators and a superintendent/head coach ran that 1,200-person, three-shift plant. Teams hired and fired their own people and did their own scheduling and training. They became a plant of soaring Phoenixes. Peter Jennings featured the plant in his ABC television network piece on "American Productivity."

Residential Energy Management Systems was another under-performer. They always delivered late. We gave them autonomy to fix the situation. They wiped out all their policies and proce-dures and selected their own leader. Within nine months they were consistently 15 to 20 percent under budget. The market kept tightening the time for new product introduction, and they kept beating the competition. They were all Phoenix leaders in charge of their own destiny—and they knew it. They saw what needed to be done—and they did it.

Stay Awake: No Reward Program Is Forever

Nothing lasts forever, least of all some management program. Be prepared to change your reward program frequently. Xaloy Inc. of Pulaski, Virginia, is a small manufacturer of plastic extrusion equipment. They've been working with various incentive pro-grams for the last ten years. Each year, Xaloy shifts the plan to reflect a new target. One year when the plant faced a particularly serious production problem, the 300 employees refocused the bonus program to target a solution to the problem. That incentive helped get everyone in the plant involved in dealing with the issue. "We even had people from data processing out on the shop floor," said president Walter G. Cox, Jr. Each year they ask, "What are the big problems, the big opportunities facing us that we need everyone to focus on?" Then they tailor their reward program to focus every nose on that issue.

American Express recently rolled out an incentive pay plan for the 10,000 employees of its consumer card and customer lending groups. But first, Amex ran a one-year pilot program so it could see exactly what would happen. The test program was a big success, especially since 98 percent of the 1,500 employees included got payouts of up to 4 percent of their base salaries. As a result of the learning from that pilot project, American Express reduced the number of measures from six to three, making it easier for employees to keep track.

The bottom line: rewards reinforce behaviors. Objectives, measures and values define those tasks and behaviors. You get what you ask for, so ask very carefully. The ultimate reward at stake may be your own. Rewards focus on behaviors where everyone wins.

PHOENIX WORKSHOP

1. THE TYPES OF REWARDS THAT TURN ME ON ARE:

_____

_____

2. THE TYPES OF REWARDS THAT TURN ON THE OTHER KEY PLAYERS IN MY NETWORK ARE:

NAME   REWARD

_____   _____

_____   _____

_____   _____

_____   _____

Summary

Vision focuses on where you want to go: the state of choice. Mission spells out how you will get there: the resources and competencies of choice. Values represent the behaviors of choice. Together these paint a picture of your future. Goals are the way stations. Strategies are the more detailed road maps that lead to the vision.

Like the vision, mission and values, we choose objectives, measures and rewards that enable us to create that future we see so clearly in our mind's eye. We live by choice, not by chance. Freedom is the great enabler in our society. We are free to make all of the choices that become the script, the game plan and the playbook for our tomorrows.

Our future will be the sum total of our choices—and our behavior based on those choices. Wishing won't make it so, though. Objectives, measures and rewards show us the performances required to win those lifetime achievement awards of the spirit. Now is the time to do it.

The goal and reward linkage drives humankind. That linkage begins with setting goals and objects that *focus on what our customers need.* These goals and objectives need to be *shared and interlocked across the network.* These goals and objectives represent real *stretch to beat the best.* Finally, *objectives and goals relate back to vision, mission and values,* the heart and soul of the Pyramid. Goals lead to strategies that *begin with customers and constituents, involve everyone in your network web* and *link to your vision, mission, values and goals in a disciplined way.*

With aligned goals, strategies, objectives, measures and rewards, we are ready to move on to constructing the last pieces of the Pyramid: business processes and communications infrastructures.

PHOENIX WORKSHOP

THINKING ABOUT MY GOALS AND STRATEGIES, THE
FOLLOWING ARE THE MOST IMPORTANT CONTRIBUTIONS
THAT I MUST MAKE TO THE SUCCESS OF THE CUSTOMERS IN
MY NETWORK, THE PURPOSES EACH CONTRIBUTION FULFILLS
AND THE BEST MEASURE OF EACH PURPOSE/CONTRIBUTION.

OBJECTIVE	PURPOSE	MEASUREMENT
What are the few most important contributions I *must* make to the success of my customers?		
No. 1:	*Performance:* *Relationship:* *Learning:*	*Performance:* *Relationship:* *Learning:*
No. 2:	*Performance:* *Relationship:* *Learning:*	*Performance:* *Relationship:* *Learning:*
No. 3:	*Performance:* *Relationship:* *Learning:*	*Performance:* *Relationship:* *Learning:*

CHAPTER 12

The Pyramid Framing: Beams, Girders and Business Processes

Those Processes from Hell—And Why They Really Need to Find Their Way Back There

How many times have you heard these words, "I'd love to help you, but our policy won't let me." Or, "The system is down. You'll have to wait." Or, "We're waiting for approval. We'll call you when we have it." Or, "The person isn't in today. Call back tomorrow." If your experience is anything like ours, you've heard these dark, disabling words all too often, the result of paralyzing processes rather than energizing processes.

These dismal experiences underscore the unfortunate truth: processes in virtually every organization desperately need re-vivolution. We must revivolute our processes to support the Pyramid's vision, mission, values, goals, strategies and objectives.

The Glacial Phone System

We ordered a new phone system for our small office. The very pleasant phone representative seemed genuinely anxious to please. "It will take twelve weeks to process your order," she told us. "I know that sounds like a long time, but we want to get it precisely the way you want it." It did sound like an awfully long time for a twelve-phone unit. Ah, but what a lovely voice she had. We cringed a bit and crossed our fingers.

About two weeks after we placed the order we hired a new person. We called the phone company to add a phone line. "Sorry, you can't do that," she said. "We'll have to wait until the end of the order-processing time, and then put in a change order. That will take another seven weeks to process. Let's hope that the engineers don't think that the additional line requires reconfiguration of your system. Because if that's the case, it'll take another twelve weeks."

Of course, the phone company had all the right Pyramid piece parts. They had a customer-focused vision. They had great-sounding mission and value statements. They had all the "right" parts, except for the processes to make those fine-sounding words come alive. PROCESS ERROR.

What's Wrong with This Picture?

Because we fly so much we buy blocks of miles in advance at discount prices from a major airline. It's a win-win deal: the airline gets its money early, and, having paid for the flights on this airline, we book their flights rather than a competitor's leaving-at-the-same-time flight. We get a cheaper price per mile when we fly, so it's better for us. Sounds great.

But their poor business processes often give us fits. Last month's statement, for instance, contained five billing errors. Four of the five errors were charges, at full retail price, for flights booked last month but billed to last year's account, which was closed eleven months ago. When we called, the accounting clerk couldn't explain how it happened. He just kept insisting that we owed them the retail price for the flights, even though we had sufficient miles in our prepaid discount account to cover those flights. He explained, "I'd love to help you out, but I can't transfer the cash charges from your old account into miles charges in your new account. The system won't let me." The airline has great-sounding vision, mission and value statements. Problem is, their business processes don't support them. PROCESS ERROR.

The same airline pushes their affinity travel charge card. On the meal tray last time we flew was an advertisement to "charge your flight and get double miles." Sounded too good to be true. Turned out it was. Ordered another block of prepaid discount miles and charged them to my airline's travel charge card. Received a form letter three weeks later informing me that they don't take credit cards. Five calls later—the accounting department administers the discount mileage program and they only list their regular office number, which is continually busy—the person at the other end said, "Sorry, that's our policy." "Not even your own card?" I asked. The broken-record answer came back, "Sorry, that's just our policy." PROCESS ERROR.

We could go on and on. Everyone has their "system from hell" stories. And that's only from the customer's perspective. Imagine what it looks like from the inside out.

Don't Rain on My Parade: The Red-Faced CEO

The new CEO of a mid-sized computer company visited a customer and learned that the customer's last order was five weeks late. "Don't worry, I'll track it down and break it loose," she said confidently, reaching for the phone in her host's office—the president's. This was a golden moment. She phoned her factory manager in South Carolina and said in her carefully articulated presidential voice: "Hi, Art, this is Sue. I'm here with Herb, the president of the Total Company. He says his last order is five weeks late. Could you tell me where it is—and what it'll take to move it to the head of the line."

Her face fell as she listened to Art's response. "Sorry, Sue, can't tell you where it is. Our system doesn't track to that micro a level. If you hang on a minute I'll look it up and see when it's due to ship." Ninety painful seconds of silence later Art came back on the line, "System says we shipped that order four weeks ago. Are you certain he doesn't have it and just doesn't know he has it?"

"No, Art," Sue said softly. "I've been down there myself and it's nowhere in sight."

"Well," Art replied, "I'll check it out. It will take me several hours to sort through the paper files to find it. Shall I call you back there?"

"No," said Sue, stifling the angst. "Let's talk when I return." PROCESS ERROR.

A Dream Deferred:
The Nonaccountable Cost Accounting System

Andy is a manufacturing engineer with a large aircraft engine components manufacturing company. His boss asked him to find ways to reduce costs in several products. Andy loved this kind of assignment. He was very good at ferreting out inefficiencies and he received lots of kudos for doing it. He was devastated, though, when he asked the management information systems analyst for the detailed cost breakdowns for the targeted products.

"Sorry," the analyst told Andy, "our systems don't provide that data. Our cost systems were set up prior to that product family coming onstream. We didn't have the resources to add that family to the mainframe, so all we have is total cost data. If you want anything more specific it would likely take several man-years and $150,000 to $200,000—neither of which we have in the MIS budget." PROCESS ERROR.

Millions in Inventory Lost in Space

A large organization bought a company about its size. They merged the two very different computer systems. During the first year-end close for the merged companies they "lost" $275 million of inventory. Three weeks of frantic top to bottom search failed to find the "lost" inventory. They finally wrote it off, taking a big hit to earnings. BIG PROCESS ERROR.

In all of these examples, the best of intentions, expressed by the best of people, were destroyed by business processes from hell. Time to get out the process blueprint.

Processes: The Organization's Primary Structural Framework

All buildings begin with framing. One-story garages and hundred-story skyscrapers begin by hammering together the 2x4s, 2x10s and 2x12s that outline and support the structure. Walk through a framed building and you can see the outline of the house. "Here's the living room. Here's the bedroom. Here's the bathroom." In construction, the framing provides the structural beams on which the doors, windows, floors and fancy kitchen cabinets hang—the outer surfaces everyone sees.

Acrobats depend on a stable and sound trapeze superstructure to support them as they fly through the air with the greatest of ease a hundred feet above the hard ground. In reality, all of us perform in the context of a process framework. In the Pyramid, processes provide the supporting framework for the other elements: vision, mission, values, goals, strategies, objectives, measures and rewards.

For instance, Supply Company's vision was "Doing whatever it takes to create success for customers." To implement that vision they developed (among other processes) a direct order business process that electronically linked store operators with both Supply Company and manufacturers. Store owners ordered replacement merchandise directly with Supply Company, who daily placed consolidated orders with manufacturers. Manufacturers shipped direct to the store and were paid by Supply Company upon electronic notification of receipt of the correct order by the store owner.

In turn, Supply Company developed an information technology infrastructure that used an intranet to connect store operators' personal computers, their client server and the manufacturers' mid-range computer. Supply Company delivered their vision using the framing of the direct order business process and the computer information infrastructure. Without this framing, the pretty words on the wall would have remained just that—pretty words on the wall.

BUSINESS PROCESSES: BEAMS AND GIRDERS

Delivering Outcomes to Customers: Processes Defined

Everyone's talking processes these days. Lots of best-sellers have the word "Process" in the title. Unfortunately, overuse blurs the real meaning of a concept. Let's get back to basics.

The dictionary defines process as "a series of actions conducive to a result." In his book *Beyond Reengineering: How the Process-Centered Organization Is Changing Our Work and Our Lives,* Michael Hammer defines process as "a related group of tasks that together create a result of value to a customer." We'd go a step further: *a process is a sequential series of interrelated repetitive tasks that usually cross functional and departmental boundaries, and delivers a desired outcome to customers.*

Get the Big Process Picture from the Space Satellite

Begin by painting a picture of the process, that "series of sequential interdependent repetitive tasks." Identify every single task and activity it takes, for instance, to translate a customer's order into a fully delighted customer. Put those steps into an overall picture called a flow chart. Usually a flow chart fills walls. We discovered more than 1,100 steps in the flow chart mapping the process of ordering and delivering a telephone system. We papered an entire hallway in mapping that process. No wonder it took three months to complete the order-install cycle.

A large insurance company found that its ordering process took 756 steps and consumed fifty-two calendar days, during which time only ninety-seven minutes of work on the order actually occurred. The rest of the time the order spent either moving from one desk to another or sitting in an in-box somewhere waiting for action to take place. No one in the company ever suspected that there was so much time consumed doing so little to advance delighting the customer. The flow chart is the satellite picture, exposing the reality of the process for all to see.

The flow chart is just what the name implies, a chart of the flow of activities. It's a simple visual aid that shows who performs each activity, the sequence of those activities, the outputs of each activity and the measurement standard for the output. Measurement is vital. Flow chart measurements help us make fact-based decisions about improving the process to support the other facets of the Pyramid. Measurements answer two questions: "Is this the most efficient activity to deliver the vision, mission, values and so on?" and "Does the outcome delight the customer by helping him create success?" The internal measure is called a process measure (indicating internal efficiency), and the external measure is called a results measure (indicating external effective-ness). Both are critical to erecting strong beams and girders for the enduring Pyramid.

Processes Aren't Only for Business, They're for Us People as Well!

Everything we do is a process, a series of interrelated tasks that delivers a desired result for a customer. Companies search for customers to create revenue. Individuals search for a job or pro-fessional assignments to create an income. A computer maker searches for a dependable supplier of chips. Individuals search for a dependable remodeling contractor. The company searches for a reliable shipper. An individual searches for a reliable auto-mobile. A business recruits employees. An individual makes new friends. Processes are the stuff of life.

Architect an Effective Process for an Enduring Pyramid

Most of us know an effective process on sight. It produces satis-fying results with predictable consistency. We see an acrobatic performance, a smooth delivery, a seamless execution. Like a trapeze team, the most incredible feats are accomplished with speed, grace and virtuosity.

But the best processes only appear to be fluid and acrobatic. In fact, they are constructed of solid material—according to a rec-ognizable pattern. The best ones share six very important char-acteristics.

1. *Driven from the customer in.* Everything begins with the question "What must this process deliver to our customers?" Talk to them. Discover what's important to them. Work with them to identify the processes that will deliver the best total value and experience for your customers.

2. *Follow the work flow, not the departmental functional structure.* Begin from what customers want and work back. Busi-ness processes are horizontal and cross-functional, not vertical and hierarchical.

3. *Involve everyone who touches the process.* Get input from everyone involved. For example, the customer acquisition process involves not just salespeople, but also service people, accounts payable people and even manufacturing people. Why? Because everyone touches or influences the acquisition and retention of customers. Involve everyone to encourage widespread ownership.

4. *Find a "champion."* Deputize an evangelist, whose passion for the process will energize everyone around her. We've learned the importance of an executive sponsor to champion the cause, to coach, lead and be a highly visible and accountable role model.

5. *Reflect the Pyramid's vision, mission, values, goals and strategies.* Processes are the "walk" that prove the commitment to the "talk" of the vision, mission, values and other portions of the Pyramid. Processes must look, feel and *act* the words of the vision, mission and values.

6. *Utilize systematic disciplined tools.* Use flow charts, wishbone diagrams and other scientific tools to gather data. Systematically use the data to describe the current process, identify customer needs and surface opportunities to do what needs to be done more effectively and efficiently. Ask and seek fact-based answers to such questions as, "What value does this step/operation/activity add? How does this activity/operation/step implement the vision, mission, values, goals and strategies? How does this benefit the customer?"

GET YOUR MARCHING ORDERS FROM THE BOSS: THE CUSTOMER

In designing processes, listen to the boss. We've all heard about the "Golden Rule." The person with the gold, makes the rules. In building strong Pyramid-supportive processes, the customer has the "gold," so the customer is the one who makes the rules. Consider three dimensions of involving customers.

Open the Customer Input Floodgates

Begin by asking customers, "What must this process do for you? In the best of all worlds, how could this process best support your success?" Then, whip out your pen and get ready to write furiously. Our experience is that customers can't wait to tell you.

In fact, they've been secretly preparing their answers for years, mostly when swearing under their breath after we've done something to mess up their lives with our processes from hell. You know the feeling. It's usually preceded by such words as, "If only they'd do . . ." Or, "It sure would help if they . . ."

Listen to Your Toughest Customers: They Just Might Save Your Life

Seek out your toughest, most dissatisfied customers. Find customers who are really ready to tell it like it is. Find those customers whom your mess-ups have pushed beyond the bounds of politeness and political correctness. And get past the plush chairs of the executive offices. Find out what life is really like in the trenches. There's nothing to be afraid of, really. It may be the beginning of a whole new way of life for you.

Ask the folks who have to make the process work at the punch press, in the warehouse, at the call center and at the accounts payable desk. They'll tell you things you'll never hear from the executive vice president who hasn't personally used the process in ten years. Get down to the details and get real. You may not like what you hear. We didn't. But we had to hear it if we were going to build a Pyramid that provides a strong base for future success.

Slice and Dice Your Customers and Listen to Them *All*

Get feedback from all customers. Since everyone is connected to everyone—remember principle number two—there's lots of customers for every process. Within an organization, the next person in the process is a customer, as are all the next persons in all the next steps of the process. That means lots of internal customers.

External customers break down into two major segments and a whole host of smaller subsegments. There are both different kinds of customers—segmented by size, geography and market focus—and different internal customers within each customer. Different customer segments want different outcomes from the process and use the process is a different way. At Supply Company we discovered that the larger store owners valued the just-in-time nature of our delivery for standard products, while the smaller store owners valued the direct ordering that saved them time and energy. Each customer segment wanted something different from our ordering and delivery process, so we designed the process to meet each of their different needs. All too often we've seen processes designed for the top 5 or 10 percent of the customer population that either serve the rest of the customers poorly, or not at all.

Then within each customer there are a host of internal customers, all with different interests and needs. For a computer company, the person on the shipping dock receiving the computer is a customer, as is the person in accounts payable processing the payment request, as is the secretary calling with a "how do I reboot my computer" question. A purchasing person may place the order and the computer may sit on an engineer's desk, but there's a whole string of internal customers that stand between that order placer and the delighted computer user. All of these customers within the customer want/need different outcomes and methodologies. Get input from everyone in the customer chain.

That's exactly what we did at both AT&T/NCR and AT&T/GBCS. We videotaped customer interviews at AT&T/NCR and used their suggestions to develop the customer-focused business model. Based on that customer feedback we learned that many of our processes earned featured spots in the Processes from Hell Hall of Fame. We launched a major process revivolution activity focused first on the "quote to cash" process. That process began with a qualified customer opportunity and continued through needs analysis, proposal (the "quote"), contract, product and software configuration and manufacture, solution installation, customer education and training, invoicing and collection (the "cash"). It was the heart of AT&T/NCR's customer acquisition process.

We assembled an associate team drawn from sales, order fulfillment, manufacturing, distribution, installation and accounting. They analyzed more than 3,500 customer comments, quantifying what was most important to customers. Then they went nose-to-nose with customers ranging from shipping personnel to vice presidents in end-user organizations, retailers and third-party resellers. Since activating the third-party reseller channel was one of the major strategic pillars, they interviewed lots of reseller firms. They conducted over a thousand interviews in more than 400 customers' firms. They asked questions, shut up and wrote customer responses.

The result: customers told us—loud and clear—what they wanted: knowledgeable people who could make on-the-spot decisions, consistent processes across locations and solutions, clear project ownership (one person to call to correct whatever was wrong), project-managed installs and upgrades that were timely and worked the first time, and complete, accurate and easy-to-understand order confirmations, bills of lading and invoices.

Based on this customer feedback the team rolled up their collective sleeves and went to work reframing the quote to cash beams and girders. Their efforts touched virtually every AT&T/NCR department and location. We made several organizational changes, eliminating product-based units and adding a project management activity in sales. These organizational changes both provided a single point of contact for the implementation process and enabled the sales force to focus on selling activities. We developed new IT applications that automated hardware and software configurations to generate a more well-defined installation package and created a common ordering and manufacturing database. These new software packages furnished more timely and accurate product availability, pricing and profit information. We dramatically streamlined the sales proposal system. We provided gobs of training to associates in using the new processes. All of these substantial changes were triggered by initial customer input and constantly reviewed by customers throughout the planning and implementation phases. The voice of the customer was heard throughout the transformation of the quote to cash process at AT&T/NCR.

The Ride to School: A Very Important Personal Process for a Very Important Customer

Sam worked hard at his administrative assistant job. He liked it, but it took ten to twelve hours a day. His wife also worked. Between them they sandwiched in time with their nine-year-old daughter, Jessica. It worked, mostly, until recently when Jessica began to exhibit signs of being unhappy and discontent. Sam and his wife, Sheila, talked about the situation and concluded that Jessica was feeling neglected. They needed to spend more time with her. Jessica took a forty-five-minute bus ride to school every day. Sam and Sheila decided that they'd rework their schedule to drive her to and from school and spend that forty-five minutes with her, one-on-one in the car.

Sam spoke with his boss, one of the most important customers of this process, and Sheila talked to hers. Based on that customer input they decided to modify their work hours so that Sam dropped Jessica off every day and Sheila picked her up. Because he would come in late every day, Sam planned to stay later in the office at night to organize it for the next day. That meant that he'd miss Jessica's bedtime. To prevent missing that important bedtime story time, he arranged with the Information Services Department, another customer, for a computer and modem connection so he could handle administrative matters in the evening from home and still be there for bedtime story time.

Sheila arranged her hours to pick Jessica up at school at the end of her shift. Unfortunately, her shift ended just a little too late to pick Jessica up at the precise end of school. So Sheila spoke with the teachers—other customers—and arranged for Jessica to participate in some extracurricular activity after school. Sheila had previously arranged for Jessica to spend time in the afternoon with Sheila's mother, who lived nearby. Sheila thought her mother would be pleased when she proposed changing the process and relieving her of her Jessica-sitting responsibility. Just the opposite occurred. Her mother looked forward to spending the time with Jessica and was disappointed with the new turn of events. Sheila modified the proposed process to drop Jessica off at her mother's house three days a week. That gave Sheila some unexpected time, so she arranged with her office to do some work at home, using Sam's computer and modem hook-up.

All throughout this process-redesign activity, the voice of one "customer" was unheard—Jessica's. Jessica was terribly upset when she discovered that she'd no longer ride the bus with her friends. She also wasn't thrilled with the thought of spending all that time alone with one of her parents either. Though she didn't say that to them, they sensed it. Her reaction threw Sam and Sheila into a tizzy. After days of fretting and stewing and discussing, first between Sam and Sheila and then with Jessica, everyone agreed to try it for three weeks, until the end of the term. As it turned out, everyone liked the new schedule and Jessica's attitude brightened. Lesson: involve all the customers, early and often in the process design (particularly nine-year-old daughters).

PHOENIX WORKSHOP

I WANT TO REBUILD/RENEW THE FOLLOWING PROCESS:

_____

FOR THAT PROCESS, THE MAJOR CUSTOMERS AND THEIR NEEDS/INTERESTS ARE:

MAJOR CUSTOMERS   WHAT THEY NEED/WANT FROM THE PROCESS

_____   _____

_____   _____

_____   _____

_____   _____

HAVE I LISTED *ALL* CUSTOMER SEGMENTS (NOT JUST THE LARGEST OR MOST VOCAL) AND ALL THE CUSTOMERS WITHIN THE CUSTOMER?

_____

_____

GO WITH THE FLOW: THE WORK FLOW, THAT IS

Follow the work flow. Want to understand how orders are processed in your organization? Staple yourself to an order and follow it through. Notice how you pass through virtually every department in the place. Notice how many different people touch you, most to just pass you on to someone else. Notice how long you spend waiting in in-boxes, on desks and in files. The trip is a real eye-opening education. When we did, it left us wondering why customers put up with us so long.

The Best Processes Work Horizontally

We had to fix the problem. So we called in the head of the sales department and told her to "fix it." She took the assignment grudgingly. Seven frustrating months later we found out why. After much wrangling and little progress we surfaced the issue during our monthly review discussion. When we asked, "How come there's been so little progress?," she just shrugged her shoulders and sighed, "Just can't get it done under present conditions. Give me the resources and I will, though. Get that blankety-blank service group to report to me. Transfer the inventory and warehouse people and the accounts payable folks to me, and I can get it done. Otherwise, I don't have the clout to do it."

Her words hit us like a wet fish across the face. Of course, she was correct. The process involved every department in the organization. She only controlled sales. Giving her the wrong assignment was a recipe for disaster. She taught us a powerful lesson: processes are horizontal, not hierarchical.

We applied that lesson at AT&T/NCR. Rather than asking one executive to champion the quote to cash process redesign that we talked about a few pages back, we built a team that included representatives from every relevant function—sales, marketing, finance, services and manufacturing. We went across the organization, following the work flow, rather than up and down the organization, following the authority flow. It worked.

Focus on the Leverage Points

AT&T/NCR's and AT&T/GBCS's customers both gave us the same marching orders: "Get us sales and customer support people who are knowledgeable about our business and our problems, and how your products and services can help us win in our markets. And, while you're at it, give us one point of contact who can really solve problems." We identified several leverage points that could deliver what customers demanded. We provided industry training for the sales force to bring them up to speed on the customers' business and industry. We automated the configuration process to relieve the sales force from performing all those calculations. We created a project management position in sales to be that one point of contact. There are many steps in every process. But there are usually a few steps, most often those in direct face-to-face contact with the customer, that provide the greatest opportunity to improve the process's deliverable to customers. Focus on those leverageable few.

Hallmark Cared Enough and Got the Very Best

Michael Hammer and James Champy, in their book *Reengineering the Corporation: A Manifesto for Business Revolution,* report that Hallmark created a whole new line of cards based on a horizontal approach. They grouped people together who had historically been separated by disciplines, departments, floors and buildings. Their aim: cut down on queue time, spur creativity and end the "throw it over the wall, it's their problem" mentality. The new, horizontally integrated team approach got half the new line to market eight months ahead of plan and the other half two months ahead of plan. Follow the work flow and build better process beams and girders, faster.

Include Bosses and Grandmothers

Sam and Sheila discovered the importance of following the horizontal flow of their process for transporting Jessica to and from school. They went from their bosses at their two work locations to the grandmother who baby-sat after school, passing by teachers and specialists within their respective organizations. They even included Jessica, and that's our next point.

PHOENIX WORKSHOP

THESE ARE THE STEPS IN THE WORK FLOW FOR THE PROCESS
I WANT TO RENEW:

STEPS	PERSON(S) INVOLVED
1. _____	_____
2. _____	_____
3. _____	_____
4. _____	_____
5. _____	_____
6. _____	_____
7. _____	_____
8. _____	_____
9. _____	_____
10. _____	_____

THERE ARE NO SPECTATORS: INVOLVE EVERYONE WHO TOUCHES THE PROCESS

Principle number two: everyone's connected to everyone. We're all part of many interconnected and interdependent systems. If so, then everyone needs to participate in laying the beams and girders that will support the new Pyramid. That's good logic. It's also great business.

We successfully applied that logic at Supply Company in the redesign of the product realization process. Being in the distribution business, their product realization process involved ordering product from the manufacturer, receiving it, warehousing it, delivering it to customers and both paying manufacturers and collecting from customers. The process touched every single aspect of the small company: sales, purchasing, warehouse, accounting and logistics. We solicited volunteers from each department to serve on a revivolution task force. More than half the company volunteered. We took them all. They divided themselves into smaller working groups with a ten-person central coordinating council.

The entire group met initially to flow-chart the process. They took their completed flow chart back to their departments and reviewed it with everyone, getting each person to sign the flow chart indicating that he or she had reviewed the chart and agreed with it. Each working group worked on a subprocess and coordinated with each other to put Humpty Dumpty back together again into the big macro process. For instance, a working group focused on the accounting subprocesses of accounts payable and customer billing and collections. They coordinated with the working groups handling ordering, delivery and logistics.

All this culminated in a two-day session involving all the volunteers where they reviewed the recommended new process. Then the entire company met for a day to approve it, signing the flow chart to indicate commitment to making the new process work. And work it did. Within seven months, days in supply dropped 52 percent, costs dropped 21 percent and back orders dropped 89 percent. Involving everyone paid off for Supply Company.

In their March 18, 1996, issue, *Fortune* reported how Hewlett-Packard used a similar approach in their redesign of their order fulfillment process. After a two-week orientation, a cross-functional team talked to everyone involved in the process. They worked across departmental and organizational boundaries, reaching out to include consulting and distribution partners. Working with this extended organization, they redesigned the process and developed a single, unified database covering everything from the customer order through credit check, manufacturing, shipping and warehousing to invoicing.

They tested their new process with the distributor that accounted for the largest share of this multibillion-dollar product line. Before beginning, the order fulfillment process took an average of twenty-six days. After this process revivolution, it took eight. Moreover, rather than the two-year delivery date they were given, they delivered the new process in eight months. And by cutting the process cycle to eight days, they enabled the distributor to cut inventories by 20 percent while increasing service levels to customers. Involving everyone paid off for everyone.

Two great examples of the "involve everyone" principle. Always invite those to the party who will be hosting it. Involve everyone in defining and implementing the new process, especially those who will be held accountable for making it work!

Get the Straight Scoop from Those Who Do It

Most managers think they know how their processes work. They're usually dead wrong. A U.S. Postal Service site manager said, "I thought I knew how we processed mail down there in the factory. I did it for many years myself. I've seen the manual. I thought I knew. Boy, was I surprised when I saw the process layout the employee team did. It turned out I knew how it was supposed to be done years ago but hadn't a clue about how it was actually done today."

We were unsurprised by her surprise. Most managers do not know how the processes they lead actually function. Like rabbits, processes tend to breed additional steps that increase complexity. Problems arise and immediate managers add extra "controls" or "approvals" or "reviews" to assure that the problems don't recur, such as "Better include production control in the order review process to make sure that we have the material to ship on time." These additional steps grow like weeds in the garden. In one process we know, the manual called for 472 distinct steps. Over a period of seven years that number proliferated to 862, mostly added to address specific problems in the past that became incorporated into the present operating procedures.

Associates also develop work-arounds and shortcuts to overcome informally the roadblocks and switchbacks built into most long-ago designed and proliferated processes. But yesterday's work-arounds become today's obstacles. In the same overgrown 862-step process, we discovered that several years ago one associate decided to call her counterpart in another division to verify that he had also received the order form, and if he hadn't she sent him a copy. Sending a copy to that sister division became a part of the normal process, even though both received copies of the same now-computerized order form.

The horror stories multiply, like those additional complexity-spinning steps in most processes. That's why the "involve everyone" approach works. You can't tweak a process. It needs complete redesign. Create a new tomorrow with a clean sheet of paper. Get together all of those who really know how the process actually works with those whom the process serves—the customers—and let them have at it.

PHOENIX WORKSHOP

RETURN TO THE IMMEDIATELY PREVIOUS WORKSHOP (PAGE 382) AND ADD THE PERSON(S) INVOLVED IN THE PROCESS WHO WILL ASSIST IN ITS REDESIGN.

_____

_____

PROCESS CHAMPIONS BRING OUT THE BEST IN PROCESSES AND PEOPLE

Nothing happens without leadership. Without leadership a collection of highly qualified individuals are just that, a collection of highly qualified individuals. They are not an effective team. Ask George Steinbrenner about that: he's an expert. In the 1980s and early 1990s he spent millions trying to buy a championship baseball team. He paid top price for the best talent, and never won the ring. Commentators said he had the best second-rate team money could buy. They were great first-rate individual contributors who together made up a second-rate team. What they lacked was leadership.

Same results happen in organizations. One company we know has very talented people. They've done a good job of recruiting talent. Yet the business struggles and consistently loses market share and margin points. Why? The talented people don't work together very well. Each one works hard on his or her own solutions. Problem is that one person's solution often conflicts with another person's solution, thus canceling out any positive effect. The CEO is losing his hair, and will soon lose his job.

Successful construction of the process beams and girders also requires leadership, but not the kind of hierarchical leadership most organizations rely on. Rather, we've discovered—the hard way—that process champions are the most effective form of leadership for building a strong, Pyramid process frame. Unlike a traditional hierarchical leader, a process champion has no formal authority over the process for which she is the champion. Rather than formal authority, they rely upon the tact of a Kissinger, the inquiring mind of an Einstein, the toughness of a Patton and the compassion of a Mother Teresa. They are the point person to whom process members bring their obstacles for removing, their concerns for coaching, their conflicts for guidance and their teamwork issues for direction. A process champion is a Phoenix leader who provides coaching, direction and facilitates personal growth, not easy answers and quick solutions.

We've met many excellent process champions in our life. At AT&T/GBCS, the vice president of sales was the process champion for the order fulfillment process redesign. She stepped forward and voluntarily took responsibility for the end-to-end creation and implementation of the process redesign activity. She agreed to help the design team eliminate obstacles, free up resources, open customer doors and stay focused on developing a process that lived the other facets of the Pyramid. She had no formal authority over the entire process, but she used her influence to help build a strong framing of process beams and girders that lived the vision and values and accomplished the strategies and goals of the organization. And her job didn't end when the process was redesigned. She voluntarily kept championing her process for years to ensure that it continued to change to meet new marketplace realities.

It doesn't take being a vice president to be a process champion. Anyone can do it. We know a sales administrator, Sheila, for a growing medical products firm. Sheila's not a manager. Sheila's job: champion the order fulfillment process. Several years ago she led the process redesign team that shortened the fulfillment process from twenty-eight days to six. There's a plaque that hangs on Sheila's wall from the CEO of her company thanking her for her efforts. Sheila's real treasure, though, is the framed letter from a seven-year-old patient that hangs right next to her CEO's letter.

In that letter, printed carefully in the seven-year-old's own hand, she thanked Sheila for getting the company's product to her that saved her life. Sheila's job as process champion didn't end when the girders and beams were in place. The process champion's job continues after the construction phase is complete.

Spend a day with Sheila and watch a process champion at work. She is on the phone with customers 60 percent of each day, resolving problems, orchestrating rush deliveries, obtaining FDA approvals and doing whatever it takes to make the order fulfillment process work. To the unenlightened spectator, she coordinates order entry and facilitates customer service. To the experienced insider, she champions the broad process of creating customer and organization success by getting customers' orders filled quickly. She deals with turf-protecting organizational warlords and a variety of personalities—the good, the bad and the moody. She communicates with the skills of a talk show host, and operates with the business focus of a Fortune 100 CEO.

She brings out the best in others, and brings out the best in her organization to create success for all those in her personal/organizational network. She is not a "manager"; she's much more. She's a Phoenix leader and a process champion! As we've said before, anyone and everyone can and must be a Phoenix leader/process champion, not just during the construction phase, but during the entire life of a process.

PHOENIX WORKSHOP

I KNOW THE FOLLOWING PROCESS CHAMPIONS:

_____

_____

I'VE LEARNED THE FOLLOWING GREAT LESSONS FROM THEM:

_____

_____

I WILL SEND THEM A NOTE OF APPRECIATION ON THE FOLLOWING DATE:

_____

_____

PROCESSES ARE THE PYRAMID IMPLEMENTATORS: VISION AND VALUES IN ACTION

Vision, mission and values talk sweetens the air. Processes reflect the commitment to the well-intended and well-fashioned statements concerning vision, mission, values, goals, strategies and objectives. Processes integrate people and activities horizontally across the organizational landscape. They also integrate with and support every facet of the Pyramid.

Visions, missions and values that emphasize people development need processes that support on-the-job and off-the-job learning, such as tuition reimbursement, required training hours per year and the accomplishment of learning plans as a prerequisite for bonus payments. Visions that stress customer focus need a customer-focused business model type of organization structure and customer-centered ordering, billing and installation activities.

See Processes Through the Lens of Vision, Mission, Values, Goals, Strategies and Objectives

It's amazing what you'll see. We saw a disturbing picture when we looked at Supply Company's processes. The right words were on the wall. Associates could repeat the vision, mission and values statements. But it took customers days to get product, and almost one quarter of the orders were backlogged. Customers constantly complained about billing errors and misshipments. In fact, the accounting department turned their phones to voice mail the week they sent out bills as a way to deal with the flood of complaints. We needed to rebuild the process framework so it supported, rather than frustrated, the rest of the Pyramid activities, as explained a few paragraphs back.

At AT&T/NCR we designed processes to support the vision, mission, values, goals, strategies and objectives incorporated in the customer-focused business model. For instance, we modified financial accounting processes to deliver full-stream profit statements that measured profitability by customer, team, industry, area, channel, line of business, business unit and product. The new process reported the value of the customer relationship, rather than just the individual business unit's financial results. It provided multiple views of profitability that linked directly to the goals and strategies. The full-stream profit financial accounting process enabled us at AT&T/NCR to implement its customer-focused business model, which reflected our new vision, mission and values.

AT&T/NCR's quote to cash process redesign team aligned their activities with the organization's goals and strategies. AT&T/NCR had four goals: associate delight, customer delight, profitable growth and shareholder delight. The process reinvention team related their activities to all four. In associate satisfaction we asked associates if they felt more empowered, were able to innovate, felt more in control of being able to satisfy customers and whether they were more satisfied in their work. We did pre- and post-measurements of the answers to determine whether we accomplished the associate delight goal.

We followed that same pattern in measuring our progress toward the customer delight goal. We surveyed customers pre and post asking for their evaluation of the knowledge ability of the salesperson and customer service person, the ease of doing business with us and the willingness to recommend and repurchase product.

Moving to the indirect channel was one of AT&T/NCR's major strategies for achieving its third goal: profitable growth. We knew that implementing that strategy would change many pieces of the quote to cash process. We designed a process that supported the new indirect channel strategy. To measure our success in accomplishing the profitable growth goal we used the amount of profitable business from that new indirect channel and the feedback from those indirect channel distributors.

AT&T/NCR's fourth goal was shareholder delight. We aimed to improve profitability in several ways through the quote to cash redesign, and we measured changes for all dimensions. We figured the redesign would reduce direct costs by reducing head count through eliminating non-value-added work, so we measured head count reductions. We calculated that the redesign would reduce provisioning costs by reducing inventories, so we measured inventory levels.

We figured that manufacturing costs should be reduced because of fewer change orders coming to the factory due to poor configurations in the field. So we tracked numbers of change orders and manufacturing costs. We also figured that better field configurations and customer support work would help customers understand what they really purchased and that that understanding would reduce the number of accounts receivable problems. So we tracked average number of days accounts were outstanding. We assumed that paying salespeople on the basis of margin rather than volume would decrease the discount rate, so we recorded average discount rate. At every major process step we used an activity-based cost measure to determine not only what direct costs we were saving, but also what profitability we were adding by increased manufacturing, financial and distribution cycle times and improved margins from more knowledgeable sales and customer support people.

The results amazed us. Head count in the process came down. Inventory levels plunged. The number of change orders fell. The average number of days receivables were outstanding fell precipitously. Average discount rates fell in region after region when we installed the new quote to cash system. Associate delight almost doubled. Customer willingness to repurchase soared. We met the indirect channel sales and profit numbers. The process redesign was a big success, because we related it to all the other dimensions of the Pyramid.

Food, Animals and Fun: Processes That Work

We know a successful entrepreneur in the "eatertainment" business—providing food and entertainment together, like a Planet Hollywood or Hard Rock Cafe. His restaurants combine live animal shows with a finger food menu. In the food business, pennies in food costs mean the difference between profit and loss. And the entertainment value of the show, combined with the entertaining service of the wait staff, is the difference between having customers or talking to yourself seven nights a week. They have a well-developed, customer-focused Pyramid, with all the right words in all the right places. But two key framing processes drive the business's success: a daily customer feedback process and a daily incentive bonus process.

Customers complete a simple five-item questionnaire at the end of every show. The card evaluates the customer's reaction to the show, the food, the wait staff, the environment (rest rooms, cleanliness, theming) and the intention to return and recommend to others. The accounting department tabulates the results at the end of every shift and posts results by the next shift. In addition, there are cost targets for every area, such as food preparation, maintenance, drinks and so forth. Actual costs compared with targeted costs are also posted every day for the last shift. This customer feedback process keeps everyone tightly focused on both delighting customers and controlling costs.

There's also an incentive bonus process tied in with the feedback process. Employees earn a daily incentive bonus based on these cost and customer feedback results. For example, the kitchen staff's bonus is based on customers' food evaluations and food costs; the entertainer's bonus is based on customers' entertainment evaluations and entertainment costs. Both processes help to build a strong framing support for the rest of the Pyramid facets.

Share the Pyramid with the Nine-Year-Old and Get Agreement

Sam and Sheila had several long talks with Jessica. They told Jessica that they wanted her to be happy (their vision) and feel like a member of their little three-person family (their mission). They loved her and wanted her to feel that love (their values). They told her that they were afraid that they weren't spending enough time with her and wanted to spend more quality time together (their goals). They confessed that they saw driving her as the best way to spend that time together (their strategy). They also told her about all the arrangements they'd made to change work hours and take work home (processes and infrastructure). Jessica was touched, even if she was annoyed. Wanting to do what her parents wanted her to do, she agreed to a test period of several weeks of driving, on the condition that she could play with her friends when she got home. Everyone seemed pleased with the outcome.

```
┌─────────────────────────────────────────────────────────────┐
│                    PHOENIX WORKSHOP                          │
│                                                              │
│   THE NEW PROCESS WILL SUPPORT THE OTHER FACETS OF           │
│   THE PYRAMID:                                               │
│                                                              │
│   VISION: _____ │
│   MISSION: _____ │
│   VALUES: _____ │
│   GOALS: _____ │
│   STRATEGIC IMPERATIVES: _____  │
│   OBJECTIVES/MEASURES/REWARDS: _____  │
│                                                              │
└─────────────────────────────────────────────────────────────┘
```

EXERCISE THE DISCIPLINE MUSCLE TO BUILD THAT STRONG FRAMING

"No pain, no gain." "No sweat, no muscle." We've heard those words forever. We wince every time we do, because we know how true they are. We're runners, three, four miles a day, sometimes wearing a special miner's hat with a flashlight in it during the early morning hours so we don't run into a coyote or some other dangerous two- or four-legged animal. It's a ritual and a rigor and a discipline.

Self-Discipline Is the Only Discipline That Works

Now there's an emotionally laden word: "discipline." Use the word and it conjures up pictures of whips and visits to the wood-shed and tough drill sergeants. The toughest discipline we've ever encountered, though, is self-discipline: the kind that gets you up at 5:00 A.M. to run several times a week, or pushes you away from the table before dessert. It's also the only kind that works. The Pyramid is built on that kind of discipline.

Imagine the discipline it took to build the pyramids in Egypt: moving all those stones hundreds of miles, shaping them into a perfect size, lifting them from the desert floor, fitting them precisely together. We'd be hard-pressed to do it with our technology today. Imagine the great effort and attention to detail it took five thousand years ago.

Use the Discipline Tools Readily Available

We need that kind of discipline to build our Pyramid. Process construction, like any other construction activity, uses scientific tools. We have a plethora of good ones to use in our process construction and management activities. Bar graphs illustrate the factors that contribute most to a particular outcome. Fishbone diagrams isolate causes that produce particular outcomes. Histograms display performance variations. Scatter diagrams show relationships among process characteristics. Flow diagrams pictorially present the steps in a process. A line graph displays changes in a characteristic over time. We don't suffer from a lack of tools. We mostly suffer from a lack of discipline to use the tools systematically. Develop the discipline to examine recurring patterns, tasks, procedures, cause-and-effect relationships, and identify how the process creates or destroys value throughout the organization.

It takes disciplined work to design and operate business processes that support the Pyramid. It takes lots of detailed diagnosis and analysis. We've all heard it said that "the devil is in the details," but that's incorrect. It should be: "God is in the details." Discipline, then, is about attention to details and commitment to execute. Exercise the discipline to map the complete current process, examine all customer needs and involve everyone who touches the process. Discipline is planning and following through.

From Surfer to Fish Taco Entrepreneur with Discipline

One of our former students learned this lesson. Ralph was a surfer, spending most of his free time (and we figured some of his class time as well) surfing in Mexico. Every time he went he'd pig out on the fish tacos that one vendor sold on a street corner. They were delicious. One day, swept by a fit of entrepreneurial spirit, Ralph asked for the recipe. The vendor scribbled it down on the back of an envelope. Ralph stuffed it into his pocket and drove off to get back across the border and make class.

Several years later Ralph found the scribbled recipe—still on the back of that ragged envelope—and decided that he'd go into the fish taco business. In truth, his dad was pushing him to do "something productive" now that he was out of school, and this idea sounded as good as any. With the help of several family members, and his dad's financial backing, Ralph opened a fish taco shop. After an initial rush of customers, the taco stand floundered. He had a recipe, but he did not have a systematic process for making tasty fish tacos time after time. Some tacos were very good, some were very bad, and many were just passable. Ralph needed more than a recipe. He needed a disciplined process. God was in the details, and talking to him. Ralph listened.

Ralph closed his shop for thirty days and went to Mexico. He found the same vendor on the same street corner selling fish tacos. The student offered to hire him and bring him to America to make his fish tacos in the store. The vendor declined. "I live in Mexico, not America," he said. But he agreed to teach Ralph how to make consistently good fish tacos every time. So Ralph stayed off the surfboard and went to work for the vendor free for thirty days. Believe it or not, it takes a complex, detailed process to make consistently good fish tacos. Ralph learned it well. He came back and taught the family. Today, he has twenty-eight restaurants. Understanding the process details and a commitment to execute them faithfully every time made all the difference.

"Plan, Do, Check, Act" is one discipline tool we've used in our organizations. It's simple and effective. Begin with "Plan" by determining goals and targets and methods to reach those goals. Continue to "Do" by educating people in the methods and implementation. "Check" the outcomes and review the methods. "Act" to correct errors and continuously maintain and improve the process.

Discipline Works to Do God's Work Also

We used this simple discipline methodology in our church with excellent results. Publishing the weekly bulletin is a chore for a small church office. The one full-time and five part-time employees and the pastor struggled every week to get the bulletin in the mail by Tuesday so it could be received by Thursday at the parishioner's home.

The pastor asked us to help. We met with the small staff and a committee of church members to determine what each wanted to accomplish in publishing the bulletin. Each person had a slightly different goal, and we listed them all. Then we flow-charted the process, identifying several areas of overlap, duplication and unnecessary activities. We developed a new simplified process, completing the "Plan" phase.

Next, we implemented the new process, tweaking it over the next several weeks. We kept histograms at three particularly key activities to check for performance variations. This completed the "Do" phase. We used parishioner feedback and scatter diagrams to continuously "Check" the process to make certain that we were accomplishing our goals. We "Acted" simultaneously to improve it. The entire activity took fifteen hours of the staff's time over six weeks. The bulletin now gets in the mail, on time, with less stress on the staff and more relevant information for the parishioners.

Disciplined analysis and consistent execution builds the framing that supports the enduring Pyramid.

PHOENIX WORKSHOP

I WILL USE DISCIPLINE TO RENEW AND EXECUTE THE NEW PROCESS IN THE FOLLOWING WAY:

_____

_____

_____

Summary: Processes and Our Quality of Life

Throughout history, processes have been central to the evolution of society. More effective processes always raise the quality of life. The first process redesign consultant in history was Jethro, Moses' father-in-law and CEO of Midian Consulting. Read about it in the Old Testament, Exodus, Chapter 18. Jethro proposed and became the champion of the redesign for the executive decision-making activity. The problem: the demand for Moses' decision making exceeded his capacity to supply it, resulting in stress for Moses, and frustration to Moses' clients, who had to wait excessive periods of time for decisions.

Like it or not, in the wilderness there were no other decision makers with Moses' credentials. Jethro outlined a process that would redistribute Moses' knowledge and satisfy Moses' customers. He proposed finding able men who would rule thousands, and hundreds, and fifties, and tens and judge the people of the "small matters," so Moses might reserve his time to judge "hard causes." Jethro proposed a hierarchy and a new judicial process that improved the quality of life for an entire nation. Jethro had simply proposed a new process enabled by an information and communications infrastructure. We will examine this infrastructure concept in the chapter ahead.

CHAPTER 13

Information and Communications Infrastructures: Power Lines That Energize the Pyramid

Infrastructures Defined: Wiring the Pyramid

"Without my laptop I'd be dead," a salesperson told us recently. "It's my pipeline to 'The Source.'" She's absolutely correct. Information is the key source of all power. The soaring Phoenix achieves just-in-time information access through such *information infrastructures* as executive information systems, intranets, data warehouses, financial reporting systems (including budgeting), customer information systems, human resource information systems and competitive intelligence information. These infrastructures reach beyond the boundary of any single organization to include customers, suppliers and government agencies (taxing and regulatory agencies, for instance).

In fact, an organization's information infrastructure is a vast and rapidly growing "extended enterprise." It's a far-reaching network of employees, partners, suppliers, customers and contractors linked together by data and IT systems.

Communications infrastructures determine *who* talks to *whom* about what subject. In developing the vision, for instance, communications infrastructures enable all associates in the organization to provide input into the vision, discuss vision drafts, clarify meanings of vision wording and link day-to-day actions with it. Similarly, communications infrastructures enable widespread discussion of the strategic plan's development that facilitates rapid deployment and execution.

Taken together, both the information and communication infrastructures are the power lines that capture knowledge and transmit it to the right person at the right place at the right time in the best way to support and integrate the other elements of the Pyramid, including: business processes, objectives, strategies, goals, values, missions and visions. These vital power lines connect people—and carry the organization's energy—so people can see what needs to be done, providing them the knowledge to do it.

The Pyramid's Wiring Diagram: Information and Communications Infrastructures

The infrastructure for the powered-up Pyramid features seven key design characteristics.

Associates own the infrastructures. Associates design, build and own the infrastructure, which provides an open line to all of the people. Everyone is live and on stage, connected together to deliver the performance of a lifetime for customers.

Informationalize data into useful, easy-to-use, fact-based knowledge. Translate all the data floating around an organization into useful, meaningful, measurable information that's linked to performance on the other facets of the Pyramid. Keep everyone up-to-date and in-the-loop.

Provide immediate access to what matters most. Develop information and communications connections that provide everyone the information he or she needs to execute the other integrated elements of the Pyramid. Connect everyone so they get what they need when they need it. Let each person decide, for himself or herself, what's relevant or not. No big brothers in corporate to decide what's best for anyone, except themselves.

Display public "scoreboards" everywhere. Build scoreboards from the measures explained in Chapter 11. Every organization, team and individual needs scoreboards to keep them continuously focused on their performance.

Create face-to-face contact. E-mail, voice mail and other forms of impersonal communication fill our lives. They're all good and efficient ways to stay connected. But nothing beats old-fashioned face-to-face, eye-to-eye contact for depth of communication. You can't watch the facial expression over voice mail, can't sense the nuances over e-mail. Research shows that personal contact is the most effective means of information transfer. Want the whole story? Get "live and on stage"—and in your customers' and teammates' faces.

Thrive on the thrill of what you are becoming. Focus everyone on accomplishments, achievements and progress toward their objectives, goals, strategies, values, mission and vision. Use the infrastructure to focus on the thrill of the quest. The world changes so quickly that every day, every organization is virtually a start-up. Every dawn is an opportunity for renewal.

Promote learning. Design and build infrastructures that develop the knowledge capability of all the interconnected and interdependent people in the network. Develop the bandwidth of the people and the power lines that move information to handle ever-increasing levels of learning and collaboration. Leverage the power lines to create and share knowledge.

Beware Power Outages

How important are these connections? Ask America Online, the large internet service provider. When America Online suffers a brownout, everything on their network comes to a halt, and they lose subscribers. Ask NCR. A construction crew in Dayton, Ohio (home of NCR), inadvertently hit a trunk phone line that cut off world headquarters from the rest of the organization for hours. It was downtime chaos!

Cut off the power of the communications and information infrastructure—and entire organizations full of people have a virtual near-death experience. Without the power lines provided by these infrastructures, no one can accomplish the Pyramid's vision, mission, values, goals, strategies, objectives and business processes.

```
┌─────────────────────────────────────────────────────────────────┐
│                     PHOENIX WORKSHOP                              │
│                                                                   │
│  I WILL WORK ON IMPROVING THE FOLLOWING INFORMATION               │
│  AND COMMUNICATIONS INFRASTRUCTURES:                              │
│                                                                   │
│  INFORMATION INFRASTRUCTURE: _____          │
│  _____     │
│                                                                   │
│  COMMUNICATIONS INFRASTRUCTURE: _____         │
│  _____     │
└─────────────────────────────────────────────────────────────────┘
```

DESIGNED AND OWNED BY AND FOR THE PEOPLE

Infrastructures are great democratizers. They provide the lines that connect everyone to everyone. Infrastructures provide everyone with the power to execute the fine words and well-intentioned phrases contained in the vision, mission and values statements. They create the opportunity to build an infrastructure—in Lincoln's words, "of the people, by the people, for the people." Seize the opportunity. Our experience tells us that only those infrastructures owned by the people will enable the Pyramid to be the strong base for future success.

We learned early, and practiced it often, to put the wiring of the information and communications power lines in the hands of associates. At AT&T/NCR a broad functional and multilevel cross section of the associate population took responsibility for communicating the new customer-focused business model. They designed the power lines and wiring infrastructure of the new AT&T/NCR Pyramid. They were responsible; not the managers or the CEO. They set up training programs. They published a 300-page "CFBM Transition Help Book" explaining the new ways of doing business. They ran information sessions. They recommended changes in planning procedures, resource allocation processes, customer response processes, supply procurement, compensation plans and a number of other policies. They modeled the new customer focus way of life. They told us what we needed to do to preach and model the new behavior. They were in charge, and we followed their lead.

Not that we were idle. Far from it. We worked overtime preaching, modeling and communicating the vision, mission, values, goals, strategies, objectives and business processes. Our continuous actions gave legs to our words that "people are our only sustainable competitive advantage." We demonstrated our intention to do whatever it took to support the associates' wiring and power line infrastructure activities.

People Can't Own What They Don't Know: Tell, Tell, Tell the Story so Everyone Knows

At Square D, we used the "Vision College" to make certain everyone knew the Pyramid and their role in making it work. An associate ran the college with the help of a team of trainers and facilitators drawn from our own ranks. More than 25,000 associates attended two-day classes, over a two-year period, to learn about our vision, mission and values.

Executives opened and closed every session. We focused on teamwork, a common set of values, mutual respect and problem solving. The classes were all off-site, away from the pressures of daily work. People flew great distances and stayed at hotels, many for the first time. We remember receiving a call from a husband who wanted us to personally confirm that his wife was indeed traveling to Chicago from South Carolina for a training program—and not for a rendezvous with a secret lover. We had a great talk. He called after her return to say that the program literally changed their life together! To this day, more than ten years later, we still get Christmas cards from people sharing stories of how Vision College changed their lives at work and at home.

We used a similar approach at both AT&T/GBCS and AT&T/NCR. An associate group put together four-hour "Vision and Value Forums" led by senior executives. The senior executive presented two hours of vision, mission, values, goals, objectives and strategic pillars, followed by two hours of discussion.

Every associate received a fold-out Pyramid card that contained the vision, mission, values, goals, objectives and strategic pillars. We used these Pyramid cards as our business cards. They were an excellent communication tool. They launched great conversations with customers.

Customers loved to be part of the communication loop. We used the Pyramid cards as a way to share with customers what our company is all about. It built rapport and a common sense of direction. In fact, many *customers* asked to participate in our Vision College and strategic forum activities. We were glad to oblige.

Some people learn best by hearing stories about ordinary people who do extraordinary things. So communicate success stories about everyday heroes living the new vision. How do you find these stories? Ask the people. People do wonderful, memorable things all the time, most of which is never shared. Identify and publicize the deeds of real people who have done real things to live the elements of the Pyramid. We've done that in every company we've led, very successfully. Organizational success stories from real life help engage and involve everyone.

PHOENIX WORKSHOP

HOW CAN I GET ASSOCIATES TO OWN THE DESIGN AND IMPLEMENTATION OF THE INFORMATION AND COMMUNICATIONS INFRASTRUCTURES?

INFORMATION INFRASTRUCTURE: _____

_____

COMMUNICATIONS INFRASTRUCTURE: _____

_____

INFORMATIONALIZE EVERYTHING:
MAKE INFORMATION EASY TO GET AND USE

The world is awash in data—unorganized bits of data buzzing around like a swarm of mosquitoes on a summer night, looking for someplace to land. We are all eaten alive by the mosquito bites of data that's unorganized, nonfactual and difficult to understand. We save our skin by arranging the data into useful, meaningful, measurable and easy-to-use information packages.

We have incredible technology resources today to put together information that is fact-driven, fact-focused and provides line of sight to import results and people; particularly concerning customers, competitors, important performance outcomes and relationships. Above all, make the data easy to understand and use. Immediate understanding of data is key to rapid access and use.

Customers, Customers, Tell Me About My Customers

We need information about customers: who they are, what they buy, why they buy it, how they use it. There's knowledge about customers all over the organization. Marketing has some. Sales has some. Finance has some. Operations has a lot. Everybody has some. But usually nobody has it all, and nobody knows what anyone else has. That's why "data warehouse" is the high-tech buzzword of our age.

Data Warehouses Tell Us All the Same Story About Our Customers

Use data warehouses to informationalize customer data. Many organizations do. *CIO* magazine in their June 1, 1996, issue reports how Citicorp's data warehouse creates a complete profile of each customer. They use nine NCR parallel processing machines to merge data about checking and savings accounts, credit cards and mortgages. Citicorp mines this data to market products like home equity loans.

For example, they may identify mortgage customers in Albany, New York, in those zip codes where property values have increased for two consecutive years who have not taken out a home equity loan. Direct mail advertising can then be targeted to that group, who are most likely to want/need a home equity line of credit. MasterCard's member banks' formal requests for customer information normally took weeks to process. Now, with their data warehouse that has desktop data mining functionality, member banks find customer information that's easy to understand and use with the touch of a few keystrokes.

Data warehouses provide line of sight to a common organization-wide version of the truth. That consistent view gets everybody on the same page and supports horizontal processes. For example, at the financial services arm of one of our companies, we used a data warehouse to get all the players on the same page: the product developers who created new financial product offerings, the risk managers who decided on credit issues, the marketing folks who searched for buyers and the channels of distribution folks who were in direct contact with the customers. We reduced the product realization process by more than 50 percent by sharing easy-to-use information across departments.

Data warehouses also provide line of sight competitive data. For example, a major shipping company's chief competitor drastically lowered rates. Salespeople demanded matching reductions. Top executives turned to their data warehouse and discovered that the competitor was severely undercapitalized. Despite strong pressure for price cuts from sales executives, top management held firm. Within a few months the competitor, unable to meet the financial requirements of the loss-creating business it won, dropped out of the market completely, sending customers back in droves at higher prices.

General Mills understands the value of line-of-sight, easy-to-understand, fact-based information concerning customers and organizational performance. They informationalize customer data in their three restaurant chains, the Olive Garden, Red Lobster and Bennigan's. General Mills uses this data to customize food menus by specific region. They pretest menu items using their database developed from U.S. Census data and individual surveys to discover which items will be most successful in given areas. They also informationalize their operating data, tracking detailed performance indicators for every location and making it easy to access and use by all employees at all locations.

Know Who, What, How, and Why: Informationalize Relationship Data

For example, most organizations hold regular meetings with customers. They discuss what's happening in the relationship, and then go back and share with everyone the good and the bad about the present and the future. Again, these are the power lines. Everyone needs them. Create easy-to-use fact-filled information to informationalize the customer relationship.

Similarly, informationalize associate relationship data. Align actions within teams and across units by providing visibility to individual and team visions, values, objectives and performance results. At Supply Company, for instance, we use e-mail as the major power wiring mechanism. Every employee lists on the e-mail his or her visions, values, individual and team objectives and monthly achievements. The e-mail system is accessible to all associates. Every associate knows what other associates are doing, thinking and desiring. Informationalizing associate relationship data helps everyone work together more effectively.

Know Who, What, How and Why: Informationalize Family Data

The same kind of wiring works for our households. We talk often among ourselves about our family visions, values and goals. We share the hits, runs and errors that make up the game of life. Informationalizing our relationships enables all of us to help any one of us. The health and stability of the family resides in the strength and reach of its information and communication power lines.

With the right information, we can better cheer when we win, console when we lose and help others climb the next mountain. It's a matter of mutual reinforcement. When the children were younger, we'd take every Friday evening as family night to talk about what each of us was doing. As the children have grown and launched families of their own, we use our frequent visits as sharing times. We continue informationalizing our relationships to

maintain the commitment to each other that keeps the family
powered on our individual and collective flight.

PHOENIX WORKSHOP

HOW CAN I INFORMATIONALIZE EVERYTHING, MAKING
INFORMATION EASY TO USE AND FACT-BASED?

COMMUNICATIONS INFRASTRUCTURE: _____

_____

INFORMATION INFRASTRUCTURE: _____

_____

THE INFORMATION SMORGASBORD:
GET YOUR CUSTOM-DESIGNED DATA MEAL PIPING HOT

Information is instantaneous. Everyone watched the bombing of
Baghdad, in real time. Everyone could see Jack Ruby shoot Lee
Harvey Oswald, as it happened. Anyone anywhere in the world can
know the price of virtually any stock traded on any stock exchange
in the world, immediately after it is traded. Information moves at
the speed of light. Access must also operate at the same speed. But
to paraphrase George Orwell's *Animal Farm,* while all information
is important, some information is more valuable than others.
Power wiring provides speed-of-light access to the information that
matters most to each and every person. Use the power wiring to deliver customized, nutritious information-rich meals.

We learned to sort through the information we receive and pick
out those few information tidbits that mattered most. As a production control manager we learned to value hourly reports on
orders, shipments, inventory at every work station, parts shortages and production rates by major area. That data enabled us to
spot developing problem areas before they erupted into a major
crisis. We got rapid responses because everyone in traffic, customer service and the distribution center also received the same

data. Everyone had immediate access to the same information that mattered most. We used that information to work together and orchestrate the fastest turnaround in company history.

Boeing used light-speed access to important information to radically reduce cycle times. Their groupware software connected 2,800 engineers in five separate organizations. They completely eliminated the prototyping stage, going directly from design to build rather than the traditional design, test and then build. Using computer-assisted design (CAD), they computerized wind tunnel testing and manufacturability. The result: they produced the new 777 in nineteen months, 80 percent faster than they ever produced a plane before.

Longs Drug Stores provided access to what mattered most and gained seven points in market share. They'd tried unsuccessfully for years to teach their store managers to use category management to make merchandising decisions. They failed because the store managers couldn't get the right information to make good merchandising decisions. That all changed when Longs installed an enterprise data warehouse that enabled store managers to find out exactly what merchandise was most likely to appeal to customers in their areas. Using the right information, store managers stocked their stores with the merchandise their customers wanted, and they gained market share.

The English retailer WH Smith learned the importance of access to important information. Their 430 locations across the world carried 150,000 different products. Like most major retailers, the huge amount of detailed daily sales information overwhelmed them and forced them to work with data summaries. They collected a large amount of information, but lost the value of it through summarization. They couldn't tell what product was selling in what locations to what kinds of customers. Worse yet, the summary data was slow in coming. In short, WH Smith had lots of data, but couldn't access the data that mattered most.

NCR created a massively parallel processing hardware solution along with a customized software application that included an accessible database. This system provided product line sales data by store and customer group matched with stock levels and ordering information. The system redeploys inventories by automatically reordering fast-moving goods and delaying slower movers, even transferring them to other locations. WH Smith discovered that associates in every organization at every level need immediate access to the information that matters most in helping them create success for customers.

Beware the Centralizers

Many organizations talk about unleashing ownership, but have a very centralized information and communications infrastructure. They talk about giving people opportunity to make decisions. But like the aging hippie searching for his fortune on the beach in Hawaii, their actions belie their words. Associates are disempowered by heavily centralized data systems that provide low-grade summary data only.

We unfortunately encountered one of those organizations that talk about empowerment but use highly centralized information systems as a control device. Central budget folks handed "the numbers" to middle managers, who were told, "Make it or else." The company was in a numbers business. Data was everywhere. But useful, meaningful, helpful, applicable information was scarce and carefully controlled by the central office. Very few in the organization knew about margins, market share, product line performance or other critical performance data. Even the senior officers were kept in the dark. Information was power, and that power was carefully controlled by a few people at the top and a large financial control organization that guarded the information gates. Today that organization continues to lose market share and margins, all the while professing to be a very associate-centered and empowered organization. It presents a real short-selling opportunity.

Turn on the Power of the Family Network

One of our grandsons is applying to college and looking for a soccer scholarship. We mobilized the family network to help. Each of us contacted people we know to gather information about good undergraduate business schools with good soccer programs. We scoured the Net to locate as much information as possible. We shared this information, exchanging e-mails, and discussed it during one of our weekly family conference calls. Grandson Eric decided (with some coaching from his dad no doubt) on several schools he both liked and felt he could qualify for. We then put Eric in touch with our contacts and coached him on how to present himself. We gave him immediate access to information he needed most, and then coached him to maximize his use of that information.

Bottom line: applied information is the secret of the self-renewing Phoenix. Keep discarding the old data and embrace the fresh updates. Keep creating knowledge.

PHOENIX WORKSHOP

HOW CAN I DELIVER TO MY PEOPLE JUST-IN-TIME ACCESS TO THE INFORMATION THEY NEED MOST?

INFORMATION INFRASTRUCTURE: _____

_____

COMMUNICATIONS INFRASTRUCTURE: _____

_____

HOW ARE WE DOING? SCOREBOARD MIRRORS EVERYWHERE YOU LOOK

The wiring infrastructure gets the right information to the right people. But what is the "right" information? As we've said over and over again, the right information focuses performance on the few performance bits that matter most to customers. Infrastructure provides the line of sight to customers.

But it's more than that. The infrastructure wires up the very public-stadium-like scoreboards that tell everyone how everybody—including themselves—is doing. You'll find these scoreboards in offices, on the production floor, in the lobby, by the time clock and back in the kitchen. The infrastructure power lines provide the riveting and performance-shaping organization's vital statistics. Make those vital statistics visible to everyone—everywhere.

At NCR we posted scoreboards everywhere. Every customer

lobby had a scoreboard. Every office had one. Every time clock had one. Every lunch room had one. Someone even suggested putting scoreboards in the toilets, but we drew the line at that. People want to know how they are doing. Make it easy for them to find out.

Apples to Apples: Report the Multidimensional Reality

Scoreboards report several statistics. There are *business results,* like revenue per employee or market share. We also see *process performance measures,* like the cost to process a payroll check. Then there's *individual performance data,* comparing productivity of CFOs or machine operators against their best-in-class counterparts. Scoreboards report both customer feedback data, like customer willingness to recommend, statistical marketplace information, like market share, as well as traditional financial data, like sales per employee.

Different statistics describe different parts of the same beast. Yes, the elephant has a long trunk, short legs, big ears and weighs several tons. To some the length of the trunk is most important. To others the weight matters most. Performance is multidimensional. The scoreboard reflects that multidimensionality.

Focus on Both Individual and Organizational-Wide Scores That People Can Impact

Not all information is equally important or valuable to all people. Percent of on-time delivery matters most to the distribution folks. It matters relatively little to the finance people since they can't move that needle. On the other hand, the time it takes to close the books every month matters a lot to the finance folks because they can make a difference in that measure. Each group needs scoreboard statistics that reflect its few most important measures in which they can make a difference. At the same time, we need common measures that tie everyone together. We've used profit margins, market share, associate growth and customer delight as across-the-organization common scoreboard statistics. This portion of the scoreboard reinforces the discussion of common goals, objectives, measures and rewards.

It's important to report both the global unifying measures, sales per employee as an example, and granular information relevant to each individual, team, product line or customer. Scoreboards focus attention. Focus that attention on those factors that the group/team/individual can influence.

Banks, these days, face intense competition, mostly from money management firms like Vanguard, Fidelity and Merrill Lynch. These investment firms today manage more money than the banks, and their overhead costs are significantly lower than those of most banks. One bank we know compares their overhead costs to Vanguard on their system-wide scoreboard. Each department then identified one specific metric they controlled that could drive down the overhead costs. That item is reported on the departmental scoreboard.

The bank-wide comparison number is awful. Vanguard is many times cheaper to run than the bank, but the CEO said, "I know that number can be discouraging. You see the wide gap between us and them and you want to throw up your hands and walk away. But that gap is real, and wishing it would go away won't make it go away. Unless we figure out ways to narrow that gap by getting much more efficient we'll get the privilege of closing this place. That's why each department has a share of cutting this elephant down to size. Together we can make a big difference. We have already." In fact, in an effort to lower costs to be more competitive this bank is installing ATM machines that dispense loans, opening branches in supermarkets while closing the crystal and marble branch office palaces. Generate a scoreboard that unites everyone in a common goal (such as lowering costs to meet Vanguard) while focusing team efforts on items they impact that contribute to the overall goal.

See the Score Through the Customer's Eyes

Like the magic mirror in Snow White, scoreboards show performance comparisons; only the scoreboard that matters most reports the comparisons through the customers' eyes. Ask, "What's really important to customers?" Then hang those numbers on the scoreboard. Make certain that the numbers reflect the customer's reality. It's all too easy to report from the internal perspective, not the customers'.

One company we know reported that their nine-member distribution crew achieved 100 percent of their distribution objective. "How can that be?" we asked. "Back orders run 12 percent. That means we're only shipping 88 percent of the products customers ordered. Warehouse errors run another 3 percent, meaning that we send the right product only 85 percent of the time. Promised next-day delivery only occurs in 82 percent of the instances. That means that only 70 percent of the customers got what they ordered when we promised to deliver it." The culprit? Hanging internal numbers on the scoreboard. The associates had the wrong measuring stick and were, therefore, performing to the wrong standard. Distribution performance changed dramatically when we changed the scoreboard numbers to a more customer-based "percent of next-day correct delivery at the customer's site."

To win on that scoreboard, distribution associates changed what they did. They worked with suppliers to eliminate back orders. They recruited new delivery companies that guaranteed next-day delivery. They followed up with customers to make certain that the order was correct and on time. The number on the scoreboard climbed from 70 percent to 93 percent within weeks.

The lesson: hang customer-based numbers on the scoreboard to win with customers. Everyone wants to win. Use customer-based scoreboard numbers to focus attention on those few performance contributions that help everyone win.

Measure Against the Best Anywhere

If you're the Dallas Cowboys, against whom do you compare yourself, the local Pop Warner team or the San Francisco 49ers? The answer is obvious: the 49ers. Why? Because they're the best of your real competition. Always compare against the best competitor, the 49ers of the world.

Also think benchmarks beyond current industry definitions. Often the biggest and best competitor isn't even in our own industry. The business landscape changes so rapidly that new, non-traditional competitors emerge with every sunrise. Hospitals today compete with Marriott in providing hospitality services like patient registration, housekeeping and food service. Marriott comparisons need to show up on hospital scoreboards. Banks today compete with Vanguard for managing customers' financial assets. You'd better benchmark against them if you're Bank of America. Take into account all of your potential competitors, those quiet little foxes who may be raiding your hen house—your customer base—next year.

At NCR we put in place a set of benchmark comparisons that represented best practices at each major process step. These external benchmarks included best-in-class companies, not necessarily in our business, that had similar characteristics to us: they were global in scope; they had many component pieces to their solutions; their solutions were customized; and they used both direct and indirect channels of distribution. We used these benchmarks as our report card, posting them prominently, so we could all keep focused on the best-in-class target.

Scoreboards focus attention on winning. Scoreboards are a public description of what winning looks like: whether it's more points on the board than the opposition at the end of the game, or friends to call for a Saturday afternoon picnic. Scoreboards answer the question "Have we created success for everyone?" Make certain everyone knows the answer.

PHOENIX WORKSHOP

HOW CAN I INSTALL SCOREBOARDS THROUGHOUT THE ORGANIZATION THAT REPORT THE FEW MOST IMPORTANT RESULTS FROM THE CUSTOMERS' PERSPECTIVE THAT MEASURE US AGAINST THE BEST?

_____

_____

_____

_____

FACE-TO-FACE COMMUNICATION: WHEN YOU CARE ENOUGH TO GIVE YOUR VERY BEST

People talking to people; that's the most effective information and communication connection. E-mail is great. Voice mail is fine. Memos are okay. But nothing beats face-to-face. Business and life is a contact sport. Be live and on stage.

We live on stage. In every situation we promote weekly "Juice with Jerre" sessions. We gather twenty or so associates from different teams and functions to discuss what's happening in the business. We give a brief report on the state of the business and then open it up for questions. The sessions usually last an hour or an hour and a half. Most sessions have lots of questions and discussion. Oftentimes associates would ask, "How come we're not doing this or that?" Or, "I heard that Company A pays more money. What are we going to do about it?" Or, "Why can't we get a new machine/office/person/etc.?" Any topic is fair game. Any question acceptable. This gives us the opportunity to teach the realities of the business to associates and address their fears and concerns. When we don't have a ready answer we promise to get back to that person personally and then publish the answer in the company newspaper so everyone can see it.

We learn a lot in these meetings about what's going on in the hearts and minds of associates. The associates learn a lot about what's going on in the business and the marketplace and in their leader's heart and mind. It's a heart check and a trust-building experience. They look in our eyes. We look in theirs. We validate the words and learn together to rely upon one another in making our joint business a success. These personal communication experiences step up the power in the Pyramid's wiring infrastructure.

Other managers establish personal communications through "bagels with Bob," "croissants with Carl" and "doughnuts with Donna." When the leader models personal communication, most other managers follow. And we strengthen the personal bond that facilitates communication and information transfers.

We'd do the same personal connection with customers. It's not unusual for us to spend three or four days out in the field with customers and associates. A typical day begins with a Juice meeting and a following managers session. Then it's off to see three or four customers, typically with the customer focus team or salespeople. All of these face-to-face contacts enhance and energize the Pyramid's wiring connections.

We've even brought customers live and in person to meet with associates. One factory was engaged in a tough competitive battle with two very strong competitors. The only way we had any chance of winning was to dramatically cut costs and provide value-added services that customers truly wanted. So we brought our key customers into the factory to tell us all what was most important to them and how we could win with them. Using this information everyone went to work shaping processes, reducing costs and adding value that was clearly important to the customer.

Non-U.S. firms also use face-to-face communication. The French president of French carmaker Renault, Jean-René Fourtou, wrote in his book *The Passion of the Entrepreneur* how he used personal communication to excite passion in his company. Fourtou would buy tickets to local soccer games and invite employees and customers to join him. He'd spend the game engaging customers and employees in passionate discussions about their company. He demonstrated his passion for the success of the company and used personal communication to infect others with his passion.

Personal connections play a huge role in our personal lives. We talk with our grown children at least twice a week, anywhere in the world—and our grandchildren at least that often. On the road we'll talk with our wives at least twice a day. Ear-to-ear or face-to-face, there is no substitute for that personal touch. It says more loudly than all the words and all the diamonds, "I truly care for you." What's true in our personal life is also true in our business life. To paraphrase Hallmark, when you care enough to give your very best, you will do it personally yourself.

```
┌─────────────────────────────────────────────────────┐
│                 PHOENIX WORKSHOP                      │
│                                                       │
│  HOW CAN I INCREASE THE AMOUNT OF PERSONAL FACE-TO-   │
│  FACE TIME WITH MY CUSTOMERS, TEAMMATES AND FAMILY    │
│  MEMBERS?                                             │
│                                                       │
│  _____  │
│                                                       │
│  _____  │
│                                                       │
│  _____  │
│                                                       │
└─────────────────────────────────────────────────────┘
```

THRIVE ON THE THRILL OF WHAT YOU ARE BECOMING!

Mountain climbers always focus upward, on the next hill to climb. They don't look back at where they've been. They focus on where they are going. Similarly, eagles don't have rearview mirrors. They focus on the sky ahead, not the ground behind. Unfortunately, messages from the past reporting where we've been jam the information and communications wires. Look at most scoreboards and what do you see: last month's sales, last quarter's profits, the last semiannual associate satisfaction ratings. If that's as far as it goes, we've missed the biggest value of that scoreboard. Rather than reporting what we've done, the scoreboard needs to help us focus on what we're on the way to becoming.

In one situation we set the goal of securing 51 percent of what A customers (those with sales volumes exceeding $250,000 per year) spent for products we delivered (we call that customer wallet share); and 25 percent of the B customers (those with potential sales volume of $25,000 to $200,000 per year). Currently we had that 51 percent wallet share for 6 percent of that customer grouping. The first report card we received showed that we had attained 51 percent wallet share with 8 percent of the target group. That may not sound like much improvement, but we were thrilled with the progress. We held a pizza and soda party for the sales crew to celebrate. We didn't celebrate the 8 percent. That's not worth celebrating. We celebrated our progress on the road to becoming what we said we wanted to be. We celebrated becoming, not achieving.

Similarly, in another setting we established a very aggressive goal for associate satisfaction, almost 40 percent higher than the current scores. The first six months' scores showed some movement, but not nearly enough to make the 40 percent goal. We celebrated the movement at the next managers meeting. We stressed that we were on the road to becoming world-class in associate satisfaction. We weren't there yet, but we were making progress toward that goal—we were becoming.

It's all in your mind-set. Is the glass half empty or half full? Is it partly cloudy or partly sunny? We'd rather emphasize the progress we are making and focus on the future steps we need to take to get ahead, rather than the missteps or missed steps of the past. We figure that we can't change the past. But we are determined to make the future different by focusing on what we are becoming, not what we aren't.

PHOENIX WORKSHOP

HOW CAN I FOCUS PEOPLE ON THE PROGRESS ON THE JOURNEY OF WHAT THEY ARE BECOMING?

_____

_____

_____

USE KNOWLEDGE TO PROMOTE LEARNING: POWER LINES THAT REACH INTO TOMORROW

Life is about learning. We are both perpetual students, always looking to learn and grow. We look to leverage the Pyramid's information and communications wiring to enhance our learning. The injunction is: learn more so we can be more valuable to our interconnected, interdependent network.

Devise a learning plan that spells out what you need to learn to be more effective in helping others create success. Communicate that plan with everybody in your network. Get their input and support for your learning. We do that routinely in our businesses. In one case, a German engineer offered to coach a young Chinese Singaporean in learning molecular plastic forming. She laid out a reading plan for her colleague halfway across the world and set up regular coaching/teaching sessions over the intranet. Within nine months the Singaporean associate was able to handle a plastics project on his own with only oversight coaching from his mentor in Germany. The intranet provided the connection that enabled that learning. Interestingly, several other associates listened in on the intranet exchanges. One of them in South Africa said, "I learned a lot by just watching the exchange. It sharpened my own understanding of the subject."

At another organization we set up an electronic Knowledge Center that was the repository of all customer and industry knowledge. We entered everything anyone learned about customers, industry trends or best industry practices into that database, which was part of our data warehouse. Once we needed to find out quickly the best industrial practice for fighting a polyethylene fire. The fire department was on the line with a live hookup to a fire truck on its way to a polyethylene fire. It took exactly ten seconds to locate the best-practice procedures and best-in-class organization name. Within twenty-five seconds the procedures were faxed to the fire truck. Within seventy-five seconds they had been revised with input from the best-practice firm and were in the fire truck before it arrived at the disaster scene.

The psychologist Abraham Maslow said that "a person is both an actuality and a potentiality." Learning translates potentiality into actuality. We thrill to the anticipation of what we can learn to become. That learning is the Phoenix's driving force. Peter Senge got it right in *The Fifth Discipline* when he equated the thrill of what we are becoming with the thrill of what we are learning. He said: "To learn is to continually enhance the capacity to realize one's highest aspirations." The information and communications wiring provides the power for each and every one of us to learn to be all that we can be.

```
┌─────────────────────────────────────────────────────────────┐
│                    PHOENIX WORKSHOP                          │
│                                                             │
│  HOW CAN I USE THE INFORMATION AND COMMUNICATIONS           │
│  INFRASTRUCTURES TO ENCOURAGE LEARNING?                     │
│  _____  │
│                                                             │
│  _____  │
│                                                             │
│  _____  │
└─────────────────────────────────────────────────────────────┘
```

THE GREAT CHALLENGE WE FACE:
A WORLD SO TECHNOLOGY-RICH, DATA-RICH AND COMMUNICATIONS-POOR

It's easy to talk about the glories of vision and values. It's even fun to spend long hours debating the future. But it's hard work to get out the hammer, nails and spools of wire and sweat up a storm framing that future and wiring it up. That's exactly what needs to be done, however, if we are to lay all the stones to build the Pyramid that will be the strong base for our future success. It's the hard-work framing and wiring that enables the Phoenix to soar and the Pyramid to be its strong base.

Everywhere we go, we see people in dire need of better information and communications. Organizations die early deaths due to lack of information and communication. People lose opportunities to live better lives due to a simple lack of information. See yourself as an information and communication paramedic—rescuing people from ignorance and isolation—while connecting more and better power lines. With the powerful technologies we have today, there is absolutely no excuse to leave anyone—ever—without the information and interpersonal connections they need to be successful.

We know how to design information and communications infrastructures that provide the power lines, the connections and the energy that get the right knowledge to the right person, at the right place, at the right moment. Perhaps the greatest tragedy of our time is that we are opportunity-rich, technology-rich and data-rich—while still so communications-poor!

Our worlds of work and family both need power lines to ensure stability, security and high-synergy relationships. Apply the principles in this chapter to create success for everyone.

The last stone is now in place. Let's step back and admire the product of our long hours of sweat and toil: our Pyramid. *Vision* is the 30,000-foot beacon, illuminating what we want to be, to create in our future. *Mission* is the 10,000-foot binoculars that focuses us on what and how we will deliver to whom. *Values* are the 10,000-foot compass that guides our everyday behavior as we strive to create the vision and mission. *Goals* are the 1,000-foot targets of choice that specify the intermediate steps on our climb toward the vision. *Strategies* are the 1,000-foot roads we follow toward our goals, mission and vision. *Objectives, measures and rewards (the disciplined management system)* are the five- to ten-foot steps we take to travel down the strategic road map toward the intermediate goals and eventually back to the vision and mission. *Business processes* are the 2x4 and 2x12 framing we build to facilitate the execution of the other Pyramid elements. Finally, *information and communications infrastructures* are the wiring that ties all the interconnected folks together and enables the Phoenix to soar.

The Pyramid represents the solid base from which the Phoenix continues to soar into the future. It is at one and the same time the Phoenix's resting place and its launching pad.

CHAPTER 14

Leave a Timeless, Personal Legacy: Your Finest Hour Is Yet to Be!

The Great Continuously Recurring Question

The graying, tall, statuesque man gazes serenely out his picture window at the manicured lawn and decorative iron gates beyond. He stands behind his huge walnut desk, his fingers drumming along the buttons on his chair, symbols of the power of his of-fice—an office he leaves this day, forever. The air is filled with the sounds of scurrying people and moving furniture—yet he is obliv-ious to it all, immersed a light-year away in his own thoughts.

He turns abruptly, catching us off guard, and blurts out, "How do you think they'll remember me?"

"Say again," we ask, startled by the suddenness and directness of the question.

He slumps into the chair, heaves a big sigh and says softly, "Oh, never mind. It doesn't matter anyway."

We come around the huge desk—like traveling through the Panama Canal to get from Los Angeles to New York—put our hands on his shoulder and say softly, "It absolutely does matter. Ask again."

Straightening up in his executive posture, he repeats, "How do you think I'll be remembered?"

Here's a man who sat at the pinnacle of almost absolute power. He commanded the stage, parried and thrust with the best of them, and won more than his share of the engagements. And here he is, in his waning moments, worrying about the legacy he is leaving.

He was a great man. We were privileged to have worked with him. He did many things for the people he served, and the networks in which he was involved. Yet despite the power he commanded, he shares the common human concern of measuring the footprints he leaves behind. All of us have but a moment on the stage. All of us ask his eternal question, "And how will they remember me?"

Look Closely: Endings Are Beginnings in Disguise

However, are endings really endings? Our friend moves out of the big house and the big desk and become "Mr. Average Citizen." No more private planes and fawning minions hanging on his every word. His vote and voice no longer count for more than just one of hundreds of millions. Is it really over for him?

The Phoenix teaches us otherwise. Endings are really beginnings, part of the eternal cycle of life. The sun sets every evening, only to rise again next morning more beautiful than ever. The dankness of winter is but a necessary step toward the freshness of spring. The natural cycle teaches us that endings are merely beginnings in disguise.

As humans, we are loath to leave our future to nature alone. We want to help nature out a bit, provide a little extra shove in the right direction, get the river to flow by us, not over us, and deposit all that rich silt in the field, and not our living room. We want to control things. But in the back of one's mind, the nagging questions reverberate: "Can we shape and determine the future? Is it ever really subject to control?"

Renew Yourself—Just Like President Carter

Our answer is a resounding, "Yes, perhaps . . . If you are willing to renew yourself." Look at President Jimmy Carter. Historians generally agree that he was not a strong president: he barely defeated a nonelected president, presided over one of the worst periods of stagflation in U.S. economic history, ordered the embarrassing helicopter rescue attempt of American hostages in Iran, and then lost soundly to Ronald Reagan.

He could have crept back to his home in Georgia, nursed his wounds, grown his peanuts and faded from view. Instead, he followed his heart and his values, renewing himself as a great humanitarian and peacemaker. His work with Habitat for Humanity, building homes for the homeless, and bringing peace to several troubled parts of the world will likely write his name in large letters in the history books—much larger than his record as president might merit. Through self-renewal, the ending of his presidency was the beginning of his glory.

You also can be a Phoenix, revivoluting your organization, life and relationships. Renew yourself, as President Carter did, and snare the golden ring. Here are our closing thoughts.

BE YOUR OWN METAPHOR: BE A PHOENIX

The Phoenix symbolizes the countless cycles of renewal we see everywhere around us. And yet renewal is not a random process. Causes produce effects, which in turn cause other ripple-like effects. Cycles begin somewhere, with someone who possesses the courage to launch the renewal process. We each possess the resources and tools to revivolute our organizations and ourselves. We have the power to create self-renewing Phoenix organizations and self-renewing Phoenix lives. What we need is a spoonful of courage.

We have done it before. When exploited by an oppressor, America's founding fathers proactively revivoluted a new system. Instead of promoting incremental change, they initiated radical innovation. They shocked and stunned the world. The Declaration of Independence tolled the obituary for obsolete, imposed control systems. It was the ringing birth announcement for a freer way of life and government in which more people than ever could be successful.

The Phoenix is the ultimate symbol of optimism. It says to

each and every one of us: "YOU CAN DO IT!" The Phoenix is about revivolution and renewal. The mythic bird symbolizes people and organizations that emerge, rise, soar, rebound, return, make amazing comebacks, reappear and spring eternal. The Phoenix is the symbol of not only the possibilities in today's turning world, but of new worlds, awaiting our discovery, use and service.

Our challenge is to harness the power of renewal and direct it toward building success for all those with whom we are connected. The Phoenix mentality teaches us to think big, think grand and think in totalities. And that's great news, because today we all have more opportunities to revivolute than ever before. These are indeed the very best of times. We all can create a more beautiful and prosperous tomorrow than ever before. Step forth and take command: become a Phoenix leader surfacing issues, engaging people, priorities, resources, unleashing ownership and energizing learning. Build your Pyramid of integrated and aligned visions, missions, values, goals, strategies, disciplined management systems, business processes and information and communications infrastructures. Use that Pyramid to launch your ever-brighter future—every day.

LEAVE A LEGACY—MAKE A DIFFERENCE

Everyone wants to make a difference. Parents yearn for children of whom that they can be proud. President Clinton worries about his place in history. So does Jack Welch, current leader of powerhouse General Electric. And John Akers, former leader of IBM. Visit any retirement dinner and listen to the "How will I be remembered?" comments. They come—not just from the retiree, but from all the participants. Why this preoccupation with what people will think of us after we're gone? Easy. Everyone wants to make a difference, leave a mark, be remembered.

Leave a Legacy of Constantly Improving People

We traveled through Europe recently, meeting with 400 people in five countries. An experience at our German facility reminded us that our ultimate legacy would be to leave a group of people who continued to better their professional and personal lives after we were gone. There are great folks at the German office, competent, motivated, concerned, real Phoenixes, willing to continually renew themselves to help others succeed. When we asked them, "How can we help you better learn and grow and serve all of your customers more effectively?" they stammered a lot and finally blurted out, "No boss ever asked us that before. We don't know, because we never thought about it."

"Well, think about it, and please tell us," we said.

One woman raised her hand from the back of the room and piped up, "How do you think you can help us?"

We instantly recognized another *Phoenix leadership moment.* "By helping you learn what your customers need and how to more effectively provide it to them. And how can we best do that?" we volleyed back.

More uncomfortable silence prompted another hand. "We need a better computer system. We can't tell a customer where his order is because we don't track orders back to the supplier. We only know when it hits our warehouse."

"That information is in the purchasing system," we responded. "Don't you have access to that system?"

"Well . . . I didn't know it was there," was the surprised response.

We saw another *Phoenix leadership moment.* "Thanks for bringing up that example. There's likely lots of information buried in files that many people don't know exist, but would help them do their jobs better. How can we get everyone to know what information we have available?"

A lively discussion followed that resulted in forming a group of volunteers to put together an information index. Furthermore, the people agreed to meet monthly to continue the dialogue we started about how they might improve their service. Ownership swirled around the room as the people took charge of solving their own problems, and established a mechanism to continue their learning and improvement. We smiled as we boarded the plane heading for the next city, leaving behind a cadre of people

committed to constantly improving themselves. We were grati-
fied that leadership was exercised, a difference was made and a
legacy was left.

Christmas Cards from the Past Remind Us of Our Legacy

We received two Christmas cards in particular this year from
Square D employees that really warmed our hearts: one from Lincoln, Nebraska, and another from Lexington, Kentucky. Both pro-
duction team associates shared how much they enjoyed going to
work these days, learning new things and improving old ways. A
decade ago we installed self-directed work teams at Square D.
Prior to that the plants were very traditional command-and-
control facilities. Today, teamwork professionals benchmark the
Square D self-directed work teams in Raleigh and Columbia,
South Carolina, and Asheville, North Carolina, and Lexington,
Kentucky, and Smyrna, Tennessee, and Lincoln, Nebraska, and
Tijuana, Mexico. Those Christmas cards, though, mean more to
us than all the accolades from the professionals, because they tell
us that we created an environment for people that still encour-
ages them to constantly improve themselves a decade after we
left the scene. The greatest feeling is that our legacy lives on at
Square D.

The Parents' Bumper Sticker Legacy

What's really important? Ask our wives and they'll tell you:
bumper stickers reading "My Child Was Citizen/Scholar of the
Month." Those adhesive-mounted paper declarations of family
accomplishment are more treasured than a beautifully decorated
house, a private pilot license or an expensive automobile.

Higher, Further, More: A Father's Legacy

We recall the tears of pride in my father's eyes when we gave the valedictorian address at the high school graduation. Why? Children are a parents' legacy. Our speech was living proof of our father's legacy of an achieving progeny. He told us often, "Your job is to do better than I did, and raise your children to do better than you do. Reach higher, go further, do more than me—and pass that injunction on to your seed." His last words to us on his deathbed were, "Reach higher, go further, do more."

Decades later his words still echo through our lives. We work hard to live up to our father's precious legacy.

Dad to Son: "I Work Hard to Earn Your Respect"

It's not just in our families, either. Listen to the preoccupation with leaving a legacy of constant growth in the following vignette. Kevin, a former student, shared an experience with us over breakfast recently. Kevin's an accomplished engineer, recorded in the *Guinness Book of World Records*. His work on the photographing of the sunken *Titanic* won international acclaim. Kevin's sixteen-year-old son asked him one day, "Dad, why do you work so hard, taking all those classes and writing and studying all the time?"

Kevin's answer: "Son, I work hard studying and learning so you'll be as proud of me as I am of you." Kevin constantly works to improve himself so he can leave a legacy of which his son can be proud. By the way, the reason for our breakfast was to discuss Kevin's interest in future educational activities. At forty-four, and with two children and a wife, Kevin's contemplating getting a Ph.D. so he can teach technology management at a university. He's becoming a self-renewing Phoenix in order to leave a legacy.

Plant Trees, Grow People, Not Monuments

Every year we plant trees in Third World countries to acknowledge the special people with whom we've worked during the past year. That gift is prompted by a story we heard.

An emperor was on a road when he saw an old man digging in the fields. "What are you doing, old man?" he called out.

"Planting fruit trees," was the old man's response.

The emperor laughed and replied, "Old man, you are foolish. This soil is terrible. It will never grow trees. And, even if it does, you will die before the trees bear fruit."

"But sir," the old man replied, "I believe that the ground will provide the nourishment to enable the trees to grow and that I will be here when they bring fruit. If not, my children will benefit."

"You are an old fool," said the emperor. "But if the trees do grow, and you are still here, bring me some of the crop and I will give you a reward."

Years went by and both the trees and the old man flourished. The old man gathered some of his first crop and took it to the emperor's palace.

The emperor remembered the old man and his promise. "Your faith has been rewarded, old man," he said. "What do you wish? You may have virtually any treasure in my kingdom."

The old man stared at the floor for a moment, turned his face toward the emperor sitting on his golden throne, smiled and said, "Just some more seeds, sir, so my children may learn my valuable lesson."

We are planters of trees and growers of people. Trees provide a Phoenix-like, self-renewing crop of nurture and food and eventually shelter and warmth. Trees help people learn the valuable lessons of self-reliance and active engagement in building their *future*. Planting trees—like growing people—yields a bountiful legacy.

Seed Capital Grows Houses, Skills and Pride

In other settings we provide seed capital that enables individuals to build their own homes. The people provide the sweat equity and we provide the training and building materials. People get off the street and into their own homes: for the first time in many of their lives they own something of value that they helped create. In addition, they learn a valuable skill that can help them earn a living—gaining self-confidence and pride. This is a legacy that creates value for many members of our interconnected, interdependent network.

Next year at our Super Bowl event, together with our top customers and vendors, we plan to build a house for Habitat for Humanity. Several people asked, "Do you think the customers will really like doing that, getting dirty and all, working with their hands?" "Absolutely," we answered. "They will create something in a day that will stand there for a lifetime. Everyone will take away a legacy of working together and contributing to making a difference." That legacy will outlive the house—and be more valuable.

Statues Don't Grow—Only People Grow

It's often said, "There's no limit to what we can accomplish, if we don't care who gets the credit." Lots of people leave a name on an endowed chair at a university, or a hospital wing, or a building, and feel that that's their legacy. We support a University Center of Ethics and Values. We've resisted their efforts to name the center after us. After all, fifty years from now what difference will our name on the door make? None. "Choose a name that best reflects your vision and purpose and will attract the best, most creative people," we urge. "Use the name to give power to your mission and help people focus on doing those things that will help others in the future." Don't worry about building statues; focus on building people.

Growing, Motivated, Educated People Are Your Company's (And Your Own) Best Legacy

Every business is a people business, whether you're an undertaker or a chip manufacturer. It's people that manufacture the product, move the product, sell the product, install the product and service it afterward. Every organization, therefore, is a vehicle to grow people.

Many economists and financiers would fire back: "That's an interesting, humanistic point of view, but unfortunately, it's not good economics."

Wrong, folks. That's just plain not true—growing people is very good economics—and finance. The empirical evidence is overwhelming that motivated people produce better economic results than poorly motivated people. Furthermore, educated people produce better economic results than uneducated people. Developing motivated, educated people, therefore, maximizes long-term economic returns—for both an individual organization and society as a whole. Growing people is Adam Smith's invisible hand at its best.

The best legacy is growing people and communities. In addition to creating customer delight today, also develop people who are more confident and capable of meeting the challenges that lie five to ten years in the future. Ensure your legacy by developing people to create more and more jobs for more and more successful people in the coming years. Don't worry about leaving your name inscribed on a building. Only a few people have the resources to do that. But each and every one of us has the resources to leave a legacy inscribed in the hearts and the minds of the people with whom we've worked and lived, leaving them better because we've touched their lives.

POWER UP THOSE HUMAN LEARNIN' MACHINES

Cultivate the Love of Learning

People love to learn and grow. Ask people about their best experiences or happiest times and they inevitably mention learning and growing. A Midwest theme park organization we know closes during the winter months, as people don't want to walk outside when it's ten degrees and snow covers the roads. Last year, they offered classes in crafts over the winter season and attracted more than 3,000 people. Executives, bank presidents and housewives paid hundreds of dollars to learn how to shape metal, carve wood, make baskets and throw pottery. What was their motivation? A bank executive from Cleveland said, "I've been wanting to learn how to blacksmith for years. This was a great opportunity for me to master a new skill."

"Will this help you in your career?" the interviewer asked.

He reflected for a moment, smiled and said, "Don't know. But I do know that I'm inordinately proud of my newfound ability, and believe that I can take the focus and lessons I learned here and use them in life—and at the bank as well. My son and I are coming back next year to learn wood carving together."

He came to learn, and he's a better person for having done so.

Learn to Grow and Grow to Earn

We encourage the love of learning in our family. Mothers read to children. Older children read to younger children. Frequent trips to libraries and museums reinforce learning. All of our travels emphasize learning. Whether it's Greece or Australia, Paris, France, or Paris, Wisconsin, we learn about the area before we visit and discuss what we learned during our visit after we return home. The adults prepare a photo album and corresponding text explanations; the children write a school report. Learning is an ongoing and integral part of our family lives.

Learning is always linked to building future earning capabilities. The trip to Australia, for instance, triggered conversations about medical care delivery and education in the remote bush country. One child followed that interest and modified her community college program as a result.

Reach Beyond the Grave Through the Learnin' Machines You Leave Behind

A founder and president of an organization we know wants his organization to remain a family-held business forever. He can make certain that the family retains control as long as he's around. But what happens after he passes on? Seven children and thirteen (and still counting) grandchildren may not share the founder's commitment.

We spent two days with him recently, helping him see that his principal legacy will be a vibrant business that reflects his vision and his Christian values. That organization may not always bear his family name, but it can live as a Christian organization that makes a difference in the lives of guests, employees and the communities in which it operates.

He now sees that the best way to ensure the survival of his organizational vision and values is to educate his progeny in the business of his business. He's now determined to create twenty "learnin' machines" who fluently understand the ins and outs of the business, so they see the value it has in advancing their—and his—shared vision and values. Helping his heirs learn about the business is his best shot at keeping the business in the family.

Learning Improves Your Value—And Your Self-Esteem

An interviewer asked us recently, "Do people want to learn so they can get a bigger paycheck, or is there really some more personal motivation?"

The answer is, "Yes, yes." Learning *is* a self-esteem issue. The more confident you feel doing a certain task, and the more confident other people perceive you as being, the higher your self-esteem. It doesn't matter what you get paid to do the task. One of us actually loves mowing his lawn, for instance. He's good at it and gets self-esteem from doing it. The earthy fragrance of freshly cut grass, the neat look of a newly mowed lawn and the knowledge that "I did it"—all add up to real satisfaction. And he doesn't earn a dime doing it.

That said, however, there's no doubt that college is the door to economic success. Over a working life, high school graduates earn less than 20 percent of college graduates. No wonder there's such a press to open college enrollments to minorities and underrepresented groups. A college degree changes everything. It changes your social status: you go from making beds to making decisions, you join different clubs and live in different neighborhoods. With a college degree you're a member of the mainstream, a part of the establishment, an insider. All the trappings of the "good life" can be purchased with those extra dollars.

At the graduation address at a large Midwestern university not long ago, more than 80 percent of the class were first-generation college graduates. Families came from across the globe to celebrate the first of their clan earning a sheepskin. Button-popping pride and tears of joy filled the stadium, along with student "learnin' machines" and family "learnin' machines."

Americans value education as the route to a better tomorrow. Parents sacrifice to get their kids through school. Remember that picture of our great-grandfather standing in front of his windowless mud house in Kansas? He worked sunup to sunset to put our grandfather through college—the first college graduate in our family. Education is the key to upward mobility, both socially and economically, and a source of great pride and self-esteem. Yes. People love to learn because it pays off at the teller window . . . in the neighborhood . . . and in the mirror.

Build a Learning Infrastructure

While learning is natural, too many organizations tell people what to do, instead of teaching them how to do it. Too many organizations insist on people following the rules rather than using their minds. Great organizations open up learning by remembering that people are learnin' machines and want to grow. For example, and it embarrasses us to report this, we have a group of very hard-to-get technicians in one of our companies that a just-

completed compensation study shows we pay less than market
value.

People weren't scrambling to leave, so we had no idea that we
were behind the market. When we asked them what kept them
here, they told us that, most of all, it was the classes they attended and their ability to learn new, interesting material and
skills. Incredible as it may seem, they were willing to pay for the
privilege of learning. Over time, we've learned that the smarter
the person, the more likely they are to willingly pay for that privilege.

Set Learning and Personal Development Goals

Build organizational life so that it focuses on learning, growing
and being more effective. Find ways to help people live their own
dreams while contributing to the organization's work. We've laid
out many different methodologies to align individual and organizational visions and learning plans. Recall the objectives, measures and rewards discussion, and the learning and development
plan discussions. There's also a whole host of more informal activities, like our constant asking about "What should we keep
doing? What should we start doing? What should we stop doing?"
Those questions create a positive learning environment.

Get everyone to pick three or four key things in which they
really want to make a difference. For example, one mid-level
manager in Buffalo wanted to become more of a coach and less of
a supervisor. We urged her to stencil the two words, "coach" and
"supervisor," on 3x5 cards, and post them at eye level right on
her desk. Another manager in France wanted to work on being
more "multinational" rather than "global."

Then we urged them to choose the top three priorities that will
make the difference in moving them from where they are to
where they want to be. Post that list right next to the words.

This learning emphasis definitely works. In one recent acquisition we closed down two very large operations of the acquired
company. Many of the folks at those two locations were not able
to make the move to our facility. For the first time, that could
have resulted in many people being unemployed in these two
communities. We made certain that we placed every one of the

people who didn't make the move with us. Earlier in our career, we likely wouldn't have even thought about the community impact. The emphasis we've put on learning about our interconnectedness really worked.

Provide Feedback to Stimulate Learning

Back in the early 1970s the technicians at Honeywell's mechanical maintenance unit faced a challenging conundrum. The better they did their job, the less feedback they received from customers on how well they were performing. The lack of feedback cut down on their learning and growing opportunities. We gave the technicians business cards to drop off on the administrator's desk, along with a note saying something to the effect that "I was here, fixed the problem. Call me if anything goes wrong."

The results were incredible. Not only did the technicians walk a lot taller, filled with pride of ownership, but their productivity soared better than 20 percent as well. In addition, the technicians were much better able to track which repair worked and which didn't, and that triggered additional classes and educational activities. They got the feedback that built pride, productivity and additional learning requirements.

Many other businesses use a similar approach. Inside the underwear you order from a catalogue is a slip of paper with the following message, "I made your garment. If there's any problem please call me." And it's signed "Carlos." We called Carlos and told him that we really liked the product and appreciated his taking care to make it so well. Later that day we received a call from Mike, the product manager, to thank us for our call to Carlos. "Few people call with compliments," Mike told us. "You made Carlos's day." "He's made lots of days for us," we responded.

"Tell us something," we continued. "We're consultants. What do you do with complaints?" "It usually means that we've missed something in either our process or our training, so we work to fix both. Customer complaints are very valuable signals on our dashboard," Mike told us. Great point. Direct customer feedback builds pride and productivity, and surfaces learning opportunities.

Learning Is a Personal Experience: Feed It Personally

The best learning takes place person-to-person, on the job. Learn-by-doing isn't only a catchy phrase, it's essential to effective learning. The best learning takes place between the coach and the coachee, both actively engaged in learning and growing together. That kind of learning doesn't happen once or twice a year.

You don't have a meeting once a year and write down some goals and check off the box. Learning between coach and coachee is an ongoing, day-in, day-out, week-in, week-out kind of activity. It's everything from hallway encounters, to one-on-one meetings, to dinners, to voice mails. Learning, like Phoenix leadership, is a contact sport, best conducted eyeball-to-eyeball. When carried out personally, learning stimulates the desire to learn even more.

Performance Evaluations Are Ultimate Personal Learning Opportunities

It's *that* time again—performance evaluations are due. You've put it off as long as you can, but you can't ignore those persistent calls from HR anymore. Just suck it up and get them done—as quickly as possible, so you can move on to the truly important issues in your job.

Unfortunately, this describes all-too-many performance evaluation experiences. Yet discussing performance with your coach—and coachee—should be the ultimate personal learning experience. It's critical to get an outside perspective on how things are going and what needs to be improved. Current performance evaluation systems don't meet that objective very well; they're all pain and no gain.

Continuous Engagement in
Performance Discussions Works Best

The best performance evaluation systems engage coaches and coachees in a continuing dialogue about performance and learning: every day, every week, every month. "But how do I do that?" a chairman asked us recently after we spoke those words at a meeting. "We've got a marvelous company. Good margins. Great people. But we're stuck in this annual ritual. I'd like to get rid of the formal review process, because it allows people to postpone the everyday performance discussions. The flip side is that I don't have anything to replace that awful system—and I'm concerned that without it, we won't get any performance discussions."

"Begin with the future and manage backward," we suggested. "Announce that two years from now the performance evaluation system will be an annual goal setting with customers, teammates and coaches, followed up with monthly action plans and reviews with the same folks. Tell everyone that you'll migrate to this new system over the next two years, so people know exactly what's coming and it's not a surprise.

"Then, find the disciples to model the new system this year, and start teaching it to others next year. Involve your excellent HR person in putting together the mechanics of the new program—the forms, training materials and handbooks—and the systematic support for it throughout the organization."

Even Voice Mails Can Be Personal Learning Opportunities

We're expanding in Latin America, looking to be the largest organization of our kind in that part of the world by the end of next year. Craig's working the acquisitions for us. We got a voice message from him about a pending acquisition which he'd been negotiating.

Listening to his voice and reading the brief he put together, we saw that he'd gotten locked into a certain purchase price number that wasn't necessarily the only number that could work for us. We left him a voice mail—after failing to reach him personally several times—and urged him to reconsider the purchase price number in light of what we're trying to accomplish in the region.

We passed on some other thoughts about how to integrate the acquisition with other activities, and he came back with a voice mail within hours saying, "Got it. Lost sight, sorry. Back on track." You've got to be personally engaged in a continuous coaching/learning process. Most performance issues that really matter can't wait for annual reviews.

In fact, most performance issues that really matter need to be handled right now. Many years ago, we had a very capable sales executive on our team. He was a gem of a salesman. Did a great job in the engineering, male-dominated world of that decade. But times changed, and female salespeople began to show up in his workforce, and in his engineering/purchasing customer base. He struggled to make the transition from dealing with "the guys" to working with "people."

We worked hard to help him acknowledge and deal with diversity. It was a minute-by-minute, day-to-day, week-by-week personal coaching process. At one point he asked us to review all his memos, and we'd send them back to him with handwritten notes scrawled all over them. It took a lot of time, but it was worth every minute. Two and a half years after we started working with him he was selected by the local Woman's Council as "Boss of the Year" upon the recommendation of three of the women he'd brought into the sales organization. Most importantly, he was real proud of himself.

Take the Time to Learn About Your Network People—As People

Learning in a family setting is a personal experience that takes time and conservation to develop. We've found in our family that our weekly sharing sessions engage each of us in each other's lives in a positive, supportive way. That engagement, and the in-depth personal knowledge of each other that that engagement brings, lays the platform for continued learning from each other. Sons teach daughters, daughters teach sons and everyone teaches parents. We all learn together from each other.

Think about the relationship with your spouse. Spend time sharing each other's dreams—and actively supporting each other's actions to realize those dreams—or you don't have much of a marriage. How many people do you know who cohabit under the same roof, but share little else? Too many, is our answer. Life is too short to merely cohabit. Make the commitment to a marriage, and invest the time and personal effort to reap the rich rewards of learning and personal growth that come from that relationship.

Beyond your family, the many other folks in your network possess incredible epic tales, experiences and valuable insights to share with you—valuable learning that cannot be duplicated anywhere else. Take the time to plumb the depths of the wisdom existing in the hearts and minds of all the others with whom you are interconnected and interdependent. There's gold out there in your network, waiting to be mined. Ask the questions and listen well, and you will be enriched with the answers. To adapt a few lines from John Greenleaf Whittier: "The saddest words of tongue or pen—are, 'I had no idea . . .' Ah, what might have been!" Have you ever heard someone say, "I didn't know you could help. I didn't realize you'd been there and done that. I didn't know you knew." Listen. Ask. Communicate. Get up front and personal with the people in your network to maximize your learning.

Facts Are Our Friends That Help Us Learn— Particularly Those Contained in the Hearts and Minds of Our Network Connections

We've said it often throughout this book, "Facts are our friends, surround yourself with them." However, our concern is not just hard, cold, impersonal facts—but also the warm, caring, personal facts that deeply affect people's behavior. Our mission is to discover the truth about tomorrow, and that truth is buried in the hearts and brains of the people with whom we live and work. Engage your network connections in shining their collective lights to find those facts about tomorrow—facts that are our friends and will help us create the Pyramid together.

Facts About Tomorrow Are Our *Real* Friends

Focus on facts about tomorrow, because those help us learn. We still see too many leaders who bury themselves and others with numbers from the past, and dig, dig, dig up facts that are not friends, because they do not lead to productive learning.

Coaches Don't Communicate, They Engage

For a long time we said that communication was 50 percent of our coaching responsibilities. We were wrong. It's really 95 percent. But we also misled people into thinking that by "communication" we mean "talking to my people more." Nothing could be further from our real meaning. Communication does not mean *talking to* people. Rather it means *engagement with* people, mostly about performance.

A sports coach is the best example. A great sports coach, and it doesn't matter whether it's football, soccer or tennis, is actively involved in every play. Coaches don't pass the ball or score points, but they are actively involved in watching, evaluating, planning the next move, noting who's performing and who isn't—on both offense and defense.

Coaches don't manage by numbers. They don't look at their plan and say, "Since this is the forty-second play, let's run the forty-second play we scripted." No coach would be foolish enough to attempt to plan that far into any game. They rely upon their ability to monitor the game situation and make adjustments on the fly.

Personal Engagement Coaching Is Not Micromanaging

Don't misunderstand. Personal-engagement coaching is not micromanaging. It's not saying, "Do it this way, or that way. Check back with me in ten minutes, tell me how it went and then I'll give you the next assignment." Coaches engage in an ongoing dialogue focused on helping the coachee learn. The coaching/learning model spells out the questions that stimulate learning, not micromanaging. Remember, the purpose in coaching is to help people grow so they can be more confident and competent on their own.

People are powerful and wonderful learnin' machines, ever pushing the boundaries of their own comfort zone, hungry for more and more knowledge. Expect, measure and reward that learning to feed that wonderful horn-of-plenty-creating machine.

ESTABLISH HEART CONNECTIONS

What has made young men and women risk their lives charging an enemy machine gun nest? What gets people to work crazy hours to meet a customer's design deadline? What gets people to redesign an entire show in forty-eight hours? Is it money? Can't be. They can't pay you enough to die. Is it power? What kind of power can you exercise looking up at the daisies? Is it the thrill? Not much thrill in a hospital bed. The answer's amazingly simple. It's leadership. Phoenix leadership makes the difference. Which is a piece of good news, because each of us can be a Phoenix leader. What does it take to be a Phoenix leader? The shorthand answer? It takes heart.

"Come on guys, give me a break," you're likely saying to yourself. "What do you mean by heart? Is this some kind of *Wizard of Oz* double-talk?"

Leadership vs. Management:
The Latest "Angels-Dancing-on-Pins" Academic Debate

Well, in a limited sense maybe it is a sort of *Wizard* thing. Tune into the academic debate about the difference between leadership and management. Some academics say that "leaders do the right thing, while managers do things right." Others point out that leaders see the big picture while managers handle the details. Still others equate leadership with strategy and management with tactics. Whatever.

Academics have debated for centuries about how many angels can dance on the head of a pin. Strikes us that whether it's one or one million doesn't much matter. Similarly, the debate over management versus leadership also doesn't much matter. Whatever you call it—and we choose to call it leadership for no real reason other than we like the term . . . lead/manage with your heart, if you want people to be willing to crawl over ground glass and break through brick walls for you.

Rewrite the Show Overnight—For the Right Leader

We watched the Phoenix leader of an entertainment company at a recent grand opening of one of his theaters. After the show, he went backstage and talked to the cast. "Great show," he said. "But something's missing. What do you think?"

The people said, "You're right. The reviews didn't come in as positive as we'd like. It seems to drag a little in the fourth, seventh and tenth scenes. Second act is a little slow-starting also." He looked at them and said, "Let's see what you can do." The entire troupe worked sixty hours straight and got the show all changed around. It became the hit of the season.

Why did they work sixty consecutive hours to change the show? Was it the great money they were getting? Absolutely not. They don't get any more than other performers in the area, and a lot less than their colleagues in Hollywood and Vegas. Was it the hope for future income? Perhaps. Good reviews will help everyone get more and better assignments in the future. Was it pride? Absolutely! The performers' names are on the marquee and in the reviews.

Most of all, however, it's their respect and caring for that Phoenix leader. He's a quiet, soft-spoken man who looks you in the eye and you know that he cares about you as a human being and that he respects and values you for your contribution. He says it with his words, his touch and his willingness to go out of his way to help you be all that you want to be. He leads with his heart—and people work insane hours to make him proud of them.

Real Phoenix Leaders Really Care

One of our senior officers is a super-smart individual. She's likely in the top 1 percent of the IQs in the world. We've been coaching her to let her heart show through more in her dealings with teammates and customers. She has such a big intellectual engine that's served her so well in her climb through the hierarchy that she has trouble relating on a person-to-person basis.

She wants to be president of an organization someday. We've counseled her that not showing her deep caring—and she has it in abundance, but it's buried—is the mountain that stands between her and her goal. We're working hard to help her see that an honest expression of caring is not a sign of weakness, but of strength.

Platoon-Mates Matter More Than Generals and Flags

Phoenix leaders really care about people, and that real caring shows through. What makes an army effective? Is it all that high-tech weaponry? No, not really. At the end of the day the army is effective because the people really care about their platoon-mates. Soldiers risk their lives in battle because of their commitment to the person on their left, the person on their right, the rest of the people in their platoon and their platoon leader.

The army's fighting unit is the platoon. The platoon will fail—and the rest of the army along with it—if the people in that platoon don't truly care for each other. They must also bond with the platoon leader, and feel cared for by that leader. Military orders can't command the courage to take out the machine gun nest in the face of blazing gunfire, or the courage to hover your helicopter behind enemy lines to rescue a downed flier. Rules and regulations can't compel people to sacrifice their lives. The willingness to give your all—whether it's time or energy or your life—comes from the heart connection among people. We work, live and die for other people.

Great Phoenix leaders build that heart connection. Remember World War II's General George Patton, who moved his entire army to do what people said was physically impossible—and win the Battle of the Bulge. The army did the impossible because they loved Patton. As tough as he was, they loved Patton because they knew he loved them.

Speaking of Issues: Soft Is Hard and Hard Is Soft

There's lots of debate about "soft" issues and "hard" issues—soft issues being "people" issues and hard issues being "financial and market" considerations. People frequently ask, "Where do you focus your time—on the soft, people issues, or the hard, financial/market issues?" Our usual answer is "Yes, yes. On both." It's impossible to separate the two. If you make a deal to buy a company at a great price and it's got a dominant market position and a great product line, once you mishandle the people issues and watch the brains walk out the door, your profits and market position go right down the drain.

A friend of ours bought a great trophy hotel in Miami Beach at a bargain basement price, and invested millions in refurbishing the down-at-the-heels property. He then opened the doors with great fanfare and waited for the guests to come. He waited, and waited and waited. Nothing as lonely as an empty hotel lobby, and a rapidly draining bank account. We stopped by for a look-see, registering as guests to sample the wares. The problem was obvious to us within the first fifteen minutes of our stay. Nobody cared at that hotel. No one smiled. No one asked about what we needed. They all did their jobs, mechanically and unemotionally. It was robots at work.

We discovered later that our friend closed the hotel during refurbishing and laid off the staff. The best ones found jobs elsewhere, and took their local following with them. Furthermore, the owner was a somewhat humorless sort, inordinately focused on finances and numbers. He didn't know any employee names, for instance. The hotel staff accurately reflected the owner's personality.

"You have three options," we told him. "Either change your style, hire a different GM who is more of an emotional leader or sell the property." He choked a bit, thanked us for our advice and paid our bill. We soon saw a small news item in the *Wall Street Journal* reporting that he sold his hotel for a fraction of what he paid. Soft versus hard? Our friend learned a very expensive lesson: it had better be . . . both soft *and* hard.

Engage, Challenge, Support and Care

People sometimes accuse of us being demanding. We do set high standards for ourselves, and for all those with whom we work. World-class is the standard that we work to exceed. It is challenging. But we'd like to think we exercise that challenge with caring and love as opposed to doing it with a sledgehammer.

The entire process we've described throughout this book is based upon helping people achieve what they want to achieve. We work hard to identify people's hopes and dreams and then challenge them, engage them and support them in realizing their hopes and dreams. We work with other people's hopes and dreams for themselves, not our hopes and dreams for them. We know it is difficult to separate out our interests and keep focused on the interests of others.

Raising children is a wonderfully humbling experience. These are your progeny, your legacy. They carry your genes, your name. In a biological and social sense they are an extension of you. Yet they are also independent of you. They have different needs and often march to different drummers. In talking about our children we've often said to our wives, "Where did that child come from?" and adding in jest: "Couldn't have been from my side of the gene pool."

It also isn't easy living in the middle of a large organization. The rules and systems and structures all seem to be oppressively omnipresent, preventing you from using your God-given talents. It's analogous to being buried alive. We wish we had a penny for everyone who came up to us during a presentation and said, "Gee, what you're saying is absolutely right. But you know, I'm just a small cog connected to this big wheel and I can't do what you're suggesting. If only my leader would do it, that would be great."

Do people suffer from a lack of courage? Does it take courage to take on "the system" and change it? Do people suffer from an absence of ownership? Are they caught up in their own victimitis? What does it take to really be a Phoenix? Does it take courage? Does it take ownership? Does it take leadership? Does it take learning? How many yeses can you handle?

Courage: When You Care Enough to Make a Difference

Let's talk about courage. What does it take to have courage? Is courage a limited commodity, available to only a chosen few? Do you have to endure a marine boot camp to develop courage? Don't think so. Courage is widely distributed. Most of us have it in abundance. We bury it, or cover it up, much like we bury and cover up our emotional, caring side.

Simply put, courage is staying the course. Caring is the taproot that nurtures the courage to stay the course regardless of the costs. You stay the course because the course is important to the people you care about. You pay the price because the people you care about need what the course provides and they need you to provide it. You stay the course because the course contributes to the legacy you want to leave.

You have the courage to do what needs to be done because you really care about the other people in your network, you really want to make a difference and you really want to leave a legacy of other successful people. We often get enamored with people who do a one-time heroic event and call that courage. However, real courage is sticking to something you know is important, that will make a true difference for the people you care about, and sticking with it until it really happens.

Courage Is When You Care Enough to Be Different

Stephen Covey said, "I care about the things you care about, as much as I care about you." So there are activities that our wives want to do that make us uncomfortable. They're not bad things, but they are out of our comfort zone. Take line dancing, for instance. It's not our cup of tea. When it comes to that kind of group dancing, we've got two left feet, and constantly trip over ourselves. We would not seek out opportunities to go line dancing, but our wives care about line dancing. So we go line dancing with them because we care about line dancing as much as we care about them—which is a whole lot. We summon up the courage to look foolish because we care about what our wives care about.

Our goals are to be world-class husbands. Our picture is that every one of our wives' family and friends will say, "He's the best husband ever." It takes courage to say that out loud and let everyone know that that's our goal. It takes courage to make the difficult and sometimes embarrassing choices to achieve that goal.

Commitment to leaving a legacy of caring, more successful people, combined with the heart connection, provides the courage to do whatever it takes to live the vision. It's a circle. Courage comes from commitment and caring: commitment to something you want to create and something you want to be, combined with the caring for others to help them be all that they want to be. That courage, in turn, produces heightened caring and commitment.

BE THE WORLD YOU WANT TO SEE

The world is filled with might-have-been people: people who just missed the train to successville, people who promise to deliver their résumé "tomorrow," people whose dog ate their homework. You know them. You've met them. At one time or another we've all been one of them. There is another side, however. There are lots of Phoenix leader/owners out there as well—people who step up to the line, take responsibility, plan for the future and work to improve the present. The world is filled with Phoenixes in varying stages of revivolution. They don't wait for permission. They don't search the rulebook to see if a proposed action falls within the acceptable policy guidelines. They see a need and use I words to describe what they're going to do: I'll fix it; I'll take care of it; I'll make certain you get it tomorrow.

Someone said that there are ten two-letter words that make all the difference. Maybe you've heard them: "If it is to be, it is up to me." Those who know this and practice it will change the world. Many already have.

When the final history of the twentieth century is written, a handful of people will stand out as the giants of our millennium. One of the handful will be a frail little man in a white loincloth. This man never held elective office. He never commanded an army, never fired a single shot. Yet with his deeds he freed more than 500 million people, and created the largest democracy on the face of this earth. His name: Mohandas K. Gandhi.

Gandhi lived the quintessence of Phoenix self-renewal. He spun his own cloth to demonstrate to his fellow Indians that they, too, could be self-sufficient. He made his own salt to demonstrate that others could also avoid paying the hated British salt tax that kept everyone poor.

In words of stirring Phoenix ownership he said, "I MUST BE THE WORLD I WANT TO SEE." Hear the Phoenix ownership words of one of the greatest people to ever live. Irrespective of others, despite what others said, did or tried to get him to say or do, he committed to *be* the world he wanted to see. He recognized that it was his responsibility to live his life in his way. Never was he the recipient of self-imposed victimitis.

Every night we ask ourselves, "Have we been the world we want to see? Have we done the things that will leave a better world for our children and our grandchildren? Have we lived the exemplary life so that they will be proud to carry our name?" As the owners of our lives we can ask—and do—no less. Can you?

Your finest hour is yet to be. We wish you the joys of self-renewal.